GRAMMAR
IN THE
CLASSROOM

Mark Lester

Eastern Washington University

MACMILLAN PUBLISHING COMPANY

New York

For all the M's and the A, too

Macmillan Publishing Company
866 Third Avenue, New York, New York 10022

Credits

The following publishers and organizations have generously given permission to refer
extensively to and quote from copyrighted works:

From *Syntactic Maturity in Schoolchildren and Adults,* Monographs of the Society for
Research in Child Development by Kellogg W. Hunt, Serial No. 134, Vol. 35, No. 1,
February 1970, University of Chicago Press. From *Grammatical Structures Written at Three
Grade Levels,* by Kellogg W. Hunt. Copyright © 1965 by the National Council of Teachers
of English. Reprinted with Permission. From *Creative Approaches to Sentence Combining,*
by William Strong. Copyright © 1986 by the National Council of Teachers of English.
Reprinted with permission.

Library of Congress Cataloging-in-Publication Data

Lester, Mark.
    Grammar in the classroom / Mark Lester.
      p. cm.
    Bibliography: p.
    Includes indexes.
    ISBN 0-02-370060-2
    1. English language—Grammar—1950-2. English language—Grammar—.
    Study and teaching. I. Title.
    PE1112.L45 1990   89-33800
    428'.007—dc20   CIP
Printing: 1 2 3 4 5 6 7   Year: 0 1 2 3 4 5 6

To the Instructor

This book grew out of my attempts to meet the needs of prospective English teachers (upper elementary and secondary English education majors) in a one semester course in English grammar. *Grammar in the Classroom* is uniquely teacher-oriented. That is, users of this book are both at the same time college students who need to understand the information presented here and prospective teachers who need to be able to draw upon this information for use in their own classrooms.

Grammar in the Classroom meets the needs of prospective English teachers in six key areas by:

- ☐ teaching students the traditional grammar they need to know as classroom English teachers
- ☐ giving students an innovative, practical methodology for successfully teaching traditional grammar in their classrooms
- ☐ giving students the basics of structural linguistics and transformational grammar
- ☐ giving students a solid understanding of both the grammatical processes of sentence-combining and the research literature on the application of sentence-combining to composition
- ☐ showing students how to relate grammar to writing
- ☐ discussing in depth the problems of teaching grammar in the classroom

As prospective teachers, students need to have an active, rather than passive command of the terms and concepts of grammar. Most students have difficulty learning how to consciously analyze grammatical constructions, as opposed to the ease with which they intuitively use these constructions. This class-tested book shows students how to use practical, operational tests for identifying the elements of grammar. These tests help students tap into their unconscious knowledge of language, in effect, serving as a field guide to grammatical identification. Students find these tests to be quite helpful; moreover, many students who have gone on to become teachers have found that the tests are at least as helpful to their students. Thus, the book models a methodology that prospective teachers can use in their own classrooms.

An important feature of the book is that it applies grammatical concepts directly to related problems of mechanics and usage. For example, the techniques used to define the subject of a sentence can also be used to help monitor for subject-verb agreement errors. The sentence combining rules that govern joining sentences with coordinating conjunctions are a natural vehicle for dealing with problems of parallelism.

The book is divided into two parts:

PART I: TRADITIONAL GRAMMAR

Part I consists of four chapters: Chapter 1, "Parts of Speech;" Chapter 2, "The Sentence;" Chapter 3, "Phrases;" and Chapter 4, "Clauses". The content of these chapters is conventional: the topics presented are the ones found in every secondary grammar textbook, and they are presented in the traditional order.

The presentation in these chapters presumes that the students have little, if any, prior knowledge of traditional grammar. The presentation further assumes that their mastery of traditional grammar will be greatly facilitated by extensive hands-on experience with carefully controlled exercises. Accordingly, every point is reinforced by an exercise that requires students to manipulate the information presented. Since answers to all exercises are provided at the end of the book, students can assume more responsibility for their own learning than is usually the case. The numerous self-correcting exercises enable the class to cover more material in greater depth than would be possible if all exercises had to be corrected in class.

PART II: ALTERNATIVES AND OPTIONS

Chapter 5, "A Short History of English Grammar," traces the origins of traditional grammar and the evolution of two modern grammars: historical-descriptive grammars and structural linguistics. This chapter shows students that different grammars make very different contributions to our understanding of English grammar. Chapter 5 closes with a detailed examination of three aspects of English grammar (word formation, phrasal verbs, and the meaning of 'present' and 'future' tense) that are particularly well described from the perspective of structural linguistics.

Chapter 6, "Transformational Grammar," provides an overview of the theory underlying transformational grammar, the most important modern approach to grammar. As an in-depth sample of how transformational grammar works, the chapter concludes with an analysis of the English tense and helping verb system, an analysis that most students find very enlightening. The model of transformational grammar used is the "classical" version of Chomsky's *Aspects of the Theory of Syntax*, 1965. I have chosen this model for several reasons: it is relatively easy to understand without many linguistic prerequisites; it is still the best known form of transformational grammar; and it fits nicely with sentence combining. There is a brief annotated bibliography of books with more current approaches in the Appendix.

Chapter 7, "Sentence-Combining," deals with the process of joining simple sentences together to form more complex sentences. The first part of the chapter examines three sentence combining processes—noun modification, nominalization, and absolutes—from the perspective of transformational grammar. These three processes have been identified as being of particular importance in our ability to form more complex and sophisticated sentences as we mature.

The second part of the chapter deals with the classroom use of sentence-combining. The section begins by tracing the history of sentence-combining. It then surveys the extensive research literature on the relation of sentence-combining to writing. The chapter closes with a detailed discussion of how sentence-combining can best be used in the classroom to teach both grammar and style.

Chapter 8, "Grammar in the Classroom," deals with two main issues: the role of grammar in the secondary classroom, and ways in which grammar can be taught more effectively in the classroom. The key points are the following:

- ☐ traditional grammar can be taught more effectively if it incorporates certain insights from modern grammars,
- ☐ those aspects of grammar that directly relate to writing are the best way to introduce the formal study of grammar, and
- ☐ sentence combining is an effective vehicle for teaching both traditional and transformational grammar.

An instructor's manual is also available from the publisher.

ACKNOWLEDGEMENTS

I would like to thank Dr. Robert Olafson, Chair of the Department of English at Eastern Washington University, for the support provided by the department, and my colleague at Eastern, Dr. Robert Riddings, for his advice.

I would also like to thank the following reviewers for their most helpful input: Douglas Alley, Auburn University; Miriam Chaplin, Rutgers University–Camden; Carol Croxton, University of Southern Colorado; John Schwetman, Sam Houston State University; Ann W. Sharp, Furman University; Sylvia Bailey Shurbutt, Shepherd College; Anne O. Soter, Ohio State University; David Sonstroem, University of Connecticut; Robert Sweazy, Vincennes University.

To the Student

This book is designed to give you what you need to know about grammar in order to be an effective, professional classroom teacher—a thorough knowledge of how grammar works and methods for teaching and using it effectively in the classroom.

The content of *Grammar in the Classroom* is divided between traditional grammar (the eight parts of speech; the sentence and its parts; phrases; and clauses) and modern approaches (with an emphasis on transformational grammar and its main application to teaching: sentence combining). The traditional grammar component (Chapters 1–4) covers—point for point in the customary order and using the conventional terminology—all the topics of traditional grammar that are taught in junior and senior high schools, including sentence diagraming.

An important feature of this book is that it does not treat you just as a student; it treats you as a prospective teacher who must teach and use what you are being taught. You need to have an active, rather than passive command of the terms of concepts of traditional grammar. It is not enough, for example, that you can recite the definition of the parts of speech; you must be able to identify them correctly and confidently and lead your students to do the same. Accordingly, the book relies heavily on practical, operational tests that help you identify parts of speech and other grammatical constructions by observing their characteristics. That is, a word is a noun because you can show that it acts the way nouns act. It is not enough to be right; you must be able to show your students why you are right. These same tests are also enormously helpful to your students. Thus, the book gives you an effective methodology that you can use in your classroom.

Every point made in the text is reinforced by an exercise. It is only by dealing in detail with many actual examples of sentences using a particular grammatical construction that you will gain a real command of that construction. A word of warning: since the answers to the exercises are provided, there is a natural temptation to check your understanding of a topic by running through the answers without first doing problems for yourself. The danger here is that you will think that you have understood the topic when you really have not. No two sentences are exactly alike. It is only by working through many examples on your own that you will really internalize the topic and be able to deal with it in different guises in new sentences. Remember, when you are in front of a class, you will not have the option of going back and checking your notes. Either you know it then and there, or you do not know it at all. And your students will have no doubts about which is the case.

The second half of the book moves beyond traditional grammar to modern approaches.

Chapter 5 gives a history of English grammar. It traces the origins of traditional grammar and the evolution of the more modern approaches. The chapter describes the ways each type of grammar has contributed to out understanding of English.

Chapter 6 introduces transformational grammar, the most important modern approach to grammar. The chapter then gives a detailed transformational analysis of the English tense and helping verb system, an analysis found to be extremely helpful.

Chapter 7 focuses on sentence combining, the most important practical application of transformational grammar. Sentence combining is the process of combining simple sentences together to form longer and more sophisticated sentences. The chapter covers both the technical grammatical process of sentence combining (focusing on three important types of sentence combining) and the extensive research literature on the use of sentence combining in teaching composition.

Chapter 8 deals with how you can teach grammar more effectively in the classroom. The chapter argues that traditional grammar can be taught more effectively by (1) incorporating new insights from modern grammars, (2) directly relating grammar to teaching writing, and (3) using sentence combining to teach grammar for its own sake.

An important theme that runs throughout the book is the application of all forms of grammar to the writing problems that your students will have. For example, the techniques used to identify the subject of a sentence can also be used to help your students control certain types of subject-verb agreement problems. Sentence combining is a very powerful tool for dealing with many punctuation problems; for example, comma splices, run-ons, fragments, dangling modifiers, and errors of parallelism.

I would like to gratefully acknowledge the many excellent suggestions that my students have given me during the evolution of this book.

I would be happy to receive any feedback about the book. I am especially interested in hearing how you were able to use ideas from this book in your own classrooms. Please forward your comments to: English Editor, Macmillan College Publishing, 866 Third Avenue, New York, NY, 10022.

Contents

PART I

Traditional Grammar

Parts of Speech

INTRODUCTION

The foundation of traditional grammar is the identification of each word in a sentence in terms of the eight parts of speech: *noun, pronoun, adjective, verb, adverb, preposition, conjunction,* and *interjection.* Thus, all traditional grammar books begin with definitions and examples of the eight parts of speech (usually in the order that they are listed above).

A word of caution: part of speech resides in the way that a word is used; it is not inherent in the word itself. For example, the names of concrete, everyday objects such as *table, chair,* and *book* would seem to be inherently nouns, but in the following sentences they are used as verbs.

> The committee <u>tabled</u> the motion.
> Mr. Smith <u>chaired</u> the meeting.
> A travel agent <u>booked</u> the ticket for me.

Consequently, we must be careful to discuss a word's part of speech in terms of the context in which it is used. Beware of talking about the part of speech of a word used in isolation.

The eight parts of speech fall into two different classes: *open* and *closed.* These terms refer to the number of words that belong to each of eight part of speech classes. Open classes contain large numbers of words and freely allow new words to be added; conversely, closed classes contain relatively few words and do not allow new words to be added. Nouns, for example, are an open class. There are many thousands of nouns. No one even knows how many nouns there are. Even the most current dictionary would not include many nouns, particularly the names of new products, inventions, and discoveries, let alone the names of new rock groups. Adjectives, verbs, and adverbs are also open classes, each with a large and unknown number of words.

The remaining parts of speech, on the other hand, are closed classes. For example, there is only a small number of personal pronouns; any grammar book of English will give a complete list of them. Moreover, the list has not changed for hundreds of years, nor is it likely to change for hundreds of years into the future.

Open and closed classes are defined in quite different ways. Three closed classes (pronouns, prepositions, and conjunctions) are defined primarily by listing all the members of the class. Since it is obviously impossible to list and memorize all the nouns, verbs, adjectives, and adverbs, the four open classes can be defined only in terms of some set of properties or characteristics that distinguishes each part of speech class from the others.

The traditional definitions of open classes are valid and useful, but not easy for all students to learn. Part of the difficulty is in the way that traditional grammar defines terms. It is not that the definitions are wrong; it is that they are abstract and hard for many students to apply in practice. For example, the traditional definition of a noun emphasizes the fact that nouns are names. The definition works well for the names of proper nouns and for common nouns when the common nouns refer to tangible things such as people, places, and concrete objects. However, students run into trouble when they apply the traditional definition of noun to intangible things. For example, the fact that *blue* is the name of a color does not mean that *blue* (in its usual meaning as a term describing a color) is a noun. Likewise, the fact that *jump* is the name of an action does not mean that *jump* (in its normal use) is a noun. The problem with the traditional definition is that, if it were applied literally, it is so broad that it seems to apply to intangible non-nouns such as *blue* in "I'm feeling blue" and *jump* in "Jump higher."

It may be impossible to give an abstract definition that works perfectly for all nouns—a definition that is broad enough to correctly identify 100% of all nouns, but at the same time is narrow enough to exclude all words that are not nouns. In this book, we supplement the traditional definition with practical tests, which students can use to see if a particular word is a noun.

The tests work because students do not have much difficulty *using* nouns; their problem is consciously *identifying* them. *The key to all tests of part of speech is tapping into our unconscious ability to use words correctly.* Since we know how to use nouns correctly, we can exploit our intuitive knowledge of nouns as a way of consciously identifying them. That is, if students can intuitively use a word in a way that they consciously know is characteristic of nouns, then they can exploit that usage to establish that the word must be a noun. Students can then prove a word is a noun by showing that it acts in ways that are characteristic of nouns. [If it walks like a duck and talks like a duck, it must be a duck.]

The traditional definitions of the four open part of speech classes (noun, verb, adjective, and adverb) are supplemented in this book by certain "operational" tests. There are three types of tests:

1. *Word form tests*: the open part of speech classes often have distinctive endings by which the class can be identified (e.g., verbs have a distinctive past tense ending).
2. *"Tip off" word tests*: certain words can occur only with specific open part of speech classes (e.g., *the* can be used only with nouns and *will* with verbs).
3. *Substitution tests*: certain words can substitute only for specific open part of speech classes (e.g., *it* and *they* can substitute only for nouns and their modifiers).

Students need to know the traditional definitions of the part of speech classes. For many students, however, the traditional definitions are so abstract (and have so many built-in hidden assumptions about grammar) that the students are unable to actually use the traditional definitions to identify parts of speech with any confidence. These same students, however, can achieve a high degree of success by learning a few simple tests that they can consciously employ to determine part of speech. The tests work because they draw on the students' existing intuitive knowledge of English. One of the main benefits of using the tests is that students come to realize that they really already know the answers, if they only knew how to approach the questions.

NOUNS

Traditional definition: A noun is a word used to name a person, place, thing, or idea. [A summary of main terms is given at the end of each chapter in Part I.]

There are two main types of nouns: *common* and *proper*. A common noun names a class or type of persons, places, or things and is not capitalized. A proper noun names a particular person, place, or thing and is capitalized.

	common noun	*proper noun*
Example:	inventor	Thomas Edison
	city	Spokane
	month	April

In general, the distinction between common and proper nouns is straightforward. However, the conventions for the capitalization of proper nouns are surprisingly arbitrary. Following are some of the main categories of nouns that are capitalized.

☐ Names of persons, places, businesses, organizations, and institutions:

John Smith	the South
Xerox Corporation	Public Broadcasting Service
Columbia University	Department of English

☐ Civil, military, religious, and professional titles are capitalized when they are part of the name.

General Smith	Judge Bean
Senator Fogghorn	Cardinal Newman

If the title is used in place of a name in speaking directly to a person, it is capitalized.

Please come in, <u>General</u>.

If the title is used to refer to a person, it is not capitalized.

Show the <u>general</u> in.

Even if a noun refers to only one person, the noun is a common noun unless the noun is used as a title. For example, compare these two uses of the noun *mother*.

Call me when you get home, <u>Mother</u>.
My <u>mother</u> called me when she got home.

In the first sentence, *Mother* is used as a title in directly addressing the person. In the second sentence, however, *mother* is used to name a third person. Even though the person uttering the second sentence has only one mother, the noun is still a common noun because it is not used as a title or form of address.

If a professional title is used *following* a name, it is not capitalized.

George King, <u>president</u> of Snowflake College
Alfred Gray, <u>chairman</u> of the Department of English

☐ Courses (but not branches of learning).

I am taking <u>Math</u> 260 this term.
I am taking <u>mathematics</u> this term.

☐ Specific historical and cultural events are generally capitalized.

the Sixties   Prohibition
Civil War   Renaissance

However, historical periods are generally not capitalized unless derived from a proper name.

eighteenth century   the twenties
baroque period   Victorian era

☐ Cultural movements and styles are capitalized only if derived from proper nouns.

Aristotelian   Gothic
Epicurean   Platonic
romanticism   realism
surrealism   classical

☐ Days, months, and holidays (but not seasons) are capitalized.

Monday   July
Christmas   Columbus Day
fall   summer

☐ Names of mountains, rivers, oceans, and islands are capitalized. Geographical terms—for example, *mountain, lake, ocean*—are also capitalized if they are used as part of the name.

Walden Pond   Rocky Mountains
Pacific Ocean   Silver Lake
Great Barrier Reef   Cape York
Windward Islands   West Coast

However, geographical terms used descriptively are not capitalized.

the desert   the Mississippi valley
the Kansas prairie   New England coastline

While the preceding rules governing capitalization are helpful, there are inconsistencies. For example, historical events are usually capitalized, but the *cold war* and *civil rights movement* are not capitalized. Many terms are inconsistently capitalized. For example, sometimes *industrial revolution* is capitalized and sometimes it is not.

Perhaps the moral of the story is, if in doubt, check a comprehensive dictionary. One of the most detailed and authoritative sources for checking on capitalization is *The Chicago Manual of Style* (13th ed. Chicago: University of Chicago Press, 1982).

■ **Exercise 1.1. Identifying proper nouns**

Underline the proper nouns in the following sentences and capitalize those proper nouns not at the beginning of the sentence. The first sentence is done as an example. (Answers to exercises are found on page 373.)

       J   B   H

1. Thursday, journalism 103 will meet in bilger hall.
2. Henry is an army officer stationed in greenland.
3. They live in maryland, just outside washington, DC.
4. Democrats will have a hard time in the west this year.
5. Lodi is west of here.
6. My brother will be going back to school next fall.
7. The sierra club is an environmental organization.
8. The statues date from the early fifteenth century.
9. Norman Smith, chairman of the board of caltex corporation, will speak.
10. There is always a spring storm in the northern plains.
11. I am majoring in secular humanism.
12. Next month we change to daylight saving time.
13. The secretary of state has his office in foggy bottom.
14. For more information on our program, please contact the department of planning.
15. He hoped to get on the staff of a museum that specialized in classical and medieval art.
16. He is a student of the new deal and the war on poverty.
17. We are taking a class in late eighteenth century and early romantic poets.

Identifying common nouns

Students rarely have difficulty recognizing common nouns that refer to concrete objects, such as *computer* or *applesauce*. The difficulty they encounter is with common nouns that refer to intangibles and abstractions. Following are some tests that students have found helpful in recognizing common nouns.

1. *Distinctive form:* Most (but not all) common nouns can be used in the plural; for example: *absence/absences*; *facility/facilities*. Thus, we can determine if a word is a noun by seeing if we can grammatically use it in the plural form.

2. *"Tip off" words:* Most (but not all) common nouns can be preceded by *the*. For example, *the expense; the variety; the measure*. If we can put *the* directly in front of a word, that word is a noun.

3. *Substitution words:* The personal pronouns *he, she, it,* and *they* replace nouns (more accurately, nouns and the words that modify nouns). Thus, if we can replace a word (or the word and its modifiers) with one of the personal pronouns, then that word must be a noun.

The tests will rarely give a false positive—that is, the tests will seldom identify a word as a noun when, in fact, it is not a noun. Occasionally the first two tests will give a false negative—that is, the tests will not be able to identify a word as a noun when it really is a noun. However, when all three are used together, the combined tests identify nouns with a high degree of certainty. In the following section, each of the three noun tests is discussed in detail.

1. Distinctive form: plural. The vast majority of nouns in English can be used in the plural. The regular plural ending is *-s* or *-es: cat/cats; dog/dogs; hero/heroes*. A small number of nouns have irregular plural endings. These nouns fall into two distinct groups: (1) native English words that have preserved old ways of forming plurals (*man/men; child/children; sheep/sheep; calf/calves*) and (2) foreign words that have retained foreign plural forms (*radius/radii; thesis/theses; cherub/cherubim*).

However, English also has an important group of nouns that do not have plural forms because they can never be used in the plural. These nouns are called *mass* or *uncountable* nouns (as opposed to normal nouns, which are called *countable* nouns). The term *mass* means nouns that refer to things that occur in undifferentiated aggregates. Mass nouns are also called *uncountable* because quite literally they refer to groups of things that occur in numbers too large to be individually counted. For example, compare the following two sentences.

Wheat is good for you.

*Wheats are good for you.[1]

The noun *wheat*, like the names of the other cereal grains, cannot be used in the plural. *Wheat* is an uncountable, undifferentiated aggregate. It is a mass or uncountable noun.

---

[1] The asterisk identifies a word or sentence that is ungrammatical. This footnote will not be repeated.

The names of many liquids are mass or uncountable nouns.

Milk is good for you.
*Milks are good for you.

The names of many natural phenomena are mass nouns.

Thunder scares my dog to death.
*Thunders scare my dog to death.

There are also mass nouns that do not seem to fit any semantic category. For example, compare *assignment* and *homework* in the following sentences.

I have two assignments due Monday.
*I have two homeworks due Monday.

Assignment is a countable noun. It has a singular and a plural form. *Homework*, however, is a mass noun and cannot be used in the plural.

The easiest way to distinguish regular nouns from mass nouns is to try to use number words with the noun.

one assignment   *one homework
two assignments   *two homeworks

Another characteristic that will help you recognize mass nouns is that they cannot be used with the indefinite article *a/an*.

I have an assignment.
*I have a homework.

The reason we cannot use *a/an* with mass nouns is historical: the indefinite article *a/an* comes from the number word *one* (the form *an* preserves the *n* from the word *one*).

Do not confuse mass nouns with the small group of irregular nouns that for historical reasons have no overt ending in the plural: for example, *sheep, deer,* and *fish*. These nouns can be counted.

one sheep   one deer   one fish
two sheep   two deer   two fish

They can also be used with plural verbs.

The sheep are in the meadow.

Some mass nouns can be used in the plural with the meaning "different kinds of," as in the following sentence.

A good nursery carries many grasses.

The noun *grasses* means something like "different kinds of grass."

Many nouns can be either countable or uncountable, but with completely different meanings. For example, compare the word *nickel* in the following sentences.

> The pencil cost a nickel.
> They extract nickel from the ore.

In the first sentence *nickel* is a countable noun, the name of the five-cent coin. In the second sentence *nickel* is a mass or uncountable noun, the name of a metal. We can prove that *nickel* is a mass noun in the second sentence by trying to paraphrase it as a plural and use it with *a/an*.

> *They extract nickels from the ore.
> *They extract a nickel from the ore.

The following is another, less obvious example. Compare the word *paper* in the following two sentences.

> What paper do you take?
> He packed his dishes in paper.

In the first sentence *paper* means "newspaper," and in this meaning *paper* is a countable noun.

> What papers do you take?
> He takes a paper.

In the second sentence *paper* means "paper material," and in this meaning *paper* is a mass or uncountable noun.

> *He packed his dishes in papers.
> *He packed his dishes in a paper.

■ **Exercise 1.2. Identifying mass/uncountable nouns**

Underline the mass/uncountable nouns in the following sentences, and paraphrase the sentence to demonstrate that your answer is correct. The first sentence is done as an example. (Answers to excercises are found on page 374.)

1. Get me the ink, will you?
   Paraphrases: *Get me an ink, will you?
                  *Get me inks, will you? (gramatical only if used in the sense "different kinds of ink")
2. There is a huge deposit of copper in Arizona.
3. It is very difficult to eliminate smoke completely.

4. It is made of iron.
5. I need to press some clothes. Are you done with the iron?
6. I didn't like his talk to the club at all.
7. All that talk amounts to very little.
8. Lightning struck a tree in Easton.
9. I love music.
10. The applicant for the job has a great deal of experience.
11. Photography is obviously not his strength.
12. The applause must have overwhelmed him.
13. Dust gets into my contact lenses.
14. They were doing research on comets.
15. We finally got some sunshine.
16. Cast your bread upon the water.
17. The lamb is too hot to eat. (a trick question—two answers)

---

2. "Tip off" word: the. A small class of "tip off" words, called *articles*, can be used with nearly all common nouns. Articles include *an* and *the*. Of these two articles, *the* is the less restricted since *a* can be used only with singular nouns. The only common nouns that cannot be used with *the* are a handful of abstract nouns. For example, *honesty* is an abstract noun that we cannot use with *the* in the following sentence.

> *The honesty is the best policy.

Outside this small group of abstract nouns, *the* is a very reliable "tip off" word for identifying nouns.

A word of caution: in an expression like *the old man*, the article *the* modifies the noun *man*, not the adjective *old*. If in doubt, you can test which word the article modifies by pairing it up with the following words. That is, we can paraphrase the phrase *the old man* as *the man*, but we cannot say *the old*. Thus we can show that *man* is a noun even though there is a word (*old*) in between the noun and its modifying article.

3. Substitution words: third person pronouns. All nouns—proper as well as common—can be replaced by third person personal pronouns (*he/him, she/her, it,* and *they/them*). The personal pronoun test replaces the suspected noun with the appropriate third person pronoun. If the resulting substitution is grammatical, the word is a noun. For example, in the sentence *Honesty is the best policy*, we can replace *honesty* with the personal pronoun *it*.

> It (= honesty) is the best policy.

The personal pronoun substitution test is a little complicated in one respect: the personal pronoun does not replace just the noun but the noun together with its modifiers. For example, in the preceding sample sentence, *it* can replace the *best policy*, both the noun *policy* and the modifiers *the* and *best*.

Honesty is <u>it</u> (= the best <u>policy</u>).

As long as you remember to strip away the modifiers from the noun, the personal pronoun substitution is a completely reliable test.

With some practice the three noun tests are easy to use and when used together are very reliable. For example, let us examine the word *prize* in the following sentence.

The committee will award a <u>prize</u> for the best entry.

We can prove that *prize* is a noun by applying the three tests.

1. *Plural form:* We can paraphrase the original sentence by creating a new sentence that differs from the original sentence only in that the noun *prize* is plural.

The committee will award <u>prizes</u> for the best entry.

Note that in paraphrasing the sentence, we deleted the article *a* from the original sentence because *a* cannot be used with the plural noun *prizes*.

2. *"Tip off" word the:* We can paraphrase the original sentence with a new sentence in which we use *the* with the word *prize*.

The committee will award <u>the</u> prize for the best entry.

3. *Substitution of third person pronoun:* We can substitute *it* for the word *prize* (and its modifier).

The committee will award <u>it</u> for the best entry.

Now we need to ask ourselves two questions about these paraphrased sentences.

1. Do the paraphrased sentences have the same basic meaning as the original sentence, differing *only* by the changes we have made?
2. Are the paraphrased sentences grammatical?

If the answer to both of these two questions is yes, then we have demonstrated that the word *prize* in the original sentence is a noun. Our proof is that *prize* demonstrates the typical behavior of nouns; that is, it (1) can be made plural, (2) can be used with *the*, and (3) can be replaced with *it*. In all of these three paraphrases the sentence retains its basic meaning, and the resulting new sentences are grammatical.

Let us now try the same three tests on the word *award* in the same sentence.

The committee will <u>award</u> a prize for the best entry.

The resulting paraphrases are all ungrammatical.

1. Plural: *The committee will <u>awards</u> a prize for the best entry.

*2. **The***:   *The committee will <u>the award</u> a prize for the best entry.

*3. **It***:   *The committee will <u>it</u> a prize for the best entry.

These three tests show that the word *award* is not a noun in the preceding sample sentence. However, the fact that *award* is not a noun in this sentence does not mean that *award* could not be used as a noun in some other sentence, such as the one that follows.

The committee gave an <u>award</u> to the best nail clipper.

In this instance, *award* is a noun, as we can demonstrate by the three noun tests.

1. Plural: The committee gave <u>awards</u> to the best nail clipper.

*2. **The***:   The committee gave <u>the award</u> to the best nail clipper.

*3. **It***:   The committee gave <u>it</u> to the best nail clipper.

When testing a word, we need to be very careful that we keep the same sense in the test that is used in the original sentence.

These tests are especially helpful in dealing with words that look like nouns but that do not behave like nouns. For example, consider the word *home* in the following sentence.

John went <u>home</u>.

The word *home* has the nounlike characteristic of being the name of a place—the place where John lives. However, when we apply the three noun tests, we can see that *home* is not a noun.

1. Plural: *John went <u>homes</u>.

*2. **The***:   *John went <u>the home</u>.

*3. **It***:   *John went <u>it</u>.

Compare the preceding use of the word *home* with the same word used in the sense of "retirement home" in the following sentence.

John visited a <u>home</u>.

In this sentence the word *home* is now used as a noun, as the three tests demonstrate.

   1. Plural: John visited <u>homes</u>.
   *2. **The**:*   John visited <u>the home</u>.
   *3. **It**:*   John visited <u>it</u>.

Paraphrase tests will often require you to make adjustments elsewhere in the sentence. For example, if the word you are testing is the subject of the sentence, you may have to change the verb to make it agree with the new subject.

   Original: The <u>idea is</u> OK with me.
   Plural test: The <u>ideas are</u> OK with me.

In the preceding example, when the word *idea* is made plural in the paraphrased version, the verb must also change from singular to plural.

If you did not know English, these tests would not work because you could not tell which paraphrased sentences were grammatical and which were ungrammatical, nor could you tell which paraphrases kept the basic meaning the same and which ones did not. In other words, these tests require your intuitive knowledge of English to make them work. (Think how difficult it would be for us to apply comparable tests for sentences in a language that we do not know very well.) You do not need these tests to *intuitively* use nouns correctly. That is what all native speakers of a language do by virtue of being native speakers. However, you will find that the tests are very useful when you need to *consciously identify* nouns.

■ **Exercise 1.3. Identifying common nouns**

In the following sentences, demonstrate that the underlined words are common nouns by using the three noun tests. (Remember, not every test will work with every noun.) The first sentence is done as an example. (Answers to exercises are found on page 375.)

  1. We bought a valuable <u>lot</u> in Camden.
     (1) *Plural*:   We bought valuable <u>lots</u> in Camden.
     (2) ***The***:   We bought <u>the</u> valuable lot in Camden.
     (3) ***It***:   We bought <u>it</u>.

  2. A <u>merger</u> may be against the law.
  3. They would not pay any attention to a <u>warning</u>.

   4. Clear <u>formulation</u> of the problem is essential.
   5. The instrument measures <u>velocity</u>.
   6. They registered a <u>protest</u> against the decision.
   7. I was attracted by an unusual <u>texture</u>.
   8. We recorded a <u>discontinuity</u>.
   9. <u>Departure</u> is always a sad occasion.
  10. The problem was discovered after a quick <u>inspection</u>.
  11. A <u>stitch</u> in time saves nine.
  12. It is hard to catch an <u>error</u> of that type.
  13. An <u>assistant</u> came to the door.
  14. <u>Slavery</u> was common in the classical world.
  15. We had <u>fish</u> for dinner last night.
  16. We all admired a <u>drawing</u> he got in Rome.
  17. He was considered to be singularly lacking in <u>insight</u>.

■ **Exercise 1.4. Identifying nouns**

Underline the nouns in the following sentences. (Answers to exercises are found on page 375.)

   1. Chicago is known as the windy city for obvious reasons.
   2. Mass is a technical concept in physics.
   3. A good plumber can fix any sink ever made.
   4. A pound of hamburger will not feed us.
   5. We loved the south of France.
   6. He is always looking for grants.
   7. The good fairy granted her wish.
   8. Economists issued dire predictions at regular intervals.
   9. Profits were heading south.
  10. The army steadily advanced on Moscow.
  11. He forgot to telephone his office.
  12. What he lacked in intelligence he made up for in courage.
  13. Garth used knives and forks in strange new ways.
  14. His interpretation of the act was upheld by the court.
  15. His trip to Dallas was an unmitigated disaster.
  16. His fastball quickly became feared by every batter in the league.
  17. Henry could write essays as fast as he could talk.
  18. Garrick is a demon at Trivial Pursuit.

Using the apostrophe to indicate possessive nouns

Nouns have a second distinctive form: the possessive -*s*. Generally speaking, the possessive -*s* indicates possession or ownership. Thus, *John's cat* is a cat that John possesses or owns. There are two problems connected with the possessive: (1) how to spell it and (2) how to distinguish the possessive -*s* from the identically pronounced -*s* plural; for example, the /s/ sound in the word *cats* could represent either the possessive marker or the plural marker.

1. How to spell the possessive In the written language, we distinguish the two different -*s*'s by using an apostrophe (') to mark the possessive.

Plural: cats

Possessive: cat's

A complicating factor is that a noun can be both plural and possessive at the same time. In this case, the spelling convention is to place the apostrophe *after* the plural -*s*, giving us -*s'*. Now we have a three-way contrast in the written forms for an identical /s/ sound.

Plural: cats

Singular possessive: cat's

Plural possessive: cats'

For nouns with irregular plural forms, the plural possessive is also formed in an irregular way: the singular form -*'s* is added onto the irregular plural form.

Singular: child

Singular possessive: child's

Plural: children

Plural possessive: children's

In this example, the -*'s* has been added to the irregular plural form *children* to produce the plural possessive form *children's*.

For nouns that end in vowel sound spelled -*y*, the plural and possessive forms of the word (although they sound exactly alike) are spelled differently: in the plural form, the -*y* spelling changes to -*ie*, whereas in the possessive form the -*y* spelling does not change.

Singular: spy

Plural: spies

Singular Possessive: spy's

The plural possessive is spelled in the usual manner by adding an apostrophe to the end of the plural -*s: spies'*.

The real problem with spelling possessives, however, is with names that end in a sibilant sound (/s/, /sh/ or /z/). In this situation, there are conflicting conventions. One convention is to add -'s to one-syllable names ending in a sibilant sound, but the apostrophe (without the -s) to names with more than one syllable.

one syllable:	Keats's poems
	Marx's theories
	Ross's family
two or more syllables:	Dickens' novels
	Surtees' fiction
	Socrates' philosophy

The difficulty with this convention is that it produces strange-looking forms for some names of two or more syllables that end in an /s/ or /sh/ sound.

? Maria Callas' singing
? Roy Harris' operas
? Dylan Thomas' poetry
* Parrish' drawings

Another convention is to forgo consistency of spelling in favor of more accurate representation of the sound of the possessive form. One-syllable names are generally spelled -'s as in the preceding examples, but some names of two or more syllables would be spelled just with an apostrophe while others would be spelled -'s; thus, besides the preceding apostrophe-only forms (*Dickens' novels, Surtees' fiction,* and *Socrates' philosophy*) we would have possessives like the following with -'s.

Maria Callas's singing	Berlioz's ballet
Roy Harris's operas	Margaux's outrageous price
Dylan Thomas's poetry	Bruce Willis's picture
Parrish's drawings	Angus's voice

Proper nouns can also be used as plural possessives. The process of making proper nouns plural follows the regular pattern of making common nouns plural: merely add -s, unless the singular form ends in a sibilant sound (/s/, /sh/, or /z/), in which case the plural is spelled -es. Fortunately, the plural possessive is formed in the regular manner by merely adding an apostrophe to the plural form.

	Singular	*Plural*	*Plural possessive*
end in sibilant:	Jones	Joneses	Joneses'
	Ross	Rosses	Rosses'
	Parrish	Parrishes	Parrishes'
	Williams	Williamses	Williamses'
	Dickens	Dickenses	Dickenses'

■ Exercise 1.5. Spelling possessive nouns

For each of the following nouns, give (1) the singular possessive, (2) the plural, and (3) the plural possessive forms. Some nouns will have more than one correct singular possessive form. Proper nouns are capitalized; common nouns are not. The first question is done as an example. (Answers to exercises are found on page 376.)

	Singular Possessive	*Plural*	*Plural Possessive*
1. James	James' (or James's)	Jameses	Jameses'
2. fly			
3. Price			
4. man			
5. Marx			
6. Smith			
7. Hopkins			
8. puppy			
9. George			
10. Gibbons			
11. Holmes			
12. Dobbs			
13. woman			
14. Robins			
15. Kris			
16. Davis			
17. boss			

2. How to distinguish the possessive -'s from the identically pronounced -s plural. Many students have a more basic problem than how to spell proper nouns ending in a sibilant sound: they cannot tell when the /s/ sound represents the plural and when it represents the possessive. Typically, students at this level do not use the apostrophe to write the singular possessive form.

*The <u>boys</u> father was kind to him.

*Water covers most of the <u>earths</u> surface.

*I finally saw my <u>sisters</u> new boyfriend.

The apostrophe is a somewhat unusual mark of punctuation in that—unlike periods, question marks, and commas—it does not correspond to anything in the spoken language. Our intuitive knowledge of spoken English guides us about when to add an /s/ sound onto nouns to form a plural or a possessive. However, in the written language we must consciously distinguish between the two meanings of the /s/ sound because the possessive /s/ is marked by the use of the apostrophe. [For the sake of simplicity, we will ignore the plural possessive.] Thus the problem for many students is not adding the /s/ to a word, but deciding whether the /s/ represents the plural or the possessive, so that they know whether or not to use the apostrophe.

The basic meaning of the possessive, not surprisingly, is possession or ownership. There are two useful tests for this meaning. One test is to paraphrase the possessive with the verb *have*.

Possessive	*Paraphrase with* **have**
John's book	John has a book.
the baby's smile	The baby has a smile.
my sister's friends	My sister has some friends.
the team's goal	The team has a goal.
the candidate's policy	The candidate has a policy.
the teacher's pet	The teacher has a pet.

Thus, one way to determine if an /s/ sound represents a possessive is to see if there is a paraphrase with *have*.

A second test for this meaning of possessives is to see if it is possible to ask a *whose* question and get back a phrase containing a possessive pronoun.

Possessive	**Whose** *question*	*Possessive pronoun answer*
John's book	*whose* book?	his book
the baby's smile	*whose* smile?	his/her smile
my sister's friends	*whose* friends?	her friends
the team's goal	*whose* goal?	their goal
the candidate's policy	*whose* policy?	his/her policy
the teacher's pet	*whose* pet?	his/her pet

After students have learned to identify when an /s/ sound represents a possessive and should thus be spelled with an apostrophe, some students encounter a second layer of difficulty with the apostrophe: they overgeneralize the meaning of possession or ownership. They are able to correctly use the apostrophe when the /s/ sound indicates possession or ownership, but they fail to recognize that the so-called possessive has other meanings. Part of the problem is the term *possessive* itself; it is misleading. What we call the possessive form in modern English is actually the descendant of the genitive case in Anglo-Saxon (Old English). In Anglo-Saxon, the genitive case had a wide range of meanings. While the most important single use of the genitive case was to indicate possession or ownership, there were a number of other meanings. For example, a common use of the genitive case was for measuring and counting (especially time). Some modern English descendants of this use of the genitive are the following.

> a week's work
> ten days' leave
> your money's worth
> a day's wages
> a good night's sleep
> today's world

Students who have associated the use of the apostrophe only with the meaning of possession or ownership quite logically do not use apostrophes with the preceding examples of counting and measuring genitives because they recognize that the /s/ sound does not mean possession or ownership; for example, the relationship between *week* and *work* in the phrase *a week's work* is not at all like the relationship between *John* and *book* in the phrase *John's book*. Ironically, the set of tests that help students identify the /s/ sound as marking the possessive in *John's book* will fail with many of the examples given of measuring and counting genitives.

	a week's work
have *test*:	*A week has work.
whose *test*:	*<u>whose</u> work? *<u>its</u> work
	today's world
have *test*:	*Today has a world.
whose *test*:	*<u>whose</u> world? *<u>its</u> world

The fact that these genitive constructions fail the possessive tests leads students to conclude that these constructions do not require an apostrophe in their written form.

Modern English has a number of other uses of the genitive /s/ that are quite hard to classify. For example, *the suspect's release* does not mean that the suspect owns or possesses release. It means something like "Somebody released the suspect." Most of these other non-possessive uses of the genitive case will also fail the *have* paraphrase test.

	the suspect's release
have *test*:	*The suspect has release.
	her parents' consent
have *test*:	*Her parents have consent.

Fortunately, there is a useful test that will identify most of the genitive (i.e., non-possessive) uses of the apostrophe: the *of* test. This test involves reversing the two nouns and putting *of* between them.

a week's work
of *test*:   the work of a week
a day's wages
of *test*:   the wages of a day
today's world
of *test*:   the world of today
the suspect's release
of *test*:   the release of the suspect
her parents' consent
of *test*:   the consent of her parents

The *of* test will often (but not always) work with apostrophes that have a possessive meaning.

my sister's friends
of *test*:   the friends of my sister
the candidate's policy
of *test*:   the policy of the candidate

Probably most experienced writers have created their own versions of the various tests to govern their use of apostrophes. Inexperienced writers often seem to go through the following stages in gaining control over apostrophes.

1.   Never use an apostrophe (except in contractions like *don't* and *I'll*).
2.   Use an apostrophe to mark possessives where there is a strong sense of ownership or possession.

Typically, the first apostrophes will be used with proper nouns (*John's car*), then extended to common nouns (*teacher's pet*), and finally extended to inanimate common nouns for which the concept of ownership *of* possession is metaphorical (*the earth's atmosphere*).

3.   Use apostrophe with non-possessive genitives.

Like all tests, the tests for apostrophe work best when used together. Where one test may fail, another test may succeed. Let us briefly review them. The *have* test is very effective when the apostrophe signals possession or ownership. It is relatively poor for non-possessive genitives, especially genitives of counting or measurement. The *whose* test works well for apostrophes that signal possession or ownership and well for non-possessive genitives except for genitives of counting and measurement. The *of* test will often work where the other two tests fail. It works well with all non-possessive genitives and with many apostrophes that signal possession and ownership.

■ **Exercise 1.6. Using apostrophes**

The following phrases (exactly as they were written) were taken from essays written by junior and senior high school students. All of the phrases contain words that require apostrophes. Add the necessary apostrophe, and demonstrate that your revision is correct by applying the applicable apostrophe tests. The first question is done as an example. (Answers to exercises are found on page 376.)

1. The guards job
   - Revised: the guard's job / or the guards' job (ambiguous)
   - *have* test: The guard has a job. / The guards have a job.
   - *whose* test: whose job? his/her job or their job
   - *of* test: the job of the guard / the job of the guards
2. Todays society
3. The players head
4. The devils helper
5. Every childs life
6. A persons height
7. Favorite teams shirt
8. The fighters hands
9. The skiers weight
10. The states rule
11. The guards defender
12. A womans world
13. Another teams word
14. The umpires decision
15. The bodies major muscles

PRONOUNS

Traditional definition. A pronoun is a word used in place of one or of more than one noun.

There are five major classes of pronouns that are discussed in this chapter (a sixth class, relative pronouns, is discussed in Chapter 4).

- ☐ *Personal*: *I, you, he, she, it, they,* and so on.
- ☐ *Reflexive*: Reflexive pronouns are used to refer to somebody already mentioned in the same sentence. The reflexive pronouns

are personal pronouns which end in *-self* or *-selves*; for example, *myself, yourself, themselves*.

☐ *Indefinite*: Indefinite pronouns refer to an unspecified person, thing, or group; for example, *all, any, anyone, anybody, everybody, few, many*.

☐ *Demonstrative*: Demonstrative pronouns are used to point out a specific person or thing. This small closed class consists of only four pronouns: *this, that, these, those*.

☐ *Interrogative*: Interrogative pronouns are used in making questions. This class consists of five pronouns: *who, whom, whose, what, which*.

Personal pronouns

Personal pronouns are the most complex and important group of pronouns. Personal pronouns have many different forms according to three factors.

1. Person (first person, second person, third person). First person refers to the person who is speaking (*I, we, me, us*). Second person refers to the person being spoken to (*you*). Third person refers to somebody or something that we are talking about (*she, he, her, him, it, they, them*).

The traditional definition of pronoun as "a word used in place of one or of more than one noun" can be misleading for two reasons.

1. The first and second person pronouns are more like names than noun substitutes in that the first and second person pronouns are determined automatically by the speaker-hearer relationship (*I* = speaker, *you* = listener—more vividly, "Me Tarzan, you Jane").

2. Third person pronouns do more than replace nouns. Certainly the third person pronouns can be noun substitutes. For example, in the following sentence, the third person pronouns *she* and *him* replace nouns.

> <u>Lois</u> saw <u>Clark</u> in a phone booth.
> She   him

However, often the third person pronoun is a substitute not for a noun by itself, but the noun along with all of its modifiers. Consider the following sentence.

> The <u>guy</u> in the phone booth dressed in a silly-looking costume with a cape attracted a curious crowd.

The third person pronoun that replaces the subject *guy* also replaces along with the subject all the modifiers of the subject.

> <u>He</u> attracted a curious crowd.

In this case the third person pronoun *he* replaces *the guy in the phone booth dressed in a silly-looking costume with a cape.*

2. Number (singular or plural). English has the following pairs of singular and plural pronouns.

First person:	*Singular*	*Plural*
Subject	I	we
Object	me	us
Second person:	*Singular*	*Plural*
Subject	you	you
Object	you	you
Third person:	*Singular*	*Plural*
Subject	he, she, it	they
Object	him, her, it	them

Note that in the second person, the singular pronouns are identical in form with the plural pronouns. There is no grammatical way to distinguish singular *you* from plural *you* except by the context of the sentence.

3. Form (subject, object, possessive). *Subject* refers to pronouns (*I, you, he, she, it, we, they*) that are used as the subject of a sentence.

I answered the phone.
She answered the phone.

Object refers to the pronouns (*me, you, him, her, it, us, them*) that are used as the object of a sentence or the object of a preposition.

The boss heard me.
The boss talked about her.

In earlier periods of English the subject form of the pronoun was regularly used after the verb *be* and similar verbs (e.g., *it is I* and *it is we* rather than the modern spoken forms *it is me* and *it is us*). In formal writing, most people would prefer the subject forms after the verb *be*.

[*Joke:* Question: How do kings answer the telephone?
Answer: It is we.]

Possessive refers to the pronouns (*my, your, his, her, its, our, their*) that are used as a modifier of a following noun.

That is my book.	That is our book.	That is your book.
That is his book.	That is her book.	That is our book.

Since possessive pronouns function as noun modifiers, most books classify them as adjectives, though some books hedge the issue and call them pronominal adjectives. In this book we have classified possessive pronouns (along with possessive nouns) as adjectives.

Possessive pronouns also have a second form in which the noun that the possessive pronoun modifies is understood.

| That is <u>mine</u>. | That is <u>ours</u>. | That is <u>yours</u>. |
| That is <u>his</u>. | That is <u>hers</u>. | That is <u>ours</u>. |

These possessive forms (as opposed to the modifying possessives discussed in the preceding paragraph) are clearly pronouns since they stand for understood nouns, (e.g., *mine = my book*).

Following are the different personal pronouns arranged by person, number, and form, including the pronoun form of the possessive.

Personal Pronouns

First person pronouns

	Number	
	Singular	*Plural*
Subject	I	we
Object	me	us
Possessive		
Used as adjective	my	our
Pronoun	yours	yours

Second person pronouns

	Number	
	Singular	*Plural*
Subject	you	you
Object	you	you
Possessive		
Used as adjective	your	your
Pronoun	yours	yours

Third person pronouns

	Number	
	Singular	*Plural*
Subject	he, she, it	they
Object	him, her, it	them
Possessive		
Used as adjective	his, her, its	their
Pronoun	his, hers, its	theirs

■ **Exercise 1.7. Personal pronoun terminology**

Put in the proper personal pronoun according to the terms below the line. *1, 2,* and *3* refer to first, second, and third person; *Sg* and *Pl* refer to singular and plural number; and *Sub, Obj* and *Pos* refer to subject, object, and possessive form. Gender (e.g., *he/she*) is up to you. The first is done as an example. (Answers to exercises are found on page 378.)

1. Don't ___I___ know ___you___?
   1-Sg-Sub   2-Sg-Pos

2. Excuse _____, that coat is _____.
   1-Sg-Obj   1-Sg-Pos

3. _____ gave _____ the book back.
   3-Sg-Sub   3-Pl-Obj

4. _____ saw _____ at the movie last night.
   1-Pl-Sub   2-Pl-Obj

5. The cat left _____ on the porch.
   3-Sg-Obj

6. Give _____ to _____.
   3-Pl-Obj   1-Sg-Obj

7. _____ is _____.
   3-Sg-Sub   2-Sg-Pos

8. What is _____ is _____; what is _____ is _____, too.
   1-Sg-Pos   1-Sg-Pos   2-Sg-Pos   2-Sg-Pos

9. _____ gave _____ the brush-off.
   3-Sg-Sub   3-Sg-Obj

10. _____ sold _____ to _____.
    1-Pl-Sub   3-Pl-Obj   3-Sg-Obj

11. _____ is _____.
    3-Sg-Sub   1-Sg-Sub

Reflexive pronouns

Reflexive pronouns refer to a noun (usually the subject) in the same sentence. For example, compare the following two sentences.

> John saw him.
> John saw himself.

In the first sentence, *him* cannot refer to *John*; it must refer to somebody else. In the second sentence, *himself* can refer only to *John*.

Reflexive pronouns can also be used for emphasis.

> I wouldn't kiss Miss Piggy <u>myself</u>.
> I <u>myself</u> wouldn't kiss Miss Piggy.
> <u>Myself</u>, I wouldn't kiss Miss Piggy.

Following is a list of all the reflexive pronouns:

Reflexive Pronouns

First Person
Singular	myself
Plural	ourselves

Second Person
Singular	yourself
Plural	yourselves

Third Person
Singular	himself
	herself
	itself
Plural	themselves

Indefinite pronouns

There are a number of indefinite pronouns. One group of them is composed of *any, every, no,* and *some* followed by *-body, -one,* and *-thing.*

	-body	*-one*	*-thing*
any	anybody	anyone	anything
every	everybody	everyone	everything
no	nobody	no one	nothing
some	somebody	someone	something

The remaining common indefinite pronouns are the following.

all	many	one
another	more	other
both	most	several
each	much	some
either	neither	such
few	none	

The indefinite pronouns beginning with *every-* (*everybody, everyone,* and *everything*) pose a special problem of number. These three indefinite pronouns have a collective meaning, but are grammatically singular. Thus, there is a conflict between their meaning and their form. Some beginning writers will think that since these pronouns are plural in meaning, they must also be plural in form, and they will create sentences like the following.

*Everybody in school <u>were</u> there.

The problem is not really a subject-verb agreement problem; it is a problem in what the writer perceives to be the number of the subject.

Some of the words used as indefinite pronouns can also be used as modifying adjectives. For example, compare the use of *most* in the following sentences.

<u>Most</u> people find Watson slightly comical.
<u>Most</u> find Watson slightly comical.

In the first sentence *most* is used as an adjective modifying the noun *people*. In the second sentence *most* is used by itself as an indefinite pronoun.

Demonstrative pronouns

The four demonstrative pronouns, *this, that, these, and those,* can also be confused with the same words used as modifying adjectives. For example, compare the use of *this* in the following sentences.

I wanted to buy <u>this</u> book.
I wanted to buy <u>this</u>.

In the first sentence *this* is an adjective modifying *book*. In the second sentence *this* stands by itself as a demonstrative pronoun.

Interrogative pronouns

The pronouns that are used to begin questions are called interrogative pronouns. The interrogative pronouns that stand for nouns are *who* (together with its object form *whom* and its possessive form *whose*), *what*, and *which*. [There are four other words also used to begin questions: *when, where, how,* and *why*. Since these words stand for adverbs rather than nouns, they are usually not included in lists of interrogative pronouns.]

Like indefinite and demonstrative pronouns, interrogative pronouns can be easily confused with adjectives. Compare the following sentences.

<u>Which</u> frog are you?
<u>Which</u> are you?

In the first sentence, *which* is an adjective (technically, an interrogative adjective) modifying *frog*. In the second sentence *which* is an interrogative pronoun.

■ Exercise 1.8. Using pronoun terminology

Put an appropriate pronoun of the type called for into the blank. *P* = Personal; *R* = Reflexive; *I* = Indefinite; *D* = Demonstrative; ? = Interrogative. The first question is done as an example. (Answers to exercises are found on page 378.)

1. __This__ is another fine mess __you__ have gotten __me__
      D   P   P
   into.

2. _____ are _____?
     ?   P

3. _____ injured _____ while playing chess.
     P   R

4. _____ is a better buy than _____.
     D   D

5. _____ knows _____ name. _____ is the Lone
        I   P   P
   Ranger.

6. _____ never told _____ _____.
     P   P   D

7. _____ can _____ tell _____ about _____?
     ?   P   P   P

8. _____ is not what _____ meant.
     D   P

9. _____ of the third graders were worried about the calculus test.
     I

10. If _____ are not careful, _____ will cut _____.
        P   P   R

11. Well, _____ do _____ know about _____?
          ?   P   D

12. _____ delightful place is _____?
      ?   D

■ Exercise 1.9. Identifying pronouns

Underline the pronouns in the following sentences. Above the pronoun, identify which type it is by the following symbols: *P* = Personal; *R* = Reflexive; *I* = Indefinite; *D* = Demonstrative; ? = Interrogative. The first sentence is done as an example. Treat all modifying words as adjectives and not pronouns. (Answers to exercises are found on page 379.)

  P   P   R
1. I would rather do it myself.
2. What do you know about that?

 3. One for all and all for one.
 4. What can I do for you?
 5. That is the last thing I would do.
 6. Who asked him to come?
 7. Nobody knows the trouble I have seen.
 8. That contraption will never get off the ground, Wilbur.
 9. Can we get you anything at the store?
10. Another victory like that and we are done for.
11. Would you like another?
12. He is a friend of her sister.
13. She is a friend of ours.
14. Someone took all of the clean cups.
15. Your logic is impeccable but despicable.
16. Many are called, but few are chosen.

Personal Pronoun Problems

Two aspects of personal pronouns pose quite troublesome problems:
(1) the proper selection of subject/object form, and (2) avoiding sexist
use of personal pronouns. The first problem occurs when personal pronouns are used in compound constructions. When we use this particular
construction it is very easy to substitute a subject form for an object
form and vice versa. The following are examples of each type of error.

Subject for object: *Between you and I, liver turns my stomach.

Object for subject: *Fred and me are going to the store.

A common characteristic of the preceding examples is that one element in the compound is a word that does not distinguish between subject and object form. In the first example, the first element in the compound is the personal pronoun *you*. *You* does not change form whether
it is used as a subject ("*You* should call Sam.") or an object ("Sam
should call *you*.")

In the second example sentence containing a pronoun error, the first
element in the compound is the proper noun *Fred*, which, like all proper
nouns, does not distinguish between subject and object form.

For whatever reason, we seem to have great difficulty in using the
proper personal pronoun in compounds that contain an element that
does not distinguish between subject and object form. It is almost as
if the unchanging form of the element blocks us from naturally and
effortlessly selecting the correct form of the pronoun that does change
form.

Fortunately, there is a simple test that will instantly show if the compound construction is correct: substitute a plural pronoun (*we* or *us*; *they or them*) for the compound. Our sense of which plural pronoun sounds correct is very strong. If the correct plural pronoun substitute is the subject form *we* or *they*, then the singular subject forms *I*, *he*, and *she* will be correct. Conversely, if the correct plural pronoun substitute is the object form *us* or *them*, then the singular object forms *me*, *him*, and *her* will be correct. The plural pronoun test would identify the error in the first example sentence as follows.

    Subject for object: *Between <u>you and I</u>, liver turns my stomach.
                                       us

Since we know that the phrase *between us* sounds right and that *between we* sounds incorrect, we know we need to change the form of the singular pronoun from its subject form *I* to the object form *me* in order to agree with the corresponding plural object form *us*. The plural pronoun test helps us correct the error in the second example sentence in a similar way.

    Object for subject: *<u>Fred and me</u> are going to the store.
                                 we

Since we know that the subject-verb relation *we are going* sounds correct and that **us are going* sounds incorrect, we know we need to change the form of the singular pronoun from its object form *me* to the subject form *I* in order to agree with the corresponding plural subject *we*.

A similar test that you may also find helpful with your students is to delete (or cover up) the first word in the pair and the coordinating conjunction *and*.

    Subject for object: *Between you and I, liver turns my stomach.
    Revised: *Between I, liver turns my stomach.

    Object for subject: *Fred and me are going to the store.
    Revised: *Me are going to the store.

This test works especially well for object-for-subject pronouns, but as you can see, sometimes it is a little artificial with subject-for-object because the preposition (*between* in the preceding example) cannot be used with a single pronoun.

■ **Exercise 1.10. Pronoun case**

The following sentences contain compounds with pronouns. In some of the compounds, the case of the pronoun is correct; in others, the case is incorrect. If the pronoun is correct, label the pronoun with *OK*; if the pronoun is incorrect, make the necessary revision. In either case, show that your answer is correct by using the plural pronoun substitution test. An example of each type is given below. (Answers to exercises are found on page 379.)

1. <u>My brother and me</u> used to be good friends.
    We
   Revision: My brother and I used to be good friends.

                            OK
2. They gave it to <u>you and me.</u>
                            us
3. John and me want to be partners.
4. I hope that Fred and I can learn to get along with each other.
5. After Alice and him called, we had to change our dinner plans.
6. Above Dorrie and I was an ornate, carved ceiling.
7. The reason we are late is that Harvey and me got lost.
8. The gift was originally intended for Sally and she.
9. Our visitors went with Alfred and me to the movies.
10. The outcome of the case surprised both Holmes and I.
11. Louise answered the phone because Joel and me had already left.
12. Ludwig proudly announced that Gretchen and he had been selected.
13. Only Fred and me would have been home at the time.
14. Why did Mr. Smith ask you and I to leave?
15. Near Holmes and I was the dark tower that we had seen earlier.

The second problem, avoiding sexist use of personal pronouns, is a problem inherent in the language itself. The problem cannot really be corrected; it can only be avoided. When we refer to a person by the use of a personal pronoun, we must choose between the masculine gender forms, *he/him/his*, and the feminine gender forms, *she/her/her*. The problem arises when the distinction between genders is inappropriate. For example, in the following sentence, what pronoun should we use?

> If a doctor is available, please ask _____ to fill my prescription.

In the past, the convention was to use the masculine form if the actual gender of the person was unknown. There are two problems with this convention: (1) it treats women as though they did not exist, and (2) it tends to stereotype occupational roles. Thus, using *him* in the preceding example implies that it is normal for doctors to be males and abnormal for doctors to be females.

The solution to this problem is tricky because English, unlike many languages, does not have a gender-neutral third person singular pronoun. In other words, English forces us to pick either a masculine or a feminine pronoun. One solution is to use both forms. In the preceding example this would be

> If a doctor is available, please ask <u>him or her</u> to fill my prescription.

There is absolutely nothing wrong with this solution from a grammatical standpoint. However, many people find the compound pronoun (*him or her*) stylistically awkward. Attempts to create a combined written form (*s/he* or *(s)he*) have not been widely accepted.

Another solution is to switch the pronoun to the plural form (*they/them/their*) because the plural does not distinguish gender. This solution is widely used in spoken English. For example, imagine the following dialog.

> (Phone rings)
>
> A:　(Answers phone): Hello .
>   　　(Pauses): It's for you.
> B:　Ask <u>them</u> what <u>they</u> want.

Now, does B really think that the call is a conference call? A more likely explanation is that B uses the plural pronouns *them* and *they* to avoid choosing between *he/him* and *she/her*. This solution has become widespread in informal written English. For example, rather than writing

> As soon as a <u>student</u> finishes the exam, have <u>him</u> turn in <u>his</u> paper.

we can avoid the innappropriate gender-marked singular pronoun by substituting the gender-free third person.

> *As soon as a <u>student</u> finishes the exam, have <u>them</u> turn in <u>their</u> paper .

At some point in the future, it may also become correct in formal English. However, until that happy time, we are caught in a conflict between grammatical values (the requirement that pronouns agree with their antecedents in number) and social values.

The use of *they/them* to refer to a singular antecedent when we do not know the gender of the antecedent or when the gender of the antecedent is irrelevant solves one problem but tends to create another. The problem arises when we use a possessive pronoun to refer to these subjects.

> <u>Everybody</u> should hang up _____ coat.
>
> <u>Everyone</u> had already turned in _____ assignment.

The technically correct possessive pronoun to use in these sentences is the singular.

> <u>Everybody</u> should hang up <u>his</u> coat.
>
> <u>Everyone</u> had already turned in <u>his</u> assignment.

The formal solution, however, forces us to use a gender-marked pronoun, *his*, where gender-marking is inappropriate. The less formal solution is to use the plural pronoun.

Everybody should hang up their coat.

Everyone had already turned in their assignment.

These two indefinite pronouns are inherently genderless; thus, they are often used as subjects of sentences precisely when we do not know or do not want to specify the actual gender of the subject. The use of the plural possessive pronoun *their* to refer to singular indefinite subject pronouns tends to reinforce the subject-verb agreement problems that some students already have with indefinite pronouns. [You may recall that the indefinite pronouns beginning with *every-* (*everybody* and *everyone*), although they have a collective meaning, are grammatically singular.] Because some students perceive *everybody* and *everyone* to be plural, they write sentences like the following.

*Everybody in school were there.

Using the plural form *their* to refer to *everyone* and *everybody* may reinforce the tendency to view these indefinite pronouns as being plural forms. Thus this solution to the gender problem of personal pronouns may make the subject-verb agreement problem of indefinite pronouns worse.

While the gender problem may be partially solved using a plural pronoun (albeit awkwardly), the problem may be avoided altogether by using another alternative: change the subject noun from singular to plural so that the plural pronoun correctly agrees with it in number. For example, rather than writing

*As soon as a student finishes the exam, have them turn in their paper.

change the subject noun to its corresponding plural form (and make corresponding changes in the rest of the sentence).

As soon as students finish their exams, have them turn in their papers.

This solution focuses on the number of the subject noun rather than on the number of the pronoun. If the subject is plural, the problems of number and gender both disappear. The following example sentences can be revised to avoid sexist pronouns by making the subject plural.

If a doctor is available, please ask him to fill my prescription.

Revised: If any doctors are available, please ask one to fill my prescription.

When a person laughs too loudly, he makes me nervous.

Revised: When people laugh too loudly, they make me nervous.

Everybody has his own opinion on the matter.

Revised: They all have their own opinions on the matter.

■ **Exercise 1.11. Eliminating sexist pronouns**

Rewrite the following sentences to eliminate the inappropriate gender-marking of pronouns. The first question is done as an example. (Answers to exercises found on page 380.)

1. If you have a friend who might be interested, give him the information.
   Revised: If you have <u>friends</u> who might be interested, give <u>them</u> the information.

2. A native speaker of a language instantly understands whatever is said to him.

3. A successful politician always remembers the names of his constituents.

4. Someone in the next office was letting his phone ring.

5. When a person doesn't look at you when he is talking, we tend not to trust him.

6. An expert is someone who charges you for listening to him.

7. A man is known by the company he keeps.

8. Everyone had to put his two cents in.

9. Each member of the group indicated his first choice.

10. The agent who is in charge of the case will make his determination.

11. When a patient is in pain, he needs immediate attention.

12. Everybody has his weaknesses.

13. A procrastinator is someone who never finishes his work on time.

14. If a student wants to get good grades, he must study hard.

15. A customer always gets his way.

16. Each member of the task force had completed his assignment.

ADJECTIVES

Traditional definition: An adjective modifies a noun or a pronoun.

Adjectives are a difficult part of speech to deal with because there are numerous adjective subclasses, many of which behave in different ways. Nevertheless, the basic fact to remember about all adjectives is that they modify (or can be paraphrased to modify) nouns—just as the traditional definition states. There are two main ways that adjectives can be used, as *predicate adjectives* and as *modifying adjectives*.

Predicate adjectives

Predicate adjectives are adjectives that are used after linking verbs. Linking verbs are the verb *be* (in all its forms—*am, are, is, was, were, being, been*) and a few other verbs of sense perception or state of being. [Linking verbs are discussed in the section on verbs.] Virtually all predicate adjectives can also be used as modifying adjectives. Following are some examples of linking verbs and predicate adjectives with the same adjectives used as modifying adjectives.

Predicate Adjectives	*Modifying Adjectives*
The day was <u>hot</u>.	It is a <u>hot</u> day.
The cat is <u>frightened</u>.	It is a <u>frightened</u> cat.
Some children were <u>noisy</u>.	They were <u>noisy</u> children.
The soup tasted <u>strange</u>.	It was <u>strange</u> soup.
His tie seemed <u>crooked</u>.	He had a <u>crooked</u> tie.

A useful test for recognizing predicate adjectives is to put *very* (or *quite*) in front of the suspected adjective. If the word really is a predicate adjective, the result will be grammatical.

The day was <u>very</u> hot.
The cat is <u>very</u> frightened.
Some children were <u>very</u> noisy.
The soup tasted <u>very</u> strange.
His tie seemed <u>quite</u> crooked.

The *very* test is particularly useful for distinguishing predicate adjectives from certain verb forms, as in the following example sentence.

The children were <u>working</u>.

The word *working* follows a form of the verb *to be*. Yet *working* is not a predicate adjective, as the *very* test shows.

*The children were <u>very</u> working.

Nearly all predicate adjectives can also occur in a *comparative* and *superlative* form. The comparative either adds *-er* or *more* to the *base* (or *positive*) form of the adjective; the superlative adds either *-est* or *most* to the base. (There are also a few irregular forms of the comparative and superlative.) Following are some examples.

Base	*Comparative*	*Superlative*
hot	hotter	hottest
frightened	more frightened	most frightened
noisy	noisier	noisiest
strange	stranger	strangest
crooked	more crooked	most crooked
good	better	best
bad	worse	worst

Predicate adjectives often (but not always) have a corresponding adverb of manner that ends in *-ly*. Here are some examples:

Predicate adjective	*Adverb of manner*
She is swift.	She runs swiftly.
She is polite.	She acts politely.
She is nasty.	She acts nastily.
She is firm.	She acts firmly.

In summary, predicate adjectives can be identified by testing to see if the word has the following characteristics.

☐ Can be used with *very* or *quite*
☐ Has a comparative and superlative form
☐ Can be paraphrased as a modifying adjective
☐ Has a corresponding adverb of manner form ending in *-ly*

While not every predicate adjective will have all of the preceding characteristics (particularly the adverb of manner), taken as a whole, these characteristics quite reliably identify predicate adjectives.

■ **Exercise 1.12 Identifying predicate adjectives**

Underline the predicate adjectives in the following sentences. Demonstrate that your answer is correct by (1) applying the *very* test, (2) making the adjective comparative and superlative, (3) paraphrasing the predicate adjective as a modifying adjective, and (4) changing the predicate adjective into an adverb of manner. The first sentence is done as an example. (Answers to exercises are found on page 381.)

1. The patient was alert
   1. *Very* test: The patient was very alert.
   2. Comparative: more alert
      Superlative: most alert
   3. Modifying adjective: an alert patient
   4. Adverb of manner: alertly
2. Her entry into the water was graceful.
3. His sense of humor is strange.
4. The attack was unprovoked.
5. The investigation of the incident seemed thorough.
6. His gestures were often dramatic.
7. The approach to the problem seems practical.
8. The children were disappointed.
9. The society has been active for many years.
10. At that altitude the air becomes thin.

11. The proposal was interesting.
12. The kids were playing football.
13. The issue was dead.
14. The issue was deadly.
15. The students were resting.

Modifying adjectives

There are many ways that modifying adjectives can be analyzed. We have classified adjectives in terms of the relative order in which they occur before nouns. To take a simple example, we can say *the old man* but we cannot say **old the man*. In other words, the fact that *the* and *old* are not interchangeable (i.e., that they are in a fixed left-to-right order with respect to each other) is used to establish that *the* and *old* belong to two different classes of modifying adjectives.

The classes are also established by the fact that words from the same class are usually mutually exclusive. For example, we can say *a man* or *the man* but we cannot say either **a the man* or **the a man*. Adjective classes are something like a menu in a Chinese restaurant: one choice from Column A, one from Column B, and so on.

On the basis of relative order and mutual exclusion, there are at least seven major classes of adjectives. In order from left to right the classes are as follows.

1. *Articles, Determiners, and Possessives:*
   Articles: *a, the* (also like articles are the adjective uses of *some* and *much*, and the adjective *many*)
   Determiners: *this, that, these, those*
   Possessive nouns and pronouns: *my, our, your, his, her, its, their, John's, Mary's*

2. *Quantifiers:*
   Numbers: *first, second, third*, and so on
   Other quantifying words: *only, last*, and so on

3. *General adjectives:*
   gracious, beautiful, peculiar, splendid, and so on. This is by far the largest class of adjectives. Included in this group are "participle" adjectives, that is, adjectives ending in *-ing* (e.g., *dripping, alarming, disgusting*) and *-ed* or *-en* (e.g., *wounded, amused, discouraged, broken, frozen*). This class includes many minor subclasses.

4. *Age: young, old, new, elderly, ancient*, and so on

5. *Color: blue, green, aquamarine, white*, and so on

6. *Material: stone, wooden, wool, silk, cotton*, and so on

7. *Origin: British, American, Parisian, foreign, native*, and so on

Following are some sample phrases illustrating the relative order of adjectives.

1	2	3	4	5	6	7	
Det.	*Number*	*General*	*Age*	*Color*	*Material*	*Origin*	*Noun*
the	two	wretched	old				textbooks
	several	beautiful		red	cotton		prints
Fred's		shiny	new			Swiss	coins
the	last	surviving			wooden		ship
		long		blonde			hair
a		little	old			Canadian	lady
our	only	mutual					friend
a		wealthy	young				bachelor
the	dozen	special	aged	red		French	wines

■ Exercise 1.13. Recognizing modifying adjective classes

Following are scrambled groups of modifying adjectives and the noun that they modify. Put the adjectives and noun back in the right order and put the number of the class above each adjective. In each question, all adjectives belong to different classes. The first question is done as an example. (Answers to exercises are found on page 382.)

1. so-called problem Russian the
   1   3   7
   the so-called Russian problem
2. ship a wood old huge
3. primitive the societies first European
4. sensitive pink some tissue new
5. cape valuable feather red Sir Roderick's
6. evil that idol stone old
7. finish popular new its satin
8. continental innovative our design new
9. population entire urban the
10. broken several crates wooden
11. new problems these frightening technical
12. pizza our sausage hot
13. annual the dinner German third
14. old our desks two massive oak
15. explorers the European known first
16. cotton my clean shirt white only

Modifying adjectives are not nearly as regular as predicate adjectives. While virtually all predicate adjectives can be paraphrased as modifying adjectives, the reverse is often not true. There are several classes of modifying adjectives that cannot be used as predicate adjectives. A simple example is the modifying adjective *the*. We can say *the idea*, but we cannot say **an idea is the*. Nor do all modifying adjectives have a comparative and superlative form. For example, there is no comparative or superlative form for *the*. Finally, not all modifying adjectives can be identified by the use of *very*: we cannot say **very the*. The following table summarizes which classes of modifying adjectives (1) can be used as predicate adjectives, (2) have a comparative and superlative form, (3) can be used with *very* and *quite*, and (4) have a corresponding adverb of manner.

Adjective Class	Predicate Adjective	Comparative/ Superlative	Very/ Quite	Adverb of Manner
1. Article	No	No	No	No
2. Quantifier	No	No	No	No
3. General	Yes	Yes*	Yes*	Yes
4. Age	Yes	Yes	Yes	Yes*
5. Color	Yes	Yes	?Yes	No
6. Material	Yes**	No	No	No
7. Origin	Yes	?Yes	?Yes	No

* Many exceptions
** Grammatical, but the meaning shifts. See following discussion.

Following is an illustration of each adjective class.

Adjective Class
1. Article: <u>some</u> pencils

Predicate adjective:	*the pencils were some
Comparative/superlative:	*more some/*most some
Very/quite:	*very some/quite some
Adverb of manner:	*somely

2. Quantifier: <u>second</u> notice

Predicate adjective:	*the notice was second
Comparative/superlative:	*more second/*most second
Very/quite:	*very second/*quite second
Adverb of manner:	*secondly
	(grammatical in different use; for example, *secondly, I would like to say...*)

3. General: <u>swift</u> car

Predicate adjective:	The car is swift
Comparative/superlative:	swifter/swiftest
Very/quite:	very swift/quite swift
Adverb of manner:	swiftly

4. Age: <u>ancient</u> mariner

Predicate adjective:	the mariner was ancient
Comparative/superlative:	more ancient/most ancient
Very/quite:	very ancient/quite ancient
Adverb of manner:	*anciently

5. Color: <u>blue</u> dress

Predicate adjective:	the dress is blue
Comparative/superlative:	bluer/bluest
Very/quite:	?very blue/?quite blue
Adverb of manner:	*bluely

6. Material: <u>stone</u> wall

Predicate adjective:	the wall was stone (with different meaning "was made of" stone rather than "is" stone)
Comparative/superlative:	*more stone/*most stone
Very/quite:	*very stone/*quite stone
Adverb of manner:	*stonely

7. Origin: <u>American</u> ship

Predicate adjective:	the ship was American
Comparative/superlative:	?more American/?most American
Very/quite:	very American/quite American
Adverb of manner:	*Americanly

One small group of adjectives, sometimes called *absolute adjectives*, fail some of the adjective tests because of their meaning. Most adjectives describe a quality that admits of degree. For example, *Fred is polite*, but *Ralph is more polite than Fred*, but *Tom is the most polite of all*. In other words, *polite*, like most adjectives, implies a scale of politeness. This point is also made in the expression "No matter how *good* you are, you can always get *better*." A few adjectives, however, are already at the end of their scale and cannot be improved—hence the term *absolute*. *Main* and *chief* are two examples of such absolute adjectives. We can say *the main chance* or *the chief idea*, but both *main* and *chief* fail the adjective tests.

Very test:	*very main chance;	*very chief idea
Comparative:	*mainer/*more main;	*chiefer/*more chief
Superlative:	*mainest/*most main;	*chiefest/*most chief

■ Exercise 1.14. Identifying adjectives

Draw a line under every adjective in the following sentences. Put *A* above each modifying (i.e. pre-noun) adjective and a *PA* above each predicate adjective. (Answers to exercises are found on page 383.) The first is done for you as an example.

   A   PA
1. His teeth were yellow.
2. His first book was about early rural development in England.
3. The first subject was only of academic interest.
4. The next proud owner of a new portable hot tub will be announced soon. (Note: *hot tub* is a compound noun that has been in use since about 1975.)
5. Finally, the bathtub was clean.
6. Eighteenth-century Latin grammar is the source of modern grammar.
7. His new coat was in a sorry state after the thunderstorm.
8. The semi-liquid steel is poured out in a continuous mass.
9. The questions seemed odd.
10. A successful swindler often has polite manners.
11. They selected an accurate new machine.
12. The hand-made wool suit looked expensive.
13. The dark stranger was a rough, tough hombre.
14. His incoherent explanation was unsatisfactory.
15. The possible junior partnership sounded promising.
16. Often the early bird gets the worms.
17. A word to the wise is sufficient.
18. His insulting behavior almost created a major diplomatic incident.

The relative order of the seven classes of modifying adjectives is important to understand because this order is reflected in our punctuation of adjectives. Compare the following two sentences.

> The six thin black cats slipped through the door.
> It was a sunlit, windy day in April.

In the first sentence the adjectives are not separated by commas, whereas in the second sentence *sunlit* and *windy* are separated. Clearly, it is not the *number* of adjectives that determines whether we use a comma; it is the *kind* of adjectives. In the first sentence each of the four adjectives belongs to a different class: *the* is a class 1 article; *six* is a class 2 quantifier; *thin* is a class 3 general adjective; and *black* is a class 5 color adjective. In the second sentence, however, both *sunlit* and *windy* are class 3 general adjectives. The following rule applies.

> *Multiple adjectives from the same class (called* **coordinate adjectives***) must be separated by commas; adjectives from different classes are not separated by commas.*

The use of coordinate class 3 general adjectives is quite common—more common than coordinate adjectives from all other classes put together. Following are some more examples of coordinate, class 3 adjectives.

His work has a strange, haunted quality.
He works for a small, energetic company.
The region is a dry, flat, barren land.
The command was given in cold, harsh, threatening tones.

Two useful tests to help identify coordinate adjectives are (1) reversing the adjectives and (2) putting *and* between them. If you can reverse the adjectives and put *and* between them (while keeping the same basic meaning), then they must belong to the same class and are thus coordinate adjectives. The tests work because adjectives from the same class (usually the "general" class) have no inherent order with one another. Order holds only for adjectives from different classes. Applying the tests to the first of the preceding example sentences, we get the following results.

Example: His work has a strange, haunted quality.
Test 1:   His work has a haunted, strange quality.
Test 2:   His work has a strange and haunted quality.

When we try to apply the same tests to adjectives from different classes, the result is very odd sounding. For example, when we apply the tests to *thin* and *black*, the results either sound strange or mean something we did not mean to imply.

The six thin black cats slipped through the door.
*The six black thin cats slipped through the door.
* The six thin and black cats slipped through the door.

The last test sentence might imply that there were twelve cats: six thin cats and six black ones.

■ **Exercise 1.15. Punctuating adjectives**

Provide the appropriate commas to indicate coordinate adjectives. (Answers to exercises are found on page 384.)

1. The young lad had a cheerful happy smile for everyone.
2. As far as I am concerned, he is a regular old crook.
3. Dracula had an ordinary normal childhood.
4. He answered the detective's questions in halting accented English.
5. His suggestion provided an effective convenient solution.
6. He was a proper English butler of the old school.
7. He was a difficult contrary obstinate child.
8. She decided that her basic black dress was appropriate.
9. Lady Mortlock's heart was smitten by the tall dark stranger.
10. It is a dangerous dirty job, but someone has to do it.
11. We all noticed her delicate smooth complexion.
12. She toyed with her beautiful new pearls.
13. Holmes fixed the cabbie with a remarkably steady cold eye.
14. Alexander had a terrible horrible no-good very bad day.
15. Lady Dedlock was hopelessly attracted by the lawyer's sophisti-cated witty conversation.
16. The mysterious dark shape had been seen in the abbey again.
17. The original American musical was changed into a British novel.
18. Unfortunately, we attended a disorganized sloppy unprofessional performance.

The following are some final observations concerning adjectives and their uses. Modifying adjectives can only modify nouns; they cannot modify other adjectives. A word that modifies an adjective is, by defi-nition, an adverb. Be sure in a given phrase that all words in front of a noun are actually modifying that noun. An easy way to check is to pair up the adjectives with the noun one adjective at a time. Consider the following sentence.

The six thin black cats slipped through the door.

We can show that *the, six, thin,* and *black* are adjectives by pairing them, one word at a time, with the noun *cats*.

the cats
six cats
thin cats
black cats

However, the same test produces different results on the words in front of the noun *cooks* in the following sentence.

Too many cooks spoil the broth.

We find that *many* is an adjective, but that *too* is not.

many cooks
*too cooks

Too is an adverb modifying the adjective *many*. This construction, an adverb modifying an adjective, is common—and easily overlooked.

Do not be confused by having to change *a* to *an* or vice versa when you pair up adjectives with nouns, as in the following sentence.

An enormous black dog appeared out of the fog.

The noun *dog* is modified by three adjectives, as we can determine by pairing each of them with the noun.

a dog
enormous dog
black dog

Note that we must change the form of the indefinite article from *an* to *a*. This change has nothing to do with the difference between adjective and adverb modifiers; the reason for this change is that the use of *a* or *an* is determined by whether the following word begins with a consonant or a vowel sound: *an enormous dog, a dog*. The change of form of the indefinite article is one of the small adjustments we must make when we use any kind of paraphrase test.

When a possessive noun is used as a modifier, the distinction between adjective and adverb is surprisingly tricky. For example, in the following sentence the word *detective's* is a possessive noun.

The famous <u>detective's</u> movements became precise.

While the *form* of the word *detective's* is a possessive noun, its *function* is that of a modifier of the noun *movements*. As a modifier, *detective's* is an adjective. However, if *detective's* is classified as an adjective, the word *famous* that modifies *detective's* must be an adverb, since a word that modifies an adjective must be an adverb.

Nevertheless, *famous* has all of the formal characteristics of an adjective modifying a noun.

<u>famous</u> detective

Predicate adjective:	The detective was famous.
Comparative/superlative:	more famous/most famous
Very/quite:	very famous/quite famous
Adverb of manner:	famously

Traditional grammar is faced with a conflict between form (*famous* as an adjective and *detective's* as a possessive noun) and function (*famous* as an adverb and *detective's* as an adjective). In this particular situation, traditional grammar considers *detective's* to be an adjective with respect to *movements*, and a noun with respect to its modifier *famous*. In other words, possessive nouns have a dual nature—they are both nouns and adjectives. No traditional grammar book, however, would consider the modifier of a possessive noun to be an adverb. All modifiers of possessive nouns are (quite reasonably) treated as adjectives. The situation is similar to possessive pronouns, which are pronouns in form but adjectives in function.

■ **Exercise 1.16. Identifying adjectives and adverbs that modify adjectives**

Draw a line under every adjective in the following sentences. Put *Adv* above each adverb that modifies an adjective. The first sentence is done as an example. (Answers to exercises are found on page 384.)

1. The urbane Holmes offered Watson a crushingly logical explanation.
2. The thought of a day in the country was an extremely good idea.
3. Their unorthodox proposal brought a very swift response.
4. They bought a quite beautiful old print of a square-rigged ship.
5. No one expects the Spanish Inquisition!
6. The mad professor had struck again.
7. The new bargaining agreement was easily ratified.
8. Their first trip across the Atlantic Ocean was a terrifying experience.
9. The public's reaction to the work was a definitely cold one.
10. The government attempted a surprisingly bold diplomatic initiative.
11. The profusely grateful clients thanked Holmes.
12. The surprising new claim was given a thoroughly demanding test.
13. I didn't think the idea seemed very funny at all.
14. In spite of his undoubtedly heroic efforts, Watson didn't have a clue.
15. Donald memorized tediously long lists of Anglo-Saxon kings.
16. The perpetually damp British summer weather became depressing.
17. A successful mystery writer makes us miss the clearly obvious facts.
18. In a well-known early story, Holmes was completely outwitted by an apparently naive young woman.

VERBS

Traditional definition: A *verb* is a word that expresses action or otherwise helps to make a statement.

There are two main classes of verbs in traditional grammar: *action verbs* and *linking verbs*.

Action verbs

The term *action* refers to the action performed by the subject of the sentence, i.e., an action verb states what the subject of the sentence *does*, as in the following sentences.

> Peter Piper <u>picked</u> a peck of pickled peppers.
> Rudolph <u>wrote</u> a riddle.
> Sally <u>scorched</u> her skirt.

The action in an action verb does not have to be physical action; it can also be mental action.

> Belinda <u>believed</u> the bulletin.
> Randolph <u>remembered</u> the riddle.
> Nell <u>knows</u> the number.
> Fred <u>forgot</u> his flippers.

Linking verbs

In sentences with linking verbs there is no action that the subject performs. Instead, the linking verb *describes* the subject as in the following examples.

> Uncle Harry <u>is</u> awful.
> The sandwich <u>smells</u> good.
> The kids <u>are</u> snotty.
> John <u>feels</u> awful.
> The children <u>became</u> angry.

In the first preceding example sentence, Uncle Harry is not doing anything. Rather, the linking verb *is* (a form of *be*) helps describe what Uncle Harry is like. In the second sentence, the sandwich is not doing anything; the linking verb *smells* helps describe what the sandwich is like, and so on.

There is only a handful of linking verbs. Nevertheless, linking verbs are extremely important because they occur so frequently. By far the most common linking verb is *be*. *Be* is the most irregular verb in English. Following are the various present and past tense forms of *be*, along with the traditional names for them.

be

Present system:

	Singular	*Plural*
1st Person	I am	we are
2nd Person	you are	you are
3rd Person	he/she/it is	they are

Past system:

1st Person	I was	we were
2nd Person	you were	you were
3rd Person	he/she/it was	they were

■ **Exercise 1.17. Recognizing forms of *be***

Provide appropriate words for the blank spaces. The first blank space in each sentence is for a subject pronoun. The second blank space is for a particular form of *be*. 1st, 2nd, and 3rd refer to person; *Sg* and *Pl* refer to number; and *Past* and *Pres* refer to tense. The subject pronoun must agree with the required form of *be*. Do the verb first. The first exercise is done as an example. (Answers to exercises are found on page 385.)

1. ____It____ ____was____ stuck up in the tree again.
   Subject / 3rd-Sg-Past

2. _____ _____ in very bad shape.
   Subject / 3rd-Pl-Past

3. _____ _____ not your sweet baboo!
   Subject / 1st-Sg-Pres

4. _____ _____ a menace to the public.
   Subject / 2nd-Sg-Pres

5. _____ _____ such good friends.
   Subject / 3rd-Pl-Past

6. _____ _____ an only child.
   Subject / 1st-Sg-Past

7. _____ _____ absolutely mistaken about that!
   Subject / 3rd-Pl-Pres

8. _____ _____ in such a hurry to finish.
   Subject / 2nd-Pl-Past

9. _____ _____ a pain in the neck.
   Subject / 3rd-Sg-Past

10. _____ _____ able to leap tall buildings at a
    Subject / 1st-Sg-Pres
    single bound.

11. _____ _____ sixteen.
    Subject / 2nd-Sg-Past

Many linking verbs are verbs of sense perception.

sight: Alice <u>appeared</u> angry about something.
Luke <u>looked</u> lost.
Sam <u>seemed</u> sad.

sound: The note <u>sounded</u> flat.

smell: The dog <u>smelled</u> awful.

taste: The sandwich <u>tasted</u> stale.

The remaining linking verbs describe the state or condition of the subject.

He <u>became</u> angry.
They <u>grew</u> strong.
The patient <u>remained</u> weak.
We <u>got</u> angry.
I <u>feel</u> sick.
The cheese <u>turned</u> green.

In the preceding example sentences, notice that all the linking verbs are followed by predicate adjectives. Indeed, one of the most important characteristics of <u>linking verbs</u> is that they <u>can be followed by predicate adjectives</u>. Predicate adjectives cannot be used with action verbs. Notice, for example, the difference between the following sentences.

linking: I am <u>angry</u>.
action: I answered <u>angrily</u>.

Angry is a predicate adjective, whereas *angrily* is an adverb. It is not grammatical to switch them.

linking: *I am <u>angrily</u>.
action: *I answered <u>angry</u>.

Some verbs can be either a linking verb or an action verb, depending on how they are used.

linking: The detective <u>felt</u> sick.
action: The detective <u>felt</u> the body for a gun.

In the first sentence *felt sick* describes the detective's state. In the second sentence *felt* is the action that the detective was performing.

A helpful (but not foolproof) test for determining whether a verb is an action or a linking verb is to ask a question with *do* (or *does/did*, depending on the sentence). If the verb is an action verb, there will be a grammatical answer beginning with the verb, as in the following example.

Sentence:	The detective felt the body for a gun.
Do *question*:	What did the detective do?
Answer:	felt the body for a gun.

If we ask the same kind of *do* question with a linking verb, we get an ungrammatical answer to the *do* question.

Sentence:	The detective felt sick.
Do *question*:	What did the detective do?
Answer:	*felt sick.

We can use the same test for sentences with nouns following the verb.

Sentence:	The detective observed the suspect.
Do *question*:	What did the detective do?
Answer:	observed the suspect. (action verb)

Sentence:	The detective was the suspect.
Do *question*:	What did the detective do?
Answer:	*be the suspect. (linking verb)

Another test that often helps identify linking verbs is to see if you can replace the linking verb with the appropriate form of the verb *be*. Most linking verbs can be reasonably well paraphrased by *be*, which action verbs cannot. Following are some examples.

Linking verbs:

Luke looked lost.
Luke was lost.

The sandwich tasted stale.
The sandwich was stale.

He became angry.
He was angry.

I stayed awake.
I was awake.

Action verbs:

Sam stole second base.
*Sam was second base.

We unplugged the lamp.
*We were the lamp.

When checking for linking verbs, remember the following points.

- ☐ Predicate adjectives can be used only with linking verbs.
- ☐ *Be* as a main verb (as opposed to *be* as a helping verb) is a linking verb.
- ☐ All linking verbs help describe the subject.
- ☐ Verbs of sense perception and state are usually linking verbs.
- ☐ Action verbs can use *do/does/did* to form questions.
- ☐ Linking verbs can be paraphrased with a form of *be*.

■ **Exercise 1.18. Identifying action and linking verbs**

Underline the verbs in the following sentences. Put an *A* above action verbs and *L* above linking verbs. The first sentence is done for you. (Answers to exercises are found on page 386.)

  A
1. I <u>wandered</u> around all afternoon.
2. Mr. Brown confirmed his reservation.
3. Mr. Brown grew angry at the delay.
4. The noise in the room was absolutely overwhelming.
5. The Feds stimulate the economy through the interest rate.
6. I am not an alarmist!
7. Dr. Rodgers classified the specimens by chemical composition.
8. His categories seem correct to me.
9. The engineers initiated the process.
10. It gets worse every day.
11. Next, soften the butter.
12. The visitors looked grateful.
13. The visitors looked around gratefully.
14. I went first.
15. She gazed out the windows.
16. The ideas seem OK to me.
17. Leon gets upset easily.
18. They recruit string players from the nearby colleges.

Finite tenses—present and past

Verbs (whether action or linking) can be used either by themselves or they can be used with one or more helping, or auxiliary, verbs. When a verb is used by itself as a main verb, it is called a *finite* verb. When a main verb is used with a helping verb, the main verb is said to be in a *nonfinite* form. In this section we are dealing only with finite verbs. There are two finite forms for all verbs: a *present* tense and a *past* tense. There is no future tense carried by a single verb by itself: in traditional terminology the future tense is expressed by adding the helping verb *will*, making the future a nonfinite verb form. For example, compare the form of *love* in the following sentences.

Present tense: He <u>loves</u> his new cookbook.

Past tense: He <u>loved</u> his new cookbook.

Future tense: He <u>will love</u> his new cookbook.

In the present and past tense, *love* is a finite verb—it stands alone without a helping verb. In the future tense, however, *love* cannot stand alone—it requires the helping verb *will* to make a complete sentence. In the future tense *love* is a nonfinite form. Combinations of helping verbs and nonfinite verbs make up a number of additional constructions that are described in Chapter 3 when we deal with verb phrases.

Present tense

The present tense has a distinct ending *-(e)s*. However, this ending is used only in certain circumstances; otherwise, the present has no distinctive form by which it can be recognized. The *-(e)s* ending is used only when the subject is a third person singular pronoun (*he, she, it*) or noun for which a third person singular pronoun can substitute.

<u>John</u> look<u>s</u> terrific.
　He

<u>Mary</u> look<u>s</u> terrific.
　She

<u>The dog</u> look<u>s</u> terrific.
　　It

The third person singular *-(e)s* is quite regular in form. The only two verbs that are irregular in the third person singular are *be* (third person singular: *is*) and *have* (third person singular: *has*).

Otherwise, the present tense has no distinct form: it is identical with the *dictionary* form (also called the *infinitive* form). For example, the remaining personal pronouns are used with verbs that have no distinctive present form by which they can be recognized.

I <u>look</u> terrific.

You <u>look</u> terrific.

We <u>look</u> terrific.

They <u>look</u> terrific.

All plural nouns are also used with verbs that have no distinct present form.

> The dogs <u>look</u> terrific.

We might say that in all the preceding examples *look* is an "unmarked" present. That is, it is present tense, but it has no distinctive form to signal the fact that it is being used as present tense. Remember, an infinitive verb form can never be used without a helping verb. Thus any verb used without a helping verb cannot be an infinitive; it must be either a present tense or a past tense.

Past tense

Historically, there were two main ways of forming past tenses, called *regular* and *irregular*. Regular verbs formed a past tense by adding *-(e)d* to the dictionary or infinitive form of the verb.

Dictionary form	*Past tense form*
pass	passed
cough	coughed
smile	smiled
dread	dreaded

Irregular verbs did not add the *-(e)d* ending but instead changed the vowel of the dictionary form.

Dictionary form	*Past tense form*
dig	dug
ring	rang
freeze	froze
see	saw
run	ran

However, over time there were so many changes that today we have a crazy patchwork of past tense forms. For example, there are verbs with past tenses that are a mixture of regular and irregular forms, i.e., they have both a vowel change and a regular ending (*sell-sold*). There is a group of verbs that have no distinct past tense form at all; the verbs in this group are single-syllable verbs that end in *-t* or *-d*; for example: *hit-hit; slit-slit; cut-cut; rid-rid; shed-shed*. There is even a verb with a past tense that is not historically related to its infinitive form (*go-went*).

The verb *be* is unique. It is formed from four historically different verbs. One verb, *be*, provided the infinitive form and the two participle forms, *being* and *been*; a second verb provided the forms that begin with *a—am* and *are*; a third verb provided *is*; and a fourth verb provided the past tense forms—the forms that begin with *w—was* and *were*. The verb *be* is also unique among verbs in that it distinguishes between first, second, and third persons in the present tense and has two different forms in the past.

Once you consciously notice verb tense markers, third person singular and past tense are easy to recognize because of their distinctive forms. The problem in recognizing verbs is with the present tense forms that are not third person singular, because these forms have no distinctive ending that indicates that they are a verb. There are two very simple tests to see if a word is a verb: (1) change the suspected verb from the present tense form to the past tense form or (2) add the helping verb *will* to form a future tense. For example, suppose that we want to find out if the word *love* in the following sentence is a verb.

> The children <u>love</u> New York.

We can show that *love* is a verb by recasting the sentence into the past or by adding *will*.

> *Past tense*:   The children <u>loved</u> New York.
>
> ***will***:   The children <u>will love</u> New York.

Since verbs are the only words that can have past tense forms and can be used with the helping verb *will*, we know that *love* must be a verb. When we try to use these two tests on a word that is not a verb, the result is ungrammatical. For example, suppose that for some strange reason we thought *spinach* might be a verb. Notice what happens when we apply the tests.

> *Sentence*:   Children love <u>spinach</u>.
>
> *Past tense*:   *Children love <u>spinached</u>.
>
> ***will***:   *Children love <u>will spinach</u>.

■ **Exercise 1.19. Testing for verbs**

Underline the verbs in the following sentences. Demonstrate that your answer is correct by (1) changing the verb from the present tense into the past and (2) adding *will*. The first sentence is done as an example. (Answers to exercises are found on page 387.)

1. The wheels <u>slide</u> into that groove.

  > *Past*:   The wheels <u>slid</u> into that groove.
  >
  > ***will***:   The wheels <u>will slide</u> into that groove.

2. They score more points in the second half.
3. Critics characterize his plots as simplistic.
4. My fingers become stiff in cold weather.
5. The rules generate a number of sentences.

6. The cookies look strange.
7. South-bound trains usually depart from Platform 2.
8. Red wines generally improve with age.
9. Time and tide wait for no man.
10. They meet our requirements.
11. The aches and pains persist for several days.
12. They are strange bedfellows.
13. Crop rotation and good tilling reduce soil loss.
14. They reproduce like rabbits.
15. The salesmen exaggerate.
16. The wines go with the food very well.
17. Grammarians classify words by part of speech categories.

ADVERBS

Traditional definition: An adverb is a word used to modify a verb, an adjective, or another adverb.

The class of adverbs is large and diverse. It is safe to say that if a word is a modifier but does not modify a noun, then the word must be an adverb. Adverbs modify (in order of frequency) (1) *verbs*, (2) *adjectives*, and (3) *other adverbs*.

1. Adverbs modifying verbs

Adverbs modifying verbs can be classified according to their meaning: time, place, manner, extent/degree, means, and so on. The most useful way of recognizing adverbs modifying verbs is by rephrasing the sentence as a question that elicits the adverb as the answer.

time:	They unloaded the truck <u>yesterday</u>.
adverb question:	<u>When</u> did they unload the truck?
answer:	<u>Yesterday</u>

This test demonstrates, by the way, that the names of the days of the week, despite the fact that they look like nouns, can function as adverbs; for example:

time:	They unloaded the truck <u>Tuesday</u>.
adverb question:	<u>When</u> did they unload the truck?
answer:	<u>Tuesday</u>

Here are examples of other categories of adverbs that modify verbs:

place:	John left his books <u>here</u>.
adverb question:	<u>Where</u> did John leave his books?
answer:	<u>Here</u>
manner:	We washed the plants <u>carefully</u>.
adverb question:	<u>How</u> did we wash the plants?
answer:	<u>Carefully</u>

How is actually ambiguous. In addition to asking adverb of manner questions, it also asks adverb of means questions, that is, by what means something is done. A lot of not very funny jokes depend on this ambiguity.

question:	How do you take an atomic bomb apart?
answer:	Carefully.

The joke (such as it is) turns on the fact that *how* seems to be asking an adverb of means question ("By what means do you take an atomic bomb apart?") but is answered by *carefully*, an adverb of manner.

How has another role unconnected with adverbs: *how* also asks questions that are answered by predicate adjectives.

predicate adjective:	John is <u>angry</u>.
how *question*:	<u>How</u> is John?
predicate adjective answer:	<u>angry</u>

Watch out for *how* questions that are answered by predicate adjectives; these are very easy to overlook.

Adverbs of manner are the only adverbs that have a distinctive form: they consist of an adjective + *-ly*; for example: *quiet-quietly; firm-firmly; rapid-rapidly; sentimental-sentimentally*. However, not every word that ends in an *-ly* suffix is an adverb of manner. A few adjectives are formed by adding *-ly* to certain nouns; for example: *scholar-scholarly; king-kingly;* and *queen-queenly*.

Adverbs of extent or degree answer questions with *how far, how often* and so on.

extent/degree:	She ran <u>miles</u>.
adverb question:	<u>How far</u> did she run?
answer:	<u>Miles</u>
extent/degree:	Harry comes here <u>frequently</u>.
adverb question:	<u>How often</u> does Harry come here?
answer:	<u>Frequently</u>

■ **Exercise 1.20. Identifying adverbs that modify verbs**

In the following sentences, underline the adverb that modifies the verb. Show that your answer is correct by converting the sentence into an adverb question and answer. The first sentence is done as an example. (Answers to exercises are found on page 388.)

1. Watson <u>hastily</u> jotted down the secret message.

    adverb question: How did Watson jot down the secret message?
    answer: <u>hastily</u>

2. The vet had examined the horse recently.
3. The ants crawled everywhere.
4. The children were plainly dressed.
5. The pilot looked down.
6. He quickly unzipped the tent flap.
7. She answered the questions correctly.
8. The operator will return your call immediately.
9. Gradually they became accustomed to the altitude.
10. Recently we sent you a letter.
11. I played badly today.
12. We rarely watch TV.
13. Leon invariably sleeps through his 8 o'clock class.
14. She told the story effectively.
15. It had to happen eventually.
16. I left my glasses somewhere.
17. There will be a full moon tonight.

2. Adverbs modifying adjectives

Adjectives cannot modify other adjectives; adjectives can modify only nouns (and occasionally, pronouns). If a word modifies an adjective, the modifying word must be an adverb. Most adverbs that modify adjectives are *intensifiers*, words that emphasize the adjective.

<u>completely</u> wrong   <u>extremely</u> bright
<u>very</u> accurate   <u>quite</u> dangerous
<u>rather</u> unusual   <u>too</u> sharp

With a few important exceptions (*too* and *rather*—and most important of all—*very* and *quite*), the adverbs that modify adjectives are very much like adverbs of manner, that is, they are composed of an adjective + *-ly*.

<u>roughly</u> even   <u>unusually</u> good
<u>strangely</u> silent   <u>terribly</u> hot

3. Adverbs modifying other adverbs

A word modifying an adverb can only be another adverb. Adverbs that modify other adverbs are often intensifiers (*very* and *quite*), but they may also be words that qualify or limit the meaning of the second adverb.

> He always answers his mail <u>very</u> promptly.
> Holmes' deductions are <u>almost</u> always correct.

In the first sentence, *very* is an intensifier adverb modifying the adverb of frequency *promptly*. In the second sentence, the adverb *almost* qualifies the meaning of the adverb *always*, which in turn modifies the adjective *correct*.

■ **Exercise 1.21. Identifying adverbs that modify adjectives and adverbs**
Underline the adverbs that are modifying adjectives and other adverbs. If the adverb modifies an adjective, write *Adj* above the adjective. If the adverb modifies another adverb, write *Adv* above the adverb that is being modified. The first sentence is done as an example. (Answers to exercises are found on page 389.)

1. We saw the movie <u>rather</u> recently. *[Adv]*
2. Fred is dreadfully serious about the whole business.
3. You are quite right.
4. The down-payment was unusually large.
5. We will be done pretty soon.
6. We were nearly ready.
7. He was at that terribly awkward age.
8. We played surprisingly well.
9. It was a remarkably strong performance.
10. She talks so softly.
11. They are seldom ready.
12. Cinderella has become dreadfully fat in her old age.
13. The dog was strangely silent.
14. They didn't want it that badly.
15. The changes have occurred somewhat irregularly.
16. Lestrade was entirely correct in his opinion.
17. Harvard fought rather fiercely.

■ **Exercise 1.22. Identifying adverbs**

Underline all the adverbs in the following sentences. (Answers to exercises are found on page 389.)

1. The swampy camp was constantly infested with savagely stinging bugs.
2. They are very suspicious of unusually glib strangers.
3. I went home early.
4. We saw that program just recently.
5. They usually come to see us afterwards.
6. Comparatively few speakers have done so well here.
7. They have often been working on the road lately.
8. Recently he has been tardy less often.
9. Nearly every company had already issued its final report.
10. The disgustingly dirty water eventually evaporated.
11. The two events were very closely related.
12. It is necessarily true.
13. Boy Scouts are almost always prepared.
14. He usually gives me too many green beans.
15. They were very sorry about the unfortunate accident.
16. Invariably Aunt Harriet gets slightly embarrassed.
17. The coins were nearly equally divided.
18. John came home Thursday.
19. She smiled very sweetly.

■ **Exercise 1.23. Review: Identifying nouns, verbs, adjectives, and adverbs**

In the following sentences, identify the nouns, verbs, adjectives, and adverbs. Write *N* above nouns; *V* above verbs; *Adj* above adjectives; and *Adv* above adverbs. (Answers to exercises are found on page 390.)

1. The airplane landed smoothly.
2. The Constitution protects free speech.
3. Sarah always makes a good impression.
4. Dracula is always polite.
5. The Count appreciated his neighborly attitude.
6. The cleaner nearly ruined my new sweater.
7. A new conductor led the orchestra today.
8. Unfortunately, the tuba player had a bad cold.
9. Holmes carefully examined the pocket's contents.

10. The unusually dry summer threatened many crops here.
11. The rookie cop seemed very embarrassed.
12. The explorers eventually chose the northern route.
13. Artificial intelligence studies formal systems.
14. The class passed the history examination easily.
15. The first seven questions were the hardest.
16. Leon enjoys debating now.
17. The Boy Scouts helped the old lady.
18. Every dark cloud has a silver lining.

PREPOSITIONS

Traditional definition: A preposition is a word that shows the relationship of a noun or a pronoun to some other word in the sentence.

Prepositions cannot stand alone. They are bound together with following nouns (or pronouns) in constructions called *prepositional phrases*. A prepositional phrase consists of a preposition plus a noun or pronoun (together with their modifiers, if any). Here are some examples of prepositional phrases of various semantic types with the preposition underlined:

Space: above the desk; by the desk; in the desk; under the desk
Time: after class; during the week; until Sunday; at dawn
Other: for your benefit; about your question; by Shakespeare;
   to the point; like that; of them; concerning the problem

Prepositions can also be made up of several words; prepositions of this type are called *compound prepositions*. Following are some examples.

as of today; in addition to the assignment; next to Fred;
in spite of your objections; because of the budget; aside from that;
in place of Alice; on account of the bad weather; in front of the
fireplace; in case of an accident; on behalf of the management

Following is a list of commonly used single-word prepositions.

aboard	about	above
across	after	against
along	among	around
as	at	before
behind	below	beneath
beside	between	beyond

but (=*except*)	by	concerning
down	during	except
for	from	in
inside	into	like
near	of	off
on	out	over
past	since	through
throughout	till	to
toward	under	underneath
until	up	upon
with	within	without

The list of single-word prepositions can be misleading because some of these same words can be used as adverbs. Nevertheless, the distinction between adverb and preposition is straightforward: adverbs stand alone, but prepositions occur only in prepositional phrases. Here are some examples of the same word used first as both an adverb and then as a preposition in a prepositional phrase.

Adverb: John looked around.
Preposition: John looked around the corner.

Adverb: John went out.
Preposition: John went out the door.

Adverb: John came near.
Preposition: John came near the table.

■ **Exercise 1.24. Identifying prepositional phrases**
Underline the prepositional phrases in the following sentences. (Answers to exercises are found on page 391.)

1. He answered the reporter's questions during the flight.
2. The typewriters in the library were repaired over Christmas.
3. I walked by the window in the kitchen.
4. Except for the ending, I like your idea about the poem.
5. Certain words in a sentence function as modifiers.
6. I haven't had a minute to myself since breakfast.
7. Holmes placed a nasty problem in front of Inspector Lestrade.
8. The car in the lot behind the building was finished as of noon.
9. John's uncooperative attitude toward the project is part of the problem.
10. A friend of mine received an award for his writing.

11. You must come and see us during your vacation.
12. We ended on good terms in spite of our differences.
13. According to the butler, she had been in the library at the time.
14. Everybody but me solved the crime within the required time.
15. Under the cover of darkness, we crossed the field without incident.
16. Holmes examined the cloak with the red trim on the bottom.
17. Holmes examined the cloak with his powerful hand lens.
18. There is a tavern in the town.

CONJUNCTIONS

Traditional definition: A conjunction joins words or groups of words.

There are two main types of conjunctions: (1) conjunctions that join words or groups of words together as equals, and (2) conjunctions that join groups unequally, that is, that subordinate one group of words to another. Conjunctions of this latter type are called *subordinating conjunctions*. We deal with subordinating conjunctions in Chapter 4.

The conjunctions that join words or groups of words together as equals are divided into two classes: *coordinating conjunctions* and *correlative conjunctions*.

1. Coordinating conjunctions

There are seven coordinating conjunctions: *and, or, but, so, for, yet,* and *nor.* The first two, *and* and *or,* can be used to join words, phrases, and sentences, whereas the remaining coordinating conjunctions are normally used to join sentences. Following are some examples of *and* and *or* used to join words and phrases.

Words: John and Mary
John, Mary, and Sally
apples or oranges
apples, oranges, or bananas

Phrases: He went up the stairs and down the hall.
He went up the stairs, down the hall, and into the room.
He went to Chicago or to New York.
He went to Chicago, to New York, or to Boston.

Following are examples of the first six coordinating conjunctions used to join sentences together.

<u>but</u>

<u>and</u>

John loves Mary, <u>or</u> Fred loves Alicia.

<u>so</u>

<u>for</u>

<u>yet</u>

Note that when a coordinating conjunction joins two sentences, a comma is used before the conjunction. A common error of beginning writers is to omit this comma. The reverse error, putting in a comma before a conjunction joining two phrases is also common. Compare the following sentences.

Sentence: John opened the icebox, and he took out the salami.

    *John opened the icebox and he took out the salami.

Phrase: John opened the icebox and took out the salami.

    *John opened the icebox, and took out the salami.

The remaining coordinating conjunction, *nor*, is in a class by itself. It requires a negative in the first sentence and reversal of the subject and verb in the second sentence; for example:

John does <u>not</u> love Mary, <u>nor</u> does Fred love Alicia.

■ **Exercise 1.25. Commas with coordinating conjunctions**

Combine the following sentences by joining the second sentence to the first with a coordinating conjunction in the following manner: (a) as a sentence (i.e., retain the subject as a pronoun), and (b) as a phrase (i.e., delete the subject), and punctuate accordingly. The first question is done as an example. (Answers to exercises are found on page 391.)

1. The governor vetoed the bill.
   The governor sent it back to the senate.
   a. <u>The governor vetoed the bill, and he/she sent it back to the senate .</u>
   b. <u>The governor vetoed the bill and sent it back to the senate .</u>

2. The performers dazzled the crowd.
   The performers amazed the critics.

3. The editor compiled a list of typographical errors.
   The editor sent the list to the grateful author.

4. The workers stacked the crates in the warehouse.
   The workers labeled them according to their contents.

5. The candidate invoked the names of the founding fathers.
   The candidate promised to follow in their footsteps.

6. The Boy Scouts synchronized their watches.
   The Boy Scouts oriented their maps.
7. The astrologer forecast the future of the stock market.
   The astrologer called his broker.
8. Dripping wet, Leon got out of the shower.
   Leon answered the phone for the third time.
9. A couple in a brand-new BMW wheeled into the filling station.
   The couple paid for their gas with nickels and dimes.
10. Glinda took off the witch's ruby slippers.
    Glinda gave them to Dorothy.
11. Holmes sent a wire to Scotland Yard.
    Holmes told Watson to pack his service revolver.

---

2. Correlative conjunctions

Correlative conjunctions are very similar to coordinating conjunctions. The main difference is that correlative conjunctions are two-part conjunctions. The most common correlative conjunctions are *both . . . and*; *either . . . or*; *neither . . . nor* and *not only . . . but also*. All four correlative conjunctions can be used with words and phrases, though sometimes they sound like a logic textbook.

Words: John loves both Mary and Alicia.
John loves either Mary or Alicia.
John loves neither Mary nor Alicia.
John loves not only Mary but also Alicia.

Phrases: Mary went both up the stairs and down the hall.
Mary went either up the stairs or down the hall.
Mary went neither up the stairs nor down the hall.
Mary went not only up the stairs but also down the hall.

Either . . . or and *not only . . . but also* can be used to join sentences:

Either Mary loves John, or Alicia loves Fred.
Not only does Mary love John, but also Alicia loves Fred.

Notice that with *not only . . . but also* the first clause must reverse the subject and verb. The two remaining correlative conjunctions cannot normally be used to join clauses:

?*Both Mary loves John, and Alicia loves Fred.
?*Neither Mary loves John, nor Alicia loves Fred.
?Neither Mary loves John, nor does Alicia love Fred.

■ **Exercise 1.26. Identifying conjunctions**

Circle the coordinating and correlative conjunctions in the following sentences and underline the words or group of words that the conjunctions join. The first two sentences are done as examples. (Answers to exercises are found on page 392.)

1. Mary <u>planned the wedding</u> (and) <u>made up the guest list.</u>
2. <u>We were tired,</u> (so) <u>we went home early</u> (and) <u>watched a little TV.</u>
3. This is either very good cheese or very bad meat.
4. I'm sure that he is right, yet I can't help worrying about it.
5. We waved and signaled, but no waiter would pay any attention to us.
6. We got into the car and drove to the station.
7. Did you want coffee, tea, or milk?
8. Holmes fooled not only Watson but also Inspector Lestrade.
9. Thanks to careful planning and more than our share of good luck, we were successful.
10. John neither smokes nor watches daytime soaps.
11. Either you give me my money back, or I'll hold my breath.
12. Henry jumped to his feet and ran to the door.
13. Unfortunately, I am neither rich nor famous.
14. Mary planned the wedding, and her mother made up the guest list.
15. He is either a fool or a knave.
16. They had better hurry, for the game is about to start.
17. I saved my money and bought both a rod and a new reel.

Parallelism

Coordinating conjunctions join together elements that have the same grammatical structure. These elements are said to be *parallel* structures. Following are some examples of various types of parallel elements.

nouns:	I saw <u>John</u> and <u>Sally.</u>
adjectives:	She was <u>hungry</u> and <u>thirsty.</u>
verbs:	I <u>turned</u> and <u>ran.</u>
adverbs:	The group responded <u>quickly</u> and <u>appropriately.</u>
prepositional phrases:	We went <u>up one side</u> and <u>down the other.</u>
sentences:	<u>She set the table,</u> and <u>I lit the candles.</u>

Faulty parallelism is when a coordinating conjunction joins two elements that do not have the same grammatical structure.

*The train was <u>early</u> and <u>on track 3</u>.

The coordinating conjunction joins an adjective, *early*, with a prepositional phrase, *on track 3*. Since adjectives and prepositional phrases are not the same parts of speech, the sentence has faulty parallelism.

A good way to teach parallelism is by drawing a double vertical line (double lines–parallel lines) at the point in the sentence where the parallelism begins. Then stack the parallel elements on top of one another so that their similarity (or lack of similarity) becomes obvious. Following is how this technique works with the preceding example sentences.

nouns: I saw ‖ <u>John</u>
   and ‖ <u>Sally</u>.

adjectives: She was ‖ <u>hungry</u>
    and ‖ <u>thirsty</u>.

verbs: I ‖ <u>turned</u>
  and ‖ <u>ran</u>.

adverbs: The group responded ‖ <u>quickly</u>
       and ‖ <u>appropriately</u>.

prepisitional phrases: We went ‖ <u>up one side</u>
        and ‖ <u>down the other</u>.

sentences: ‖ <u>She set the table</u>
   and ‖ <u>I lit the candles</u>.

faulty parallelism: *The train was ‖ <u>early</u>
      and ‖ <u>on track 3</u>.

The advantage of this technique is that it enables your students to actually see the parallel structures within a sentence. It also helps your students spot where a parallel structure has gone off the track.

INTERJECTIONS

Traditional definition: An interjection is an exclamatory word that expresses emotion.

An interjection is a word that has no grammatical relation to the rest of the sentence. In other words, it is not really part of the grammar of the sentence. Don't confuse interjections with imperative sentences. An imperative sentence is a command with an understood *you* as a subject. Even one word imperatives (e.g., *Stop!* or *Duck!*) are still full sentences. An interjection can never be a verb and therefore can never be expanded to a full sentence by an understood *you*.

If the emotion that the interjection expresses is strong, the interjection is set off from other sentences by an exclamation point.

> <u>Ouch!</u> I just stubbed my toe!
>
> <u>Wow!</u> We won!
>
> <u>No!</u> Don't do it!

If the emotion that the interjection expresses is less dramatic, the interjection can be joined to the sentence by a comma.

> <u>Damn,</u> I'm good.
>
> <u>Well,</u> what do you know?

■ **Exercise 1.27. Review I: Identifying parts of speech**

In the following sentences, identify the parts of speech of every word. Write *N* above nouns; *V* above verbs; *Adj* above adjectives; *Adv* above adverbs, *P* above pronouns; *Prep* above prepositions; *C* above conjunctions; and *I* above interjections. (Answers to exercises are found on page 393.)

1. The overall effect was quite disappointing for us.
2. The new mystery completely baffled Holmes and Watson.
3. Almost all professional writers keep a daily journal.
4. The FDA carefully evaluated the new French drug in their labs.
5. The Sun Belt had a massive population growth recently.
6. Good entry-level positions are usually scarce.
7. These old flashbulbs often fail at the worst possible time.
8. The young witness was visibly nervous.
9. Holmes located the missing bullet in the wainscot.
10. The agency often hired too many consulting firms and experts.
11. Oh, Jason missed the bus again today.
12. Scientists discovered a new particle recently.
13. Shelf space and storage are always limited here.
14. The commission expected a more favorable outcome from the hearing.
15. Holmes always quizzed Watson unmercifully about the methods of scientific deduction.
16. The slope seemed terribly steep to me.
17. Godzilla ordered the poached fish and artichokes.

■ **Exercise 1.28. Review II: Identifying parts of speech**
In the following sentences, identify the part of speech of every word. Write *N* above nouns; *V* above verbs; *Adj* above adjectives; *Adv* above adverbs, *P* above pronouns; *Prep* above prepositions; *C* above conjunctions; and *I* above interjections. (Answers to exercises are found on page 393.)

1. Diagram this sentence.
2. I found a map in the glove compartment.
3. Fred went to a college out of state last year.
4. Sally sold Sarah some sandwiches.
5. We were happy about the decision.
6. John and I finished the project in the library.
7. Nonsense, the paint on that bench is perfectly dry.
8. The answer to the first question is 42.
9. Underline the subject and the simple predicate.
10. The young blonde found a nice apartment in the city for King Kong.
11. The kid at the counter finally bought a liver and onion ice-cream cone.
12. They were completely wrong about the size of the lot.
13. Holmes's deductions in criminal cases are almost always accurate.
14. Give me a coke, please.
15. A rolling stone gathers no moss.
16. In a complex society like ours, the issues are often very confusing.
17. Jones singled in the first inning and walked in the third.

SUMMARY OF TRADITIONAL GRAMMAR

Eight parts of speech: *noun, pronoun, adjective, verb, adverb, preposition, conjunction,* and *interjection.*

Noun: A noun is a word used to name a person, place, thing, or idea.

There are two types of nouns: *common* and *proper.* **Common** nouns name any one of a group of persons, places, or things and are not capitalized. **Proper** nouns name particular persons, places, or things, and are always capitalized.

Pronoun: A pronoun is a word used in place of one or more than one noun.

There are five types of pronouns: *personal, reflexive, indefinite, demonstrative,* and *interrogative* (a sixth type, *relative* pronouns, is covered in Chapter 4).

Personal pronouns are categorized by **Person** (1st, 2nd, 3rd), **Number** (Singular, Plural), and **Form** (Subject, Object, Possessive).

First person refers to speaker (*I, me, my, mine, we, us, our, ours*), 2nd person refers to hearer (*you, your, yours*), and 3rd person refers to person or thing spoken about (*it, its, they, them, their, theirs*).

Reflexive pronouns refer to someone or something already mentioned in the same sentence. They always end in *-self* or *-selves*.

Indefinite pronouns refer to unspecified persons, things, or groups; for example, *all, anyone, few*.

Demonstrative pronouns point out a specific person or thing, for example, *this, that, these, those*.

Interrogative pronouns begin questions, for example, *who, what, which*.

Adjective: An adjective modifies a noun or a pronoun.

Predicate adjectives are adjectives used after linking verbs. Most predicate adjectives (and some modifying adjectives) have three forms: a *base* or *positive* form (e.g., *tall, beautiful*), a *comparative* form (e.g., *taller, more beautiful*), and a *superlative* form (e.g., *tallest, most beautiful*).

Articles are modifying adjectives. There are two types: *definite (the)* and *indefinite (a/an)*.

Coordinate adjectives are two or more modifying adjectives from the same class. Coordinate adjectives are separated by commas.

Verb: A verb is a word that expresses action or otherwise helps to make a statement.

There are two types of verbs: *action* and *linking*. **Action** verbs express an action. **Linking** verbs serve as a link between words.

Adverb: An adverb is a word used to modify a verb, an adjective, or another adverb.

Preposition: A preposition is a word that shows the relationship of a noun or a pronoun to some other word in the sentence.

Compound prepositions are made up of more than one word, for example, *in spite of.*

Conjunctions: A conjunction joins words or groups of words.

There are two main types of conjunctions: *coordinating* and *subordinating*. **Coordinating** conjunctions join words or groups of words together as equals, for example, apples *and* oranges. **Subordinating** conjunctions (which are discussed in Chapter 4) join groups of words as unequals.

Correlative conjunctions are coordinating conjunctions that consist of two parts, for example, *either* he leaves *or* I do.

Interjection: An interjection is an exclamatory word that expresses emotion, for example, *Hey*, I can relate to that.

2

The Sentence

INTRODUCTION

Chapter 1 examines the eight parts of speech. Chapter 2 examines how nouns and pronouns (and occasionally adjectives) are used together with verbs to form the basic sentence. Chapter 1 deals with how we recognize the various parts of speech. Chapter 2 deals with how certain parts of speech work together to make a sentence.

In this chapter we begin with the definition of *sentence* and then move to a more detailed discussion of the three major sentence elements—*subject, predicate,* and *complement*. The chapter concludes with an introduction to sentence diagraming.

Traditional definition: A *sentence* is a group of words expressing a complete thought. A sentence consists of two parts: a *subject* and a *predicate*.

The key part of the traditional definition is the term *complete*. Complete means that the sentence stands alone without being included in some larger unit. For example,

I ordered a shake.

is a sentence because it can stand alone as a grammatical unit. Even a very long group of words is not a sentence if it cannot stand alone.

For example, even though the following group of words has two finite verbs and numerous nouns, it is not a sentence because it cannot stand alone.

> despite the fact that Angus often has very perceptive little insights into how things really work in this world

In order for it to be free standing, we can add another whole sentence for it to lean on.

> Despite the fact that Angus often has very perceptive little insights into how things really work in this world, <u>he really doesn't have a clue.</u>

We can instead get rid of *despite the fact that* and make the remainder free standing.

> Angus often has very perceptive little insights into how things really work in this world.

All language is based on our ability to use and recognize sentences. In fact, our sentence-sense is so strong that the biggest problem we have in consciously identifying sentences is that we automatically put *fragments*—words or phrases that are less than complete sentences—into some context in order to make implicit sentences out of them. For example, some students would identify the fragment *on the desk* as a sentence because they would supply some context in which *on the desk* is part of a complete sentence. For example, a student might supply an "understood" question *Where are the papers?* In the context of this imaginary question, *on the desk* is a part of an implicit complete sentence answer.

> The papers are <u>on the desk.</u>

When students supply a context, they are using their intuitive knowledge of language to make communicative sense out of the fragment. Their "mistake" is to do what all speakers of a language do—supply a context to make sense out of the language with which they come into contact. Their "mistake" does not mean that they do not understand what a sentence is; it means that they do not understand the rules of the game for consciously identifying sentences and fragments.

For a group of words to stand alone as a complete sentence, the words must not be an answer to some understood question or part of some implicit complete statement. One way to teach this concept is to imagine that you are awakened in the middle of the night by a phone call. The first utterance must be a complete sentence since there is no previous context. For example, the caller might say

> The papers are on the desk.

But the caller cannot convey any message by saying a part of a sentence:

on the desk

This preposterous situation is a way to help students see whether a supposed sentence can stand alone or not. Students rarely identify full sentences as fragments, but some students have great difficulty in learning how to recognize a fragment because they unconsciously supply a context that makes the fragment part of an implicit complete sentence. The middle-of-the-night phone call test may help them.

■ **Exercise 2.1. Recognizing fragments and complete sentences**

Below is a mixture of complete sentences and fragments. Mark the complete sentences with *C*. Expand the fragments to make complete sentences. Underline the fragment in your complete sentence. The first fragment is expanded as an example. (Answers to exercises are found on page 394.)

1. After the party
   Expansion: We decided to go out for some pickled herring after the party.
2. Whatever you want
3. We were completely confused about the situation
4. Safe at home
5. You can be sure of that
6. OK by me
7. As soon as you can
8. On top of old smoky
9. More or less
10. By noon, if not sooner
11. Understood
12. Not a chance
13. When the Christmas rush is over
14. I couldn't believe it
15. After you called about the package from the mail room
16. If it's OK with you

SUBJECT

Traditional definition: The *subject* (also called the *complete subject)* of the sentence is the part about which something is being said.

The *simple subject* is the main noun (or pronoun) within the complete subject. (The term subject implies simple subject unless specified otherwise.) The simple subject is always a noun or pronoun. All of the other words in the complete subject are modifiers of the noun that is the simple subject.

Those <u>stupid old cats</u> are always dragging dead mice in.
<u>Those stupid old cats</u>   (complete subject)
    <u>cats</u>   (simple subject)

<u>The truck in the left lane</u> suddenly slowed down.
<u>The truck in the left lane</u> (complete subject)
    <u>truck</u>   (simple subject)

A very important technique for identifying the complete subject is to replace it with a pronoun. For example, replacing the complete subjects in the two preceding example sentences, we get the following.

<u>Those stupid old cats</u>   are always dragging dead mice in.
        They
<u>The truck in the left lane</u> suddenly slowed down.
    It

What makes this test so useful is that the pronoun will not substitute for adverbs that are not part of the complete subject. Consider the following sentence.

Every day after school all the kids in the neighborhood come by.

We can discover the complete subject by replacing it with the appropriate pronoun.

Every day after school <u>all the kids in the neighborhood</u> come by.
            they

The complete subject is the part of the sentence that the pronoun *they* has replaced.

they = all the kids in the neighborhood

The simple subject is the main (or head) noun in the complete subject. Typically the simple subject will have modifiers with it— adjectives in front and adjective prepositional phrases after it. The complete subject in the preceding example follows this pattern.

<u>all the</u>   <u>kids</u>   <u>in the neighborhood</u>
Adj   Simple Subj   Adj Prep Phrase

A useful rule to remember is that the simple subject can *never* be inside a prepositional phrase (even though sometimes this seems strange). Consider the following sentence.

All of the children were playing soccer.

The simple subject is *all*, not *children*, because *children* is in the prepositional phrase *of the children*.

When two or more subjects are joined together by a coordinating conjunction, the combined subjects are called a *compound subject*. In the following sentences the complete subject is underlined and the simple subjects are in italics.

> *Fred* and *Harry* finished cleaning the windows.
>
> The *guy* in the yellow pick-up and the *couple* in the van were stopped by the police.
>
> *You* and *I* should go there some time.

Compound subjects joined by *and* are replaced by plural pronouns. For example, the pronouns for the preceding sentences would be the following.

> Fred and Harry finished cleaning the windows.
>   *They*
> The guy in the yellow pick-up and the couple in the van were
>   *They*
> stopped by the police.
>
> You and I should go there some time.
>   *We*

■ **Exercise 2.2. Identifying subjects**

Underline the complete subject and circle the simple subject. Underneath the complete subject put in the pronoun that substitutes for the complete subject. The first sentence is done as an example. (Answers to exercises are found on page 395.)

1. A first-class college (education) is worth its weight in rubies.
      It
2. The modern art world was shocked by Fred's use of bananas.
3. The unions in this area have traditionally opposed open shops.
4. The program has been canceled.
5. An announcement of a major new project will be made this week.
6. Naturally, the major sources for his story are a closely guarded secret.
7. The proposed new industry standards are likely to be controversial.
8. The economic conditions of the country depend on the balance of trade.
9. The so-called window of opportunity for the launch is this month.
10. The dock and the buildings near the river have become quite valuable.
11. The secretary, the treasurer, and the vice president are flying to Brazil.

12. A stitch in time usually saves nine.
13. The tax rate for purchases made after March 1 has been lowered.
14. As always, the list of suspects in her new novel is overwhelming.
15. Several large cold fronts from Canada will affect our weather.
16. Increasingly, the internationalization of trade in commodities makes us an economic global village.

PREDICATE

Traditional definition: The *predicate* (also called the *complete predicate*) is the part that says something about the subject.

The *simple predicate*, or verb, is the main word or group of words within the complete predicate.

	Those stupid old cats	are always dragging dead mice in
(complete predicate)		are always dragging dead mice in
(simple predicate)		are dragging
	The truck in the left lane	suddenly slowed down
(complete predicate)		suddenly slowed down
(simple predicate)		slowed

The term *simple predicate* includes the main verb plus all helping or auxiliary verbs (*but no adverbs*). The term *verb* is used more often than the term *simple predicate*. For example, we talk about subject-verb agreement, not the more logically consistent subject-simple predicate agreement. [If we were consistent, we would use either part of speech terms—*noun-verb* agreement—or function terms—*subject–simple predicate* agreement; instead we mix a function term—*subject*—with a part of speech term—*verb*.] Adding to the confusion, the term *verb phrase* is also used to refer to the main verb and all its helping or auxiliary verbs. Thus, the terms *verb, verb phrase,* and *simple predicate* mean the same thing.

In a manner similar to compound subject, two or more verbs joined by a coordinating conjunction are called *compound verbs*.

We nailed and painted the wallboard.

In this sentence *nailed* and *painted* are compound verbs.

The normal sentence can be divided into two parts: the complete subject and the complete predicate.

The normal sentence	can be divided into two parts.
complete subject	complete predicate

For emphasis or for stylistic variation we sometimes change the normal order of sentences. A very common variation is to move an adverb from its place in the complete predicate to the first position in the sentence. The following example shows the normal order.

> We can go shopping <u>after school</u>.

We can emphasize *after school* by moving it out of its normal place in the complete predicate and putting it in front of the complete subject.

> <u>After school</u> we can go shopping.

It is important to realize that sentences have a "normal" or basic form. When we deviate from this normal form, we call attention to that portion of the sentence that does not fit in with our expectations. Such variations from the norm are not bad as long as they are done deliberately for a particular purpose. In fact, good writers have a very strong sense of normal expectations and are able to deviate skillfully from these expectations to focus the reader's attention on important ideas.

■ **Exercise 2.3. Putting sentences into normal order and identifying complete predicates**

Put the following inverted sentences into their normal subject–complete predicate order, and then underline the complete predicate. The first sentence is done as an example. (Answers to exercises are found on page 396.)

1. Nowadays an awful lot of coffee is grown in Brazil.
   An awful lot of coffee <u>is grown in Brazil nowadays</u>.
2. On your way out, close the door.
3. At first you may have trouble adjusting the focus.
4. By using a coat hook Mary Ann managed to get the car door open.
5. As soon as you get there, call me.
6. Late in the day, the cashier noticed the missing bills.
7. This afternoon I have several appointments.
8. Today he shoved the oranges into the back of the refrigerator.
9. Gracefully and with no wasted motions, he put the canoe into the water.
10. Under most circumstances, you should eat your soup with a spoon.
11. Recently you were contacted by one of our sales staff.
12. Again they heard the mysterious tapping at the window.
13. With a flourish Holmes pulled out his service revolver.
14. Recently King Arthur has been having doubts about his marriage.
15. Somewhere the sun is shining.
16. If he starts talking about his snail collection, change the subject.
17. Most of the time you would be right.

SUBJECT-VERB AGREEMENT

If the subject and verb are separated from each other, many students have difficulty in monitoring the sentence for correct subject-verb agreement. The problem for identifying subject-verb agreement in sentences in which the subject and verb are separated is sometimes called the *nearest noun problem*. If the subject noun is followed by modifiers, there is a tendency for writers to make the verb agree with the nearest noun rather than with the noun that is the subject. For example, a writer would be unlikely to make a subject-verb agreement error in the following sentence because the subject and verb are next to each other.

A working <u>student is</u> asking for problems with his grades.

But if the subject noun *student* is followed by a long modifying phrase, a writer could easily make an agreement error.

*A working student carrying over twenty semester <u>credits are</u> asking for problems with his grades.

In this sentence the writer has made the verb *are* agree with the nearest noun, *credits*, rather than with the actual subject, *student*. There are two good checks for monitoring complex sentences to see if there is a nearest noun problem. One is to substitute a pronoun for the complete subject.

*<u>He</u> are asking for problems with his grades.

The other check is to delete everything in the complete subject except for the simple subject—the noun that everything else in the complete subject modifies.

*<u>Student</u> are asking for problems with his grades.

When these checks are performed, and the sentence simplified, the subject-verb agreement error becomes obvious.

■ **Exercise 2.4. Checking for nearest noun subject-verb agreement error**

All of the following sentences contain a nearest noun subject-verb agreement error. Demonstrate the error (a) by substituting a pronoun for the complete subject, and (b) by replacing the complete subject with the simple subject. The first sentence is done as an example. (Answers to exercises are found on page 396.)

1. The wages of sin is death.
   a. *<u>They</u> is death.
   b. *<u>Wages</u> is death.
2. The answers for the problems in the first section is on page 312.

3. Only one finalist out of several hundred contenders are selected.
4. Plans belonging to the city planning department is public property.
5. Three mistakes in a row means that you are out.
6. Parking in the marked spaces are forbidden by city ordinance.
7. The persons seated in the back row needs to move forward.
8. The number of accidents caused by drunk drivers increase at night.
9. One of these three classes are required for your major.
10. The heavy fall rain in the mountains have washed a lot of soil away.
11. The boxes in the back of the trailer goes in the storage room.
12. The luggage belonging to the transit passengers are now available.
13. The radio shown in their new catalogs were just what we wanted.
14. The experts that we polled at the university has confirmed our opinion.
15. Parking in the downtown lots overnight are prohibited.
16. Pain in the joints of the fingers and toes signal arthritis.

COMPLEMENT

Traditional definition: A *complement* completes the meaning begun by the subject and the verb.

A complement is a noun, pronoun, or (in the case of linking verbs only) predicate adjective *that is required by the verb in order to make a complete sentence*. By definition a complement cannot be an adverb or a prepositional phrase, or be inside a prepositional phrase. Only nouns, pronouns, and predicate adjectives can be complements.

Traditional grammar uses a complex vocabulary to refer to different types of complements. Complements are divided into two main subcategories depending on whether the complement follows (1) an action verb or (2) a linking verb. We deal with each type in turn.

1. Action verb + complement

Action verbs that require a complement to make a complete sentence are called *transitive* verbs. For example, the following sentences all contain transitive verbs.

Jack <u>met</u> a stranger at the fair.
Jack <u>sold</u> the cow yesterday.
Jack <u>bought</u> some beans then.

Action verbs that do not require a complement to make a complete sentence are called *intransitive* verbs.

Sam <u>snores</u> loudly.
All of the flowers <u>wilted</u> in the heat.
The children in the back of the room <u>snickered</u> behind their hands.
The old cow <u>died</u> yesterday.

Note that intransitive verbs (like any verbs) can be followed by adverbs and prepositional phrases. These adverbs and prepositional phrases are not required to make the sentences grammatical. For example, the preceding intransitive sentences are still fully grammatical if the adverbs and prepositional phrases are removed.

Sam <u>snores</u>.
All of the flowers <u>wilted</u>.
The children in the back of the room <u>snickered</u>.
The old cow <u>died</u>.

Many action verbs can be either transitive or intransitive, depending on their meaning and the way that they are used.

intransitive: John <u>returned</u>.
transitive: John <u>returned</u> Bjorn's serve.

In these examples, the verb *return* has two different meanings. As an intransitive verb, *return* means something like "go back to place of origin." As a transitive verb, *return* means something like "send back" or (in the case of tennis) "hit back."

The complements that follow action verbs are called *objects*. There are two types of objects: *direct objects* and *indirect objects*.

Direct Object

Traditional definition: a *direct object* is a noun or pronoun that receives the action of the verb or shows the result of the action.

Following are some sentences with the direct object underlined.

Sally answered the <u>question</u> easily.
Rudolph defeated his <u>opponent</u> in straight sets.
The accident spoiled the <u>party</u>.
The ends justify the <u>means</u>.
A stone hit the <u>side</u> of the car.

Direct objects can be recognized by their ability to be used as a subject in a passive sentence. Passive sentences are formed from active sentences by (1) switching the position of the subject and direct object, (2) adding *by* in front of the original subject, and (3) adding the helping verb *be* and putting the main verb into the past participle form. For example, compare the following active sentence with the corresponding passive version.

Active: John saw Mary.

Passive: Mary was seen by John.

In order for a sentence to be put into the passive, it *must* contain a direct object to serve as the subject of the passive. Thus, the ability to create a passive sentence is a very reliable test for identifying a direct object. If a sentence can be turned into a passive, it must contain a direct object. If a sentence cannot be turned into a passive, it does not contain a direct object complement. We can demonstrate that the five preceding example sentences contain direct objects by turning them into passives.

Sally answered the <u>question</u> easily.

The <u>question</u> was answered easily by Sally.

Rudolph defeated his <u>opponent</u> in straight sets.

His <u>opponent</u> was defeated in straight sets by Rudolph.

The accident spoiled the <u>party</u>.

The <u>party</u> was spoiled by the accident.

The ends justify the <u>means</u>.

The <u>means</u> are justified by the ends.

A stone hit the <u>side</u> of the car.

The <u>side</u> of the car was hit by a stone.

What makes the passive test so useful for identifying direct object complements is that the very similar appearing predicate nominatives that follow linking verbs cannot be used in the passive.

Active: John was a <u>detective</u>.

Passive: *A <u>detective</u> was been by John.

Active: Her brother seemed a <u>nuisance</u>.

Passive: *A <u>nuisance</u> was seemed by her brother.

Active: Johnson became the <u>President of the United States</u>.

Passive: *The <u>President of the United States</u> was become by Johnson.

The failure of these sentences to be converted into the corresponding passives is proof that the nouns are not direct objects; they are predicate nominatives following linking verbs.

Indirect Object

Traditional definition: an *indirect object* is a noun or pronoun that comes between the verb and the direct object and that tells *to whom* or *for whom* the action of the verb is done.

A small but very important group of verbs can have not one but two objects. For these verbs it is necessary to distinguish between direct object and indirect object. (The term *object* used by itself implies the direct object.) Both direct and indirect objects are identified in the following sentences.

Sally gave ___Fred___ ___the answer.___
          Indirect object   Direct object

She left ___him___ ___a note.___
       Indirect object   Direct object

Recall that the traditional definition says that an indirect object comes between the verb and the direct object. One implication of this definition is that an indirect object must always precede a direct object; that is, an indirect object can never be used without a direct object. The reverse, of course, is not true. Direct objects usually occur without indirect objects.

An indirect object can *always* be recognized by paraphrasing the sentence with *to* or *for*.

Sally gave Fred the answer.
Sally gave the answer <u>to</u> Fred.

She left him a note.
She left a note <u>for</u> him.

If the paraphrase is grammatical, then the original sentence must contain both a direct and an indirect object.

■ **Exercise 2.5. Identifying objects**

Underline the objects in the following sentences (if any). Label the direct object *DO* and indirect object *IO*. If the sentence contains both a direct object and an indirect object, paraphrase the sentence with *to* or *for*. The first sentence is done as an example. (Answers to exercises are found on page 397.)

                IO   DO
1. Alice gave <u>Mary</u> a <u>present.</u>
   Paraphrase: Alice gave a present <u>to</u> Mary.
2. Babar ruled the land of the elephants.
3. The elephants befriended young Tarzan.
4. Leon displayed a surprising knowledge of the situation.
5. Stark terror concentrates the mind wonderfully.
6. She parked my car on the street.
7. Garrick sold me Boardwalk.
8. Igor began the operation confidently.
9. You cannot alter the situation.

10. Holmes always solved the mystery.
11. He finally told me the answer.
12. The investigation confirmed Holmes's worst suspicion.
13. We drew Anne a picture.
14. The farmer killed a duckling for us.
15. The wizard granted them three wishes.

---

2. Linking Verb + Complement

The complement that follows a linking verb is called a *subject complement*.

Traditional definition: A *subject complement* is a noun, pronoun, or adjective that follows a linking verb. It describes or explains the simple subject.

Subject complement is a collective term for the nouns (or their pronoun substitutes) or adjectives that are required by a linking verb to make a complete sentence. A noun that is used as a subject complement also has a special name: it is called a *predicate nominative*.

Their child was an <u>actor</u>.

The noun *actor* follows a linking verb and refers to the subject, *child*. It is thus a subject complement. Since *actor* is a noun, we can further specify that *actor* is a predicate nominative. Following are some more examples of predicate nominatives.

Frankenstein resembles a <u>zombie</u>.
Sally was a <u>seamstress</u>.
Dick became a <u>detective</u>.
Fred looked the <u>part</u>.

The term predicate nominative also includes pronouns, as in the following sentences.

Our first choice is <u>you</u>.
The reporter is <u>she</u>.

When the subject complement is an adjective, the subject complement is called a *predicate adjective*.

The trout tasted <u>terrible</u>.
The soup seemed <u>sour</u>.
The wine was <u>watery</u>.
Bob became <u>belligerent</u>.
Ichabod is <u>idiotic</u>.

Let us briefly summarize what we know about subject complements. *Subject complement* is a collective term for the nouns, pronouns, and adjectives that follow linking verbs and are required to make a complete sentence. A noun or pronoun that is used as a subject complement is called a *predicate nominative*; an adjective that is used as a subject complement is called a *predicate adjective*.

The sentences with linking verbs pose a special problem. Recall that the definition of *complement* includes only nouns, pronouns, and predicate adjectives; the definition excludes adverbs and prepositional phrases. Thus, by definition, the adverbs and prepositional phrases in intransitive linking verb sentences cannot be part of the complement. To see the problem that this definition creates, let us compare several sentences containing intransitive action verbs and linking verbs without subject complements—all of which also contain adverbs or prepositional phrases.

> *Intransitive action verbs*:
> Sam <u>snores</u> loudly.
> All of the flowers <u>wilted</u> in the heat.

> *Linking verbs without subject complements*:
> The bus <u>was</u> there.
> Your check <u>is</u> in the mail.

Both types of sentences contain adverbs and prepositional phrases. However, the adverbs and prepositional phrases seem to play different roles, as we can see when we delete them.

> *Intransitive action verbs*:
> Sam <u>snores</u>.
> All of the flowers <u>wilted</u>.

> *Linking verbs without subject complements*:
> *The bus <u>was</u>.
> *Your check <u>is</u>.

In the case of the two intransitive action verbs, the adverb and prepositional phrase are optional elements that can be deleted without affecting the grammaticality of the two sentences—as we would expect from the fact that they are intransitive. However, when we delete the adverb and prepositional phrase from the two sentences with linking verbs, the results are ungrammatical. In other words, the adverb and prepositional phrase seem to be required by the two linking verb sentences in order to be grammatical. If they are required by the verb to make a complete sentence, they would seem to fit the definition of complement.

We are caught in a paradox. The definition of complement prohibits adverbs and prepositional phrases from being classified as complements, so (by the terms of the definition) the adverb and prepositional phrase in the sentences containing linking verbs cannot be complements. Yet since the adverb and prepositional phrase in the sentences are obviously required to complete the meaning begun by the subject and verb, they seem to meet the definition of complement.

How is this paradox resolved? In adherence to the traditional definition of complement (noun, pronoun, or adjective), traditional grammar treats (and diagrams) the adverbs and prepositional phrases in linking verb sentences as though they were optional modifying elements. In other words, the adverb and prepositional phrase in the preceding example sentences are not part of the complement.

■ **Exercise 2.6. Identifying subject complements**

In the following sentences, underline the subject complements (if any). Label the predicate nominatives as *Pred Nom* and the predicate adjectives as *Pred Adj*. The first sentence is done as an example. (Answers to exercises are found on page 398.)

                                    Pred Adj
1. Throughout the ordeal, Holmes remained <u>calm</u>.
2. Thanks to his grammar teacher, Leon became a better person.
3. The new patient was in a dangerous coma.
4. Hearing the news, the general grew angry.
5. Aunt Sally was there on time.
6. His home brew tasted just awful.
7. The queen was in the parlor, eating bread and honey.
8. The cat acted crazy.
9. I am mad at myself for saying that.
10. Rudolph remained a private for several more months.
11. I answered their questions.
12. Later that year, Lady Windermere fell ill.
13. The answer to the meaning of life was 42.
14. At first the idea sounded crazy to me.
15. The winner of the contest was in a state of shock.
16. Louise looked angry.
17. Louise looked angrily at the rude waiter.

Let us now pull together all the arcane terminology of complements. All sentences are divided into two parts: a complete subject and a complete predicate. The complete predicate, in turn, consists of a verb which may or may not be followed by a complement. Following is how we could represent these relations.

Complete Subject + Complete Predicate

Verb   (Complement)

The verb dictates whether or not there is a complement and (if there is a complement) the type of complement.

☐ If the verb is an action verb, there are three possibilities: (1) no complement at all, (2) a direct object complement, or (3) an indirect object + direct object complement.

☐ If the verb is a linking verb, there are also three possibilities: (1) no complement at all, (2) a subject complement consisting of a predicate nominative, or (3) a subject complement consisting of a predicate adjective.

Altogether, then, there are six types of complete predicates.

1. Intransitive action verb (no complement)
   Example: The ship sank.
2. Transitive action verb + direct object complement
   Example: The torpedo sank the ship.
3. Transitive action verb + indirect object + direct object complement
   Example: The teacher read the class a story.
4. Linking verb (no complement)
   Example: Kilroy was here.
5. Linking verb + predicate nominative subject complement
   Example: William was a waiter.
6. Linking verb + predicate adjective subject complement
   Example: William was weary.

The complete predicates of the vast majority of English sentences belong to one of the six types in the preceding list.

■ **Exercise 2.7. Identifying complement types**

Underline the complements (if any) in the following sentences. If the complement is a subject complement, put *Sub Comp* above it and *Link* above the linking verb. If the complement is an object, put *Trans* above the verb and *DO* above the direct object and *IO* above the indirect object (if any). The first sentence is done as an example. (Answers to exercises are found on page 398.)

     Trans DO
1. Finally, he found the ad in the paper.

2. These sentences are rich in subject-verb agreements.
3. We completed the first portion of the test in good time.
4. The post office returned the package to Marty.
5. Cinderella was in a foul mood that day.
6. Alice bought Fred a new dish towel for Father's Day.
7. I smell smoke.
8. My dog smells awful.
9. The agent sold them the replacement parts.
10. Today, Leon turned 30.
11. Fred is never on time.
12. With a satisfied look, Aunt Sally fit the last piece into the puzzle.
13. Everyone likes chocolate cake.
14. Apparently no one noticed the incident in Lady Crumhorn's drawing room.
15. With deep regret, Charles declined a second helping.
16. Leon eventually became a famous and beloved grammarian.
17. The tenor sounded flat to me.

CLASSIFYING SENTENCES BY PURPOSE

In traditional grammar, sentences are classified in a fourfold manner depending on the purpose of the sentence. The following are the four types of sentences.

1. *Declarative:* A declarative sentence makes a statement. Declarative sentences are punctuated with a period.

   John went away.

2. *Imperative:* An imperative sentence gives a command or makes a request. Imperative sentences *must* have an understood *you* as subject. Imperative sentences may be punctuated with either a period or an exclamation point.

   Go away.
   Come here!
   Stop it!

3. *Interrogative:* An interrogative sentence asks a question. Interrogative sentences *must* be punctuated with a question mark.

   Did John go away?
   Where are you?

4.   *Exclamatory:* An exclamatory sentence expresses strong feeling. Exclamatory sentences are declarative sentences with an exclamation point. Remember that imperative sentences can have exclamation points too. The difference is that imperative sentences must always have an understood *you* as subject; exclamatory sentences can never have an understood *you* as subject. Exclamatory sentences *must* be punctuated with an exclamation point.

> John went away!
> Sally has no cavities!

■ **Exercise 2.8. Classifying sentences by purpose**

Classify each of the following sentences by purpose. (Answers to exercises are found on page 399.)

1. What do you know about that?
2. It seems pretty simple to me.
3. That's what *you* think!
4. Holmes warned Watson to stay back.
5. To get the mean, total the data and divide by the number of observations.
6. Is everything all right here?
7. His mission was to seek out and destroy the enemy.
8. I did not order a bottle of Chateau Yquem with my chili dog!
9. He asked if I could come in this afternoon.
10. Can you come in this afternoon?
11. Publish or perish.
12. The very existence of Bertha's Kitty Boutique was at stake!
13. He tends to get excited about little things.
14. Blend in the cream cheese until smooth.
15. We will soon be home.
16. Remember where you are.
17. The total far exceeded our most optimistic projections!
18. Has the cat got your tongue?
19. Return to headquarters at once!

DIAGRAMING

In this section we examine the way traditional grammar represents sentence relationships: *diagraming*. Diagraming is a visual representation of how all the words in a sentence fit together. The basic elements of the sentence—the subject, verb, and complement—are drawn on what is called the *main sentence line*. The only words that can appear on the main sentence line play the following roles.

- ☐ the simple subject (just the subject noun or pronoun–no modifiers)
- ☐ the simple predicate (the main verb along with any helping verbs)
- ☐ the complement: either (1) the direct object (when the simple predicate is an action verb) or (2) the subject complement–either a predicate nominative or predicate adjective (when the simple predicate is a linking verb)

Following are the diagrams for the two basic main sentence types. Note that the difference between action verbs and linking verbs is indicated by the line that separates the verb from its complement: with action verbs the line is vertical; with linking verbs the line is slanted.

| subject | action verb | object |

| subject | linking verb \ subject complement |

Compound subjects, verbs, objects, and subject complements are drawn in the following manner.

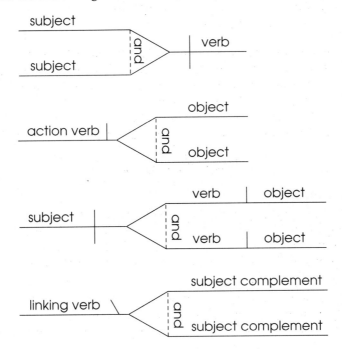

All modifiers are written on lines that slope downward and to the right. (Remember, no modifier can appear on the main sentence line.) Modifiers are attached to the main line *underneath* the words they modify. Thus, adjectives are attached to the nouns they modify and adverbs are attached to the verb or predicate adjective. Adverbs that modify adjectives or other adverbs are attached to the side of the words that they modify. Assume that all adverbs are attached to the verb unless it is clear that they modify a particular adjective or other adverb. Following are examples of modifiers.

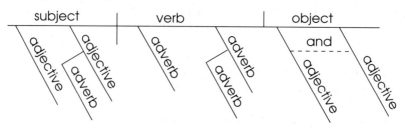

Indirect objects are not drawn on the main sentence line as one would expect. Instead, they are placed on a line drawn underneath and parallel to the main sentence line. The indirect object line is connected to the verb by a sloping line.

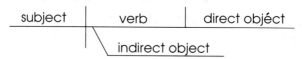

Imperative sentences have an "understood" *you*. In diagraming imperative sentences, the understood *you* is put in parentheses and placed in the subject position on the main sentence line.

Interrogative sentences (questions) are diagramed by rearranging the words so that they are in the same order as they would be in a corresponding declarative sentence.

Can John swim?

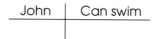

Who asked a question?

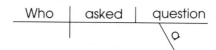

Where did Sally go?

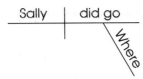

As a way of summarizing the conventions for diagraming simple sentences, the following are diagrams for the example sentences used to illustrate the six different types of complete predicates.

1. Intransitive action verb (no complement)

    The ship sank.

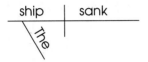

2. Transitive action verb + direct object complement

    The torpedo sank the ship.

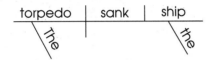

3. Transitive action verb + indirect object + direct object complement

    The teacher read the class a story.

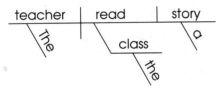

4. Linking verb (no complement)

    Kilroy was here.

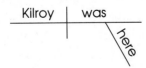

5. Linking verb + predicate nominative subject complement

    William was a waiter.

6. Linking verb + predicate adjective subject complement
   William was weary.

```
  William  |  was  \  weary
           |
```

Following are some helpful hints about diagraming.

☐ Do the main sentence line first.

☐ No punctuation is used in diagraming sentences. Capital letters and apostrophes, however, are kept.

☐ When two different adjectives or adverbs modify the same word on the main sentence line, put the adjectives or adverbs in the same left to right order in which they occur in the original sentence.

■ **Exercise 2.9. Diagraming the basic sentence: (I)**

Diagram the following sentences. (Answers to exercises are found on page 400.)

1. The Eagle has landed.
2. They lowered the lifeboats.
3. Fred always split his infinitives.
4. The room was a mess.
5. They are playing our song.
6. He became a legend.
7. Most politicians kiss babies and shake hands.
8. We went home and changed our clothes.
9. The sketch was not very funny.
10. They sought a long-range solution.
11. Usually, he is a very good little dog.
12. He tapped the glass and cleared his throat loudly.
13. Joan and I sanded the old desk yesterday.
14. The residents were constantly complaining.
15. The play was at an old theater.
16. I made Fred a sandwich.
17. Are you coming?
18. What is the answer?

■ **Exercise 2.10. Diagraming the basic sentence: (II)**
Diagram the following sentences. (Answers to exercises are found on page 403.)

1. The Count politely took a small bite.
2. The plumber flooded the basement and the garage.
3. Lady Grenville graciously greeted the humble peasants.
4. She found Anne an apartment.
5. A policeman's lot is not a happy one.
6. I had a terribly bad cold recently.
7. Williams rounded first and took second base.
8. Wasn't the rainy landscape gloomy and depressing?
9. They explored the constantly changing desert.
10. Tarzan and Jane loathe bananas.
11. Did you take your pills?
12. The mysterious red stain was there again.
13. The dog gave Holmes an idea.
14. The office resembled a movie set.
15. What is the matter?
16. Naturally, he had wanted a full-time job and reasonable pay.
17. The boss promised me a promotion yesterday.
18. Where are you going now?
19. Tell me the truth!

SUMMARY OF TRADITIONAL TERMS

Sentence: A sentence is a group of words expressing a complete thought.

Fragment: A fragment is a word or phrase that is less than a complete sentence.

Subject: The subject of a sentence is the part about which something is being said. The *simple subject* is the main noun (or pronoun) within the complete subject. The *complete subject* is the simple subject together with all the modifiers of the simple subject. A *compound subject* is two or more subjects joined by a coordinating conjunction.

Predicate: A predicate is the part of a sentence that says something about the subject. The *simple predicate* is the main verb together with any helping or auxiliary verbs. The *complete predicate* is the simple predicate together with modifiers and the complement. A *compound verb* is two or more main verbs joined by a coordinating conjunction.

Complement: A complement completes the meaning begun by the subject and the verb. A *transitive verb* is an action verb that requires an object. An *intransitive verb* is an action verb that does not require a complement. A *direct object* is a noun or pronoun that receives the action of the verb or shows the result of the action. An *indirect object* is a noun or pronoun that comes between the verb and the direct object and which tells *to whom* or *for whom* the action of the verb is done.

A *subject complement* is the complement that follows a linking verb.

A *predicate nominative* is a subject complement that is a noun.

A *predicate adjective* is a subject complement that is an adjective.

Classifying sentences by purpose:

Declarative: A declarative sentence makes a statement.

Imperative: An imperative sentence gives a command or makes a request.

Interrogative: An interrogative sentence asks a question.

Exclamatory: An exclamatory sentence expresses strong feeling.

3

Phrases

INTRODUCTION

Traditional definition: A *phrase* is a group of related words that is used as a single part of speech and that does not contain a finite verb and its subject.

There are two key concepts in the definition of *phrase*.

1. Phrases, no matter how many words they contain, act as a single unit, playing the role of one of the parts of speech, and
2. Phrases do not have the subject-predicate relation and therefore can never stand alone as sentences.

Following are the five main types of phrases along with their definitions.

☐ **Noun Phrase**   A noun phrase consists of a noun and its modifiers.

☐ **Verb Phrase**   A verb phrase is the main verb and all of its helping or auxiliary verbs.

☐ **Prepositional Phrase**   A prepositional phrase is a group of related words beginning with a preposition and ending with a noun or pronoun.

☐ **Appositive Phrase** An appositive phrase contains an appositive and its modifiers. An appositive is a noun or pronoun that follows a first noun or pronoun and that identifies or explains the first noun or pronoun.

☐ **Verbal Phrase** A verbal phrase is a group of related words that contains a verbal and its modifiers and/or complement. A verbal is a form of a verb used as another part of speech. There are three types of verbal phrases: *participial, gerund,* and *infinitive.*

NOUN PHRASE

A noun phrase consists of a noun (called the *head* noun) and its modifiers. The term *noun phrase* is not widely used in traditional grammar, although the concept is clearly present.

The usual pattern of modification in noun phrases containing common nouns (proper nouns are seldom modified) is adjectives in front of the head noun and prepositional phrases after the head noun.

Noun Phrase

the little old	man	on the bus
Adjectives	Head Noun	Prep Phrase

An important point to remember is that the head noun can never be part of a modifying prepositional phrase. Consider the following sentence.

Noun Phrase　　　　　　*Noun Phrase*

All of the elderly alligators frightened Captain Hook.

The head noun in the first noun phrase is the indefinite pronoun *all,* not the noun *alligators,* because *alligators* is inside a modifying prepositional phrase—the phrase that begins with *of.*

Noun Phrase

all	of the elderly alligators
Head Noun	Prepositional Phrase

It is very easy to overlook the preposition in a noun phrase, especially since there is often a very similar sentence without the preposition. For example, if we were to delete the preposition *of* from the preceding example sentence, we would get a new noun phrase in which *alligators* is the head noun and *all* is a modifier.

Noun Phrase

All the elderly	alligators	frightened Captain Hook.
Adjectives	Head Noun	

The sequence <u>indefinite pronoun</u> + *of* is very frequent. Following are some common ones to look out for.

all of the	few of the	neither of the
another of the	many of the	none of the
both of the	more of the	one of the
each of the	most of the	several of the
either of the	much of the	some of the

Remember that in all these examples the head noun is the indefinite pronoun, not the noun that follows the preposition *of*.

All noun phrases can be identified by replacing them with the appropriate personal pronouns. The choice of pronoun is determined by the head noun.

<u>The little old man on the bus</u> got off next.
　　　　　　　He

<u>The tall young girl in a blue dress</u> ordered <u>the asparagus shake</u>.
　　　　　She　　　　　　　　　　　　　　　　　　　　it

<u>The letter that you wrote</u> raised <u>a lot of questions</u>.
　　　　It　　　　　　　　　　　　it

<u>Most major achievements in science</u> were originally controversial.
　　　　　　They

■ **Exercise 3.1. Identifying noun phrases: I**

Underline the entire subject and object noun phrases in the following sentences. (Remember to underline also all modifiers of the head noun, including prepositional phrases.) Underneath the head noun in each noun phrase write the appropriate personal pronoun. The first sentence is done as an example. (Answers to exercises are found on page 406.)

1. <u>The members at the last meeting</u> ignored <u>the issue</u> completely.
　　　　They　　　　　　　　　　　　　　　　　it
2. Unfortunately, many of the voters opposed the new tax measures.
3. The elk in this area are protected.
4. The wet children dried their hands energetically.
5. A little girl in the first row easily guessed the answer.
6. Complex mathematical expressions defined the object's path correctly.
7. The group of volunteers finally painted the old barn.
8. These lights always attract some bugs.
9. That tree branch just snagged my pants.
10. Some girls in local costumes performed a dance.
11. The cold wind was killing most of the new plants.

12. Several guest speakers made excellent presentations last night.
13. The black prongs cover the small holes in the base plate.
14. The students had to use absentee ballots.
15. The police have established the owner of the stolen car.
16. In his dream the old man saw a long flight of stairs.
17. In English, modifying adjectives almost always precede their nouns.

■ **Exercise 3.2. Identifying noun phrases: II**

Underline the entire subject and object noun phrases and circle the head noun in the following sentences. Remember, the head noun cannot be in a prepositional phrase. The first sentence is done as an example. (Answers to exercises are found on page 407.)

1. The (men) in the silly little hats made an amazing (amount) of noise.
2. The chairman of the committee ruled the motion invalid.
3. A few of the members protested his ruling.
4. However, the chairman could cite all of the by-laws.
5. All the motions confused the poor secretary no end.
6. Finally, several of the members got *Robert's Rules of Order* out.
7. The organization thanked the members of the committee.
8. Most of us would never undergo that kind of pressure again.
9. The laundry didn't remove the stain on my tablecloth.
10. A few of us have never paid income tax.
11. The rank-and-file union members met yesterday.
12. The outcome of the case confirmed my worst suspicions.
13. A phrase is a group of related words.
14. Soon many of the bored children quit the game.
15. The fastest runners on the team could not steal second base.
16. All of the commentators predicted the results of the election.
17. Beethoven's symphonies completely dominated the next generation of composers.

VERB PHRASE

Traditional definition: A *verb phrase* consists of a main verb together with one or more helping or auxiliary verbs.

Adverbs, even adverbs in the middle of verb phrases, are modifiers of the verb phrase and thus not considered part of the verb phrase itself. Consider the following sentence.

John has already eaten.

The verb phrase is *has eaten*. The adverb *already*, even though it is in the middle of the verb phrase, is not part of the verb phrase.

Every verb phrase is classified according to its *tense*. The meaning of the term *tense* in traditional grammar is very complex. First of all we need to distinguish between "tense" referring to the *form of individual verbs* and "tense" referring to the *meaning of entire verb phrases*. The discussion of tense in Chapter 1 focuses only on the form of individual verbs. You may recall from that discussion that there are two types of individual verb forms: finite forms (verb forms that can stand alone, that is, without helping verbs) and nonfinite forms (verb forms that must be used with a helping verb).

The classification scheme for verb phrases is different. It is based on the meaning of the verb phrase as a whole rather than on the form of each verb that makes up the phrase. "Tense" in reference to the meaning of verb phrases is two dimensional: it refers both to *time*, and to *aspect*. The term *aspect* means action that is completed with reference to the time of some other action.

In the *time* dimension of tense, verbs and verb phrases are classified as being *past*, *present*, or *future*; for example, the three time forms for the verb *go* are the following.

Past: went
Present: go/goes
Future: will go

In the *aspect* dimension of tense, verbs and verb phrases are either *simple* (as in the examples preceding) or *perfect*. A verb phrase in the perfect tense always requires the helping verb *have* (in some form). A perfect verb phrase must also be classified by time: past, present, or future. Following is an example of the three perfect verb phrase forms (again using the verb *go*).

Past perfect: had gone
Present perfect: have/has gone
Future perfect: will have gone

An important point to notice about the perfect tenses is that the time dimension is signaled by the form of the helping verb *have*. In the past perfect tense, the helping verb is in the past tense form *had*. In the present perfect tense, the helping verb is in the present tense form *have/has.* In the future perfect tense, the helping verb is in the future tense form *will have.*

What is so perfect about the perfect? Something that is "perfect" is finished or completed. Compare the following two sentences.

Past:　　　　We <u>went</u> to the movies last night.

Past perfect:　We <u>had gone</u> to the movies when you called.

In the simple past sentence, the time of the action (going to the movies) is not specified further than being sometime *last night.* In the past perfect tense, however, the two events are sequential: we went to the movies *before* the time that you called. In other words, the past perfect relates two events in time—one event taking place before the other: the first action (going to the movies) was completed or finished (i.e., "perfected") before the second action (your calling) took place.

The present perfect describes an action begun in the past that continues in an unbroken manner up to the present moment.

Question:　Is John here?

Answer:　　No, he <u>has been</u> out of the office all day.

The present perfect *has been* emphasizes the fact that John has been absent from the office during the entire span of the day.

The present perfect differs from the simple present in that the present perfect implies that an action begun in the past may not continue beyond the present time into the future, whereas the simple present is essentially timeless. Compare, for example, the following two sentences.

Present:　　　　Fred <u>is</u> a great pitcher.

Present perfect:　Fred <u>has been</u> a great pitcher.

The present perfect implies that while he was a great pitcher in the past, Fred's days of greatness are numbered.

The future perfect implies that an action will be completed by some time in the future. Compare, for example, the following two sentences.

Future:　　　　We <u>will finish</u> at ten.

Future perfect:　We <u>will have finished</u> by ten.

The future tense sentence states when the action will take place. The future perfect tense sentence gives a time by which the future action will already have been completed (i.e., perfected).

To summarize, in traditional grammar verbs and verb phrases have six tenses: three simple tenses (Past, Present, Future), and three perfect tenses (Past Perfect, Present Perfect, and Future Perfect). The verb *go* has been picked to illustrate the six different tense forms. The names of the six different forms are in parentheses.

Tense .

Perfect

Past	went (Past)	had gone (Past Perfect)
Present	go/goes (Present)	have/has gone (Present Perfect)
Future	will go (Future)	will have gone (Future Perfect)

English also has another helping verb: *be*. When the helping verb *be* is used, the construction is called a *progressive*. For reasons going back to the Latinate origins of traditional grammar in the 18th century, traditional grammar does not call the progressive a "tense." Instead, the progressive is somewhat mysteriously called "a separate form of each of the six tenses." The progressive form of the six tenses follows (again illustrated with *go*).

Past progressive:	was/were going
Present progressive:	am/are/is going
Future progressive:	will be going
Past perfect progressive:	had been going
Present perfect progressive:	have/has been going
Future perfect progressive:	will have been going

The basic meaning of the progressive is something like "action in progress at a specific moment in time." For example, compare the following two past tense sentences.

Past:	John watched TV last night.
Past progressive:	John was watching TV when you called.

In the first sentence, the past tense means that sometime during the period of last night John engaged in the action of watching TV. The past progressive, however, ties the action (John's watching TV) to a specific point in time (the time that you called). Likewise for all the other uses of the progressive, this construction specifies that there is an ongoing action at some specified moment.

Following are some observations that may help you in the field identification of the various types of verb phrases.

☐ The progressive is easy to recognize because (1) the helping verb *be* (whatever form it is in) is always followed by the main verb, and (2) the main verb always ends in *-ing* (this form of the verb is called a *present participle*). [The term *present participle* and the term *past participle*, used in the following paragraph, are defined in the section on verbal phrases.]

☐ No matter how many verbs there are in a verb phrase, the first verb, and only the first verb, will be past, present, or future. Thus, the initial step in identifying a verb phrase is to identify whether the first verb is past, present, or future. Do not be misled by the forms of verbs that follow *have*: often these verbs look like past tenses, but they are really a form called the *past participle*. Consider the following sentences.

John has brushed his teeth.
Phil had ordered breakfast.

The verbs *brushed* and *ordered* are not past tenses; they are past participles. In the first sentence, *has* is in the present tense and the whole verb phrase is thus a present perfect; in the second sentence, *had* is in the past tense and the whole verb phrase is thus a past perfect. The helping verb *have/has/had* will always be followed by a verb in the past participle form.

☐ When a verb phrase contains both a perfect and a progressive, the helping verbs are always in a fixed order: first the perfect tense helping verb *have* (in some form), and then the progressive helping verb *be* (in some form). That is, we can say *has been working* but not **was had working*.

☐ Do not confuse *have* and *be* as helping verbs with *have* and *be* used as main verbs.

Helping Verb: I have gone.
Main Verb: I have a friend.

Helping Verb: I am going.
Main Verb: I am sorry.

Have and *be* can be used both ways in the same sentence.

I have   had a good time.
helping   main

I am   being patient.
helping   main

Let us now put all these observations to work classifying some tense names of complex verb phrases. [Hint: Work through the verb phrase from left to right, looking at the form of each verb, and determine why each verb is in the form it is.] Consider the following examples.

Verb Phrase: has slept
Tense name: present perfect

The tense is *present* because the first verb, *has*, is in the present tense; *perfect* because (1) *has* is a form of the perfect tense helping verb *have*, and (2) *slept*, the verb following *has*, is in the past participle form.

Verb Phrase: will be returning
Tense name: future progressive

The tense is *future* because the first verb, *will be*, is in the future tense; *progressive* because (1) *be* is a form of the progressive helping verb, and (2) *returning*, the verb following *be*, is in the present participle, or *-ing*, form.

Verb Phrase: had been working
Tense name: past perfect progressive

The tense is *past* because the first verb, *had*, is in the past tense; *perfect* because (1) *had* is a form of the perfect tense helping verb *have*, and (2) *been*, the verb following *had*, is in the past participle form; *progressive* because (1) *been* is a form of the progressive helping verb *be*, and (2) *working*, the verb following *been*, is in the present participle, or *-ing*, form.

Naming verb phrases boils down to three questions.

1. What is the tense (past, present, or future) of the first verb?
2. Is some form of *have* followed by a past participle verb used? If so, then the tense is a perfect.
3. Is some form of *be* followed by a present participle used? If so, then the tense is a progressive.

■ **Exercise 3.3. Verb and verb phrase names**
In the following sentences underline the verb or verb phrase. Underneath the sentence write the name of the verb or verb phrase (e.g., past, future perfect, present progressive). The first one is done as an example. (Answers to exercises are found on page 408.)

1. We <u>have postponed</u> the game.
    present perfect
2. The senator's aides are denying the statement.
3. They will have finished by now.
4. The doctor prescribed aspirin.
5. I will be busy all afternoon.
6. We interrupt this program for an important message.
7. I am already working on it.

8. They will have invested a fortune on it by then.
9. He had nearly wrecked the turntable.
10. He will have been sleeping all afternoon.
11. That tasted just awful.
12. He has certainly been persistent in his efforts.
13. The secretary informed the chairman.
14. He will probably argue against the measure.
15. Lady Lockridge will have collected all the insurance.
16. Watson was considering an alternative plan.
17. This is silly.

In diagraming verb phrases, remember that all helping verbs go on the main sentence line with the main verb and that all adverbs go under the main sentence line as modifiers. For example, the sentence *Newspapers will not usually publish unsigned letters* is diagramed in the following manner.

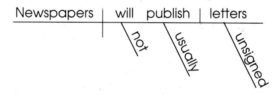

■ Exercise 3.4. Diagraming verb phrases

Diagram the following sentences. Remember that questions are diagramed in normal statement order. (Answers to exercises are found on page 408.)

1. The home team has scored first.
2. Did he ever confess?
3. Regular exercise will often ease the stiffness.
4. The company had invented a new mousetrap.
5. The bacteria will have been reproducing rapidly.
6. The problem seems impossible.
7. They have already eaten all the hamburgers and hot dogs.
8. Was the boat already leaking?
9. Holmes and Watson quickly spotted the frightfully decomposed body.
10. They did not disclose their information.
11. They were such nice people.

12. Frankenstein has been coloring his Easter eggs today.
13. They are always splitting their infinitives.
14. Holmes rapidly calculated the odds.
15. Has he aged?
16. The events had naturally discouraged him.
17. Tomorrow's quiz will be a nasty one.
18. John and Ralph have been watching the game and painting the deck.

PREPOSITIONAL PHRASE

Traditional definition: A *prepositional phrase* is a group of related words beginning with a preposition and ending with a noun or pronoun.

The form of prepositional phrases differs from the form of noun phrases and verb phrases in one important way: a prepositional phrase can have a phrase within a phrase. A prepositional phrase is a complex structure consisting of two elements: (1) a preposition and (2) a single word (a noun or pronoun) or noun phrase, bound together as a single unit. A diagram may help make this hierarchical structure clearer when the prepositional phrase contains a noun phrase.

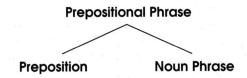

Following are some examples of prepositional phrases diagramed in the same manner.

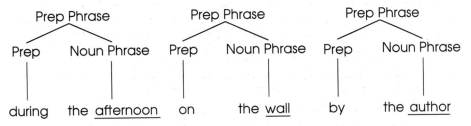

In the three examples, the underlined noun is the head noun in the noun phrase. This noun is called the *object of the preposition.*

The noun phrase inside a prepositional phrase is like any other noun phrase. The head noun of this noun phrase can be modified both by preceding adjectives and by following prepositional phrases. In the case of objects of prepositions, a modifying prepositional phrase will create a nest of phrases, one inside another, as in the following example.

We swam at the pool in the hotel.

There are two prepositional phrases: *at the pool* and *in the hotel*. The second prepositional phrase, *in the hotel*, modifies *pool*, the object of the preposition in the first prepositional phrase. Following is how we might represent the relation between the two prepositional phrases in a tree diagram.

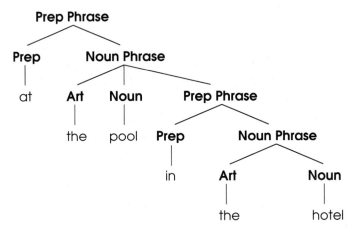

Since any common noun can be modified by a prepositional phrase, we can extend the sentence indefinitely by modifying the object of the preposition with another prepositional phrase, which contains an object of the preposition, which can be modified by another prepositional phrase, and so on.

We swam at the pool in the hotel near the shopping center by the airport.

So far we have examined only the *form* of prepositional phrases. Let us now turn to their *function*. Prepositional phrases are always modifiers. Prepositional phrases that modify nouns or pronouns are called *adjective phrases*; prepositional phrases that modify verbs, adjectives, or adverbs are called *adverb phrases*. We deal with these two uses of prepositional phrases in turn.

a. Adjective phrase

Some prepositional phrases that modify nouns have a time or space meaning.

time: the period after the war; the time before dawn;
           sometime during the movie; the years between the wars;
           the hour past noon

space: a seat next to the window; a city on a hill;
           the space underneath the roof; the chair by the wall;
           the space by the curb

However, for the most part adjective prepositional phrases defy any simple scheme of classification. Consider, for example, the different meanings conveyed by the various prepositions in the following sentences.

I read a book about The Beatles.
I read a book against The Beatles.
I read a book from The Beatles.
I read a book by The Beatles.
I read a book for The Beatles.
I read a book on The Beatles.
I read a book with The Beatles.
I read a book on account of The Beatles.
I read a book in spite of The Beatles.

Not only do different prepositions have very different meanings; the same preposition can have different relationships with the nouns it modifies. The preposition *of* undoubtedly has the most complex range of meaning. For example, *a person of courage* is someone who has courage, but *a person of science* is not someone who has science. *The arrival of the ship* is when the ship arrives, but *the schedule of the ship* is not when the ship schedules.

Prepositions that modify nouns are often ambiguous. For example, several of the preceding sentences about The Beatles can be interpreted in several ways.

I read a book by The Beatles.

The sentence can mean either "I read a book that was written by The Beatles" or "I read a book while seated next to The Beatles." Consider another example.

I read a book on The Beatles.

The sentence can mean either "I read a book that was about The Beatles" or "While I was seated on top of The Beatles, I passed the time by reading a book."

b. Adverb phrase

Adverb phrases that modify adjectives and adverbs also immediately follow the words they modify.

Modifying adjectives	*Modifying adverbs*
lucky at cards	later in the morning
happy with my job	earlier in the game
ready for dinner	
wise beyond your years	

The remaining (and largest) group of adverb prepositional phrases modifies verbs. These adverb prepositional phrases behave much like single word adverbs in that they tell time, place, manner, extent/degree, and so on. These adverb prepositional phrases can usually be recognized by adverb questions.

time:	They unloaded the truck after dinner.
adverb question:	When did they unload the truck?
answer:	after dinner
place:	John left his books at school.
adverb question:	Where did John leave his books?
answer:	at school
manner:	We washed the plants with great care.
adverb question:	How did we wash the plants?
answer:	with great care
means:	We washed the plants by hand.
adverb question:	How did we wash the plants?
answer:	by hand
extent/degree:	She ran for miles.
adverb question:	How far did she run?
answer:	for miles
reason/cause:	We closed early because of the heat.
adverb question:	Why did we close early?
answer:	because of the heat

However, there are many other functions that adverb prepositional phrases play that cannot be identified by asking questions. This is particularly true of compound prepositions. For example, there is no adverb question for the compound preposition *according to*.

That is the correct solution according to the book.

Like adverbs that modify verbs, adverb prepositional phrases that modify verbs normally occur at the end of sentences. And like adverbs, they can be moved to the beginning of the sentence.

According to the book, that is the correct solution.

Often it is hard to tell whether a prepositional phrase is an adjective phrase or an adverb phrase. If it is an adverb phrase, usually it can be moved to a different position in the sentence (as in the preceding example). If it is an adjective phrase, it cannot be moved away from the noun it modifies because adjectives are directly tied to the nouns they modify.

That is the correct solution to the problem.

The prepositional phrase *to the problem* is an adjective phrase modifying the noun *solution* and thus cannot be moved away from the noun it modifies.

*To the problem that is the correct solution.

Sometimes the prepositional phrase can be interpreted either as an adjective or adverb phrase. In this case the sentence is simply ambiguous.

My wife at the time worked for the government.

One interpretation is that *at the time* is an adjective phrase modifying *wife* (implying that the speaker is no longer married to that person). The other interpretation is that *at the time* is an adverb phrase modifying the verb *worked*. In this interpretation the adverb phrase can be moved to the first position of the sentence.

At the time my wife worked for the government.

There are two tests for telling adjective and adverb prepositional phrases apart: (1) move the prepositional phrase, and (2) substitute a pronoun for both the noun and the following prepositional phrase. Adverb prepositional phrases can usually be moved without difficulty, whereas adjective prepositional phrases are tied to the noun they modify and cannot be moved. Consider the following sentence.

We studied the map in the afternoon.

The prepositional phrase *in the afternoon* is an adverb. We can show that this interpretation is valid by moving the prepositional phrase to the first part of the sentence.

In the afternoon we studied the map.

Compare the preceding sentence with another sentence.

We studied the map from the drawer.

The most likely interpretation of this sentence is that *from the drawer* is an adjective phrase. One justification for this interpretation is the implausibility of moving the prepositional phrase to the first position.

*From the drawer we studied the map.

The fact that we cannot move the prepositional phrase to the first position is evidence that the prepositional phrase is not an adverb.

The second test involves substituting a pronoun for *both the noun and the following prepositional phrase*. [Recall that a pronoun substitutes for a noun and all of its modifiers.] If the resulting sentence is grammatical, then the prepositional phrase must be an adjective modifier of the noun since both the prepositional phrase and the noun have been replaced by the pronoun.

We studied the map from the drawer.
it (= the map from the drawer)

When we apply the pronoun substitution test with a sentence containing an adverb phrase, the prepositional phrase is not replaced by the pronoun.

We studied the map in the afternoon.
*it (= *the map in the afternoon)

These two tests are quite reliable ways of distinguishing adjective and adverb prepositional phrases. Nevertheless, prepositional phrases are often ambiguous—the prepositional phrase can be interpreted either way (as, for example, in the preceding sentence about the man's wife). Accordingly, in the answers to the exercises you will occasionally find that where you have interpreted a prepositional phrase as an adjective phrase, the book has done the opposite (and vice versa). Often in these cases the sentence is ambiguous, and thus your interpretation (and diagram) is as good as the answer in the book.

Some adverb phrases cannot be identified by moving the adverb phrase to a different position in the sentence. Consider the following sentence.

The car is at the garage.

The adverb phrase *at the garage* cannot be moved to the first position in the sentence.

*At the garage the car is.

The problem here is not so much the test itself—*at the garage* is indeed an adverb phrase. The problem is the *use* of the adverb phrase. In this sentence it is not really an optional element that can be moved or deleted; it is something more like a complement—a word or phrase required by the verb to make a complete sentence. The adverb phrase cannot be moved in this case because it is not an optional modifier; it is locked into position after the verb in the same way that a complement is.

A similar problem occurs with a group of transitive verbs that requires an adverb of place after the object in order to complete the meaning of the sentence. A good example of this group is the verb *put*.

John put the book on the table.

The prepositional phrase *on the table* does not modify *book*, as we can demonstrate by the pronoun substitution test.

John put the book on the table.
*John put   it

Nor does *on the table* behave like an optional adverb phrase since we cannot move it to the first position in the sentence.

*On the table John put the book.

The grammar of the verb *put* requires a direct object and an adverb phrase of place. In other words, it is ungrammatical to *put* something without specifying where we put it. As is the case with "The car is at the garage," the adverb phrase is part of the complement, not an optional modifier.

■ **Exercise 3.5. Identifying prepositional phrases**
Underline the prepositional phrases in the following sentences (all of the adverb phrases modify the verb). Above the prepositional phrase write *Adj* if it is an adjective phrase or *Adv* if it is an adverb phrase. Apply the adverb or adjective phrase tests to support your answer. The first two sentences are done as examples. (Answers to exercises are found on page 411.)

                    Adj
 1. The house in the movie resembles my parents' place.
    Adjective phrase: It resembles my parents' place.
                                             Adv
 2. How did you like the place aside from the yucky wallpaper?
    Adverb phrase: Aside from the yucky wallpaper, how did you like the place?
 3. I think that he overplayed the part of the tough reporter.
 4. We bought an old cabin in the mountains.
 5. He is an Englishman in spite of all temptations.
 6. We finally found substitutes for our injured players.
 7. He has attended City College for the last few weeks.
 8. The drug store in River City carries them.
 9. The prosecutor in the case convinced the jury without much difficulty.

10. I just stood there shaking after the accident.
11. I still trusted him despite all the evidence against him.
12. Everybody in town has seen the movie at the Palace.
13. The company was acquired within a week.
14. They will issue new stock in the company as of the first.
15. The Division mounted an all-out attack without air support at dawn.
16. I fell asleep during the program about whales.

Diagraming prepositional phrases.   Since prepositional phrases are modifiers, they are drawn underneath the main sentence line and are attached to the word they modify. Adjective phrases are drawn underneath the nouns they modify; adverb phrases are drawn underneath the adjective, adverb, or verb that they modify. Following are some examples.

We swam at the pool in the hotel.

(Note that the adjective phrase *in the hotel* is attached to *pool*, the noun it modifies, and that the adverb phrase *at the pool* is attached to *swim*, the verb that it modifies. We have here an adjective phrase inside an adverb phrase.)

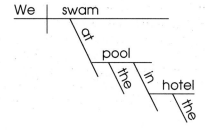

We swam at the pool in the afternoon.
(*In the afternoon* is an adverb phrase modifying *swam*.)

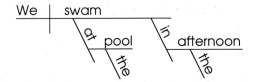

She is lucky at cards.
(*At cards* modifies the adjective *lucky*.)

We arrived late in the evening.

(*In the evening* modifies the adverb *late*. *Late* is an adverb because it answers the adverb question *when*.)

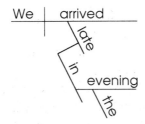

Traditional grammar does not make any distinction between optional modifying adverb phrases and those adverb phrases which are required by certain verbs. In the latter case, the adverb phrases are diagramed as though they were optional modifiers of the verb. Following are two examples.

The car is at the garage.

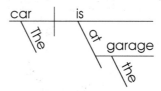

John put the book on the table.

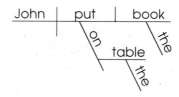

■ **Exercise 3.6. Diagraming prepositional phrases**

Diagram the following sentences. (Answers to exercises are found on page 412.)

1. Everybody in town rejected the bill.
2. The carrier delivered a package at our new house.
3. We went to the library later in the afternoon.
4. After breakfast we divided the wood into two piles.
5. Watson was terribly concerned about the incident.
6. The railroad runs through the woods and over the river.
7. He listed the many causes of the revolution in France.

8. The minister issued a statement concerning the events of the last few days.

9. We had an argument about our policy on imports of shoes from Italy.

10. Who is going to the movies besides us?

11. My seat at the concert was behind a pillar.

12. We finally located the right kind of part in a junkyard near the river.

13. My cousins have remained active in politics since college.

14. Why do we always get so many bills around Christmas?

15. Mary told John the story.

16. Mary told the story to John.

17. Could you attend the meeting instead of me?

18. He found a parking place in front of the store on 6th Street.

APPOSITIVE PHRASE

Traditional definition: An appositive is a noun or pronoun that follows another noun or pronoun to identify or explain it. An *appositive phrase* consists of an appositive and its modifiers.

The head noun in an appositive phrase is called the appositive. If the appositive has its own modifiers, then the entire noun phrase is called an appositive phrase.

Appositives (and appositive phrases) are not modifiers. Appositives rename or identify other nouns. Following are some examples of appositive phrases (the head noun, the appositive, is in italics).

Emma, the only *child* to have no cavities, smiled proudly.

Senator Smithers, a *man* in a hurry, flies his own jet.

Dr. Goldhord, a *member* of the Chicago school, urged a return to fiscal responsibility.

The head noun in the appositive phrase in the first example sentence is *child*; *child* refers to *Emma*. The appositive phrase describes or further identifies *Emma: the only child to have no cavities*. In the second sentence the appositive is *man*; the appositive phrase describes something about *Senator Smithers*. He is *a man in a hurry*. In the third sentence the appositive is *member*; the appositive phrase describes or further identifies *Dr. Goldhord*. He or she is *a member of the Chicago school*. Note that appositives and appositive phrases are normally set off from the rest of the sentence by a pair of commas. A common error for beginning writers is to omit the second comma. A way to minimize this problem is to teach your students that the pair of commas around an appositive phrase is like a pair of parentheses—you cannot have a left one without a right one.

Occasionally, when the word being renamed is (1) a proper noun or a pronoun, and (2) the subject of the sentence, the appositive phrase is moved to a place in front of the subject noun for emphasis.

> <u>The only child to have no cavities</u>, Emma smiled proudly.

> <u>A man in a hurry</u>, Senator Smithers flies his own jet.

> <u>A member of the Chicago school</u>, Dr. Goldhord urged a return to fiscal responsibility.

Since an appositive can be moved to a position in front of its noun, how can we tell which is the noun and which is the appositive? We can always tell by the punctuation. Compare the following two sentences.

> Lady Montcrief, the heir to Abbington Hall, stood aghast.
> The heir to Abbington Hall, Lady Montcrief stood aghast.

In the second sentence *Lady Montcrief* is not an appositive because if it were, it would be surrounded by a pair of commas. Since it is not, *Lady Montcrief* is the subject and *the heir to Abbington Hall* is an appositive that has been moved out of its normal position following the noun it renames.

■ **Exercise 3.7. Recognizing appositives and appositive phrases**

Combine the following sentences by changing the second sentence into an appositive or appositive phrase. The first exercise is done as an example. (Answers to exercises are found on page 414.)

1. He gave his daughter a new toy.
   The toy was a stuffed teddy bear.
   <u>He gave his daughter a new toy, a stuffed teddy bear.</u>

2. Dorothy saw her old enemy.
   Her old enemy was the Wicked Witch of the West.

3. The Pacific Ocean was unknown to the ancient world.
   The Pacific Ocean is the earth's largest body of water.

4. Export processing zones specialize in light manufacturing.
   Export processing zones are managed industrial parks.

5. The answer to the question came as a complete surprise.
   The answer to the question was 42.

6. PDQ Bach composed *The Stoned Guest*.
   PDQ Bach is an imaginary son of JS Bach.

7. Watson is the perfect foil for Holmes.
Watson is a slightly comic figure.
8. My grandfather refused to get electric lights.
My grandfather was a man with firm convictions.
9. Calvin Coolidge was known as "Silent Cal."
Calvin Coolidge was the 30th President of the United States.
10. The theater was undergoing renovation.
The theater was one of the old movie palaces.
11. She finally got around to taking the test.
The test was a multiple choice examination on philosophy.
12. They elected Leon class secretary.
Leon was a person who could hardly spell his own name.

Diagraming appositive phrases. Appositives are diagramed by putting
the appositive in parentheses and placing it immediately after the noun
or pronoun it renames. For example, the sentence *My English teacher,
Mr. Smith, loves gerunds* is diagramed in the following manner.

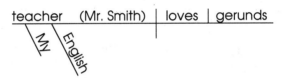

In appositive phrases only the appositive noun—the single noun that
refers to the noun being renamed—is placed on the main sentence line.
The other words in the appositive phrase are modifiers of the appositive
noun and are drawn below it. There is nothing strange about this since
the appositive is really the head noun in a noun phrase. The appositive
noun is put on the main sentence line, and all its modifiers are attached
to it from below.

A man in a hurry, Senator Smithers flies his own jet.

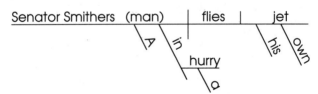

Note that in this example the appositive phrase *a man in a hurry* is in
front of the subject noun. In the diagram, however, the appositive is
put back in its normal position, following the noun to which it is an
appositive. This follows the general practice of diagraming sentences
in a normal form. You recall, for example, that questions are put back
into a normal statement form when they are diagramed.

■ **Exercise 3.8. Diagraming appositives and appositive phrases**

Diagram the following sentences. (Answers to exercises are found on page 415.)

1. The first talking motion picture, *The Jazz Singer*, was produced in 1927.
2. An excellent student, she was first in her class.
3. Oxford University, the most famous school in England, is outside London.
4. Mr. Smith, a teacher at our school, admires appositives.
5. The police found his last address, an old hotel in Denver.
6. Atolls, small coral islands, cover tropical waters.
7. Homer, the Greek poet, was blind.
8. The children loved tortillas, a type of cornmeal pancake.
9. Holmes noticed the man, a soldier in civilian clothing.
10. Oakridge, the first street after Main, will take you there.
11. Nematodes, microscopic worms, attack the roots of cotton plants.
12. The first player got 12,000 points, a high score in this game.
13. Noel Coward wrote *Private Lives*, his best-known play, in 1930.
14. The new cook, a recent graduate, was a great improvement.
15. Did the conductor see the suspect, an elderly man in a green coat?
16. Pull the switch, the red one.
17. They enrolled in the course, a five-credit class in financial accounting.
18. A hopeless romantic, I always want a happy ending.

VERBAL PHRASE

Traditional definition: A verbal is a form of a verb used as another part of speech. A *verbal phrase* contains a verbal together with its modifiers and/or complement.

Verbals are by far the most difficult type of phrase to deal with. First we need to distinguish between *verb phrases* and *verbal phrases*. A *verb phrase* must contain a *finite verb*. A finite verb, you recall, is a verb in the present or past tense form. A verb phrase is used with a subject to make a complete sentence.

A *verbal phrase*, on the other hand, never contains a finite verb. A verbal phrase contains a *nonfinite verb* that is used as another part of speech, that is, as a noun, adjective, or adverb.

Before we discuss verbals, let us examine the forms of nonfinite verbs. There are three nonfinite verb forms: *present participles, past participles*, and *infinitives*. Following are some examples of verbs in both finite forms (present and past—remember, the future is not a finite tense because it requires the helping verb *will*) and the three nonfinite forms (present participle, past participle, and infinitive).

Finite		Nonfinite		
Present	*Past*	*Present Participle*	*Past Participle*	*Infinitive*
see(-s)	saw	seeing	seen	to see
work(-s)	worked	working	worked	to work
drive(-s)	drove	driving	driven	to drive
smile(-s)	smiled	smiling	smiled	to smile
come(-s)	came	coming	come	to come

Present participles are quite regular. They always end in *-ing*.
Past participle forms, however, pose several problems.

1. Past participles of irregular verbs are hard to recognize because irregular verbs do not have a single common form for the past participle. The most common irregular verb form ends in *-(e)n*.

   eat-ate-eaten
   fall-fell-fallen
   see-saw-seen

   Many past participles, however, can only be recognized by the changes in their vowels.

   ring-rang-rung
   sing-sang-sung

   Many past participles have both an *-(e)n* ending and a vowel change.

   do-did-done
   freeze-froze-frozen
   ride-rode-ridden

   There are even some verbs in which there is no distinction at all between present, past, and past participle forms.

   hit-hit-hit
   put-put-put

2. Past participles of regular verbs pose a completely different problem. The form of the past participle in regular verbs always

ends in -*(e)d*. The problem here is that the past tense also ends in -*(e)d*. In other words, students easily confuse the past participle with the past tense. To minimize the confusion, it is a good idea to point out that the past participle form is used after *have/had*, whereas the past tense is used without a helping verb. For example, compare the following sentences.

Past: They <u>sanded</u> the floors.
Past Participle: They <u>have sanded</u> the floors.
                     They <u>had sanded</u> the floors.

Infinitives are the dictionary entry forms of verbs—the form of the verb that is listed in the dictionary (without *to*). With the major exception of the verb *be* (present: *am, are, is*), the infinitive form is the same as the form of the present tense. In verb phrases, infinitives are used without *to* (e.g., He will *go*). When infinitives are used as verbals, however, the infinitive (with a few exceptions) is used with *to*.

I wanted <u>to go</u>.
I told them <u>to leave</u>.
He asked me <u>to come</u>.

■ **Exercise 3.9. Nonfinite verb forms**

Below are past tense forms. For each verb give the following nonfinite forms: (1) infinitive (with *to*), (2) present participle, and (3) past participle (with *have*). The first is done as an example. (Answers to exercises are found on page 417.)

1. forgot
   1. to forget   2. forgetting   3. have forgotten
2. chose
3. came
4. protested
5. saw
6. faded
7. bought
8. fulfilled
9. ran
10. substituted
11. dug
12. conceded
13. dreamed
14. spent

15. inquired
16. split
17. sold
18. cut

The three nonfinite verb forms are used to form the three types of verbals in the following manner.

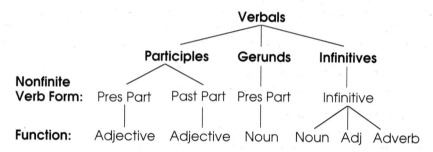

The first type of verbal, *participles*, consists of present and past participle verb forms, both of which function as adjectives. The second type of verbal, *gerunds*, consists of present participle verb forms that act as nouns. The third type of verbal, *infinitives*, consists of infinitive verb forms that act as nouns, adjectives, or adverbs. Note that present participle forms can be used as either adjectives or nouns.

a. Participle and participial phrase

Traditional definition: A *participle* is a verb form used as an adjective. A *participial phrase* consists of a participle together with its modifiers and/or complement.

There are two different types of participles: *present participles* and *past participles*. Following are some examples of each type.

Present participles	*Past participles*
<u>winning</u> coaches	<u>sanded</u> floors
<u>trusting</u> students	<u>understood</u> subject
<u>participating</u> schools	<u>reported</u> incident
<u>simpering</u> maidens	<u>injured</u> party
<u>arousing</u> speaker	<u>aroused</u> speaker

As the last example indicates, the same verb can be used to form either a present participle (*arousing*) or a past participle (*aroused*) with the same noun (*speaker*), but with a substantial difference in meaning. An *arousing* speaker is a speaker who arouses the audience, whereas an *aroused* speaker is one that is himself aroused—with unknown effect on the audience.

There is no profound difference between a participle and a participial phrase. A participle is a single word. When we add additional words to a participle, we have a participial phrase. For example, we can change the following participles into participial phrases merely by adding modifiers to the participle.

Participles:
The <u>ducking</u> runner slid into second base.
The <u>struck</u> batter went to first base.

Participial phrases:
The runner, <u>easily ducking under the tag</u>, slid into second base.
The batter, <u>struck by the pitch</u>, went to first base.

Note that the distinction between present and past participles carries over to participial phrases. Thus, *easily ducking under the tag* in the first example sentence is a present participial phrase, and *struck by the pitch* in the second example sentence is a past participial phrase. Note also that the normal position of a participle, like an adjective, is in front of the noun it modifies, whereas the normal position of a participial phrase, like a prepositional phrase, is after the noun it modifies. However, we can readily move participial phrases to a position in front of subject noun phrases.

<u>Easily ducking under the tag</u>, the runner slid into second base.
<u>Struck by the pitch</u>, the batter went to first base.

A useful way to think of participles and participial phrases is that they come from understood full sentences.

<u>Swallowing his disappointment</u>, Tom accepted defeat gracefully.

We can see how the present participial phrase can be paraphrased as an understood full sentence. Who swallowed his disappointment? Obviously, *Tom* did. Thus underlying the participial phrase *swallowing his disappointment* is the full sentence.

(Tom swallowed his disappointment.)
[We will use parentheses to indicate understood sentences.]

We can transform the understood sentence into a verbal phrase by (1) changing the finite verb *swallowed* into a nonfinite form—the present participle *swallowing*, and (2) deleting the subject *Tom*. Notice that the rest of the original sentence, the complement *his disappointment*, remains unchanged. The verbal phrase *swallowing his disappointment* describes *Tom*. Therefore, the verbal phrase has the function of an adjective.

A participle is produced in exactly the same manner as a participial phrase. The only difference between a participial phrase and a participle is that a participle comes from an underlying sentence that has an intransitive verb and no adverbs. For example, if we had the understood intransitive sentence *Tom swallowed* instead of the transitive sentence *Tom swallowed his disappointment*, the result would be the participle *swallowing*. Thus a participle is really just a "special case" form of a participial phrase. The only difference is that the verb in the underlying sentence does not have a complement or any modifiers. Now look at the following variation of the original sentence.

Smiling, Tom accepted defeat gracefully.

Underlying the participle *smiling* is the following understood sentence.

(Tom smiled.)

The finite verb *smiled* is changed into a present participle, a nonfinite verb form, and the subject is deleted, leaving us with the present participle *smiling*.

So far we have discussed participles and participial phrases formed with the present participle. The other kind of participial phrase is formed with the past participle.

Rejected by the voters, Tom burned all his bumper stickers.

Who was rejected? *Tom* was. Therefore, the past participial phrase *rejected by the voters* comes from the following understood sentence.

(Tom was rejected by the voters.)

In the case of past participles, the main verb, *rejected*, is already a past participle, so the only change in the sentence is to delete the finite helping verb (*was*) and the subject (*Tom*), leaving the past participial phrase

rejected by the voters.

Following is another example that involves a past participial phrase.

Disappointed by his unexpected loss, Tom sadly accepted defeat.

Who was disappointed by his unexpected loss? Again, obviously it was *Tom*. Thus the subject of the understood full sentence is *Tom*.

(Tom was disappointed by his unexpected loss.)

Past participles always come from understood sentences that have *be* as a helping verb. These understood sentences are always passives. The past participle or past participial phrase is formed by deleting the subject and the passive helping verb *be*, retaining the past participle form of the main verb plus whatever (if anything) follows the verb. Following are some more examples of past participles and past participial phrases with the underlying passive sentence in parentheses.

> Demoralized by his defeat, Tom thought about his future.
> (Tom was demoralized by his defeat.)
>
> Stung by the outcome, Tom demanded a recount.
> (Tom was stung by the outcome.)
>
> Dismayed, Tom swore never to run for elective office again.
> (Tom was dismayed.)

Another way that passive sentences can be turned into participles and participial phrases is by keeping the helping verb as a present participle. For example, from the understood sentence *(Tom was rejected by the voters)* we can also produce a present participial phrase by retaining the helping verb *be*.

> Being rejected by the voters, Tom burned all his bumper stickers.

Thus, from the same underlying sentence, we can produce two slightly different forms of participial phrases.

> Being rejected by the voters, ⎤ Tom burned all his bumper
> Rejected by the voters, ⎦ stickers.

We often use the present participle of *have* to emphasize that the action of the underlying sentence took place before the main sentence. The effect of this time distinction is to imply a cause and effect relationship. That is, the action in the main sentence took place *because* of the action in the underlying sentence. For example, from the underlying sentence *(Tom had been rejected by the voters)* we can produce the following sentence.

> Having been rejected by the voters, Tom burned all his bumper stickers.

The use of *have* emphasizes the fact that Tom's rejection by the voters occurred *before* he burned his bumper stickers, implying that there is a cause-and-effect relation between the two events: namely, he burned his bumper stickers because the voters rejected him. The same implication is there in the underlying sentences without *have*, but the use of *have* makes the implication much stronger.

■ **Exercise 3.10. Recognizing participles and participial phrases**

Combine the following pairs of sentences by changing the second sentence into a present or past participial phrase that modifies a noun in the first sentence. The first pair is done as an example. (Answers to exercises are found on page 418.)

1. The hikers set up camp.
   The hikers were picking their spot carefully.
   <u>Picking their spot carefully, the hikers set up camp.</u>

2. The conductor stepped to the podium.
   The conductor was greeted with warm applause by the audience.

3. The teller called the manager over.
   The teller was noticing his strange behavior.

4. The truck finally began to inch forward.
   The truck was pulled by two wreckers.

5. The event was soon the talk of the town.
   The event had been mentioned on several news programs.

6. Leon climbed to the top of the flagpole.
   Leon was trying to set a new record.

7. Leon gave up in disgust.
   Leon was endlessly bothered by pigeons.

8. They ran for shelter.
   They were grabbing the picnic basket and table cloth.

9. Leon took up gardening.
   Leon was ridiculed by his neighbors.

10. John married Marcia.
    John was forsaking all others.

11. The salesman engaged Uncle Ralph in conversation.
    The salesman was expressing a great interest in worm farming.

12. The calf soon gained its weight back.
    The calf was being fed by hand.

In diagraming participles and participial phrases, the participle is treated like an adjective: it is drawn on a slanted line underneath the noun that it modifies. However, apparently in deference to its origin as a verb, the participle's line is connected to a horizontal line parallel to the main sentence line, and the participle is elegantly draped between the slanted and horizontal lines.

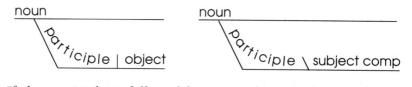

If the participle is followed by a complement, the complement is drawn on the horizontal line in the normal way as though it were following a finite verb, and the modifiers are attached accordingly. For example, the following is how the sentence *Swallowing his disappointment, Tom accepted defeat gracefully* is diagramed.

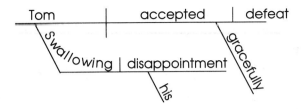

Past participial phrases are diagramed in exactly the same manner. For example, *Rejected by the voters, Tom burned all his bumper stickers* would be diagramed as follows.

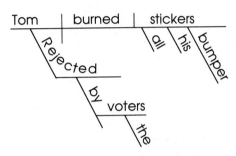

■ **Exercise 3.11. Diagraming participles and participial phrases**

Diagram the following sentences. (Answers to exercises are found on page 418.)

1. Proving his point, the professor gestured wildly.
2. Looking very uneasy, Leon checked his parachute.
3. Being concerned about his grades, Chadwick requested an appointment.
4. The owners, represented by their lawyers, filed a new motion.
5. Recognizing the value of a formal education, Leon entered college.
6. The strikers, being restrained by court order, had stayed outside.
7. We finally found the answer in a book written by Ralph Blake.
8. The new airline, started by the Blues Brothers, is based in Chicago.
9. Justice Potter, dissenting, roundly attacked the company's argument.
10. The tenor, joined by the baritone, sang a rousing duet about free trade.
11. Giving me a dirty look, she concluded her prepared statement.
12. Endowed with great natural beauty, North Dakota has become a major tourist destination in recent years.
13. Being tall, I reached the top shelf without difficulty.
14. We remembered the strange sound occurring in the night.

15. Closing his book, the teacher signalled the end of class for the day.
16. Dogged by constant failure, Leon revised his game plan drastically.
17. How could he have paid the fine, being completely broke?
18. Being ready for the exam, she had little difficulty with it.

Dangling Participles. When present and past participles and participial phrases are placed at the beginning of the sentence, the reader naturally assumes that the first noun that follows the participle or participial phrase will be the noun that the participle or phrase modifies; that is, that the first noun following the participle or participial phrase will be the subject of the understood sentence that is the source of the participial phrase. For example, compare the following two sentences.

1. <u>Having hiked all day</u>, I couldn't wait to take off my backpack.
2. *<u>Having hiked all day</u>, my backpack was killing me.

When a participle or participial phrase appears to modify a noun that is not the subject of the understood sentence that the participle or participial phrase comes from, we have what is called a *dangling participle*. Sentence 2 contains a dangling participle because it looks as if the following is the understood sentence.

*(My backpack had hiked all day.)

A dangling participle "dangles" because it is placed next to a noun that the writer does not mean for the participle to modify. In the preceding example sentence, the participial phrase *having hiked all day* is placed next to *backpack*, making it appear that the participle modifies it rather than *me*, the word the writer intended it to modify.

Now suppose that you wrote the following sentence.

<u>Having been excused from class</u>, I was not reported by the teacher.

This sentence does not contain a dangling participle because the participial phrase *having been excused from class* is properly placed next to the noun (or in this case, the pronoun) that it is intended to modify. In other words, the pronoun *I* is properly understood as the subject of the sentence underlying the participial phrase.

(I had been excused from class.)

Suppose that you then decided that you did not like the main clause's being in the passive, so you changed *I was not reported by the teacher* into its corresponding active form, *the teacher did not report me*, producing the following sentence.

*<u>Having been excused from class</u>, the teacher did not report me.

As you can see, the inadvertent result has been to create a dangling participle by incorrectly implying that the present participial phrase *having been excused from class* modifies *teacher*; that is, that the subject of the understood sentence underlying the present participial phrase is *teacher*.

*(The <u>teacher</u> had been excused from class.)

Probably the most common source for dangling participles is using the participial phrase as a kind of reduced adverb clause.

*<u>Jogging down main street this morning</u>, the sunrise was spectacular.

Following is what the writer of the sentence *meant*.

<u>As I was jogging down main street this morning</u>, the sunrise was spectacular.

Unfortunately, however, the following is what the writer *implied*.

*(The sunrise was jogging down main street this morning.)

The moral of the story is simple. *When you use a participial phrase in an initial position, the participial phrase must modify the following noun.* Otherwise, the participial phrase will be a dangling participle because, like it or not, the following noun will be perceived as the understood subject of the sentence underlying the participial phrase. A good rule of thumb in any kind of noun modification is to keep the modifier next to the noun (or pronoun) it modifies.

■ **Exercise 3.12. Dangling participles**

Many of the following sentences contain dangling participles. Correct the dangling participles by rewriting the sentence. [Many possible answers.] (Answers to exercises are found on page 422.)

1. Working all night, my term paper was almost finished.
   Revised: Working all night, I nearly finished my term paper.
2. Piled on the floor, I began sorting through my books.
3. Detouring through my old neighborhood, our house looked the same as ever.
4. Having matured, I now enjoy the Flintstones.
5. Being old Dodger fans, the outcome of the game pleased us.
6. Once considered only an average player, Don's game has improved enormously.
7. Hoping for a league championship, there was excitement in the air.
8. Disappointed by the unexpected defeat, we, nevertheless, applauded the team's efforts.

9. Working for old Mr. Green, he taught us the value of a good day's work.
10. Finishing in 2 hours and 37 minutes, John's first marathon was a terrific success.
11. Finished with my term paper, we all went out for a pizza.
12. Shining in the sun, the water looked very inviting.
13. Running across the plowed field, my ankle twisted.
14. Made from a new plastic, you cannot easily tell these artificial flowers from real ones.
15. Warped and twisted from the heat, I realized that my records were ruined.

---

b. Gerund and gerund phrase

Traditional definition: A *gerund* is a verb form ending in -*ing* that is used as a noun. A *gerund phrase* consists of a gerund together with its complement and/or modifiers, all of which act together as a noun phrase.

Here are some examples of gerunds and gerund phrases in the different noun roles of subject, object, predicate nominative, object of a preposition, and appositive.

Gerund:

Subject:	Swimming is an excellent form of exercise.
Object:	I hate swimming.
Pred Nom:	His favorite sport is swimming.
Obj of Prep:	The pool is used for swimming.
Appositive:	His favorite sport, swimming, is very time-consuming.

Gerund Phrase:

Subject:	Shouting at me won't help the situation.
Object:	We enjoyed playing Monopoly.
Pred Nom:	His idea of a good time is watching reruns on TV.
Obj of Prep:	Alicia learned English by listening to the radio.
Appositive:	His favorite sport, nude skydiving, is expensive.

The difference between gerunds and gerund phrases, like the distinction between participles and participial phrases, is merely the presence of additional words (modifiers and complements) in the gerund phrase.

Gerunds and present participles are both present participle nonfinite verb forms. In order to avoid confusion between the term *present participle* referring to a nonfinite verb form and *present participle* referring to an adjective verbal phrase, from this point on our discussion refers to the nonfinite verb form as the *-ing* form (i.e., *-ing* = present participle nonfinite verb form) and reserves the term *present participle* to refer solely to the adjective verbal phrase.

The difference between present participles and gerunds is not in their forms (which are identical) but in their functions. Present participles function as adjectives; gerunds function as nouns. For example, the *-ing* word *laughing* can be used either as an adjective (present participle) or as a noun (gerund).

Present Participle:	<u>Laughing</u>, Alice answered the question.
Gerund:	<u>Laughing</u> gives Alice a side-ache.

In the first sentence the present participle *laughing* is an adjective describing *Alice*. In the second sentence the gerund *laughing* is a noun functioning as the subject of the sentence.

Likewise, the difference between present participial phrases and gerund phrases is in how they are used. For example, the *-ing* phrase *parking his car* can be either a present participial phrase or a gerund phrase, depending on how it is used.

Present Part Phrase:	<u>Parking his car</u>, Fred ran into the store.
Gerund Phrase:	<u>Parking his car</u> is a real problem for Fred.

In the first sentence the present participial phrase is functioning as an adjective describing Fred. In the second sentence the gerund phrase is a noun functioning as the subject of the sentence.

An important characteristic of gerunds and gerund phrases is that they are always singular.

<u>Parking their cars</u> *is* a problem for them.
*<u>Parking their cars</u> *are* a problem for them.

The fact that gerunds and gerund phrases are always singular gives us an important test for recognizing them: we can *always* substitute *it* for a gerund or gerund phrase. For example, we can substitute *it* for the gerund phrase in the following sentence.

<u>Parking their cars</u> is a problem for them.
     It   is a problem for them.

Now, let's try the *it* test with a present participial phrase:

<u>Parking their cars</u>, they ran into the store.
     *It   , they ran into the store.

As you can see, the resulting sentence is ungrammatical. Since gerunds and gerund phrases always function as singular nouns, the *it* test is a simple and very reliable test for them. If you cannot substitute *it* for an *-ing* phrase, then the *-ing* phrase must be a participle or participial phrase.

However, like any test, the *it* test for gerunds can be misused. *It* can substitute for any singular abstract noun phrase. Compare the following sentences.

1. Running around campus made the students tired.
2. The rumor running around campus frightened the students.

Let us apply the *it* test to the subjects of both sentences.

1. <u>It</u> made the students tired.
2. <u>It</u> frightened the students.

Does the fact that we can use the *it* test in both sentences mean that both sentences contain a gerund? Not at all. The *it* test merely means that whatever the *it* replaced is a noun phrase. In sentence 1 the *it* test shows that *running around campus* is a noun phrase. We recognize this particular type of noun phrase to be a gerund by the fact that the head noun (*running*) is an *-ing* form of a verb. In sentence 2 the *it* test shows that *the rumor running around campus* is a noun phrase. However, the head noun in this noun phrase is *rumor*, not *running*. *Running around campus* is a modifier of the head noun. Since this noun modifier contains a verb used as an adjective (*running*), we recognize that *running around campus* is a participial phrase. So remember that in using the *it* test to identify gerunds, the head noun that the *it* refers to must be an *-ing* form of a verb, not some other noun that the *-ing* form modifies.

Gerund phrases used as predicate nominatives may seem difficult at first glance because they superficially resemble progressives, but the *it* test shows that they are gerunds.

His idea of a good time is <u>watching reruns on TV</u>.
it

Another way of distinguishing between gerunds and progressives is to change the suspected progressive into a past tense by deleting the helping verb *be* and the *-ing* from the main verb and making the main verb finite. When we try to do this with the preceding example sentence, the result is clearly ungrammatical.

Gerund: His idea of a good time <u>is watching</u> reruns on TV.

Past paraphrase: *His idea of a good time <u>watched</u> reruns on TV.

With a genuine progressive, of course, the past tense paraphrase produces a grammatical sentence.

Progressive: He is <u>watching</u> reruns on TV.
Past paraphrase: He <u>watched</u> reruns on TV.

Like participles and participial phrases, gerunds and gerund phrases come from understood full sentences.

<u>Parking their cars</u> is a problem for them.

Who is parking their cars? Clearly, *they* are. Thus underlying the gerund phrase *parking their cars* is the following full sentence.

(They parked their cars.)

Likewise, understood sentences underlie the gerund phrases in the following sentences.

<u>Shouting at me</u> won't help the situation.
(You shout at me.)

We enjoyed <u>playing Monopoly</u>.
(We played Monopoly.)

His idea of a good time is <u>watching reruns on TV</u>
(He watches reruns on TV.)

Alicia learned English by <u>listening to the radio.</u>
(Alicia listened to the radio.)

His favorite sport, <u>nude skydiving</u>, is expensive.
(His favorite sport is nude skydiving.)

■ **Exercise 3.13. Recognizing gerunds and gerund phrases**
Combine the following sentences by changing the second sentence into a gerund or gerund phrase and substituting the gerund or gerund phrase for the *it* in the first sentence. The first sentence is done as an example. (Answers to exercises are found on page 422.)

1. It is hard work in the dark.
   I fixed a flat tire.
   <u>Fixing a flat tire is hard work in the dark.</u>

2. It is their main job.
   They protect the President.

3. They tried it.
   They adjusted the starter.

4. They talked about it.
   They went out for a hamburger.

5. It isn't enough.
   You were sorry.
6. I didn't think about it.
   I was caught in traffic.
7. It got him into a lot of trouble.
   He was always late.
8. They managed to avoid it.
   They worked in the student union.
9. She was interested in it.
   She studied classical Greek.
10. It prohibits it.
    They rejected the plan.
    We develop the idea further.
11. It attracted wide attention.
    We avoided it.
    We took a stand against the proposal.

Gerunds and gerund phrases are diagramed in a manner that reflects their noun function. The convention for diagraming the gerunds and gerund phrases that function as subjects, objects, predicate nominatives, and appositives is to put them above the main sentence line and attach them to the main sentence line in the position appropriate for the noun role that they play.

Subject: Parking their cars is a problem for them.

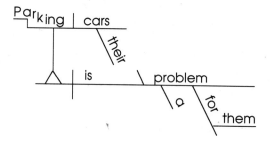

Object: I hate doing the dishes.

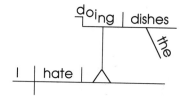

Pred Nom: His idea of a good time is watching reruns on TV.

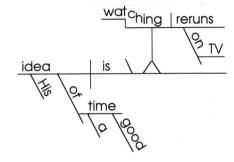

Appositive: His favorite sport, nude skydiving, is expensive.

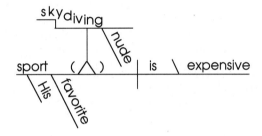

Gerunds and gerund phrases used as objects of prepositions are simply attached to the prepositions.

Object of Preposition: It is an excuse for taking a break.

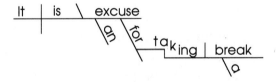

Some books use a different convention for representing gerunds and gerund phrases used as objects of prepositions: the gerund or gerund phrase is placed on a Christmas-tree stand on a horizontal line attached to the preposition line. Following is the same sentence diagramed in this manner.

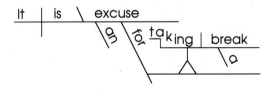

■ Exercise 3.14. Diagraming gerunds and gerund phrases

Diagram the following sentences. (Answers to exercises are found on page 422.)

1. I preferred finishing the job by myself.
2. Putting a coat of wax on it protects the surface.
3. We always dreamed about going to Hawaii.
4. Putting my ideas on paper helped me.
5. The injunction restrained them from picketing the site.
6. Getting detailed factual information always strengthens your case.
7. The staff had anticipated receiving a raise in January.
8. Getting their cooperation in this matter was not easy.
9. Coming in first exceeded their wildest expectations.
10. Leon often regretted picking a fight with all those marines.
11. They wondered about reporting the strange call.
12. His decision, selling Park Place to Garrick, was a big mistake.
13. Don't bother about returning it until the end of the semester.
14. Lowering the interest rate usually stimulates the economy.
15. He muttered something about stealing the Maltese Falcon.
16. His plan, selling iceboxes to Eskimos, was not well received by the consumers.
17. Excluding him from starting a new business in the area was a good idea.
18. Enjoying criticizing the plot in a loud voice, our friend succeeded in annoying everyone watching the movie.

---

c. Infinitive and Infinitive Phrase

Traditional definition: An *infinitive* is a verb form, usually preceded by *to*, that is used as a noun, adjective, or adverb. An *infinitive phrase* consists of an infinitive together with its modifiers and/or complement.

Infinitives look very much like prepositional phrases beginning with *to*. Remember, though, that a prepositional phrase consists of a preposition and a *noun*. In an infinitive, the *to* is followed by a *verb*. Following are examples of sentences containing infinitives in the three different functions of *noun*, *adjective*, and *adverb*.

Noun:	Our goal is <u>to succeed</u>.
	<u>To err</u> is human.
Adjective:	D-day was a day <u>to remember</u>.
	Number 17 is the player <u>to watch</u>.

Adverb: You must practice constantly <u>to win</u>.
<u>To answer</u>, I filled in the blanks with a pencil.

The distinction between an infinitive and an infinitive phrase, like the distinction between a participle and participial phrase and between a gerund and gerund phrase, is merely the presence of additional words (modifiers and/or complement) in the phrase. In all respects, infinitive phrases act just like infinitives. Following are some examples of infinitive phrases in the three different functions.

Noun: <u>To learn traditional grammar</u> takes some effort.
I always wanted <u>to play the tuba</u>.

Adjective: He is the man <u>to ask about a job</u>.
The person <u>to get the work done on time</u> is Alice.

Adverb: You must practice constantly <u>to win at basketball</u>.
<u>To answer the questions</u>, I filled in the blanks with a pencil.

Since infinitives used as nouns do not behave exactly like infinitives used as adjectives or adverbs and vice versa, our discussion in this chapter treats the three uses of infinitives separately.

Infinitives and infinitive phrases used as nouns. Infinitives and infinitive phrases used as nouns are very similar to gerunds; often, in fact, they are completely interchangeable.

Gerund: I like <u>swimming</u>.
Infinitive: I like <u>to swim</u>.
Gerund phrase: I like <u>eating pizza at drive-in movies</u>.
Infinitive phrase: I like <u>to eat pizza at drive-in movies</u>.

However, some verbs that will allow a gerund phrase as an object will not allow an infinitive phrase.

I enjoy <u>eating pizza at drive-in movies</u>.
*I enjoy <u>to eat pizza at drive-in movies</u>.

And conversely, some verbs that will allow an infinitive phrase as an object will not allow a gerund phrase.

I want <u>to eat pizza at drive-in movies</u>.
*I want <u>eating pizza at drive-in movies</u>.

As native speakers of English, you already know (unconsciously, of course) which of all the thousands of English verbs will allow infinitive phrases as objects, which will allow gerund phrases, and which will allow either.

Infinitive phrases also can be used as subjects, predicate nominatives, and appositives (but not as objects of prepositions).

Subject: To earn a million dollars has always been my great dream.

Pred Nom: My great dream is to earn a million dollars.

Appositive: My great dream, to earn a million dollars, has so far eluded me.

When used as noun phrases, infinitives and infinitive phrases, like gerunds and gerund phrases, are always singular, and therefore they can be replaced by *it*. The same *it* test we developed for gerunds and gerund phrases will work for infinitives and infinitive phrases used as noun phrases.

I like to swim.
      it

He likes to eat pizza at drive-in movies.
                it

To earn a million dollars is my dream.
       it

Our goal is to succeed.
           it

To err is human.
  it

Like gerunds and gerund phrases, infinitives and infinitive phrases come from understood full sentences—infinitives come from intransitive verbs without modifiers, and infinitive phrases come from intransitive verbs with modifiers and from transitive verbs. For example, in the following infinitive phrase, who is eating pizza?

He likes to eat pizza at drive-in movies.

Clearly, the understood subject of *eats* is *he* in the following underlying sentence.

(He eats pizza at drive-in movies.)

To form an infinitive phrase, the subject is deleted and the finite verb (*eats*) is changed to the infinitive form (*to eat*). Notice how similar this process is to the way that gerund phrases are formed.

He likes eating pizza at drive-in movies.

The sentence underlying the gerund phrase is the same as the sentence underlying the infinitive phrase.

(He eats pizza at drive-in movies.)

The difference is that in forming the infinitive phrase the finite verb (*eats*) is changed into an infinitive (*to eat*), whereas in forming the gerund phrase, the finite verb is changed into a gerund (*eating*). Since both sentences come from the same underlying sentence, it is not surprising that the two sentences mean the same thing.

■ Exercise 3.15. Recognizing infinitives and infinitive phrases

Combine the following sentences by changing the second sentence into an infinitive or infinitive phrase and substituting the infinitive or infinitive phrase for the *it* in the first sentence. The first sentence is done as an example. (Answers to exercises are found on page 426.)

1. It was a pleasant surprise for her.
   She won so easily.
   <u>To win so easily was a pleasant surprise for her.</u>

2. She expected it.
   She won the election.

3. We will manage it somehow.
   We make a profit.

4. His best opportunity was it.
   He led spades.

5. It is very foolish of you.
   You keep on smoking.

6. Everybody managed it.
   Everybody got the cans open, except you.

7. The idea was it.
   We get the place cleaned up before lunch.

8. It was beyond our wildest expectation.
   We came in first.

9. He claimed it.
   He wanted it.
   He preserved the American way of life.

10. It is it.
    You missed an inch.
    You missed a mile.

Infinitives and infinitive phrases used as nouns are diagramed very much like gerunds and gerund phrases, the only difference being that the infinitive marker *to* is drawn on a slanted line like a preposition. Since infinitives used as nouns cannot be used as objects of prepositions, infinitives are drawn above the main sentence line.

In infinitive phrases the diagram reflects the underlying understood sentence. If the infinitive is a transitive verb, the object will be drawn as a normal complement. Following are examples of infinitive phrases in the various noun functions.

Subject: To earn a million dollars has been my great dream.

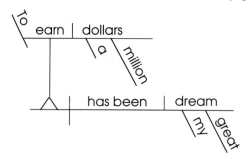

Object: I like to eat pizza at drive-in movies.

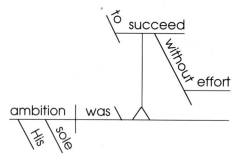

Predicate Nom: His sole ambition was to succeed without effort.

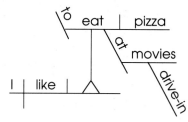

Appositive: His ambition, to succeed without effort, was unobtainable.

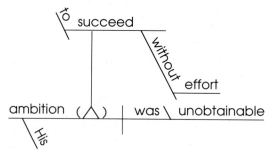

■ **Exercise 3.16. Diagraming infinitives and infinitive phrases**

Diagram the following sentences. (Answers to exercises are found on page 426.)

1. My hobby is to collect bottle tops.
2. I have always wanted to live in Australia.
3. To tell the truth is always the best policy.
4. His problem, to be incapable of telling the truth, is very serious.
5. He intends to run for governor.
6. My job, to answer the phone and take messages, could be done by a machine.
7. To never get the right answer is very discouraging.
8. He promised to clean his room at frequent intervals.
9. The plan is to leave my car at the station.
10. Leon planned to have dinner and watch some TV.
11. I want to be alone.
12. To admire the book is to admire the author.
13. Don't try to do everything at once.
14. They wanted to propose to open a new plant.
15. His one great goal in life was to try to break the bank.
16. I wanted to give a present to them.
17. She decided to plan to return to school.
18. He disclosed his life's ambition, to write the Great American Novel.

Infinitives and infinitive phrases used as adjectives. Infinitives used as adjectives always follow the nouns they modify. Following are some examples of infinitives and infinitive phrases.

Infinitives: The decision to quit was a painful one.

He was the last guest to leave.

They picked some songs to sing.

Palm Beach is not a bad place to be.

The desire to succeed is natural.

Infinitive phrases: They marked the items to be put on sale.

That is the attitude to constantly encourage.

The man to ask about a job will be back at noon.

The company resisted the demand to open its books.

Infinitives and infinitive phrases used as adjectives will fail the *it* test since, obviously, they are not nouns.

> He is the man <u>to ask about a job</u>.
> *He is the man   it

Infinitives and infinitive phrases used as adjectives usually can be recognized by asking a *which* question.

> The decision to quit was a painful one.
> Q: <u>Which</u> decision was a painful one?
> A: <u>The decision to quit</u>

> The man to ask about a job will be back at noon.
> Q: <u>Which</u> man will be back at noon?
> A: <u>The man to ask about a job</u>

> The company resisted the demand to open its books.
> Q: <u>Which</u> demand did the company resist?
> A: <u>The demand to open its books</u>

Infinitives and infinitive phrases used as adjectives are diagramed as modifiers; that is, they are attached underneath the noun they modify with the *to* drawn as though it were a preposition. For example, the sentence *The time to fix the roof is before winter* is diagramed as follows.

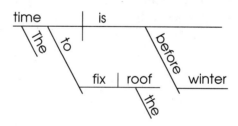

Infinitives and infinitive phrases used as adverbs. Infinitives and infinitive phrases used as adverbs have two main functions: (a) to modify verbs, and (b) to modify predicate adjectives.

When infinitives and infinitive phrases modify verbs they usually answer the *why* question.

> You must practice constantly to win at basketball.
> Q: <u>Why</u> must you practice constantly?
> A: <u>To win at basketball</u>

To answer the questions, I filled in the blanks with a pencil.

Q: Why did I fill in the blanks with a pencil?

A: To answer the questions

Another useful way of testing to see if an infinitive or infinitive phrase is an adverb modifying a verb is to see if you can paraphrase the infinitive or infinitive phrase by putting *in order* in front of it. For example, we can paraphrase the two example sentences with *in order*.

You must practice constantly to win at basketball.
You must practice constantly in order to win at basketball.

To answer the questions, I filled in the blanks with a pencil.
In order to answer the questions, I filled in the blanks with a pencil.

Infinitives and infinitive phrases used to modify verbs are drawn underneath the verb. For example, the sentence *To win at basketball, you must practice constantly* is diagramed in the following manner.

The other adverb use of infinitive phrases is to modify predicate adjectives. This construction is very common. Following are some examples.

I am ready to leave now.
We are glad to see you again so soon.
Sally is silly to slumber so soundly.
He is crazy to take that job.
They are anxious to get packed.

As you would expect, this use of the infinitive and infinitive phrase fails the *it* test since the infinitive does not function as a noun phrase.

They are anxious to get packed.
*They are anxious   it

Likewise, this use of the infinitive and infinitive phrase also fails the tests for infinitives and infinitive phrases used as adverbs modifying the main verb.

Why test: I am ready to leave now.
Q: <u>Why</u> am I ready?
A: *To leave now

In order test: I am ready to leave now.
           *I am ready <u>in order</u> to leave now.

In diagraming, as you would also expect, the adverb infinitives and infinitive phrases are attached underneath the adjectives that they modify. For example, the sentence *I am happy to be a grammar student* is diagramed in the following manner.

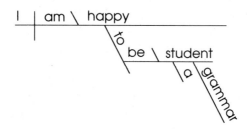

■ **Exercise 3.17. Identifying uses of infinitives and infinitive phrases**
Underline the infinitives and infinitive phrases in the following sentences. If the infinitive or infinitive phrase is used as a noun, write *Noun* above it; if it is used as an adjective, write *Adj* above it; and if it is used as an adverb, write *Adv* above it. The first is done as an example. (Answers to exercises are found on page 430.)

               Noun
1. I wanted <u>to know the answer.</u>
2. Will you have a chance to get away this weekend?
3. I went home early to get some work done today.
4. Are you ready to go home now?
5. To get to Broadway, turn left at the next light.
6. To lessen the impact of the decision was important to them.
7. We were all sorry to see the outcome.
8. It was a time to live and a time to die.
9. Weren't you sad to leave home?
10. They scanned the entire structure to locate any defects.
11. To be elected on the first ballot would be a great victory.
12. That was not the time to make your move.
13. They decided not to unload the furniture after all.
14. To take such a chance at this stage of the game, you must be very sure of yourself.
15. He wouldn't listen to anyone.

16. Luckily, the conductor refused to be distracted by the noise back-stage.

17. They tried to sell the picture to a museum.

■ **Exercise 3.18. Diagraming infinitives and infinitive phrases**

Diagram the following sentences. (Answers to exercises are found on page 430.)

1. To water the lawn at night seemed a good idea.
2. To explain the situation, I will need a pencil and some paper.
3. We were trying to correct Leon's weak backhand.
4. The effect of the ruling is to increase property taxes.
5. Did he mention the problem to you?
6. To forgive is divine.
7. I wanted to ask you a question.
8. Holmes objected to the plan to open the tomb.
9. Check the label to assure a proper fit.
10. We felt equal to the task.
11. She certainly is devoted to her work.
12. At first the idea was to examine the origins of the modern state.
13. John is easy to please.
14. John is eager to please. (Do sentences 13 & 14 mean the same thing?)
15. To make the Dean's List means a lot.
16. We finally gave the cat some milk to get some sleep.
17. The drama students arranged to take the examination later.
18. I found a perfect present to give my mother.

■ **Exercise 3.19. Review I**

Diagram the following sentences. (Answers to exercises are found on page 433.)

1. Jason was in a hurry to finish.
2. To further delay our plans would be a big mistake.
3. The farmers burned all the trees infected by the insects.
4. Fingering his cutlass and smiling, the man with the patch over his eye welcomed them aboard.
5. According to a usually reliable source, the President has switched from jelly beans to gummy bears.
6. He has been poor at organizing his work.
7. To pronounce Chinese, a tone language, is very difficult.

8. Taking too much time about making a decision implies indecisiveness.

9. We bought an insecticide intended for commercial use.

10. The official, ignoring the angry questions of the frustrated reporters, abruptly terminated the press conference.

11. Depending on the weather, we may work in the garden this afternoon.

12. He is always late for work.

13. Salting your food excessively can be bad for your health.

14. He was the first person to eat snails.

15. Shaking his burned fingers, Rollo dropped the hot pan.

16. The game was postponed on account of rain.

17. In medieval medicine each of the four humors—blood, phlegm, yellow bile, black bile—caused specific diseases.

■ **Exercise 3.20. Review II**

Diagram the following sentences. (Answers to exercises are found on page 436.)

1. The head office appreciated getting an accurate statement.

2. Selecting his club carefully, the golfer approached the tee.

3. She is very professional at her job in the bank.

4. Toward evening, the rain began again.

5. Touched by their sad plight, Scrooge gave them some good advice.

6. We thought about going by train.

7. They submitted the idea to the committee to be evaluated.

8. The play, a comedy about making movies, has been very successful.

9. Taking a shortcut caused them a lot of trouble in the long run.

10. The piece performed by the Juilliard String Quartet has hit the top of the pop charts.

11. I regret to bring you some bad news.

12. A notorious complainer, Achilles sulked in his tent, refusing to fight.

13. The weather seems normal for this time of year.

14. The Senator fumbled through his speech, constantly referring to his notes and papers.

15. We really enjoy backpacking in the mountains.

16. We wanted to get escargot shakes to take home.

17. Jerry was very concerned about finishing his paper on time.

18. The arresting officer read the suspected offender his rights.

SUMMARY OF TRADITIONAL TERMS

Phrase: A phrase is a group of related words that is used as a single part of speech and does not contain a finite verb and its subject.

Noun Phrase: A noun phrase consists of a noun and all of its modifiers.

Verb phrase: A verb phrase consists of a main verb together with one or more helping or auxiliary verbs.

Tense: There are six tenses, *Past, Present, Future, Past Perfect, Present Perfect, Future Perfect*. The *Progressive* is a separate form of each of the six tenses, but is not itself called a tense.

Prepositional Phrase: A prepositional phrase is a group of related words beginning with a preposition and ending with a noun or pronoun.

The noun that ends the prepositional phrase is the object of the preposition that begins the phrase. A prepositional phrase that modifies a noun is called an *Adjective Phrase*. A prepositional phrase that modifies a verb, adjective, or an adverb is called an *Adverb Phrase*.

Appositive Phrase: An appositive is a noun or pronoun that follows another noun or pronoun to identify or explain it. An appositive phrase consists of an appositive and its modifiers.

Verbal Phrase: A verbal is a form of a verb used as another part of speech. A verbal phrase consists of a verbal together with its modifiers and/or complement. There are three types of verbals and verbal phrases.

1. Participle and Participial Phrase: A participle is a verb form used as an adjective. A participial phrase consists of a participle together with its modifiers and/or complement. There are two types of participles: (1) *Present Participles*, and (2) *Past Participles*. A *Dangling Participle* is a participle that appears to modify the wrong noun.

2. Gerund and Gerund Phrase: A gerund is a verb form ending in *-ing* that is used as a noun. A gerund phrase consists of a gerund together with its modifiers and/or complement.

3. Infinitive and Infinitive Phrase: An infinitive is a verb form that is used as a noun, adjective, or adverb. An infinitive phrase consists of an infinitive together with its modifiers and/or complement.

4

Clauses

INTRODUCTION

Traditional definition: A clause is a group of words that contains a verb and its subject.

There are two types of clauses: *main (independent) clauses* and *subordinate (dependent) clauses.*

Main (independent) clauses

Traditional definition: A main (independent) clause expresses a complete thought and can stand by itself.

> *Examples:*   I hate Mondays.
> Can you read this?
> Stop!
> This is an independent clause.

An independent clause can always be punctuated as a free-standing sentence. Conversely, all sentences must contain at least one independent clause. An independent clause consists of the basic sentence (subject-verb-complement) and any additional modifiers.

Subordinate (dependent) clauses

Traditional definition: A **subordinate** (dependent) **clause** does not express a complete thought and cannot stand alone.

> *Examples:*   before the party is over
> when you called
> if I were you
> what you said
> because I was finished

A subordinate clause must always be attached to an independent clause in order to make a complete sentence; it can never stand alone as a complete sentence. If such a subordinate clause is punctuated with a period or semicolon, it is considered to be a sentence fragment.

Subordinate clauses are classified according to the part of speech role that they play. Subordinate clauses can be used in one of three ways: (1) as *adjectives*, (2) as *adverbs*, or (3) as *nouns*. In this chapter we discuss each of these three types of subordinate clauses in turn.

ADJECTIVE (RELATIVE) CLAUSE

Traditional definition: An adjective (relative) clause is a subordinate clause used as an adjective to modify a noun or pronoun.

> *Examples:*   The weatherman who is on Channel 7 is always wrong.
> She married a man whom she met at school.
> They called the person whose turn was next.
> The radio, which I had left on, woke me up.
> I found it in the book that you lent me.

Adjective clauses begin with a relative pronoun. The relative pronouns are *who, whom, whose, which* and *that.* They are called *relative* pronouns because they "relate" to the noun that the adjective clause modifies. In the preceding examples, *who* refers to *weatherman; whom* refers to *man; whose* refers to *person; which* refers to *radio;* and *that* refers to *book.*

All adjective clauses come from underlying full sentences.

> They identified the person who won the lottery yesterday.

The relative clause *who won the lottery yesterday* comes from the underlying sentence in which *the person* is the subject.

> (The person won the lottery yesterday.)

As you can see, the underlying sentence *the person won the lottery yesterday* tells us something about the noun *person* in the main sentence. There is an important restriction on the source sentences for adjective clauses: these underlying sentences must contain within them duplicates of the nouns in the main sentence that they modify. This restriction is much more obvious than it sounds at first. Following is an underlying sentence that violates this restriction.

They identified the person (the Bears won the Super Bowl).

Clearly, this is nonsense. In order for an underlying sentence to produce a valid adjective clause, the underlying sentence must say something about the noun in the main sentence being modified. In the preceding example, the underlying sentence does not contain the noun *person*, and thus the underlying sentence does not have any connection with the main sentence and cannot be turned into a relative clause.

What connects the underlying sentence to the main sentence is the repetition of that same noun in the modifying sentence. The repeated or duplicate noun in the underlying sentence does not have to be a subject. It could be an object or an object of a preposition. It can be any of these—but it must be there in the underlying sentence somewhere.

The repeated noun (together with its modifiers, if any) in the sentence underlying the adjective clause is replaced by the appropriate relative pronoun. When a relative pronoun replaces the repeated or duplicate noun in the adjective clause, the relative pronoun inherits whatever function the noun had in the underlying sentence—subject, object, possessive noun, or object of a preposition.

> *Subject:* I met a man (the man knows four languages).
> who
>
> *Object:* I met a man (the man you would like).
> whom
>
> *Poss Noun:* I met a man (the man's wife knows four languages).
> whose
>
> *Obj of Prep:* I met a man (about the man much is said).
> whom
>
> *or:* I met a man (the man much is said about).
> whom

Note that when the relative pronoun is the object of a preposition, there are two slightly different versions of the adjective clause, one with the preposition at the beginning of the relative clause and one with the preposition at the end. Although both versions are used, the version with the preposition at the beginning of the clause is considered by some to be more appropriate in formal writing.

We can represent the conversion of the underlying full sentence into a relative clause as a two-step process.

1. Replace the repeated or duplicate noun (along with its modifiers) in the underlying sentence with the appropriate relative pronoun.
2. Move the relative pronoun to the first position in the underlying sentence if it is not already in the first position.
   Following are some examples.

   They identified the person (the accident injured <u>the person</u>).

   1. Replace the duplicate noun and noun modifiers with the appropriate relative pronoun.

      They identified the person (the accident injured <u>whom</u>).

   2. Move the relative pronoun to the first position in its clause.

      They identified the person <u>whom</u> the accident injured.

Following is an example with the duplicate noun already in the first position.

   They identified the person (<u>the person</u> won the lottery yesterday).

   1. Replace the duplicate noun and noun modifiers with the appropriate relative pronoun

      They identified the person <u>who</u> won the lottery yesterday.

In this particular case the relative pronoun is already in the first position, so we do not need to use the second step.

The relative pronoun *whose* replaces possessive nouns and whatever adjectives modify the possessive noun.

   The man (<u>the man's</u> children go to college) had just taken a second job.

   1. Replace the duplicate noun and noun modifiers with the appropriate relative pronoun.

      The man <u>whose</u> children go to college had just taken a second job.

If the duplicate noun is not already in the first position, then the second step must be applied.

   The man (you met <u>the man's</u> children yesterday) had just taken a second job.

   1. Replace the duplicate noun and noun modifiers with the appropriate relative pronoun.

      The man (you met <u>whose</u> children yesterday) had just taken a second job.

   2. Move the relative pronoun *whose* <u>together with the noun that it modifies</u> to the first position of the underlying sentence.

> The man <u>whose children</u> you met yesterday had just taken a second job.

If the duplicate noun is the object of a preposition, then there is an option in the way that the rule is applied.

> (Much has been said about <u>the man</u>.)

The underlying sentence can form a grammatical adjective clause in two different ways. Following is the normal way in which the modification rules work.

> 1. I met a man (much has been said about <u>whom</u>).
> 2. I met a man <u>whom</u> much has been said about.

However, as we saw previously, there is a second option, in which the preposition is moved along with the relative pronoun to the first position in the underlying sentence.

> 1. I met a man (much has been said <u>about whom</u>).
> 2. I met a man <u>about whom</u> much has been said.

If the relative pronoun is an object or the object of a preposition, there is another option in the way that the relative clause is formed. After the relative pronoun has been moved to the first position within the clause, the relative pronoun may be deleted.

> *Object:* The teacher asked a question (I couldn't answer <u>that</u>).
> The teacher asked a question <u>that</u> I couldn't answer.
> The teacher asked a question I couldn't answer.
>
> *Obj of Prep:* Col. Smith was the CO (I served under <u>whom</u>).
> Col. Smith was the CO <u>whom</u> I served under.
> Col. Smith was the CO I served under.

In cases where the relative pronoun is not an object or object of a preposition, we may not delete the relative pronoun. That is, deleting the relative pronoun when it is *whose* or when it is the subject of the underlying sentence results in an ungrammatical relative clause.

> *Possessive:* The singer (you heard <u>whose</u> voice) is not a professional.
> The singer <u>whose</u> voice you heard is not a professional.
>
> *The singer voice you heard is not a professional.
>
> *Subject:* Holmes solved the crime <u>that</u> baffled Inspector Lestrade.
> *Holmes solved the crime baffled Inspector Lestrade.

■ **Exercise 4.1 Forming relative clauses**

Change the sentences in parentheses into relative clauses by (1) replacing the duplicate noun and its modifiers with the appropriate relative pronoun, and (2) moving the relative pronoun into the first position if it is not there already. When there are options in the form of the relative clause, show all possible forms. The first sentence is done as an example. (Answers to exercises are found on page 440.)

1. We sampled the dessert (you told us about the dessert).

    Step 1:   We sampled the dessert (you told us about <u>that/which</u>).

    Step 2:   We sampled the dessert <u>that/which</u> you told us about.
    We sampled the dessert <u>you told us about</u>.

2. They welcomed the visitors (they had long anticipated the visitors' arrival).

3. My uncle finally found the letter (the IRS had sent him the letter).

4. The soup (we had the soup last night) is in the icebox on the bottom shelf.

5. The scientists hoped to unify the theories (the theories had been developed over the past decade).

6. The treaty (Congress had been debating the treaty's fate for months) was finally approved in a voice vote.

7. The company returned the parts (the parts' design had proven so unsatisfactory).

8. I finally passed the exam (I was worried about the exam).

9. The story was based on documents (the government has just declassified the documents).

10. I found the book (the poem was taken from the book).

11. The objects (I found the objects in the attic) turned out to be worth several hundred dollars.

12. They were in an old trunk (the trunk had belonged to my grandfather).

Sometimes students have difficulty in deciding whether *who* or *whom* is the appropriate form for the relative pronoun. The fact that the relative pronouns replace nouns in the underlying sentence gives a simple test to tell which form is correct. For example, a student might write the following sentences.

1. *I saw the man <u>who</u> we saw on TV.

2. *I saw the man <u>whom</u> was on TV.

Teach a student who has this kind of problem to restore the relative clause back to its underlying sentence form, using either *he/him, she/her,* or *they/them* in place of the relative pronoun.

>   1. I saw the man (We saw <u>him</u> on TV).
>   2. I saw the man (<u>He</u> was on TV).

The student who has trouble with *who/whom* rarely would have a problem with the choice of *he/him, she/her,* or *they/them* in the underlying sentence.

>   1. I saw the man (*We saw <u>he</u> on TV).
>   2. I saw the man (*<u>Him</u> was on TV).

   Paraphrasing the relative clause with a subject or object personal pronoun is a quick and highly reliable way of choosing between the subject and object form of the relative pronoun. Where students can use *he, she,* or *they* in the paraphrased sentence, *who* will always be correct in the relative clause; where students can use *him, her,* or *them* in the paraphrased sentence, *whom* will always be correct in the relative clause. The object personal pronouns *him* and *them* are particularly good tests because the *-m* in *him* and *them* is historically the same *-m* in the object relative pronoun *whom*.

■ **Exercise 4.2. Distinguishing between *who* and *whom***

The following sentences all contain relative clauses beginning with *who*. If *who* is correct, write OK above it. If *who* is wrong, supply *whom*. Demonstrate that your answer is correct by replacing the relative clause with the underlying full sentence with *he/him* or *they/them* in place of the relative pronoun. The first two questions are done as examples. (Answers to exercises are found on page 441.)

                 whom
1. I have a teacher <u>who</u> my father had as a student.
   Test: I have a teacher. My father had <u>him</u> as a student.
   <u>him</u> = <u>whom</u>
                    OK
2. I have teachers <u>who</u> love to diagram sentences.
   Test: I have teachers. <u>They</u> love to diagram sentences.
   they = who

3. In class we studied the Anglo-Saxons, who originally came from Germany.

4. The king met with the bishops who had previously opposed his policies.

5. Donald became a wealthy banker who everyone envied for his amusing anecdotes about the International Monetary Fund.

6. The company employed a shipping clerk who I greatly admired.

7. The voters summarily rejected the candidates who the party had nominated at the convention.

8. The story had been filed by a correspondent who the bureau chief had personally selected because of his knowledge of the language.
9. The plot revolved around a rural sheriff who had a strange tendency for driving police cars off cliffs at high speeds.
10. Lady Lockheart graciously acknowledged the peasants who were allowed to watch their betters at play.
11. The manager called in the pitcher who the team had acquired in a trade with Tacoma the week before.
12. The long-suffering patient finally turned on the dentist who had ridiculed his brushing habits.

Restrictive and nonrestrictive clauses

Adjective clauses pose a special problem of punctuation. Some adjective clauses, called *nonrestrictive* clauses, are set off from the rest of the sentence with commas, while other adjective clauses, called *restrictive* clauses, are not used with commas. Restrictive adjective clauses do just what their name suggests—they restrict or limit the meaning of a general reference noun to just one specific thing or person. In other words a restrictive clause defines exactly which particular thing the general noun refers to. Following is a very clear-cut example of a *restrictive* clause.

People who live in glass houses should not throw stones.

Who should not throw stones—*people*, or *people who live in glass houses*? Obviously, it is the latter. *Who live in glass houses* is a restrictive adjective clause modifying the noun *people*. The noun with the restrictive clause together make a single unit, and thus, the restrictive clause cannot be set off from the noun by commas. Consider another example of a restrictive adjective clause.

The man who lives next door complained about the dog again.

The adjective clause *who lives next door* restricts (defines) who it was who complained about the dog. It was not some indefinite person who complained about the dog—it was *the man who lives next door*. If we were to ask the question *"Who complained about the dog again?"* the answer would not be just *the man* but rather *the man who lives next door*. In short, we need the information in the adjective clause to know which specific man among all the possible men in the world we are talking about.

What happens when the noun being modified is not a general noun like *people* or *man*, but is a specific thing or person? In this case the adjective clause is *nonrestrictive*. It does not restrict the noun's meaning, it *renames* the noun. In this respect nonrestrictive adjective clauses are like appositives—they rename the noun they follow, and they are set off from the rest of the sentence with commas. Consider the following example.

Mr. Smith, <u>who lives next door</u>, complained about the dog again.

The adjective clause *who lives next door* refers to a specific person—*Mr. Smith*. The name of a specific person or thing cannot be further narrowed or defined by an adjective clause. In this case the adjective clause is doing nothing more than renaming the already specified noun, and therefore it is set off with commas in the same way that an appositive is. If we were to ask the question *"Who complained about the dog again?"* the answer this time would be *Mr. Smith*, not **Mr. Smith who lives next door*.

What is so confusing about restrictive and nonrestrictive clauses is that the distinction is made solely from the standpoint of the speaker (or writer), not from the standpoint of the listener (or reader). From the hearer's standpoint there are a million Smiths in the world. How is the hearer supposed to know which Smith complained about the dog unless the speaker adds the information that the Mr. Smith who complained about the dog is the Mr. Smith who lives next door? It would seem, then, that this adjective clause also gives essential information identifying which Mr. Smith we are talking about.

This train of thinking seems perfectly reasonable, but unfortunately it is wrong. The distinction between restrictive and nonrestrictive has little to do with what the hearer (or reader) knows. The distinction really rests with what kind of noun the adjective clause is modifying. Some common nouns have inherently broad or *generic* meanings—nouns like *man, person, idea,* or *thing.* Adjective clauses used with these generic nouns narrow the generic meaning to a specific person or thing. In the preceding example about people in glass houses, the noun *people* is inherently generic. The adjective clause *who live in glass houses* narrows the broad meaning of the word *people* to a specific subclass of people—just those people who live in glass houses.

The opposite of generic is *specific*. All proper nouns, for example, are inherently specific, and thus when these nouns are modified by an adjective clause, the adjective clause will be nonrestrictive and set off with commas. Because the noun being modified is already specific, the nonrestrictive modifier cannot narrow; it can only rename the noun it modifies.

Many common nouns, however, can be either generic or specific depending on the context. For example, in the following sentence, is the adjective clause *who lives in Chicago* restrictive or nonrestrictive?

Sally's cousin <u>who lives in Chicago</u> visited her last week.

The answer depends on whether the noun *cousin* is generic or specific. In this sentence the answer depends on how many cousins Sally has.

If Sally has several cousins, the word *cousin* is generic, and thus the adjective clause *who lives in Chicago* is restrictive (no commas) because the adjective clause defines which cousin of Sally's many cousins was the one who actually visited her. If we asked the question *"Who visited Sally last week?"* the answer would be *her cousin who lives in Chicago* (as opposed to her other cousins, none of whom live in Chicago).

However, if Sally has only one cousin, then *cousin* is specific. The adjective clause cannot further define which cousin because there is only one cousin to begin with. In this case the adjective clause is nonrestrictive (commas) because the information in the clause does not narrow or reduce the scope of the word *cousin*. If we asked the question *"Who visited Sally last week?"* the answer would be *her cousin*.

Following is another example in which the noun being modified by an adjective clause is not inherently generic or specific.

The policeman <u>who knew the area best</u> led the search.

If there was only one policeman at the scene, then *policeman* is specific, and the adjective clause is like an appositive—it adds information about the policeman. The clause does not narrow a group to a single individual because there is only one individual to begin with. The clause is nonrestrictive and is set off with commas.

The policeman, who knew the area best, led the search.

If, however, there were several policemen at the scene, then *policeman* is generic, and the adjective clause is restrictive (no commas) because it tells which one of the several policemen was the one who led the search—it was the one policeman of all the policemen who knew the area best.

The policeman who knew the area best led the search.

As you can see from these two examples, the distinction between restrictive and nonrestrictive frequently depends on the context and on what the writer means.

Often restrictive clauses are said to contain "essential" and nonrestrictive clauses "unessential" information. This distinction between kinds of information sometimes confuses students. For example, the following sentence contains a nonrestrictive clause.

Mr. Smith, <u>who lives next door</u>, complained about the dog again.

The fact that Mr. Smith is the next-door neighbor may be quite essential for someone who does not know which Mr. Smith the speaker is referring to. However, *Mr. Smith* is a proper noun, and as such is *inherently* specific. Thus, by definition, any adjective clause that modifies a specific noun is nonrestrictive (commas). The fact that the hearer (or reader) does not know which Smith is being talked about is irrelevant.

Explanations of restrictive and nonrestrictive clauses should focus on the noun being modified by the clause (whether it is generic or specific) and on whether or not the clause narrows the meaning of the noun rather than on whether the information in the clause is "essential" or not.

The various relative pronouns are used with both restrictive and nonrestrictive clauses with one pair of exceptions: *that* and *which*. *Which* is preferred to *that* in nonrestrictive clauses. For example, compare the use of *which* and *that* in the following nonrestrictive clause.

Our radio, *which* had served us so well, suddenly fell silent.

*Our radio, *that* had served us so well, suddenly fell silent.

An exception to this generalization occurs when the relative pronoun is the object of a preposition.

Leon lost the map (we had depended on the map).

From the underlying sentence we can form two versions of the relative clause, one with *that* and one with *which*.

Leon lost the map *that* we had depended on.

Leon lost the map on *which* we had depended.

We cannot use *that* in place of *which* in the second version.

*Leon lost the map on *that* we had depended.

Opinions differ about the distinction between *which* and *that* in restrictive clauses. Some reference works prefer *that* to be used in restrictive clauses, whereas others absolutely prohibit the use of *which*. Kolln, for example, categorically states, "The relative pronoun *that* always introduces restrictive clauses." (Kolln 1984, 76) However, the most authoritative modern reference grammar, *A Comprehensive Grammar of the English Language* (Quirk et al. 1985, 1248), treats *which* and *that* as being interchangeable in restrictive clauses.

Following are some important points about the distinction between restrictive and nonrestrictive clauses to bear in mind.

- ☐ There are two kinds of nouns—*specific* and *generic*.
- ☐ Proper nouns are inherently specific. Some common nouns (for example, *person* and *thing*) are inherently generic.
- ☐ Most common nouns, however, can be either specific or generic, depending on the context. For these nouns, the distinction between restrictive and nonrestrictive clauses is not in the adjective clause itself, but in how the clause affects the meaning of the noun being modified.

☐ An adjective (relative) clause that follows a *specific* noun merely renames the specific noun, accordingly, the adjective clause is treated like an appositive: it is set off with commas. This kind of adjective clause is called *nonrestrictive* because it does not restrict or narrow the meaning of the specific noun.

☐ An adjective clause that follows a *generic* noun changes the meaning of the generic noun by narrowing or restricting it to a specific person or thing within the broader generic category. This kind of adjective clause is called *restrictive*. Restrictive clauses are not set off from the noun being modified by commas because the adjective clause changes the meaning of the noun it modifies. In other words, the adjective clause becomes part of the meaning of the noun and thus cannot be separated from the noun by commas.

■ **Exercise 4.3. Recognizing restrictive and nonrestrictive adjective clauses**

Combine the following sentences by turning the second sentence into an adjective clause. Punctuate the clause according to whether it is restrictive or nonrestrictive. The first sentence is done as an example. (Answers to exercises are found on page 442.)

1. Ralph forgot the present.
   I got the present for mother.
   Ralph forgot the present (that) I got for mother.
2. His carelessness caused an accident.
   The accident should never have happened.
3. The people are old friends of ours.
   We attended the people's party.
4. We settled on the wording of Section 13b.
   The wording of Section 13b had previously been in dispute.
5. They identified the person.
   The person won the lottery yesterday.
6. The first proposal was rejected by the committee.
   We submitted a first proposal.
7. The night sky was lit by the moon.
   The moon was just rising over the hills.
8. Napoleon became a French patriot.
   Napoleon was actually from Corsica.
9. Holmes found the driver.
   The driver had mysteriously vanished on the night of the murder.
10. I bumped into my boss.
    My boss was also doing some last minute shopping.

11. Charles finally found his mistake.
    Charles's error caused all the trouble to begin with.
12. We got the item.
    You had asked about the item.

Diagraming adjective clauses. All dependent clauses are put into normal sentence form. Dependent clauses are connected by a line to the main sentence line according to the relation of the dependent clause to the main clause. Following are some specifics for diagraming adjective clauses.

☐ Adjective clauses are put on a sentence line that is drawn underneath and parallel to the main sentence line.

☐ Relative pronouns are placed within the underlying sentence according to their grammatical function. For example, relative pronouns that function as objects are moved from their position at the beginning of the clause back into a normal object position, and objects of prepositions are put back inside their prepositional phrases.

☐ Relative pronouns are then connected by dotted lines to the nouns on the main sentence line that they modify.

☐ If the relative pronoun has been deleted from the adjective clause, an appropriate "understood" relative (in parentheses) is added to the adjective clause in the proper place.

☐ There is no distinction made between restrictive and nonrestrictive clauses in the way adjective clauses are diagramed.

Following are examples of adjective clauses with relative pronouns functioning in different roles.

Subject: I met a man who knows four languages.

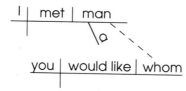

Object: I met a man whom you would like.

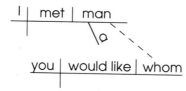

Possessive noun: I met a man whose wife knows four languages.

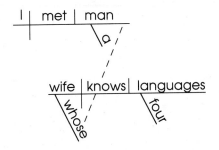

Object of preposition: I met a man about whom much is said.
   or: I met a man whom much is said about.
   [Note: the same diagram is used for both versions.]

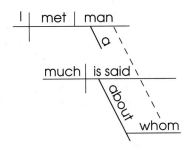

Understood relative: The teacher asked a question I couldn't answer.

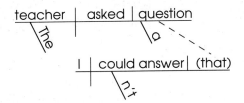

■ **Exercise 4.4. Diagraming adjective clauses**
Diagram the following sentences. (Answers to exercises are found on page 443.)

1. The person who entered the tomb first would die.
2. The cat that we found in the woods had kittens yesterday.
3. The passages that we omitted were not very important.
4. We met Garrick, whose parents live on the Eastern Shore.
5. An article we featured in our last issue has won an award.

6. Watson found the revolver that Holmes had worried about.
7. The barges that had already been unloaded were taken downstream.
8. They rejected the suggestions we had offered.
9. The union, whose offer was accepted, contacted the members.
10. I finally found a doctor who understood the problem that I have.
11. My parents thanked the students whose rooms they had used.
12. We really missed the things we had forgotten about.
13. The Council, which meets on Thursdays, will review your request.
14. The campers checked the supplies they had ordered.
15. Shift the outfield for batters who tend to pull the ball.
16. Everyone whose paper is finished may leave.
17. We listed the topics about which we would write.
18. The employers we approached liked our ideas about marketing.

ADVERB CLAUSE

Traditional definition: An adverb clause is a subordinate clause that modifies a verb, an adjective, or another adverb.

Following are some examples of adverb clauses modifying adjectives, other adverbs, and verbs.

Modifying Adjectives:	I am sorry that you are not able to come.
	She was worried that we were not going to finish on time.
	Leon was more reasonable than he usually is.
Modifying other Adverbs:	I answered more sharply than I had intended to.
	The class performed more satisfactorily than they had expected.
	The new machine performed more successfully than the standards called for.
Modifying Verbs:	I ate a whole pizza because I was hungry.
	Where there is smoke, there is fire.
	Give me a call if I can help you.

All adverb clauses are made up of two components: (1) a subordinating conjunction, and (2) an underlying sentence. Following are some examples of adverb clauses.

Adverb clause

Subord Conj	+	Underlying Sentence
after	+	I have finished washing the car
because	+	I was hungry
where	+	there is a will
if	+	I can help you
that	+	you are not able to come
than	+	he usually is
than	+	the standards call for

Adverb clauses are built in a different way from adjective clauses. In adjective clauses, the word that begins the clause (the relative pronoun) is an essential part of its clause; it is a subject, object, object of a preposition, or possessive noun. In adverb clauses, however, the word that introduces the clause (the subordinating conjunction) plays no role inside the subordinate clause. In other words, the subordinating conjunction is a bridge-word that links the subordinating clause to the main clause. Compare the following examples of adjective and adverb clauses.

Adj clause: I put away the lunch that I had fixed earlier.

Adv clause: I'll come over for lunch when I have finished the car.

In the adjective clause, the relative pronoun *that* is the object in the sentence underlying the clause.

(I had fixed the lunch earlier.)
          that

In the adverb clause, the subordinating conjunction *when* plays no role in the sentence underlying the clause.

(I have finished the car.)

Adverb clause modifying an adjective

Adverbs that modify adjectives are restricted to two patterns. In the first pattern the adverb clause modifies a predicate adjective. In this pattern, the subordinating conjunction can be only the word *that* (though *that* may be omitted). Following are some examples.

Pattern 1:	Predicate adjective	+	(that)	+	Underlying Sentence
	We were glad	+	(that)	+	you won
	John is afraid	+	(that)	+	he will not come
	I am sure	+	(that)	+	I am right
	It seemed certain	+	(that)	+	the Bears would win

In the second pattern the adverb clause modifies a comparative predicate adjective. In this pattern the subordinating conjunction can be only the word *than* (which, unlike *that*, cannot be omitted).

Pattern 2:   *Comparative adjective* + *than* + *Underlying Sentence*

It is <u>later</u> + than + <u>you think it is</u>

It was <u>more formal</u> + than + <u>I had expected it to be</u>

John is <u>stronger</u> + than + <u>he ever was before</u>

The children seemed <u>taller</u> + than + <u>they did this summer</u>

Adverb clause modifying another adverb

There is only one main pattern for adverb clauses modifying other adverbs. In this pattern the adverb clause modifies a comparative adverb. In this pattern the conjunctive adverb can be only the word *than*. Here are some examples.

Comparative adverb + *than* + *Underlying Sentence*

I answered <u>more abruptly</u> + than + <u>I had intended to</u>

She will finish <u>quicker</u> + than + <u>you can</u>

Their ships went <u>faster</u> + than + <u>any had gone before</u>

I can diagram sentences <u>better</u> + than + <u>you can slice muffins</u>

Adverb clause modifying a verb

Adverb clauses that modify verbs have an important characteristic that makes them quite easy to identify. The adverb clause behaves like a single word adverb.

I returned the book to the library <u>when I got the overdue notice</u>.

The adverb clause, *when I got the overdue notice*, can be moved *as a single unit* to the front of the main sentence just the way a single word adverb can be moved.

<u>When I got the overdue notice</u>, I returned the book to the library.

Compare this sentence with a similar sentence with a single word adverb.

I returned the book to the library <u>yesterday</u>.

<u>Yesterday</u>, I returned the book to the library.

Following are some more examples of this type of adverb clause being moved from its normal, final position to a position in front of the main clause.

I ate a whole pizza <u>because I was hungry</u>.

<u>Because I was hungry</u>, I ate a whole pizza

Let's go <u>whenever you are ready</u>.

<u>Whenever you are ready</u>, let's go.

I took it off the hook <u>after the phone rang a dozen times</u>.

<u>After the phone rang a dozen times</u>, I took it off the hook.

Note that when the adverb clauses in these examples are in their normal position after the complement, commas are not used to separate the adverb clauses from the main clauses. However, when the adverb clauses are moved out of their normal positions, they must be set off from the main clauses by commas.

Adverb clauses that modify adjectives and other adverbs cannot be moved out of their normal position.

Modifying adjectives:

We were glad <u>that you won</u>.

*<u>That you won</u>, we were glad.

It is later <u>than you think it is</u>.

*<u>Than you think it is</u>, it is later.

Modifying other adverbs:

I answered more abruptly <u>than I had intended to</u>.

*<u>Than I had intended to</u>, I answered more abruptly.

Their ships went faster <u>than any had gone before</u>.

*<u>Than any had gone before</u>, their ships went faster.

Since adverb clauses that modify verbs behave like single-word adverbs, the subordinating conjunctions that create adverb clauses can be classified in much the same manner as single-word adverbs—by semantic function. Following are the more common types of subordinating conjunctions classified by meaning.

Time:	after, as, as soon as, before, even after, even before, just after, just before, since (meaning "after" or "when"), until, when, whenever, while
Place:	where, wherever
Manner:	as, as if, as though
Cause:	as, because, inasmuch as, since, so that
Condition:	if, on condition that, provided that, unless
Concession:	although, even though, though

Following are some examples of adverb clauses illustrating the different categories of conjunctive adverbs.

> *Time:* I had finished my popcorn <u>before the movie started</u>.
> <u>Before the movie started</u>, I had finished my popcorn.
>
> *Place:* We found broken glass <u>where the accident had happened</u>.
> <u>Where the accident had happened</u>, we found broken glass.
>
> *Manner:* Marian looked <u>as if she would die laughing</u>.
> (Adverb clauses of manner usually cannot be moved to the front.)
>
> *Cause:* I decided not to go <u>since I would have to leave early</u>.
> <u>Since I would have to leave early</u>, I decided not to go.
>
> *Condition:* I would not do that <u>if I were you</u>.
> <u>If I were you</u>, I would not do that.
>
> *Concession:* We ordered pizza, <u>even though I had already eaten</u>.
> <u>Even though I had already eaten</u>, we ordered pizza.

Note that when the adverb clause follows the main clause the adverb clause is not normally set off with a comma. However, there is one exception to this generalization: adverb clauses of *concession*; that is, clauses beginning with *although, even though*, and *though*. Possibly because these adverbs signal a reversal of expectations, the subordinate clauses they introduce are set off from the main clause by a comma.

Also note that when the adverb clause is moved to a position in front of the main clause, the adverb clause is *always* set off with a comma to signal that the clause is out of its normal position. Failure to use a comma to set off an introductory adverb clause is a frequent comma error of beginning writers. Apparently many beginning writers, noticing that adverb clauses (except ones beginning with *although, even though*, and *though*) are not used with commas when the clauses follow main clauses, overgeneralize and make the erroneous assumption that commas are not needed for any use of adverb clauses.

■ **Exercise 4.5. Recognizing and punctuating adverb clauses that modify verbs**

Combine the following sentences by changing the second sentence into an adverb clause of the type indicated. Pick an appropriate subordinating conjunction. Put the adverb clause in (a) final position and (b) initial, and punctuate accordingly. The first exercise is done as an example. (Answers to exercises are found on page 446.)

1. The phone rang.
   Time: I was getting into the shower.
   a. The phone rang as I was getting into the shower.
   b. As I was getting into the shower, the phone rang.

2. We will cut your phone off.
   Condition: You pay your bill.

3. I am still gaining weight.
   Concession: I have been eating nothing but carrot sticks.

4. I bought my roommate a new ribbon.
   Cause: I use her typewriter all the time.

5. I couldn't write my paper.
   Time: I found all the references.

6. They were stripping off the old wallpaper.
   Manner: Their lives depended on it.

7. The dog followed him.
   Place: He went.

8. The coaches review the films each week.
   Time: They decide which plays to prepare.

9. I liked the movie after all.
   Concession: I hate to admit it.

10. He dehydrated.
    Cause: He does not drink enough water while running.

11. Watson tried to behave.
    Manner: He was not wearing the most ridiculous disguise.

SUBORDINATING CONJUNCTIONS AND CONJUNCTIVE ADVERBS

Subordinating conjunctions link the subordinate clause to the main clause to form a new grammatical unit. *Conjunctive adverbs*, however, establish a semantic relationship between two independent clauses without grammatically linking them. Unfortunately, subordinating conjunctions and conjunctive adverbs are easily confused. The confusion is not merely academic because the clauses they introduce must be punctuated differently. For example, compare the following sentences.

1. John was involved in the accident after he took drivers' education.
2. John was involved in the accident; however, he was not hurt.

After is a subordinating conjunction introducing an adverb clause. The adverb clause is not separated from the main clause by any punctuation. *However* is a conjunctive adverb and, as an adverb, it has no power to join clauses by any grammatical linkage. Thus, the clause that the conjunctive adverb *however* introduces is an independent clause that *must* be separated from the first independent clause by a semicolon or period. Moreover, the conjunctive adverb *must* be separated from the rest of its clause by a comma (i.e., *semicolon* + conjunctive adverb + *comma*).

When a comma is used to join the two independent clauses instead of a semicolon, the resulting sentence is said to contain a *comma* splice.

> *Comma splice:*   *John was involved in the accident, <u>however</u> he was not hurt.

Following are some common conjunctive adverbs.

again	hence	nonetheless
also	however	otherwise
besides	indeed	similarly
consequently	likewise	then
further	moreover	therefore
furthermore	nevertheless	thus

Remember, conjunctive adverbs are *adverbs*, and as such they cannot be used to join independent clauses by themselves. The clauses must be joined either by a comma and a coordinating conjunction or by a semicolon, or else each clause must be punctuated with a period.

> *Comma and coordinating conjunction:*
> John was involved in the accident, <u>and</u> consequently, he was very upset.

> *Semicolon:*
> John was involved in the accident; consequently, he was very upset.

> *Period:*
> John was involved in the accident. Consequently, he was very upset.

Subordinating conjunctions and conjunctive adverbs behave in quite different ways. As was mentioned, one of the characteristics of adverb clauses that modify verbs is that the adverb clause can be readily moved to a position in front of the main clause. Clauses beginning with conjunctive adverbs, however, cannot move.

> *Subordinating conjunction:*
> John was involved in the accident <u>after he took drivers' education</u>.
> <u>After he took drivers' education</u>, John was involved in the accident.

Conjunctive adverb:
John was involved in the accident; <u>however, he was not hurt.</u>
*<u>However, he was not hurt,</u> John was involved in the accident.

The adverb clause beginning with *after* easily moves to the first position, whereas the independent clause introduced by the conjunctive adverb *however* cannot move to the first position. [Recall that when a subordinate clause is moved to a position in front of the main clause, the subordinate clause must be set off from the main clause with a comma.]

Conjunctive adverbs differ from subordinating conjunctions in a second way. As their name suggests, conjunctive adverbs are a class of adverbs, and consequently, they can be moved around inside their clause in the same manner that single-word adverbs of time and place can be moved. In the preceding example sentence, *however* can be moved from its position at the beginning of its clause to a position in the middle or end of its clause.

John was involved in the accident; <u>however,</u> he was not hurt.
John was involved in the accident; he was, <u>however,</u> not hurt.
John was involved in the accident; he was not hurt, <u>however.</u>

Note that when a conjunctive adverb is moved into the middle of its clause (as in the second example), it is surrounded by commas.

Subordinating conjunctions, on the other hand, are locked into position at the beginning of their clause. Any attempt to move them in the same manner as a conjunctive adverb results in an ungrammatical sentence.

John was involved in the accident <u>after</u> he took drivers' education.
*John was involved in the accident he took <u>after</u> drivers' education.
*John was involved in the accident he took drivers' education <u>after.</u>

Let us now summarize the difference between subordinating conjunctions and conjunctive adverbs.

Subordinating conjunctions are *conjunctions*; conjunctions join grammatical elements together. Subordinating conjunctions join adverb clauses to main clauses. Clauses containing subordinating conjunctions can be identified by moving the entire clause to a position in front of the main clause. Independent clauses introduced by conjunctive adverbs, however, cannot be moved in front of another main or independent clause.

Conjunctive adverbs are *adverbs*; adverbs cannot join clauses together. Conjunctive adverbs can be identified by moving the conjunctive adverb around inside its clause. Subordinating conjunctions, however, are locked into the initial position within their clause and thus cannot be moved to any other position within it.

■ **Exercise 4.6. Distinguishing subordinating conjunctions and conjunctive adverbs**

Label the subordinating conjunctions by writing *Sub Conj* over them, and label the conjunctive adverbs by writing *Conj Adv* over them. Supply appropriate punctuation. Confirm your analysis by applying both tests. The first question is done as an example. (Answers to exercises are found on page 447.)

 1. Leon dropped a pass in the end zone; moreover, he fell on top of a sprinkler.

 Conj Adv is written above "moreover" in sentence 1.

   Sub Conj test: *Moreover, he fell on top of a sprinkler, Leon dropped a pass in the end zone.

   Conj Adv test: Leon dropped a pass in the end zone; he fell, moreover, on top of a sprinkler.

   Leon dropped a pass in the end zone; he fell on top of a sprinkler, moreover.

 2. I was upset because I had damaged the arm on my turntable.
 3. We are ready to leave unless there is something else you need to do.
 4. The experiment had been affected by the accident therefore we had to start all over again.
 5. Aunt Sally has been depressed since she was badly beaten at Monopoly.
 6. She passed Go nevertheless she was forced to sell her railroads.
 7. The doctor was called to testify inasmuch as she took the X-rays.
 8. The general was not able to consolidate his forces thus he lost a unique opportunity to defeat the opposition.
 9. We stayed up to watch the program even though it was getting pretty late.
10. The program was filmed near our school consequently we recognized many of the settings.
11. The kids decided to sleep on the porch as the night was quite warm.
12. The company offered compensation nevertheless we went to court.

Diagraming adverb clauses As with adjective clauses, the adverb clause is diagramed as a complete sentence on a sentence line drawn underneath and parallel to the main sentence line.

The adverb clause is connected to the main sentence line by a dotted line drawn from the verb in the adverb clause to the word in the main clause that the adverb clause modifies. For an adverb clause that modifies an adjective, the line is drawn to the adjective; for an adverb clause that modifies another adverb, the line is drawn to the adverb; for an adverb clause that modifies a verb, the line is drawn to the main verb.

The subordinating conjunction is placed on the dotted line. Remember: the subordinating conjunction is a bridge-word that links the adverb clause to the main clause; it is not part of the sentence underlying the subordinate clause.

In adverb clauses that modify adjectives, the bridge-word *that* may be "understood"; for example: *I am glad you are here.* In the diagram of this sentence the understood *that* is put on the dotted line in parentheses.

Following are examples of diagrams for the three types of adverb clauses.

Adverb clause modifying adjective (with understood that):

I am glad you can come to the party.

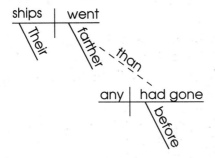

Adverb clause modifying adverb:

Their ships went farther than any had gone before.

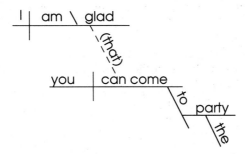

Adverb clause modifying verb:

Unless you stop that, I will leave.

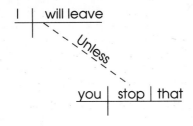

■ **Exercise 4.7. Diagraming adverb clauses**

Diagram the following sentences. (Answers to exercises are found on page 449.)

1. I am afraid that we must leave now.
2. Since we would be late, we called them.
3. As soon as their parents left, the kids began to play the stereo.
4. We finished poorer than we had started.
5. John took a taxi to the airport so that he would not miss his flight.
6. After they left, we began cleaning the apartment.
7. The movie that we saw was funnier than we had expected.
8. If you had led spades instead of hearts, we could have set them.
9. Since the undercoat was completely dry, we got a surface that was not sticky.
10. I want to finish my paper before it is due.
11. I have learned a lot since I began going to classes.
12. We were afraid that we would stick in the wet snow.
13. Although they won the battle, they have not won the war.
14. He is very snide whenever he talks about a movie he does not like.
15. The church is much older than it appears when you first see it.
16. If you look to your right, you will see the man that I told you about when you called.
17. We got another car so that everyone would have plenty of room.

NOUN CLAUSE

Traditional definition: A noun clause is a subordinate clause used as a noun.

Following are some examples of noun clauses used in the noun functions of subject, object, object of a preposition, predicate nominative, and appositive.

Subject:	What he knows about art is a mystery.
Object:	They know who we are.
Obj of Prep:	I will sell them for whatever I can get for them.
Pred Nom:	The decision was that we would go ahead as planned.
Appositive:	The decision, that we would go ahead as planned, did not make everyone happy.

Noun clauses differ from adjective and adverb clauses in one important way: noun clauses are not modifiers. Adjective and adverb clauses modify words in other clauses. Noun clauses play the role of nouns. In the first example sentence, *what he knows about art* is the subject of the verb *is* in the main clause. In the second sentence, *who we are* is the object of the verb *know*, and so on.

Noun clauses are always singular even when the nouns within the clause are plural. For example, in the following sentence, notice that while both the subject and the object within the noun clause are plural, the noun clause *as a whole* is singular.

> That they usually win all their games pleases the audience.
>   it

Since noun clauses always function like noun phrases and are always singular, noun clauses (like gerunds) can be readily identified by the *it* test.

Subject: What he knows about art is a mystery.
                            it

Object: They know who we are.
                           it

Obj of Prep: I will sell them for whatever I can get for them.
                                                    it

Pred Nom: The decision is that we will go ahead as planned.
                                                         it

There are two different types or families of noun clauses, depending on the nature of the word that begins the clause. The first type begins with one of the introductory words *that, if,* or *whether (or not).* Since *that* is by far the most common introductory word of this group, this type is sometimes called the *that*-type noun clause. Most of the words that begin the second type start with the letters *wh-* (for example, *who, what,* and *whatever*). For this reason the second type is sometimes called the *wh*-type noun clause.

That-type noun clauses. In a *that*-type noun clause, the introductory words *that, if,* and *whether (or not)* play no role in the rest of the noun clause.

> That they usually win all their games pleases the audience.

The noun clause, *that they usually win all their games,* consists of two parts, the introductory word *that* plus an underlying sentence. Following are some more examples of this type.

Noun Clause

Introductory word	Underlying Sentence
that	they usually win all their games
if	Leon calls
whether or not	you are ready

Notice that the underlying sentences within these three noun clauses are complete; the introductory words do not have any grammatical function within the underlying sentence. In this sense the introductory words in *that*-type noun clauses are like the subordinating conjunctions in adverb clauses—they both stand outside the underlying sentences that they introduce.

Following are example sentences using *that*-type noun clauses in all of the noun functions.

Subject:	Whether or not you are right remains to be seen.
Object:	I don't know if I can come.
Obj of Prep:	They debated about whether they should leave the party.
Pred Nom:	My wish is that you are right.
Appositive:	The idea, that the earth is millions of years old, is relatively modern.

Noun clauses that begin with *that* are sometimes confused with adjective clauses that begin with the relative pronoun *that*. However, the two different types of clauses are easily distinguished. For example, compare the following.

Noun clause:	I know *that* we can all accept the plan.
Adjective clause:	It is a plan *that* we can all accept.

We can recognize the noun clause by replacing the noun clause with *it*.

I know that we can all accept the plan.
              it

When we apply the *it* replacement test with the adjective clause, the result is ungrammatical.

It is a plan that we can all accept.
             *it

Conversely, we can distinguish an adjective clause beginning with *that* from a noun clause beginning with *that* by replacing the relative pronoun *that* in the adjective clause with the relative pronoun *which*.

It is a plan *which* we can all accept.

When we attempt to replace the noun clause *that* with a relative pronoun, the result is clearly ungrammatical.

*I know *which* we can all accept the plan.

Noun clauses beginning with *if* can be mistaken for the much more common adverb clauses beginning with *if*. Compare the following.

Noun:	I don't know if I can come.
Adverb:	I will meet you there if I can come.

When we apply the *it* test, we see that it applies to the first sentence, but not the second.

> I don't know <u>if I can come</u>.
> it

> I will meet you there <u>if I can come</u>.
> *it

Conversely, when we apply the movement test for adverb clauses, we see that the *if* clause in the second sentence can be moved to an initial position, but the clause in the first sentence cannot.

> *<u>If I can come</u>, I don't know.

> <u>If I can come</u>, I will meet you there.

The two tests taken together demonstrate that the *if* clause in the first sentence is a noun clause and that the *if* clause in the second sentence is an adverb clause.

That-type noun clauses when they are used as objects have one peculiarity: *that* (but not *if* and *whether (or not)*) can be optionally deleted.

> I know *that* <u>you are right</u>.

> I know <u>you are right</u>.

Obviously, when the "tip-off" word *that* has been deleted, noun clauses are much more difficult to recognize. However, the *it* test still applies equally well.

■ **Exercise 4.8. Recognizing *that*-type noun clauses**

Combine the following sentences by turning the second sentence into a *that*-type noun clause and inserting it into the first sentence in place of *it*. Use whichever introductory word *(that, if,* or *whether (or not))* is called for. The first exercise is done as an example. (Answers to exercises are found on page 452.)

1. I don't know it.
   I believe you. (if)
   <u>I don't know if I believe you.</u>

2. Lady Smyth suspected it.
   Something was afoot. (that)

3. It quickly squelched the opposition.
   The idea was endorsed by the President. (that)

4. The motion, it, passed without a dissenting vote.
   Fattening desserts should be banned from the mess hall. (that)

5. The idea was it.
   Leon would collect thousands of bottle caps. (that)

6. They argued about it.
   Dorothy should take her ruby slippers. (whether)
7. It was apparent to everyone.
   He was no friend of mine. (that)
8. They should tell us it.
   They are planning on coming with us tonight. (if)
9. The question is it.
   He can be trusted. (whether or not)
10. It strained credulity.
    He could diagram 100 sentences in 10 minutes. (that)
11. It shows it.
    She is nearly always correct. (that)
    She is well prepared. (that)

Wh-type noun clauses The most common *wh-* words that begin noun clauses are the following.

what, whatever
when, whenever
where, wherever
which, whichever
who, whoever
whom, whomever
whose
why

There are a few words that belong to this family which do not happen to start with the letters *wh-*, the most important being *how* and *however*.

Following are example sentences using *wh-*type noun clauses in all of the noun functions.

Subject:	Whatever you want is OK with me.
Object:	I don't know how you like your coffee.
Obj of Prep:	Nobody told me about what I should do.
Pred Nom:	Zen is whatever you want it to be.
Appositive:	The last question, when we should schedule the next meeting, was quickly decided.

Wh- words differ from *that* introducers in one important way: *wh-* words play a role inside the noun clause. You must be careful to distinguish between the role of the noun clause *as a whole* inside the main sentence and the role of the *wh-* word itself *inside* the noun clause.

How you do it is your own business.

The noun clause *how you do it* functions as a grammatical unit; it is the subject of the main sentence. Within the noun clause, the introductory word *how* functions as an adverb of manner—"you do it *how*."

Who, whoever, whom, whomever, whose, which, and *what* will always play noun roles inside their clause.

Subject in noun clause:	Whoever calls first will win the prize.
	We will replace *whatever* breaks.
Object in noun clause:	Whomever you called will win the prize.
	We will replace *whatever* you break.

The following *wh-* words, *when, whenever, where, wherever, why, how,* and *however,* play adverbial roles within their clause.

Adverb of manner:	How you diagram a sentence depends on its meaning.
	The diagram depends on *how* you understand the sentence.
Adverb of time:	When you called surprised us.
	Her alibi depends on *when* the butler returned.
Adverb of reason:	Why he said that is a complete mystery.
	He finally told us *why* he said that.
Adverb of place:	Where you live is your own business.
	Aunt Sally noticed *where* you put your elbows.

The distinction between the function of the noun clause as a whole and the function of the introductory word inside the noun clause requires careful analysis. For example, in the following sentences, which is correct, *whoever* or *whomever?*

1. We will sell it to whoever bids the highest.
2. We will sell it to whomever bids the highest.

The correct answer is *whoever,* not *whomever,* because the object of the preposition *to* is not just the *wh-* word *whoever* but the *whole* noun clause *whoever bids the highest.* The *wh-* word itself takes its form from its function as the subject of the verb *bids, within* the noun clause, not from the role of the noun clause as a whole as an object of the preposition *to.*

■ **Exercise 4.9. Recognizing *wh-* type noun clauses**
Combine the following sentences by turning the second sentence into a noun clause and inserting it into the first sentence in place of the *it*. Use any *wh-* word appropriate for the function indicated. The first exercise is done as an example. (Answers to exercises are found on page 453.)

1. Ralph is never worried about it.
   He will get his next paycheck (adverb of manner/means).
   Ralph is never worried about how he will get his next paycheck.

2. It is painfully obvious to us now.
   We went wrong (adverb of place).

3. We finally reached an important decision about it.
   We should have (object) for lunch.

4. We finally agreed on it.
   We should pick up the van (adverb of time).

5. It does not necessarily affect the value of the dollar.
   (subject) affects the price of gold.

6. Everyone asked it.
   They did it (adverb of reason).

7. You are it.
   You eat (object).

8. Leon agonized over it.
   He should keep all those stupid bottle caps (adverb of place).

9. It is none of your business.
   (possessive) telephone call it is.

10. He would not tell me it.
    He was (predicate nominative).

11. It depends on it.
    You stand (adverb of manner).
    You sit (adverb of place).

Diagraming noun clauses. Noun clauses are diagramed as complete sentences on their own sentence line. Noun clauses that function as subjects, objects, predicate nominatives, or appositives are drawn above and parallel to the main sentence line. These noun clauses are connected to the main sentence line by a solid vertical line with a little Christmas-tree stand at the bottom in the same manner as gerunds and gerund phrases.

Noun clauses that function as objects of prepositions are drawn below and parallel to the main sentence line. Their line is connected to the preposition line.

That, if, and *whether (or not)* are put above the noun clause on separate lines and are connected to the main verb in the noun clause by a dotted vertical line. [Remember: *that, if,* and *whether (or not)* are not part of the noun clause.] If the *that* is omitted from the sentence, an understood *(that)* is added to the diagram in the same place that an overt *that* would be put.

Wh- words are diagramed according to their function within their clause; for example, *wh-* words used as subjects are diagramed as subjects.

Following are examples of noun clauses in the different noun functions.

Subject: Whatever you want is OK with me.

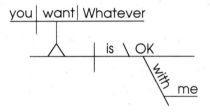

Object—with understood that: I know you are right.

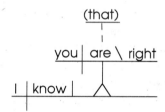

Predicate nominative: My wish is that you are right.

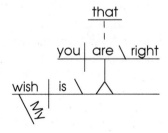

Appositive: The last question, when we should schedule the next meeting, was quickly decided.

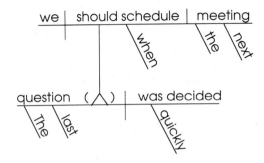

Object of preposition: Nobody told me about what I should do.

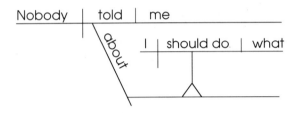

■ **Exercise 4.10. Diagraming noun clauses**

Diagram the following sentences. (Answers to exercises are found on page 453.)

1. I know who you are.
2. We have finally decided that we would quit raising chickens.
3. Whomever you elect will have a very hard time of it.
4. We all learn that we cannot always have our own way.
5. What you see is what you get.
6. Call us if you are free tonight.
7. What you said about where you had been surprised us.
8. They were able to take advantage of whatever they found.
9. Their position was that they would accept any reasonable offer.
10. How they managed to win was an absolute miracle.
11. Their explanation, how noun clauses worked, was warmly received.
12. When we got back last night was pretty late.
13. They wanted to finish what they had started.
14. How you feel about what happened is very important.
15. I do not know whether or not I will be able to leave then.
16. Whichever one that I pick will finish last.
17. Whoever sees Leon must tell him where the bottle caps are.
18. We are pleased that you understand how noun clauses are diagramed.
19. 42, what the meaning of life was, was a complete surprise to them.

SENTENCES
CLASSIFIED ACCORDING TO STRUCTURE

Traditional definition: There are four kinds of sentences according to structure: *simple, compound, complex,* and *compound-complex.*

Simple sentence

Traditional definition: A simple sentence has one independent clause and no subordinate clauses.

> *Examples:*   This is a simple sentence.
> The boy on the bank waved his hand at us with all his might.
> Sam and Sally save soda straws.
> The birds fluttered and squawked in the trees.

A simple sentence is a minimal sentence—it is a single independent clause that is not expanded by any modifying adjective or adverb clauses, nor can it contain any noun clauses. A simple sentence can have any number of modifying words and phrases. It can also have a compound subject (e.g., *Sam and Sally*) or a compound verb (e.g., *fluttered and squawked*).

Compound sentence

Traditional definition: A compound sentence has two or more main (independent) clauses but no subordinate clauses.

> John went to the store, and he bought frozen pizzas.
> Trust me; you won't regret it.

Compound sentences contain a string of at least two independent clauses joined by coordinating conjunctions or semicolons; however, none of the independent clauses can contain a subordinate clause, i.e., no adjective or adverb clauses as modifiers and no noun clauses. It can contain, of course, modifying words and phrases.

Compound sentences that are joined by coordinating conjunctions are diagramed by connecting the verb phrases of the independent clauses in the following manner:

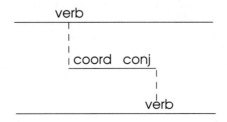

For example, the compound sentence *We had dinner, and then I went home* would be diagramed as follows.

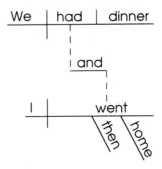

Complex sentence

Traditional definition: A complex sentence has one main (independent) clause and at least one subordinate (dependent) clause.

> *Example:* This is a complex sentence <u>because it contains a subordinate clause</u>.
>
> <u>If you are not sure of the spelling</u>, check a dictionary.
>
> The words <u>that I need to spell</u> don't seem to be there.
>
> I thought <u>that I knew how to spell it</u>.

In a complex sentence there must be at least one dependent clause—an adjective or adverb clause as a modifier or a noun clause.

Compound-complex sentence

Traditional definition: A compound-complex sentence contains two or more main (independent) clauses and at least one subordinate (dependent) clause.

> *Examples:* <u>Since he was here</u>, <u>he helped me roll up the rug</u>,
>   subordinate clause   independent clause
> <u>and we moved the piano</u>.
>   independent clause
>
> <u>We will return the car</u>, <u>and they will bring us back</u>
>   independent clause   independent clause
> <u>when we are ready</u>.
>   subordinate clause

A compound-complex sentence contains both a compound sentence (two independent clauses joined by a coordinating conjunction or a semicolon) and at least one subordinate clause (thus making it also a complex sentence).

Following is how the two example sentences are diagramed.

Since he was here, I vacuumed the rug, and we moved the piano.

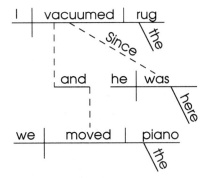

We will return the car, and they will bring us back when we are ready.

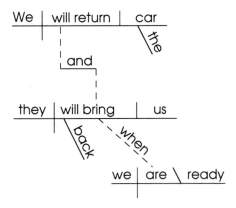

■ **Exercise 4.11. Diagraming and classifying sentences by structure**

Diagram the following sentences and classify them according to structure. (Answers to exercises are found on page 457.)

1. I did not like the program on television last night.
2. When I was your age, I had never been outside River City.
3. We argued all night about what we should do with Leon.
4. I finished my paper, but my roommate worked all night.
5. My paper was about the French who invaded England in 1066.
6. I went to bed after I finished typing it.
7. It was OK, but I did not have enough time to do a good job.

8. Working all night really wrecks me the next day.
9. The fish looked good, so I ordered it when the waiter came.
10. After we finished, I charged the dinner on my credit card.
11. Sometimes my father gets angry about how much I spend.
12. By paying the bill on time, I usually avoid credit charges.
13. I read the book and saw the movie, but I did not like them.
14. I liked the movie that we saw last week.
15. We located the device, but it was partially buried in the sand, so we could not get it.
16. What you said surprised everyone who was there.
17. We tried to get the answer, but we could not find the right book.
18. The people who were at the scene gave the police a description of what had been taken.

Exercise 4.12. Review

Diagram the following sentences. (Answers to exercises are found on page 461.)

1. Removing her glasses, she examined the questionnaire I had handed her.
2. Scratch it where it itches.
3. I will return when you are ready to start.
4. If you think you can do that, you are mistaken.
5. The candidate was bitter that he was not able to fill the seat vacated by Senator Smithers.
6. Known and loved by all his neighbors, Leon decided he had a future in politics.
7. Since you asked about what I know, I will tell you.
8. She was happier than I had seen her since her accident.
9. We saw the ad everybody had been talking about.
10. The tea was weaker than I like it.
11. While you were out, Van called about fixing his car.
12. The press received the story with suspicion that verged on disbelief.
13. Tell me when you are ready to leave the office.
14. Why you would say that about what we did is beyond me.
15. I did not respond to the question to avoid saying something that might embarrass you.
16. As I was going to St. Ives, I met a man with seven wives.
17. You must apply yourself to succeed in getting what you want.
18. The story, having been confirmed, was on the wire services.

SUMMARY OF TRADITIONAL TERMS

Clause: A clause is a group of words that contains a verb and its subject. An *independent (main) clause* expresses a complete thought and can stand by itself. A *dependent (subordinate) clause* does not express a complete thought and cannot stand alone. There are three types of subordinate clauses.

1. Adjective (relative) clause: An adjective (relative) clause is a subordinate clause used as an adjective to modify a noun or pronoun. *Restrictive* adjective clauses restrict the meaning of the words they modify and are not set off with commas. *Nonrestrictive* adjective clauses rename the words they modify and are set off with commas.

2. Adverb clause: An adverb clause is a subordinate clause that modifies a verb, an adjective, or another adverb.

3. Noun clause: A noun clause is a subordinate clause used as a noun.

Sentences classified according to structure: There are four kinds of sentences according to structure.

1. Simple: A simple sentence has one independent clause and no subordinate clauses.

2. Compound: A compound sentence has two or more independent clauses but no subordinate clauses.

3. Complex: A complex sentence has one independent clause and at least one subordinate clause.

4. Compound-complex: A compound-complex sentence has two or more independent clauses and at least one subordinate clause.

PART II

Alternatives
and Options

5

A Short History
of English Grammar

The best-known grammar of English is traditional grammar, or more accurately, the conventional schoolroom version of traditional grammar. The latter has been the mainstay of English education in America since the time of the Revolutionary War, and every educated person in the English-speaking world has at least a passing familiarity with its terms and concepts. Since at least the turn of this century, however, other ways of looking at English grammar have evolved. In this chapter we review the origins of traditional grammar and then briefly discuss two of the modern approaches to grammar: historical-descriptive grammar and structural linguistics. The most important current grammar of English, transformational grammar, is discussed in some detail in the Chapter 6.

THE ORIGINS OF TRADITIONAL GRAMMAR

In order to understand our traditional schoolroom grammar, we need to examine where traditional grammar itself came from. The first grammars of English were written in England in the late 1500s. These books did not appear out of thin air: they closely followed the organization and content of a widely used schoolroom grammar of Latin written by William Lyly with the assistance of John Colet and Erasmus. Lyly's book, in turn, was derived from a fourth-century Roman grammar by Aelius Donatus, which, in its turn, was derived from a Greek grammar written in the second century BC by Dionysius Thrax.

Lyly's grammar, which may have been written as early as 1513, had many names—*Paul's Accidence* (for St. Paul's school, where Lyly was the first headmaster and where John Milton would later be a student), the *Eaton Grammar,* and its most common name, *Lyly's Grammar.* It has been called the most influential single textbook ever to appear in England. For example, in 1542 Henry VIII made it the standard text for school use, and it was probably the Latin grammar that Shakespeare studied. Editions and revisions of this book continued to appear until 1858, a publication life span of over 350 years.

It is difficult for us today to appreciate fully the enormous prestige that Latin had in previous centuries. During the Middle Ages Church Latin was the universal language of religion, of diplomacy, and of all learning. In the Renaissance and in following periods, classical Latin was the foundation for all secular education. For instance, today we still occasionally use the term *grammar school* to refer to the elementary grades. The "grammar" in "grammar school" is not English grammar, it is Latin grammar. It is only in relatively modern times that teaching Latin grammar has not been one of the major elements of the school curriculum.

In the sixteenth and seventeenth centuries, the level of scholarly knowledge about classical Latin was very high. In fact our twentieth-century knowledge of Latin is not appreciably more sophisticated, except in our knowledge of its relation to the other Indo-European languages. Naturally enough, when scholars in the sixteenth and seventeenth centuries turned to describing English, they employed the familiar terms and concepts of Latin grammar. In other words, English was seen through the filter of Latin. An obvious consequence of this approach was to describe those features in English that most closely resembled Latin and to ignore those features of English that were very unlike Latin and thus poorly understood.

But the factor that perhaps more than any other contributed to the Latin-ness of traditional English grammars was the purpose for which the grammars were written. It is not surprising that most English grammars were intended to be used in the classroom. However, what may be surprising is that they were not used for the purpose of teaching English grammar, but for preparing to teach *Latin* grammar. The logic of this is simple: if children could learn the basic concepts and terms of grammar for their own language first, then the process of learning them for Latin would be much easier. As Greenwood and Steele put it in *The Tatler* of 1770:

I take our corrupt Ways of Writing to proceed from the Mistakes and wrong Measures in our common Methods of Education, which I always looked upon as one of our National Grievances. . . . For can any Thing be more absurd than our Way of Proceeding in this Part of Literature? To push tender Wits into the intricate Mazes of Grammar, and a Latin Grammar? To learn an unknown Art by an unknown Tongue? To carry them a dark Round-about Way to let them in at a Back-Door? Whereas by teaching them first the Grammar of their Mother-Tongue (so easy to be learned) their Advance to the Grammars of Latin and Greek would be gradual and easy; but our precipitate Way of hurrying them over such a Gulph before we have built them a Bridge to it, is a Shock to the weak Understandings, which they seldom or very late, recover. . . . (No. 234, 6 October 1770)

Since teaching English grammar was not an end in itself, but only a vehicle for teaching Latin grammar, it is not surprising that just those features of English grammar that had counterparts in Latin grammar were taught. The areas where English differed from Latin were simply ignored as being irrelevant, which they were—from the standpoint of teaching the grammar of Latin.

Present as a minor element in the sixteenth and seventeenth centuries, but coming increasingly to dominate all consideration about English grammar in the eighteenth century, was the issue of establishing standards for correct usage. As Charles C. Fries points out in his book *The Teaching of the English Language* (1927), the English grammars of the eighteenth century differed from those of the preceding two centuries in that the earlier grammars were primarily intended as an aid in teaching Latin, whereas the eighteenth-century grammars were primarily aimed at teaching English students to use correct English. It is no accident that the first important dictionary of English that also addressed questions of standard usage was published in the middle of the eighteenth century—Samuel Johnson's *Dictionary of the English Language* (1755). Lord Chesterfield in his Preface to Johnson's *Dictionary* called for the dictionary maker and grammarian to act as dictators to establish standards of correctness.

The role of grammars and dictionaries in establishing national language standards was important in also establishing a sense of national language identity. To a certain extent the English were here keeping up with the Joneses. In Italy and France scholars had already prepared dictionaries and grammars for their languages. English dictionaries and grammars were an important step in establishing English as a legitimate language on a par with the other major European languages.

Finally, grammars and dictionaries were thought to play a key role in stabilizing the language. One of the persistent beliefs of eighteenth-century English thinkers was that their period was entering a time of social and linguistic decline. A recurring metaphor in the eighteenth century for describing their society was the natural life cycle: a period of vigorous, youthful growth, a period of maturity, and a period of decline and decay. The latter part of the eighteenth century looked back at the Elizabethan age as the period of vigorous youth; the age of Dryden (or Addison or Swift, depending on the taste and period of the observer—golden ages need to be seen at a distance) as the period of maturity; and their own generation (whatever it was) as the period of decay. Change in language was seen as prima facie evidence of social decay. There was the same cycle in language as there was in society: the period of youthful vigor was found in the writing of Shakespeare and his contemporaries; the period of maturity was reached with Dryden (or Addison or Swift); and the jargon, slang, follies, affectations, and vanities of the present time were evidence aplenty that the period of linguistic decay and corruption had been reached.

Dictionaries and grammar books—particularly schoolroom grammar books—were seen as the main weapons in fighting the rearguard delaying action against the barbarians at the gate. James Burnett, Lord Monboddo, expresses this attitude in his book *The Origin and Progress of Language* (1773–92):

> ... *a language of art not only could not have been invented by the people but ... it cannot be preserved among them, without the particular care and attention of those men of art we call grammarians; whom we may despise as much as we please; but if there be not such a set of men in every country, to guard against the abuses and corruptions which popular use will necessarily introduce into every language; and if the youth of rank and fortune in the country, are not carefully instructed by such men in the principles of grammar; the language of that country, however perfect it may have been originally, will very soon become unlearned and barbarous. It is chiefly by such neglect that all the present languages of Europe are become corrupt dialects of languages that were originally good ...* (Vol. II, Part II, Book III, Ch. 14).

The main concern in settling questions of proper usage was the development of some set of uniform principles to provide a basis for making judgments about questions of divided usage. During this period two main principles emerged. One principle was the *analogy to the rules of Latin grammar*. Thus, questions of correctness in English could be settled by citing the appropriate rule in analogous areas of Latin grammar. Often quoted with approval was Dryden's method of testing a doubtful passage in English by turning it into Latin. For example, two rules derived from analogy to Latin grammar which were applied to English were (1) do not split infinitives, and (2) do not end a sentence with a preposition.

English verb phrase constructions that began with *to* were considered the equivalent of the infinitive verb form in Latin. In Latin an infinitive is a single word. Since it is patently impossible to split apart the infinitive in Latin, the infinitive being a single word, it was considered bad form to split the corresponding form in English. Consequently, schoolroom grammar books of English to this day still consider sentences like the following to be bad grammar.

A teacher's job is to carefully check papers for split infinitives.

The infinitive to check has been "split" by the adverb carefully. Thus, the "correct" version of this sentence would move the adverb to a different position.

A teacher's job is to check papers carefully for split infinitives.

The second rule, about not ending sentences with prepositions comes from the literal meaning of the term preposition in Latin: *prae* 'in front' + *pōnere* 'to place'. Since the term *preposition* literally means "to place in front," it is grammatically incorrect to have a preposition in a final position.

The problem with this approach, of course, is that English and Latin are two very different languages. The fact that both languages have verb forms that can be called infinitives does not mean that the forms behave the same in both languages. Likewise, as we discuss later in this chapter, prepositions in English have a completely different set of functions from prepositions in Latin.

Even more important, these two "rules" have never corresponded to the actual practice of many major writers. Winston Churchill was once said to have written a sentence ending in a preposition that a junior staff member bravely (but not very wisely) corrected by moving the preposition from the end of the sentence to a place in the middle. Churchill wrote him a note saying, "This is the kind of errant pedantry up with which I will not put."

The second main basis for settling questions of divided usage was an appeal to *universal grammar*. The features of language that are basic to all languages were considered to be universal. Each particular language had a number of peculiarities and special features, each of which must be learned apart from the universal base. James Harris in his *Hermes* (1751) defined universal grammar as:

> *That Grammar, which without regarding the several Idioms of particular Languages, only respects those principles, that are essential to them all.* (x)

One would think that universal grammar would be embodied in every language equally (i.e., *universally*), but such was not the eighteenth-century view. For them, universal grammar was an ideal, perfect state like a Platonic Form. All languages reflected the universal perfection, but some more than others. The older languages, especially Greek and Latin, were believed to be very close to the universal grammar, but their modern descendants were believed to have become corrupted through the passage of time. In the eighteenth century, universal grammar was often connected with universal reason. For example, in discussing universal grammar, Harris (1751) comments:

> *It may afford perhaps no unpleasing speculation to see how the same reason has at all times prevailed; how there is one truth, like one sun, that has enlightened human intelligence through every age, and saved it from the darkness both of Sophistry and Error.* (x)

Thus, the more a language deviated from universal grammar, the less pure and logical the language became. A side effect of universal grammar was to reinforce the already high status of classical Greek and Latin. However, the main effect of universal grammar was to settle questions of divided usage by appeals to universal "reason" and "logic." An example of an issue in English grammar's being settled by an appeal to "reason" is the question of double negation. For example, a child's complaint that

> Nobody don't like me

is judged to be ungrammatical on the grounds that in logic and mathematics two negatives make a positive; that is, they reverse each other. The rule for double negatives is based on the logic of the fact that a minus number times a minus number equals a positive number ($-2 \times -2 = +4$). However, one could equally argue that since a -2 *plus* a -2 is a -4, the child's sentence is an instance of additive negatives and is therefore equally valid. Multiplication is not inherently more logical or appropriate as an analogy to language than addition is.

At the end of the eighteenth century, education became increasingly open to a much broader range of socioeconomic classes. One consequence of this broadening was that English began to supplant the role of Latin in the humbler educational tracks. However, since the tradition for teaching Latin was the sole model for language teaching, it is not surprising that English was taught with the same methods and, to the greatest extent possible, the same content as Latin. As Rollo Lyman (1921) puts it:

> *When the Latin grammar school was proved to be ill-suited to the majority of pupils, and when the demand increased for a type of secondary education to supplant the Latin, English grammar came naturally to the fore. Instruction in vernacular grammar could be imparted by exactly the same methods used in the teaching of Latin grammar. The passing of Latin grammar is contemporaneous with the rise of vernacular grammar. The older order—reading, writing, spelling, and Latin grammar—now became reading, writing, spelling, English grammar, all in the Mother Tongue.* (20)

Traditional grammar was profoundly shaped by the intellectual and cultural values of the grammarians of the seventeenth and eighteenth centuries. The grammarians in the seventeenth century developed a grammar for English based on the only linguistic model available to them: Latin. Since the early schoolroom grammars of English were intended to introduce those terms and concepts necessary for the traditional classroom study of Latin grammar, the areas of English that were similar to Latin were emphasized and the many areas of English that differed from Latin were completely ignored. In the eighteenth century, grammars were called upon to play a prescriptive role—to establish and permanently fix proper usage. Many eighteenth-century grammarians, drawing on analogies to Latin grammar and on appeals to universal grammar and universal reason, gladly attempted to do just that.

The traditional grammar book in our classrooms today is the direct descendant of eighteenth-century grammar books through the work of nineteenth-century traditional grammarians, the most important in America being Lindley Murray and Goold Brown. Murray, who copied extensively from Bishop Robert Lowth's 1762 book *A Short Introduction to English Grammar,* is a particularly important link with the eighteenth-century grammarians because of his enormous popularity. Murray's numerous works, published at the beginning of the nineteenth century, had sold more than one million copies by 1850. Goold Brown published his colossal *Grammar of Grammars* in 1851. This work, containing over a thousand pages of rules and ex cathedra pronouncements in excruciatingly fine print, is the epitome of eighteenth-century grammatical traditions. As Robert Pooley (1957) puts it,

> The *Grammar of Grammars marked the pinnacle and decline of the traditional concept of language and grammar as derived from the eighteenth century. Tendencies already visible in earlier grammars become more and more pronounced, so that by the third quarter of the century a new theory of grammar was superseding the old, bringing with it a new attitude toward language itself. Yet with the changes in theory, much of the specific subject matter remained unchanged, appearing in text after text even to the present day, carried along by the weight of tradition.* (25)

Several eighteenth-century grammarians, chief among them William Ward (*Essay on Grammar,* 1765) and the scientist Joseph Priestley (*Rudiments of English Grammar,* 1761), argued against using Latin as a framework for describing English. Priestley, for example, rejected the appropriateness of Latin grammatical terms for English and denied that there was a future tense inflection in English parallel to the future tense in Latin. Even the conservative traditional grammarian Bishop Lowth rejected the validity of modeling the verb system of English on the verb system of Latin.

Priestley and the well-known eighteenth-century rhetorician George Campbell both argued against appeals to analogy and universal grammar in establishing proper usage and argued instead for the authority of custom and the practice of leading writers. In particular, they challenged the authority of grammarians to decree arbitrarily what is or is not correct usage on the basis of the grammarian's personal and unsubstantiated notions of what constituted valid analogy and universal grammar. Here, for example, is Priestley's argument (1769):

> *It must be allowed, that the custom of speaking is the original, and only just standard of any language. We see in all grammars that this is sufficient to establish a rule, even contrary to the strongest analogies of the language with itself. Must not this custom, therefore, be allowed to have some weight, in favor of those forms of speech, to which our best writers and speakers seem evidently prone; forms which are contrary to no analogy of the language with itself, and which have been disapproved by grammarians, only from certain abstract and arbitrary considerations, and when their decisions were not prompted by the genius [nature] of the language . . . . (ix)*

Campbell, in his *Philosophy of Rhetoric* (1776), roundly attacked appeals to universal grammar and the notion held by Swift, Lowth, and others that usage could offend against proper grammar. Campbell questions what the term *grammar* means and cleverly argues that since language is what is in general use, and since general use cannot offend against itself, then usage cannot offend against grammar:

> *Some notion, possibly, he [Swift] had of grammar in the abstract, an universal archetype by which the particular grammars of all different tongues ought to be regulated . . . I acknowledge myself to be entirely ignorant of this universal grammar; nor can I form a conjecture where its laws are to be learnt . . . . If he meant the English grammar, I would ask, whence has that grammar derived its laws? If from general use (and I cannot conceive another origin), then it must be owned, that there is a general use in that language as well as in others; and it were absurd to accuse the language, which is purely what is conformable to general use in speaking and writing as offending against general use. (1.342–3)*

Unlike Priestley, whose work on language was too far outside the mainstream of eighteenth-century thought to influence his contemporaries, Campbell was quite influential. His criteria for correct usage—"national, reputable, and present use"—was famous. His definition of *reputable* rested on the practice of authors of high reputation. Interestingly, his definition of *present* extended back over a hundred years to the major writers of the post-Restoration period—exactly the period that the life cycle theory considered to be the peak of maturity. The "present" did not include contemporary writers since Campbell thought their status was not sufficiently established to serve as models.

Three ideas largely shaped traditional schoolroom grammars of English: (1) that classical languages, especially Latin, provided the best model for the description of English, (2) that questions of appropriate usage could be settled by appeals to Latin grammar and universal grammar, and (3) that languages naturally decay over time if left to themselves. In the following sections of this chapter, we discuss two new approaches to English grammar that challenge these three tenets of traditional grammar: (1) the development of historical-descriptive grammars in the late nineteenth century, and (2) the development of structural linguistics in the mid twentieth century.

THE DEVELOPMENT
OF HISTORICAL-DESCRIPTIVE GRAMMARS

Eighteenth-century scholars were well aware that many languages of Europe and the Middle East were somehow related to one another, but they did not have any method or adequate theory of language by which they could make sense out of the historical relationships. The key that unlocked the mystery came from a totally unexpected source—India and the discovery of the historical significance of the ancient Indian language Sanskrit. The most famous observation about Sanskrit was made in 1786 by Sir William Jones, who was then serving as Chief Justice in Bengal in the employment of the East India Company:

> *The Sanskrit language, whatever be its antiquity, is of a wonderful struc-*
> *ture; more perfect than the Greek, more copious than the Latin, and more*
> *exquisitely refined than either; yet bearing to both of them a stronger affinity,*
> *both in the roots of verbs and in the forms of grammar, than could possibly*
> *have been produced by accident; so strong, indeed that no philologer could*
> *examine all three without believing them to have sprung from some common*
> *source, which, perhaps no longer exists.* (Quoted from Jespersen 1922, 33)

The discovery of an ancient language related to Greek and Latin led to a revolution not only in scholarly attitudes toward the classical languages but also toward the whole process of language change. Sanskrit showed that classical Greek and Latin were not immutable, perfect languages, but in fact they were languages that had undergone sweeping changes that had caused them to lose features that were preserved in Sanskrit. Thus Greek and Latin were not perfect languages, which closely reflected the purity of the original universal grammar, but were themselves the products of language change over time. In short, Greek and Latin were not unique languages whose grammars held special significance.

Beginning in the early part of the nineteenth century, scholars began to reconstruct the exact relationship of Sanskrit, Greek, and Latin to one another and to other related languages (including English). The most important reconstruction was by Jakob Grimm (one of the Grimm Brothers of fairy tale fame) of the relationship of consonant sounds in the Germanic language to the sounds in Sanskrit, Greek, and Latin. Grimm showed that there was a systematic correspondence of consonant sounds between Germanic languages and the classical languages; for example, that where Latin has a / k / sound (spelled with the letter *c*), English has an /h/: Latin *cor*—English *heart*; Latin *canis*—English *hound*; Latin *cornū*—English *horn*.

By comparing the consonants in related words in Sanskrit, Greek, Latin, and various Germanic languages, Grimm and other scholars were able both to reconstruct the pronunciation of consonants in the common ancestor language, called Indo-European, and to establish a set of pronunciation rules that showed step-by-step how the pronunciation of consonants in the Germanic language was derived from their pronunciation in Indo-European.

Grimm's research and similar discoveries by other historical linguists had far-reaching implications about the nature of language change. They showed that although language change had taken place on a massive scale, the nature of the change was regular. In complete opposition to eighteenth-century grammarians who saw change as being a random process of decay, the nineteenth-century historical linguists saw change as obeying systematic laws, which could be discovered by scientific analysis.

Historical linguistics affected the study of English grammar in two important ways. One effect was to make the study of the history of the English language a major scholarly field. By way of contrast, traditional grammarians in the eighteenth century had no knowledge of and little interest in the history of English; they saw English only through the filter of Latin. For them, the extensive areas of English that did not conform to Latin were a jumble of idioms, incapable of analysis. The history of English was the first aspect of English to be the topic of serious and systematic research. Generations of scholars learned Anglo-Saxon and worked out the systematic relations between it and the hypothetical common Indo-European ancestor language. They also described how the forms of modern English were derived from Anglo-Saxon. One important consequence of this research was to begin to look at English in its own terms and not just as a deviant and corrupted form of Latin.

The second effect of historical linguistics was to carry over the new scientific approach employed in the study of the history of language to the description of contemporary languages. Beginning in the last part of the nineteenth century and continuing to the present day, there have been a number of grammarians who, while accepting the Latinate framework of traditional grammar, wrote detailed grammars of English that accurately described the actual language of English speakers without prescribing what that language should be. [Grammars of this type are sometimes called *descriptive* grammars as opposed to *prescriptive* grammars that are more oriented toward correcting errors of usage.] Many scholars became interested in the study of regional dialects. Of particular interest to them was the preservation in dialects of older forms of the language. Other scholars described the standard language of educated speakers in comprehensive reference grammars. Two particularly important historical-descriptive grammarians in this tradition were Henry Sweet, *A New English Grammar, Logical and His-*

torical (1891), and Otto Jespersen, *The Philosophy of Grammar* (1924) and *Essentials of English Grammar* (1933). Sweet, by the way, was the model for Professor Henry Higgins in Shaw's *Pygmalion* (later adapted as the musical *My Fair Lady*).

Unfortunately, neither the findings of the historical linguists nor the excellent work of historical-descriptive grammarians like Sweet and Jespersen have had any significant impact on the content of schoolroom traditional grammars. Clearly, the pattern of schoolroom traditional grammars was so firmly established that it was (and is) fully self-perpetuating. After all, teachers teach the way they were taught, and unless there is a full-scale revolution in teaching—as nearly happened in the 1960s—nothing is going to change. An inevitable consequence of the insulation of schoolroom traditional grammar from language research is a widening gap between what is taught in the schoolroom and what is known about language. There are few disciplines in which the distance between what is taught at the secondary level and what is taught at the university level is greater.

THE DEVELOPMENT OF STRUCTURAL LINGUISTICS

In America, structural linguistics began after the turn of the century with the work of Franz Boas, the first professor of anthropology at Columbia University, and his students. Boas and his students conducted fieldwork on native American cultures. An important part of their research was concerned with describing various native American languages. Boas and his students realized that the traditional concepts of Latin grammar were often inapplicable to the new kinds of grammatical structures they encountered. There were languages in which nouns were counted according to the shape of the object the nouns referred to. There were languages in which there was virtually no distinction between verbs and adjectives. There were languages in which noun endings were added to verb stems. And there were even languages in which the Indo-European concept of word was inapplicable—languages in which each sentence was formed from a single gigantically compounded word.

Boas and his students developed new concepts for describing the vast variety of grammatical structures they encountered. Their approach is now called *structural linguistics*.

The key concept of structural linguistics (and from which it derived its name) was its emphasis on structure. For structural linguists, *structure* meant the forms of words and the arrangement of words to construct sentences. Structural linguistics drew a fundamental distinction between form and meaning. Words and sentences have both form and meaning, but it is very difficult and perhaps ultimately impossible to precisely define meaning apart from form. [Remember that structural linguistics was developed to describe languages that linguists did not already know. Linguists can directly observe the forms of words and sentences in unknown languages, but they can only infer meanings.]

To see the important consequence of the difference between school-room traditional grammar's meaning-based approach and structural linguistics' form-based approach, compare their definitions of a sentence and a noun in English.

Traditional grammar: A sentence expresses a complete thought.
Structural linguistics: A sentence contains a noun and a verb in agreement with each other.

The traditional definition of sentence is based on what a sentence means, whereas the structural definition is based on the forms (noun and verb in agreement) that are required for a sentence to be grammatical.

Traditional grammar: A noun is a name of a person, place, thing, or idea.
Structural linguistics: Nouns have the following characteristics.

☐ Nouns are formed with a distinctive set of suffixes, for example: -hood (boy + hood), -ship (friend + ship), -er (submarine + er).
☐ Nouns directly follow articles and possessive pronouns.
☐ Nouns can be replaced by personal pronouns.
☐ Most nouns have a singular and plural form.

The traditional definition of noun is based on meaning—on what the noun refers to. The structural definition is based on formal properties of word formation and the properties of word arrangement to form larger units—properties that only a speaker of English can recognize since these properties are unique to English.

The differences in the definitions of sentence and noun reflect fundamentally different assumptions about what a definition is. The definitions of traditional grammar rest not only on meaning but on the universality of that meaning. That is, traditional definitions are rooted in assumptions about universal grammar; for example, that the concepts of sentence and noun are realized in all human languages. Thus our ability to recognize the categories of sentence and noun is ultimately dependent on our intuitive, untaught knowledge of universal grammar. Structural linguistics, on the other hand, assumes that even if the grammatical categories of *sentence* and *noun* are widespread, they are not found in every language, and even for those languages in which the categories are useful descriptive devices, the embodiment of abstract concepts such as *sentence* and *noun* in the actual forms of specific languages is so amazingly diverse that the concepts must be defined uniquely in terms of the structures of those languages. [The structural description of English grammar that had the greatest impact on the classroom, Charles C. Fries's *Structure of English* (1952), went so far as to abandon the traditional names for parts of speech and substituted in their place numbered classes in order to emphasize the independence of his classification from the conventions of traditional grammar.]

The single most important work in the development of structural linguistics was Leonard Bloomfield's *Language* (1933), a lucid general introduction to the study of language from a structural point of view that can still be read today with great profit. Bloomfield's book provided an intellectual framework that essentially defined structural linguistics as a discipline in its own right—as opposed to being a subdiscipline of anthropology. Bloomfield's book brought together into a single coherent theoretical model the work of the historical linguists, the work of American anthropologists on non-Indo-European languages, and contemporary models of psychology, especially psychological models of language processing and the acquisition of language by both children and second-language learners.

Structural linguistics became the first full-blown attempt to create an integrated scientific theory of language with a well-defined theoretical base and methodology. Two things set structural linguists apart from their closest predecessors, the historical linguists and the historical-descriptive grammarians.

First, structural linguists made a major distinction between *synchronic* and *diachronic* linguistics. The former pertains to descriptions of language at one moment in time without reference to any past or future time; the latter refers to descriptions of changes in language forms across time. The historical-descriptive grammarians did not make a clear distinction between synchronic and diachronic studies of language. For them, an "explanation" of a construction in modern English was a description of how this construction evolved from an earlier stage of the language. From the standpoint of structural linguistics, this was a diachronic description. The information it provided was certainly of academic interest, but it had nothing to say about how a modern speaker of the language actually acquired and used that construction. In other words, diachronic linguistics dealt with information that was not available to speakers of a language and therefore had nothing to do with that speaker's linguistic behavior. The goal of synchronic linguistics was to describe the linguistic mechanisms of actual speakers of a language (a speech community) in real time. Thus, historical information was irrelevant to the main concern of structural linguistics—synchronic linguistics.

The second thing that set structural linguists apart from historical-descriptive grammarians was the structural linguists' belief that the linguistic behavior of a speech community was based on an orderly set of structures that members of the speaker community shared. From this point of view, the historical-descriptive grammarians were little more than data collectors searching out interesting examples of language like vacationers picking up seashells at the beach. For example, when Jespersen discusses a particular construction, he freely mixes together interesting examples of that construction from then contemporary authors, eighteenth-century writers, and Shakespeare. The structural linguists felt that this curiosity shop approach to data collecting made it impossible to describe the linguistic behavior of a speech community at any one point in time. To repeat: the fundamental idea of synchronic structural linguistics is that a speech community is defined by a shared set of linguistic structures. A linguist's analysis of the language of that community is a description of those shared structures.

Many structural linguists undertook analyses of English grammar. These analyses were most revealing in two areas: (1) areas where the new concepts and methodologies of structural linguistics led researchers to discover structures and patterns in English that were hidden from previous grammarians who saw in English only those structures that had Latin counterparts, and (2) areas where the imposition of Latin grammar had resulted in distorted analyses of English grammar. In these latter areas, structural linguistics reformulated traditional terms and concepts.

In the remainder of this chapter, we examine four case studies that illustrate how structural linguistics has contributed to our understanding of English grammar. The first three case studies are instances of structures and patterns not available in traditional grammar, and the fourth case study is an instance of how structural linguistics gains a new insight by reformulating a traditional Latin-based concept.

1. The structural approach to word formation, and how it can be used to help define parts of speech.
2. The identification and analysis of a major class of verbs, phrasal verbs, that were ignored by traditional grammarians.
3. A class of helping verbs, modals, that were also ignored by traditional grammarians.
4. A reformulation of the concept of *tense* from a structural point of view.

1. Word Formation and Parts of Speech

The structure of nouns, verbs, adjectives, and adverbs differs in important ways from the structure of the remaining parts of speech.

Compare, for example, the noun *nonswimmers* with the preposition *to*. The noun has a complex internal structure: a stem *swim* to which the prefix *non-* and the suffixes *-er* and *-s* have been added. Prepositions, on the other hand, have simple, unchanging forms, they cannot be used with prefixes and suffixes.

The prefixes and suffixes serve several functions. In our example, the *-er* suffix changes the verb *swim* into the noun *swimmer*, meaning "someone who engages in the action of swimming." The negative prefix *non-* then changes the meaning of the noun to something like "someone who cannot (or will not) swim." Finally, the *-s* suffix makes the noun plural. Note that the order in which the prefixes and suffixes were discussed is the order in which they *must* be added to the stem. That is, we can add the prefix *non-* to nouns derived from verbs.

smoker-nonsmoker

talker-nontalker

drinker-nondrinker

flyer-nonflyer

However, we cannot add the prefix *non-* directly to these same verbs.

*nonswim

*nonsmoke

*nontalk

*nondrink

*nonfly

Thus we cannot add the prefix *non-* until after we have changed the verb into a noun by means of the *-er* suffix. It is typical that prefixes and suffixes can be added only in a certain order.

Since most prefixes and suffixes can be used only with certain parts of speech, we can use these prefixes and suffixes to help identify parts of speech. For example, the prefix *de-* 'to reverse, eliminate' can be used only with verbs. Thus, one way that we can recognize that the following words are verbs is that they all begin with the prefix *de-*.

code	decode
centralize	decentralize
frost	defrost
regulate	deregulate
segregate	desegregate

Unfortunately, there is a catch to this method: other suffixes can then change the verb (along with the *de-* prefix) into another part of speech. For example, *deregulate* is indeed a verb, but the verb can be changed into the noun *deregulation* by the suffix *-(a)tion*. Consequently, we must be careful to look at the way the whole word is used. The prefix *de-* does not prove that a word is used as a verb; it may prove only that the word in question was *derived* from a verb.

■ **Exercise 5.1. Prefixes and suffixes that identify parts of speech**

In the same way that verbs can be recognized by their ability to use the prefix *de-*, the part of speech of each of the following groups of words can be identified by their ability to use a certain prefix or suffix. 1. Attach the prefix or suffix to all of the words in the group. 2. Identify the part of speech (noun, verb, or adjective) of each group. Use the test words to prove your identification of parts of speech: *the* in front of nouns; *will* in front of verbs; and *very* in front of adjectives. The first group is done as an example. (Answers to exercises are found on page 465.)

1. Prefix: mis- 'badly'
   Words used with: calculate, hear, fire, inform, lead
   Answer: 1. miscalculate, mishear, misfire, misinform, mislead
            2. Verb (proof: will miscalculate, will mishear, etc.)

2. Prefix: in- 'not, the opposite of'
   Words used with: active, considerate, elegant, sane, significant, valid, vulnerable

3. Prefix: mini- 'little'
   Words used with: cab, conference, session, skirt

4. Prefix: re- 'again, back'
   Words used with: build, form, join, locate, produce, sell, tell, turn, wind

5. Suffix: -hood 'state, status'
   Words used with: boy, brother, knight, man, mother, neighbor, widow

6. Prefix: fore- 'before, in advance'
   Words used with: doom, judge, ordain, see, stall, tell

7. Prefix: hyper- 'especially'
   Words used with: active, critical, sensitive

8. Suffix: -let/-ette 'small, unimportant'
   Words used with: book, cigar, kitchen, leaf, pig, star

9. Prefix: out- 'to do something better/faster'
   Words used with: grow, live, perform, play, sell, weigh

The prefixes and suffixes in Exercise 5.1 affect the meaning of the stems they attach to in various ways, but they do not change the stem's part of speech. However, there is another class of suffixes (and a few prefixes) that does just that: it changes the stem word from one part of speech class to another. We have already seen one example of this: the *-er* suffix that changes verbs to nouns (e.g., *swim* (verb) to *swimmer* (noun)). Nouns, verbs, and adjectives can each be formed from the other two parts of speech by prefixes and suffixes. Adverbs are much more limited. There are no productive prefixes or suffixes that change adverbs into the other parts of speech, nor can prefixes or suffixes change nouns or verbs into adverbs. However, a very productive suffix (-ly) changes adjectives into adverbs.

Adjective	Adverb
clear	clearly
dark	darkly
full	fully
great	greatly
light	lightly
narrow	narrowly
practical	practically
thick	thickly
vigorous	vigorously

The prefixes and suffixes that change words from one part of speech to another are very helpful in identifying part of speech because, in a way, we get two identifications for the price of one. For example, the fact that *clear* and *clearly* are related words and that the second word is formed by adding the suffix -ly to the first word not only tells us that *clearly* is probably an adverb, it also tells us that the stem that the -ly was added to was probably an adjective. Conversely, one proof that *clear* is an adjective is that we can form a corresponding adverb from it by adding -ly, a process of word formation that is typical of adjectives.

■ **Exercise 5.2. Prefixes and suffixes that change part of speech**

1. Identify the part of speech of each of the following groups of words.
2. Attach the prefix or suffix to the words in the group. 3. Determine what part of speech the group has now become. The first group is done as an example. (Answers to exercises are found on page 466.)

1. Suffix: -ness
   Words used with: clever, courageous, happy, kind, mean,
   righteous, selfish, slovenly, snobbish, useful

   Answer:
   1. Part of speech: Adjective (proof: very clever, very
      courageous . . .)
   2. With suffix: cleverness, courageousness, happiness,
      kindness, meanness, righteousness, selfishness,
      slovenliness, snobbishness, usefulness
   3. New part of speech: Noun (proof: the cleverness, the
      courageousness, the
      happiness . . .)

2. Suffix: -less
   Words used with: blame, care, child, hair, harm, rest, speech, tooth
3. Suffix: -ant
   Words used with: contest, defend, disinfect, inform, inhabit
4. Suffix: -ity
   Words used with: banal, curious, diverse, infirm, intense, rapid, vital
5. Suffix: -al
   Words used with: adjective, critic, logic, nation, profession, tradition
6. Suffix: -ation
   Words used with: confirm, deport, explore, fix, organize, protest
7. Suffix: -en
   Words used with: hard, mad, ripe, rough, sad, short, sweet, wide
8. Suffix: -ment
   Words used with: amaze, arrange, embody, govern, puzzle, retire
9. Prefix: en-
   Words used with: compass, courage, danger, slave, throne, vision

---

The suffixes that change part of speech often interact with the stem of the word in very complex ways. Sometimes the suffix will cause a stress shift. For example, the noun *Canada* has its stress on the first syllable: *Canada*, but the adjective has its stress on the second syllable: *Canadian*. Sometimes, particularly with words taken from Latin, the interaction of stem and suffix is so complex that it is difficult to tell what the stem really is. For example, consider the following group of related words.

Verb:	destroy
Noun:	destruction
Adjective:	destructive
Adverb:	destructively

Is the stem *destroy* or is it only *destr-*? We recognize the *-(a)tion* suffix, which changes verbs into nouns (as in *explore-exploration*), but where does the *c* in *destruction* come from? Is it part of the stem, part of the suffix, or part of neither one? Could the stem be based on the noun form *destruct-* which is somehow shortened to form the verb *destroy*? The fact that the adjective and adverb form both contain *destruct-* would be some evidence for this idea. [The real answer, of course, does not lie in English at all, but is in the complexity of Latin grammar and the accidents of history that gave rise to various French forms, which in turn were carried over into English.]

■ **Exercise 5.3. Related parts of speech**

Change each of the following verbs into at least one related noun, adjective, and adverb form. The adverbs are all based on the adjective forms. Sometimes the adjectives are based on the verb forms and sometimes on the noun forms. The first exercise is done as an example. (Answers to exercises are found on page 466.)

1. Grieve
   Answer: Verb: <u>grieve</u>; Noun: <u>grief</u>; Adjective: <u>grievous</u>;
   Adverb: <u>grievously</u>

2. Attract
3. Edit
4. Explode
5. Prefer
6. Sense
7. Offend
8. Explore
9. Refute
10. Participate
11. Specify
12. Enslave
13. Organize
14. Inform
15. Criticize
16. Credit

So far we have discussed two types of prefixes and suffixes: one type that does not change the part of speech of the word to which it is added, and a second type that does change the part of speech. Both types of prefixes and suffixes are collectively called *derivational*, as opposed to a third, completely different, type of suffix called *inflectional*. Inflectional suffixes are the endings of nouns, verbs, and adjectives.

Inflectional suffixes

Noun:	-s	(plural)	Example: boys, glasses
	-'s/-s'	(possessive)	Example: John's, dogs'
Verb:	-ed	(past tense)	Example: talked, faded
	-s	(3rd-person singular)	Example: talks, wishes
	-ing	(present participle)	Example: talking, working
	-en/-ed	(past participle)	Example: hidden, talked
Adjective:	-er	(comparative degree)	Example: faster, smaller
	-est	(superlative degree)	Example: fastest, smallest

Structural linguistics distinguished inflectional suffixes from derivational prefixes and suffixes in a number of ways.

☐ The inflectional suffixes are a small, closed class. They are limited to just the eight previously listed—there are no others. The number of derivational prefixes and suffixes is large, certainly over a hundred.

☐ The inflectional suffixes identify part of speech. That is, if a word can be used with the plural marker -s, the word *must* be a noun; if a word can be used with the past tense marker -ed, the word *must* be a verb, and so on. Many derivational suffixes, on the other hand, change a word from one part of speech to another. Other derivational suffixes can be added to more than one part of speech. For example, the negative prefix *non-* can be added to adjectives (*nonscientific*) as well as to nouns (*nonswimmer*).

☐ Only one inflectional suffix can be used per word. Since inflectional suffixes define part of speech, and since a word cannot be more than one part of speech at a time, it follows that a word can have only a single inflectional suffix. [There is one mild exception to this generalization about inflectional suffixes: nouns can be used with both the plural and possessive inflections; for example, *children's* is a plural possessive.] Derivational prefixes and suffixes, though, have no such limitation at all. For example, the word *irreplaceability* contains two derivational prefixes (*ir-* and *re-*) and two derivational suffixes (*-able* and *-ity*).

☐ The inflectional suffixes are highly productive. That is, all but a few exceptional nouns can be used with the plural marker -s; all verbs can be used in the past tense (though for historical reasons not all past tenses are marked with -ed), and so on. Derivational prefixes and suffixes, however, are just the opposite: they are typically unproductive. That is, any given prefix or suffix can be used only with a relatively small number of words. For example, there is a -ly suffix that changes nouns into adjectives: *king-kingly; queen-queenly; prince-princely.* However, we do not have these comparable forms: *princess-*princessly; duke-*dukely; earl-*earlly.* We have *man-manhood* and *woman-womanhood*, but not *person-*personhood.* We have *friend-friendship*, but not *ally-*allyship.* We have *pig-piglet*, but not *dog-*doglet*, or *cat-*catlet. Fair* and *sane* are both adjectives, but we negate them with different prefixes: we say *unfair* and *insane*, but not **infair* and **unsane.*

☐ Inflectional suffixes come as a package deal: by definition a verb is a word that can be used with any one of the family of four inflectional suffixes: the past tense marker, the third-person present tense marker, the present participle, and the past participle. No verb can be used with just one or two of these markers and not with the remaining ones. If a word can be used with any one of them, that word *must* be capable of being used with all four verb inflectional suffixes. Derivational prefixes and suffixes, of course, have no such interconnection. Each derivational prefix and suffix has an existence totally independent of any other derivational prefix or suffix.

☐ Inflectional suffixes are always at the end of a word. That is, we can add an inflectional suffix onto one or more derivational suffixes, but we can never add a derivational suffix onto any inflectional suffix. For example, we can add the derivational suffix *-ize* to the stem noun *victim* to create the verb *victimize*. We can then add the derivational suffix *-ation* to create the abstract noun *victimization*, which, if we choose, we can then pluralize by the inflectional suffix *-s: victimizations*. However, if instead we had pluralized the stem and created the plural noun *victims*, we could not then add the derivational suffix *-ize* to the stem: **victimsize*. Likewise, if we had added the inflectional suffix *-ed* to the verb *victimize* to create the past tense form *victimized*, we could not then add the derivational suffix *-ation: *victimizedation*.

2. Phrasal verbs

All languages need to create new words. Latin and the Germanic languages share a particular (and when one thinks about it, rather peculiar) technique for creating new verbs—they add prepositions to verb stems to create new verbs. In Latin the preposition is added in front of the verb. Following are some examples of verbs made this way that have come into English.

Preposition		*Verb Stem*		*English Form*
com-	'with'	pellō	'drive'	compel
de-	'down'	vorō	'swallow'	devour
ex-	'out'	cedō	'go away'	exceed

Latin can even make new verbs with multiple prepositions. For example, the English word *comprehend* is made up of two Latin prepositions—*com-* 'with' + *prae-* 'before'—and the verb stem *hendō* 'grasp'.

English can form new verbs in exactly the same manner.

Preposition	*Verb Stem*	*New Verb*
by-	pass	bypass
down-	play	downplay
for-	give	forgive
off-	set	offset
out-	last	outlast
over-	come	overcome
under-	stand	understand
with-	draw	withdraw

However, English and the other Germanic languages more commonly put the preposition behind the verb as a suffix rather than as a prefix. Since English does not write the new verb unit as a single word (though some of the other Germanic languages do), these verb units may be difficult to recognize at first. The verb stem plus preposition unit is called a *phrasal verb*. Following is a simple example of a sentence containing a phrasal verb.

> I give up.

One way to recognize phrasal verbs is to find a single-word verb (often Latin in origin) that substitutes for both the verb stem and the preposition. In this case the substitute is easy to find.

> I surrender.

Surrender, by the way, is an Old French form of a preposition plus verb stem unit in Latin.

Transitive phrasal verbs are very common. Compare the following two sentences.

> a. John turned out the light.
> b. John turned at the light.

In sentence a, *turned out* is a phrasal verb meaning "extinguished." In sentence b, *turned* is the verb followed by *at the light*, an adverb phrase of place.

Though these two sentences look alike, they have profound differences in structure and even in pronunciation. In sentence a, the preposition *out* has an extra degree of stress, whereas in sentence b, the preposition has a very low degree of stress. The difference in stress is characteristic of the two different uses of prepositions: in phrasal verbs, the preposition is stressed; in prepositional phrases, the preposition is unstressed.

There are several differences in structure. In sentence b, *at the light* is an adverb phrase of place, and, as such, it answers a *where* question.

> *Q:* Where did John turn?
> *A:* At the light.

However, when we try the same question with sentence a, the result is clearly ungrammatical, proving that *out the light* is not an adverb phrase.

> *Q:* Where did John turn?
> *A:* *Out the light.

Transitive phrasal verbs can be recognized by putting the sentence into the passive. If the preposition is part of a phrasal verb, then the noun that follows the preposition is not the object of the preposition;

it is the object of the verb. Furthermore, if the noun is the object of a transitive action verb, the object noun can become the new subject in a passive sentence. Compare the two sentences when we try to put them into the passive.

> *a.* Active: John turned out the light.
> Passive: The light was turned out by John.
>
> *b.* Active: John turned at the light.
> Passive: *The light was turned at by John.

Like Latin, English can make new verbs with more than one preposition. Following are some examples of transitive phrasal verbs made with two prepositions.

> Everyone <u>looked down on</u> us.
> The children <u>talked back to</u> their parents.
> They <u>found out about</u> it.
> John <u>came up with</u> an idea.
> We <u>faced up to</u> the problem.
> We <u>walked out on</u> them.

Since these phrasal verbs are active, we would expect them to have corresponding passive forms, as indeed they do.

> *active:* Everyone looked down on us.
> *passive:* We were looked down on by everyone.

Constructions like *give up, turn out,* and *look down on* are simply ignored in traditional schoolroom grammar. One reason why traditional grammar does not discuss phrasal verbs is because of the literal meaning of the word *preposition* in Latin: *prae-* 'before' + *pōnere* 'to place'. Since *preposition* means "to place before," the reasoning is that a preposition could not follow a word that it is connected to. [Recall that phrasal verbs in Latin are formed with the preposition in front of the verb.] If phrasal verbs are mentioned at all in traditional grammars, they are treated as "idioms."

Interestingly, Bishop Lowth, an ultraconservative eighteenth-century grammarian, rejected the conventional traditional analysis and argued instead that these constructions formed new verbs—very much the modern position. Despite Lowth's great prestige, his objections were overwhelmed by the weight of authority given to Latin.

Structural linguistics uncovered an additional striking feature of phrasal verbs: the distinction between *separable* and *inseparable* phrasal verbs. Compare the phrasal verbs in the following sentences.

> a. John depended on the answer.
> b. John found out the answer.

Some phrasal verbs are separable; that is, the preposition can be moved to a position after the object noun phrase. Other phrasal verbs are inseparable; that is, the preposition cannot be moved. *Depend on* is inseparable and *find out* is separable, as we can see from the following paraphrases of the preceding example sentences.

    a. *John depended the answer on.
    b. John found the answer out.

When the object of a separable phrasal verb is a pronoun, the movement of the preposition is actually obligatory. The sentence becomes ungrammatical if the preposition is *not* moved to the position following the object.

    John found it out.
    *John found out it.

Every speaker of English knows that the first sentence is grammatical and the second sentence is ungrammatical. Notice that these two sentences flatly contradict the rule of traditional schoolroom grammar that says that it is incorrect to end sentences with prepositions: in these sentences, it is ungrammatical *not* to end the sentences with prepositions.

■ **Exercise 5.4. Phrasal verbs**

The following sentences all contain verbs followed by a preposition. Indicate phrasal verbs by underlining the verb and the preposition. If the preposition is part of an adverb phrase (i.e., the preposition is not part of a phrasal verb), underline the adverb prepositional phrase. Remember that the passive is a very reliable test for transitive phrasal verbs. (Answers to exercises are found on page 467.)

1. John looked up the word.
2. John looked out the window.
3. They boarded up the windows.
4. She broke off our engagement.
5. The general looked over the situation.
6. We usually turn in after the 10 o'clock news.
7. I turned in my report.
8. Fred turned down the offer.
9. The truck turned down a side road.
10. The well finally dried up.
11. The assembly voted down the motion.
12. The assembly voted on the motion.
13. The assembly voted in the main ballroom.

14. We picked out the bad parts.
15. He always picked on smaller children.
16. We worked in the back yard.
17. I can't put up with that nonsense.

---

3. Modals

In the Indo-European languages (including earlier stages of English) there is a set of verb forms called the *subjunctive mood*. In modern English, only a few distinctive subjunctive forms have survived. The most common recognizable subjunctive form is the use of *were* (in place of the expected *was*) to indicate a wish (e.g., "If I *were* rich . . .") or make a statement contrary to fact (e.g., "If he *were* in your place . . ."). Another, less common, distinct subjunctive form is the use of what appears to be an infinitive in place of an expected third person singular in making requests (e.g., "The committee recommends that the motion *be* tabled"; God *save* the king!"). As the preceding examples illustrate, the subjunctive is moribund, surviving only in the somewhat literary use of *were* and in infinitives used in fixed expressions.

Possibly one reason for the decline of the subjunctive in English (and in the other Germanic languages) was the development in the Germanic branch of Indo-European of a set of helping verbs called *modals* (or modal auxiliaries) that had many of the semantic functions of the subjunctive mood. There are five modal verbs in English: *can, may, must, shall,* and *will.* The modals are used to convey *modality*, an expression of the likelihood that what is being said in a sentence will actually be true or will actually happen. In general, modality (a) reflects such human factors as permission, obligation, and volition, or (b) expresses the probability, possibility, or necessity of the statement's being true or actually happening. For example, there is a world of difference between the following statements about the weather.

It will rain.
It should rain.
It may rain.
It might rain.
It must rain.

The difference in meaning between these five verb forms is neither tense (time) nor aspect (duration), but an expression of the probability, possibility, or necessity of it raining.

The present and past tense forms of modals have very different meanings, but the differences are not related to time. For example, compare the following sentences with the present and past tense forms of the modal *can*.

> *present tense form*: Our team <u>can</u> win tomorrow.
> *past tense form*: Our team <u>could</u> win tomorrow.

The distinction between *can* and *could* is not time. The sentence with the present tense form, *can*, is a statement about our team's capability of winning, while the sentence with the past tense form, *could*, casts considerable doubt on that capability's being realized. Notice also that the past tense form of the modal, *could*, is used with a future time adverb without seeming in the slightest bit odd. This apparently paradoxical situation is possible because *could* does not imply anything about the "time" of the sentence; instead, it implies something about the speaker's confidence (or lack thereof) in the outcome of tomorrow's game.

Since the system of modals (and their range of meanings) is not found in Latin, there is no conventional terminology for describing them in schoolroom traditional grammar. It is as if this important feature of the English verb system did not exist. The one modal that is recognized is the modal *will* as a "future" tense. While it is certainly true that *will* can indicate future time, so can all of the other modal verbs (including the past tense forms).

	<u>can</u>	
	<u>could</u>	
	<u>may</u>	
	<u>might</u>	
John	<u>must</u>	leave for school tomorrow.
	<u>shall</u>	
	<u>should</u>	
	<u>would</u>	

The problem here is with the meaning of the term *tense*. In a narrow sense, the term *tense* means only the finite verb forms, that is, distinctive forms of the main verb without the use of helping verbs. If we broaden the term *tense* to include helping verb plus main verb constructions (e.g., the traditional grammar "future tense" with *will*), then all of the other helping verb combinations listed above are "future" tenses too. There would be as many future tenses as there are different modal verbs. Either we count all the modals (including the past tense forms *could*, *might*, *should*, and *would*) as "future" tenses, or we count none of them (including *will*) and restrict *tense* to finite verb forms.

4. Alternatives
to Traditional Latin-based Analyses of English: Tense

English and Latin are distantly related to each other. In many areas, features of Latin grammar are similar to the corresponding features of English grammar. In these areas the framework of Latin grammar fits English reasonably well. However, there are other areas in which Latin and English are radically different. In these areas the Latinate framework of schoolroom traditional grammars has resulted in descriptions of English that are, at best, misleading. One area with significant mismatch between the structures of the two different languages is the tense system. The terminology and concepts of verb tense that are used in schoolroom traditional grammar are directly borrowed from Latin grammar. Let us begin with a brief (and somewhat simplistic) examination of tense in Latin and then return to English.

Latin verbs have six finite verb forms; that is, forms that can be used in a sentence without the aid of other verbs. These six forms are commonly called *tenses*, named as follows: *present, past, future, present perfect, past perfect*, and *future perfect*. The Latin system is really two-dimensional: (1) *time*—past, present, and future, and (2) *aspect*—a term referring to the state of completion, duration, or repetition of the action of the verb. Latin, like many languages, makes a distinction between (a) action that is ongoing with reference to some moment in time, and (b) action that is completed with respect to some moment in time; these latter forms are called the *perfect* tenses. By way of example, following are the six Latin tense forms for the verb *aedificāre*, 'to build' (a form of which comes into English as the noun *edifice*), in the third-person singular along with approximate English translations.

	Aspect	
	Ongoing	*Perfect (Completed)*
Time		
Present	aedificāt	aedificāvit
	'(he) is building (it) now'	'(he) has built (it) by now'
Past	aedificābat	aedificāverat
	'(he) was building (it) then'	'(he) had built (it) by then'
Future	aedificābit	aedificāverit
	'(he) will be building (it) then'	'(he) will have built (it) by then'

As you can see, none of the six tense forms of Latin is the exact equivalent of any simple form in English. The ongoing state in Latin roughly corresponds to the English progressive (*be* + present participle) in English, and the perfect in Latin roughly corresponds to the English perfect (*have* + past participle). But the two languages are not parallel at all. For example, in Latin the two aspect states (the ongoing and the perfect) are mutually exclusive, but in English the ongoing (progressive) state can be used together with the perfect state; for example, *he has been building it*.

However, an even more significant difference between Latin and English is found in the concept of tense itself. The tense system of English does not make a simple three-way distinction of present, past, and future. English does not have a future tense, and while English has present tense verb forms, English does not mark present time.

In Latin, all verbs have separate finite forms (i.e., forms that can be used by themselves without helping verbs) that signify time: present, past, and future. However, one of the features of the Germanic branch of Indo-European that distinguishes the Germanic branch from all other branches of Indo-European is the complete absence of the future tense. That is, in English, German, Dutch, and the Scandinavian languages, there is no finite verb form that indicates future time. Each language has, of course, developed various helping verb constructions that can express future time, but multi-verb constructions are not *tenses* in the literal meaning of the word *tense*: tense is finite verb form that expresses time.

A second difference between Latin and English tense systems is in the English use of the present verb form. In English the present verb form does not indicate time at all; it indicates *aspect*. Consider, for example, the following present verb form sentences.

Two plus two *is* four.

The sun *rises* in the east.

We *shop* on the weekends.

The present tense form of the verb does not indicate the present time of "now, at this very moment." For example, the sentence *Two plus two is four* does not imply "now." If it did, it would also imply that two plus two was not four at some time in the past and would not be four at some time in the future. The present tense in these sentence means either "eternally true," as in the first two examples, or "habitual or customary," as in the third example. The present verb form in English does not mean "present time" at all; in fact, the present verb form really indicates an action that is outside time altogether. The present verb form belongs to the aspect system rather than the time system.

Can English refer to the present moment? Yes, but not with the present verb form. Compare the following sentences.

Present verb form: The sun *rises* in the east.

Present progressive: The sun *is rising* in the east.

The present verb form (*rises*) implies that it is always the case that the sun rises in the east. Since we can say this sentence in the middle of the night when the sun is not rising, the present tense form does not mean that the sun is in the process of rising now. If we wanted to express the idea that the sun was in the process of rising now, at this moment of present time, we would not use the present tense at all. We would use the present progressive form (*is rising*).

Structural linguistics shows that our conventional, Latin-based terminology for describing tense is misleading in two important ways.

1. Latin has a three-way contrast of finite verb form to indicate three distinct times: present, past, and future. English, however, presents a much more complex picture in its finite verb system. English (together with its Germanic cousins) has no future finite verb form. English indicates future time in the verb system only by the use of helping verbs (supplemented, of course, with future-time adverbs such as *tomorrow*).

2. The present finite verb form in English indicates aspect relation rather than time. Its basic meaning is an action that is either "eternally true" (e.g., *two plus two is four*) or "customary or habitual" (e.g., *we shop on the weekends*). English can indicate present time in the verb system only by the use of the present progressive construction.

SUMMARY

In this chapter we briefly examine the origins of traditional grammar. We have seen that the first grammars of English were deeply influenced by the grammar of Latin, partly because of the prestige of Latin but mostly because Latin grammar (and to a lesser extent, Greek grammar) provided the only available model for describing language. In the eighteenth century, traditional grammar began to play a prescriptive role in determining what was proper usage.

In the nineteenth century, the discovery that Sanskrit was related to Greek and Latin had a number of far-reaching consequences. One consequence was a change in perception of classical Greek and Latin. These languages were now perceived to have been themselves the product of extensive change. Since they could no longer be regarded as immutable embodiments of universal grammar, their grammars also lost their privileged status as universal models. A second consequence was that the process of change obeyed regular rules; change, in other words, was more than just decay and corruption from a higher state to a lower state. A third consequence was that the rules that governed this change could be reconstructed by scientific inquiry. For the first time, then, languages became the topic of systematic, scientific investigation. The historical-descriptive grammarians investigated the history of English as a phenomenon in its own right. These same grammarians began to accurately describe the structures of modern English in nonprescriptive terms.

In the mid-twentieth century, structural linguistics emerged from the study of non-Indo-European languages. Structural linguistics focused on language structures—how words are formed and how words are used in patterns to make larger units. Structural linguists drew a distinction between the study of a language's history (diachronic linguistics) and the study of the users of that language at any one moment in time (synchronic linguistics). Only through studying the latter, they believed, could they understand the actual processes of linguistic behavior—how learners acquire language and how speakers communicate meaning to listeners.

The chapter concludes with a discussion of four specific areas of English grammar in which structural linguistics has gone beyond the framework of traditional grammar: (1) the structural analysis of word formation (and how that analysis can be used to determine part of speech), (2) the identification of a large class of new verbs (phrasal verbs) made up of verb stems plus prepositions, (3) the identification and analysis of an important class of helping verbs (modals), and (4) an analysis of the English tense system that sharply departs from the traditional analysis.

In Chapter 6 we will examine the contribution of transformational grammar, the most important current grammatical theory.

6

Transformational Grammar

INTRODUCTION

In this chapter we examine *transformational grammar*, the most important modern approach to grammatical analysis. Transformational grammar is the invention of Noam Chomsky, a professor at M.I.T. The version of transformational grammar described here is sometimes called "classical" transformational grammar or the "standard theory." This version was first presented in *Syntactic Structures* (Chomsky 1957) and then expanded in *Aspects of the Theory of Syntax* (1965). While there have been extensive developments in transformational grammar since then, the classical version is presented here for the following reasons.

☐ It is the best known form of transformational grammar.

☐ It was the form of transformational grammar that was current when sentence combining (the topic of Chapter 7) was evolving. In fact, some of the features of classical transformational grammar had a profound impact on the development of sentence combining.

☐ It is still the most appropriate form of transformational grammar for dealing with questions of writing style and discussing stylistic choices.

☐ A general knowledge of the classical version of transformational grammar is assumed in most discussions of the more advanced versions.

☐ Classical transformational grammar is relatively easy to grasp intuitively. That is, it can be understood without first mastering a great deal of technical grammatical apparatus. The more modern versions of transformational grammar achieve valuable new insights at the cost of making the grammatical machinery much more complex and technical.

Transformational grammar is hard to describe briefly because, although it grew out of structural linguistics, it has some features that radically differ from all previous types of grammar. We begin this chapter with an overview of the theoretical basis of transformational grammar, and then, as an in-depth sample of how transformational grammar works, examine in detail the transformational treatment of "tense" and helping verbs. In Chapter 7 we examine the most important applied aspect of transformational grammar—*sentence combining*, the process by which a number of simple sentences can be combined to form more complex, adultlike sentences.

THEORETICAL BASIS OF TRANSFORMATIONAL GRAMMAR

All approaches to grammar are rooted in larger intellectual environments that define what grammar is and the issues with which it is concerned. Traditional grammar, with its roots in classical rhetoric and literary studies, was essentially concerned with questions of style and usage. Nineteenth-century linguistics, with its roots in history and the comparative method, was concerned with reconstructing the history of the Indo-European languages. American descriptive linguistics, with its roots in anthropology, was concerned with describing language patterns within contemporary societies.

Transformational grammar has its roots in information science and artificial intelligence. Artificial intelligence is a rapidly developing field of study. A major component of this field is the replication in artificial systems—mathematical models, computers, or robots, for example— of the kind of intelligence that humans possess. Only through attempts to replicate human intelligence artificially do we gain any real insight into the awesome complexity of what we are born to do intuitively and effortlessly. Artificial intelligence enables us to stand outside ourselves, as it were, and see how complex human cognitive processes really are.

Perhaps an example of artificial intelligence from another field will make the point clearer. A major undertaking in artificial intelligence is the development of industrial robots that can see. There is no difficulty in attaching a TV camera to a robot. The trick is in getting the robot to interpret what the camera sees. For example, a robot can be programmed to recognize the appearance of an object. However, if that object is rotated even a few degrees, the robot no longer can recognize it as the same object because it no longer looks the same. Humans, however, can recognize a known object when seen from a number of perspectives. In other words, we have a mental perception of an object in three-dimensional space that goes far beyond the two-dimensional image that each of our eyes actually sees.

Our eyes and brain are built to see and perceive the world in a certain manner and in no other—we cannot suddenly choose to see the world as a frog does. In a way we (and all other living creatures) are prisoners of our own genetically determined systems. Likewise, our genetic endowment has determined the structure that human languages can take, and we can no more go outside that structure than a prisoner can leave his cell. The language rules we have developed for English since childhood have further determined our adult language. Accordingly, since we always function within the compass of our internalized rule system for language, we are seldom aware of the limits of our rule system or that the system even exists. Eighteenth-century grammarians, for example, urged the study of English as a prerequisite for studying Latin because English was so simple. English, it was said, had no grammar. Nothing, in fact, could be farther from the truth.

However, we do become aware of the existence of our rules when we encounter people—children and non-native speakers of our language—who have a different and conflicting set of rules. Alternatively, and more to our purpose here, we can become aware of the existence and even gain some conscious insight into the nature of our internal rules by constructing an artificial set of rules that duplicates the output of our intuitive rules. In other words, if our artificial rules can produce exactly the same sentences with the same structure that our intuitive rules produce, then we have developed a powerful model for describing our internal rule system. This model is a description of our linguistic capacity; it is not, however, a model of the process that actually takes place within our brain.

This is what transformational grammar is—a set of artificial rules that mimic our intuitive knowledge of our language. Our intuitive set of rules is so fully internalized that we have little more conscious awareness of how the rules work than we have of how our eyes and brain enable us to see. By creating and studying a set of artificial rules that mimic our ability, we can gain considerable insight into our intuitive, internalized rule system. Through the approach of transformational grammar we have learned more about English and language in general in the last thirty years than we have learned in all of previous history.

Chomsky's artificial intelligence approach to language is centered around the following two questions:

☐ When we say that native speakers of a language have an intuitive knowledge of their language, what is it exactly that they know?

☐ How can we describe (i.e., replicate) that intuitive knowledge in a formal, explicit, and conscious manner?

Chomsky's answer to the first question is that native speakers of a language are able to (1) distinguish between all possible sentences that are grammatical in their language and all possible sentences that are ungrammatical in their language, and (2) recognize the structure of grammatical sentences.

The first ability, the ability to distinguish between all possible grammatical and ungrammatical sentences, is not concerned with questions of divided usage, in which the grammatical systems of different people conflict with one another (something that eighteenth-century traditional grammarians were mainly concerned with). Rather, Chomsky is talking about how each of us can distinguish between sentences that are grammatical and ungrammatical in terms of our own systems.

All of us have a strong sense of grammaticality that has nothing to do with either prior experience of a particular sentence or conscious knowledge of the "rules" of English. The number of possible sentences in English is so vast that every sentence we encounter is new to us (except for ritualized greetings and other such conventional expressions). For example, how many sentences on this page can you recall having read or heard before? To take another example, it is highly unlikely that you have ever seen the following sentence.

A number of peanut butter and jelly sandwiches have been placed into earth orbit by a powerful merry-go-round.

Yet through your intuitive knowledge of English you know that this is a grammatical sentence. Likewise, you have never seen this same sentence with the words backwards.

Merry-go-round powerful a by orbit earth into placed been have sandwiches jelly and butter peanut of number a.

Yet through your intuitive knowledge of English you know that this is an impossibly ungrammatical sentence. Our ability to make this kind of judgment is so effortless that it is easy to overlook the magnitude of the knowledge that makes the judgment possible. Perhaps shifting to an unknown language will make the idea clearer; for example, consider how much Japanese you would have to know before you could instantly and unhesitatingly decide which of millions of different combinations of Japanese words constituted grammatical Japanese sentences and which constituted ungrammatical sentences.

The point about our lack of conscious knowledge of the "rules" of English is perhaps less obvious. Most speakers of most languages in the world have never studied their own language, yet they all have very strong opinions about what is and is not correct. [A linguist friend of mine once worked on a nearly extinct native American language that had only two living speakers. The two speakers, first-cousins, each confided to my friend that the other was not a very good speaker of the language.] Likewise, few of us could cite any "rules" to explain why our language works the way it does. To take just one example, compare the positive and negative forms of the following two sentences.

	Positive	*Negative*
1.	John has taken a nap.	John has not taken a nap.
2.	John took a nap.	John did not take a nap.

In sentence 1 we can make the sentence negative merely by adding *not*. However, in sentence 2 we must add a new word: *did* in addition to *not*. Why do we add *did* to the negative of sentence 2 but not to the negative of sentence 1? What role or function does *did* play in sentence 2? Why is the main verb in the positive of 2 a past tense (*took*) while the main verb in the negative of 2 is an infinitive (*take*) while the verb forms in sentence 1 do not change similarly? All speakers of English have internalized the rules governing these sentences, yet few of us could offer any explanation to a foreigner who asked us about them.

Our ability to make judgments about the grammaticality of sentences is based on our second ability—the ability to recognize the structure of grammatical sentences. Grammatical sentences are those that are formed in accord with our intuitive knowledge of sentence structure. Ungrammatical sentences are those that are not in accord with our sense of correct structure.

Chomsky characterizes our sense of sentence structure as a huge set of internalized rules that governs the structural formation of sentences. Chomsky has illustrated both the existence and the incredible complexity of these rules by the following pair of sentences.

1. John believes he is intelligent.
2. John believes him to be intelligent.

The pronoun *he* in sentence 1 is ambiguous: it can refer to *John* or it can refer to somebody else—Fred, say. However, in sentence 2 the pronoun *him* cannot possibly refer to *John*. It must refer to somebody else not named in the sentence. All mature native speakers of English know the difference in pronoun reference in this pair of sentences without any prior explanation—and without any conscious knowledge of *how* they know. Chomsky's point, of course, is that we could have this knowledge only through our having a complex set of internalized rules that govern the structure of these and similar sentences.

It is this set of rules that children and non-native speakers often violate, producing sentences that are perfectly plausible from the standpoint of their developing systems, but that are ungrammatical from the standpoint of mature native speakers.

*There is a fly in my soup, isn't it?

*I am knowing what means that.

*I turned the radio just now on.

Even though native speakers cannot always articulate what rules these sentences have broken, we are, nonetheless, keenly aware of the fact that rules have been broken. We have so fully internalized this elaborate set of sentence structure rules that we are unaware of their existence until someone breaks them. In other words, even though we do not know the rules (consciously), we act as though we did.

Another aspect of our internalized rule system is manifested by our ability to determine when a sentence is *structurally ambiguous* or when two different sentences are *structural paraphrases* of each other. A sentence that is structurally ambiguous has one structure or form, but it has two distinct meanings. Consider the possible interpretations of the following example from *Syntactic Structures*:

the shooting of the hunters

The phrase has one form but two meanings.

1. The hunters were shooting.
2. The hunters were being shot.

Note that the ambiguity of this phrase is in the structure, not the words; neither *hunters* nor *shooting* is ambiguous in itself. It is their combination in this particular structure that creates the ambiguity.

The opposite situation, paraphrase, occurs when two different sentence forms have the same meaning and are structurally related in a systematic manner. The two different sentences are in a very real sense the same sentence. A good illustration of structural paraphrase is found in sentences with separable phrasal verbs.

1	*2*
She called up her parents.	She called her parents up.
I took back the pump.	I took the pump back.
Johnson knocked out Smith.	Johnson knocked Smith out.
They turned down the idea.	They turned the idea down.

Clearly, the sentences in columns 1 and 2 mean exactly the same thing. Moreover, the structure of the sentences in the two columns differs in a systematic way: in the sentences in column 1, the preposition precedes the object noun phrase, while in column 2 the preposition follows the object noun phrase.

The relationship between the active and the passive illustrates how complex paraphrase relationships can be.

Active: John saw Mary.

Passive: Mary was seen by John.

The two sentences have totally different forms: *John* is the subject of the active sentence while *Mary* is the subject of the passive sentence. The verb phrase in the active sentence is a simple past tense *saw* while there is a past tense helping verb (*was*) and a past participle verb form (*seen*) in the passive. In the active sentence the verb is followed by an object while in the passive the verb is followed by a prepositional phrase. These two sentences are totally unalike in form, yet every speaker of English knows that they are really variants of the same basic sentence.

To recapitulate: our knowledge of a language is manifested in our ability to (1) distinguish between grammatical and ungrammatical sentences in our language, and (2) recognize the structure of grammatical sentences, including our ability to recognize structural ambiguity within a sentence and structural paraphrase relationships between sentences. These abilities reflect a highly complex set of internalized, unconscious rules that govern the proper structure of English sentences. Grammatical sentences are those sentences whose structure conforms to the unconscious rules. Conversely, ungrammatical sentences are those whose structure violates some aspect of the unconscious rules.

In response to the second question—how we describe or characterize our knowledge of language in a formal, explicit manner—a transformational grammar creates a set of formal, explicit rules that replicate or mimic the structures that our internal, unconscious rules create. That is, the rules of a transformational grammar of English must correctly do what we do, namely, (1) distinguish between grammatical and ungrammatical English sentences and (2) determine the structure of grammatical sentences, including the recognition of structural ambiguity within a sentence and structural paraphrase relationships between sentences. The rules of a transformational grammar must produce sentences that conform to our own intuition about the grammaticality and structure of those sentences. Otherwise, the rules of the transformational grammar are wrong and must be corrected.

In this sense transformational grammar and traditional grammar are complete opposites. In traditional grammar the "rules" exist outside of and are often contrary to the intuition of native speakers. Bishop Lowth, for example, claimed that the works of even our greatest writers were filled with errors. In transformational grammar, on the other hand, when the grammar's rules and our intuition disagree, our intuition is always right and the grammar is wrong because the transformational grammarian is trying to describe that intuitive knowledge.

The linguist's rules are meaningful only to the extent that they produce sentences that conform to human intuition of their correctness and structure.

HOW CLASSICAL
TRANSFORMATIONAL GRAMMAR WORKS

The classical transformational grammar for English consists of two components—two sets of artificial rules. The first set, called *phrase structure rules*, produces abstract grammatical structures that, when married to vocabulary, generate basic sentences. These basic sentences are grammatical abstractions that underlie real sentences. For this reason these basic sentences are called *deep structures*. Following is how the deep structure that underlies the sentence *Tom painted the fence today* might be represented.

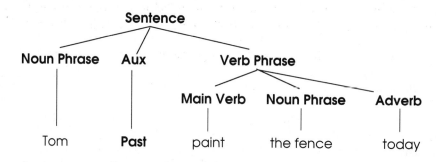

In this deep structure analysis, called a *phrase structure tree*, the sentence consists of three elements: (1) a subject noun phrase, (2) an auxiliary (Aux), the source for tense and for helping verbs, and (3) a verb phrase. [The term *phrase* in transformational grammar is used in a slightly different way from its use in Chapter 3. For example, the term *noun phrase* is used as the source point of personal pronouns and of all nouns, whether accompanied by modifiers or not. In Chapter 3 the term *noun phrase* means a head noun plus its modifiers—as opposed to a noun used without modifiers.]

The verb phrase, in turn, consists of three elements: the main verb, an object noun phrase, and finally an adverb. As you can see, except for separating out the auxiliary element, the deep structure analysis for this particular sentence is not very different from the analysis that would be given in traditional grammar.

The second set of rules, the *transformational rules*, converts abstract deep structures into representations of actual sentences, called *surface structures*. In the preceding deep structure example, a transformational rule would attach the past tense marker to the following verb, transforming Past + *paint* into the actual word *painted*, producing the surface sentence.

Tom painted the fence today.

In this case the transformational rules made minimal changes in deriving the surface structure from the underlying deep structure. A surface sentence that is derived from a deep structure with only obligatory, housekeeping transformational rules (as in the preceding example) is called a *kernel* sentence. A *nonkernel* sentence is one in which one or more optional transformational rules have been used to derive a paraphrase of the kernel sentence. For our discussion in Chapter 7, the concept of kernel sentences is especially important in sentence combining.

A single deep structure can be transformed into a number of related surface sentences by applying different optional transformational rules. To illustrate, the deep structure of the preceding example can be transformed into a passive surface structure.

The fence was painted by Tom today.

In this case, the transformational rules have considerably reshaped the surface sentence. The complexity of the transformations involved and the relative distance of the surface structure from the underlying deep structure suggest why it takes many years before children are able to construct the correct grammatical relationship between active and passive sentences in their intuitive internal rule system. [Carol Chomsky has conducted quite insightful research on children's acquisition of the passive (C. Chomsky 1969).]

In transformational terms, the active and passive have the same basic meaning precisely because they share a single common ancestor—the same deep structure. The differences in surface form between the active and passive sentences are due solely to their different derivational history in the transformational rule component. The active version is a kernel sentence—it has had only low-level obligatory transformational rules applied to it, whereas the optional passive has been formed by the application of three rules: a rule that reversed the subject and object, a rule that added *by*, and a rule that added the passive helping verb *be* (*was* in this case). Note that the transformational rules affect the form of sentences, but they do not radically affect the basic meaning. In other words, optional transformational rules create paraphrases of the kernel sentence.

Following is another example of an optional transformational rule. Whenever we have a sentence that contains both a direct and an indirect object in the deep structure, we can apply an optional transformational rule called the *dative switch*. The dative switch transformation reverses the order of the indirect object (IO) and the direct object (DO) and inserts a preposition, usually *to* or *for*.

1. *Deep structure:*   John Past give <u>Fred a message</u>
                                  IO   DO

   Dative switch: John Past give <u>a message</u> *to* <u>Fred</u>
                                    DO   IO

   Surface structure: John gave a message to Fred

2. *Deep structure:*   John Past find <u>Fred a typewriter</u>
                                  IO   DO

   Dative switch: John Past find <u>a typewriter</u> *for* <u>Fred</u>
                                  DO   IO

   Surface structure: John found a typewriter for Fred.

One of the most powerful aspects of the transformational rules is that the rules can be combined. That is, the output of one transformational rule can become the input for a second transformational rule. For example, the dative switch and the passive can be combined. From the deep structure *John past give Fred a message* we can produce this structure by the dative switch transformation:

   Deep structure: John Past give Fred a message
   Dative switch: John Past give a message to Fred
   Surface structure: John gave a message to Fred.

We can stop here, having produced a grammatical surface structure. However, we also have the option of applying the passive transformation to the output of the dative switch before the surface structure is reached to produce a new surface structure that is a passive version of the preceding example sentence.

   Dative switch: John Past give a message to Fred
   Passive: A message Past be Past Part give to Fred by John
   Surface structure: A message was given to Fred by John.

In this particular case, one deep structure underlies four separate surface structures.

   Deep structure: John Past give Fred a message
   1. *Kernel (no optional transformations):*   John gave Fred a message.
   2. *Passive of deep structure:*   Fred was given a message by John.
   3. *Dative switch of deep structure:*   John gave a message to Fred.
   4. *Dative switch + Passive:*   A message was given to Fred by John.

Note that the four surface structures, despite their rather considerable difference in form, mean the same thing—they are all *paraphrases* of one another precisely because they come from the same underlying deep structure.

■ **Exercise 6.1. Deep and surface structures**

For each of the deep structures below, provide the following corresponding surface forms: (1) kernel, (2) passive, (3) dative switch, and (4) dative switch + passive. The first is done as an example. (Answers to exercises are found on page 468.)

1. The sergeant Past hand Leon the grenade
   Kernel: The sergeant handed Leon the grenade.
   Passive: Leon was handed a grenade by the sergeant.
   Dative switch: The sergeant handed the grenade to Leon.
   Dative switch + Passive: The grenade was handed to Leon by the sergeant.
2. You Past find Aunt Sally a table
3. They Past tell me all their secrets
4. I Past order you dinner
5. The owner of the restaurant Past serve us our dinner
6. We Past reserve them a place
7. The operator Past read me the telegram
8. His thoughtfulness Past spare us a lot of trouble
9. He Past owe me some money
10. The waiter Past bring us the check
11. The IRS Past do me a big favor
12. The agency Past sell them the house
13. The pitcher Past throw the catcher the ball
14. She Past offer me her hand
15. We Past teach old dogs new tricks

The various surface structures derived from a single underlying deep structure are paraphrases of one another. We may represent *paraphrase* relationships schematically as follows.

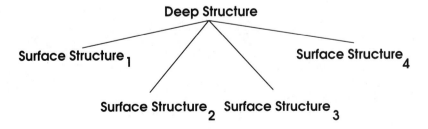

There is no absolute limit to the number of surface structures (sentences) that can be derived from a single deep structure. One textbook on transformational grammar has an example in which 128 different surface structure paraphrases could be derived from one deep structure, all of them retaining the same basic meaning of the common ancestor deep structure.

The opposite of paraphrase is *structural ambiguity* (i.e., ambiguity that is the result of grammar or structure, as opposed to the ambiguity that results from a single word having more than one dictionary meaning—e.g., *bank* of a river and a savings *bank*). Ambiguity results when two (or more) different deep structures happen to have surface forms that are identical to each other. Since the two different surface forms come from different deep structures, they must mean different things. Consider the following two different deep structures.

> *Deep structure 1:* The hunters Past shoot something
> *Kernel:* The hunters shot something.
> *Deep structure 2:* Somebody Past shoot the hunters
> *Kernel:* Somebody shot the hunters.

Each of these deep structures underlies a number of different surface structures in addition to the kernel. Among the many structures that can be derived from these two deep structures are a number of different verbal phrases. It so happens, essentially by accident, that one of the gerund phrases from deep structure 1 is exactly identical in form with one of the gerund phrases from deep structure 2.

the shooting of the hunters

In other words, the fact that the preceding gerund phrase (a surface structure) can be derived from two different deep structures means that the gerund phrase must have two different meanings. The particular surface structure gerund phrase is an example of structural ambiguity because it can be derived from two different deep structures.

We may represent structural *ambiguity* as follows (SS = surface structure).

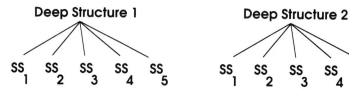

Deep Structure 1   **Deep Structure 2**

SS₁ SS₂ SS₃ SS₄ SS₅   SS₁ SS₂ SS₃ SS₄ SS₅

[Where some surface structure from Deep Structure 1 is accidentally identical in form with some surface structure from Deep Structure 2]

The existence of ambiguity and paraphrase relations among surface sentences shows that form and meaning are not related in a simple one-to-one manner. In cases of structural ambiguity, a single surface form is derived from more than one deep structure; in fact, there are as many different deep structures as there are structural ambiguities in the surface sentence. In paraphrase relationships, two (or more) different surface forms are derived from a single deep structure. The deep structure establishes the meaning of sentences, while the transformational rules establish the variety of forms that come from the deep structures.

So far we have examined how the transformational rules change the form of single deep structures. The transformational component has another important function, which we examine in detail Chapter 7: combining multiple deep structures to produce a single complex surface structure (sentence combining). However, in the remaining portion of this chapter we will examine as case studies the rules that govern the formation of tense and helping verbs and the rules that govern the formation of the passive.

TENSE AND HELPING VERBS

When Chomsky's *Syntactic Structures* was first published in 1957, perhaps the aspect of transformational grammar that won the first converts was Chomsky's highly innovative approach to tense and helping verbs.

In Chapter 5 we discussed some problems that traditional grammar has with the conventional concept of tense. As you recall, the English tense system does not at all conform to the simple three-way time distinction between past-present-future. In fact, the main verb has no tense form that signals future time, nor does the so-called present tense normally mean present time. In English a finite verb (a verb used without any helping verbs) has only two tense *forms*—present and past.

In a transformational grammar the term *tense* refers only to verb *form*, not to *meaning*. Thus, in transformational grammar when we say that *sang* is the past tense of *sing*, we are talking only about the form of the verb; we are not talking about the meaning of the past tense. Likewise, when we say that *sing/sings* are the present forms of the verb *sing*, we are talking only about the form of the verb; we are not saying anything about what that form of the verb means. This distinction between tense form and the meaning of that tense form is critically important for the following discussion. Remember, the terms *present tense* and *past tense* refer only to the form of verbs, not their meaning.

In the phrase structure component of transformational grammar, the basic sentence consists of three components: the subject noun phrase, the auxiliary, and the verb phrase. The auxiliary and the verb phrase together comprise what is called the complete predicate in traditional grammar terms.

Traditional: complete subject   - complete predicate
Transformational: subject noun phrase - auxiliary + verb phrase

One reason why transformation makes a distinction between the auxiliary and the verb phrase is that the verb phrase can appear without the auxiliary. Consider the following sentence.

John made Fred answer the question.

Answer the question is a verb phrase, but it is a verb phrase that has no accompanying auxiliary which would provide a tense marker. If there were a tense marker accompanying the verb *answer*, the result would be an ungrammatical sentence with a third-person singular *-s*.

*John made Fred *answers* the question.

The auxiliary component (Aux) in a transformational grammar must always contain a tense marker, and that marker must be either present or past. We can represent these requirements in the following manner.

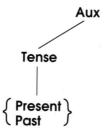

The braces {} mean a mutually exclusive choice: choose either *Present* or *Past*, but not both. Following is a sample derivation involving the present tense.

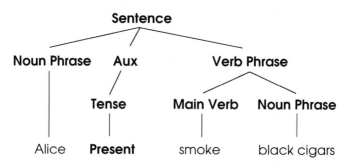

In order to convert this deep structure to a kernel surface structure, we need to apply a transformational rule called the *affix movement* rule. This obligatory transformational rule attaches *verb affixes* (present or past tense markers plus present participle and past participle markers) to the verb that immediately follows the verb affix. In this case the affix movement rule will attach the present tense marker to the verb *smoke*, producing the present tense surface form *smokes*. In the deep structure the main verb is an infinitive (without the *to* that infinitives have when they are used as verbals). In fact, all verbs in the deep structure are infinitives and stay infinitives unless the affix movement rule attaches a verb affix to them. In the example of the preceding diagram, the main verb, *smoke*, acquires tense only by the operation of the affix movement rule. If the deep structure had included a past tense marker rather than a present tense marker, the affix movement rule would attach the past tense marker to *smoke*, producing the past tense surface form *smoked*.

Following is how the affix movement rule converts the deep structure into the surface structure.

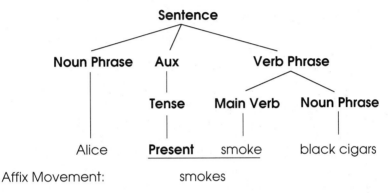

In this case, affix movement attaches the present tense marker to the infinitive verb *smoke*, producing the present tense form *smokes*.

The past tense is done in exactly the same manner.

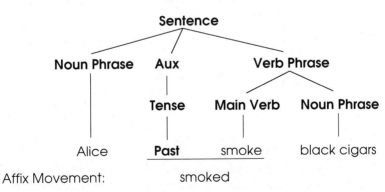

In order to save space in writing out phrase structure trees, you may use the following abbreviations in place of structure-related terms.

AM	Affix Movement	NP	Noun Phrase
MV	Main Verb	VP	Verb Phrase

■ **Exercise 6.2. Present and past tense**

Draw phrase structure trees and apply the affix movement rule to produce the following surface sentences. (Answers to exercises are found on page 469.)

1. Louise broke the record.
2. The committee offered a prize.
3. An asterisk indicates an ungrammatical sentence.
4. The students passed the course.
5. The King is a fink.
6. I lost my place.
7. We have a nuclear-powered pencil sharpener.
8. They see us.
9. We need some more coffee.
10. I love banana splits.

In addition to tense, the auxiliary is also the source for three types of optional helping verbs: *Modals*, the *Perfect*, and the *Progressive*. In order to be grammatical, every sentence must contain a present or past tense marker, but no sentence must contain a helping verb to be grammatical. If more than one helping verb appears in the same sentence, the helping verbs must be used in the order that they are given in this paragraph: first a modal, then the perfect, and finally, the progressive. Our discussion treats them one by one.

1. Modals

The modals are a family of five verbs: *can, may, must, shall,* and *will.* (Recall that all verbs in the deep structure, including modals, are in the infinitive, or dictionary, form until the affix movement rule attaches a tense marker to them.) The present and past tense forms of these verbs are highly irregular. For example, they are the only verbs in English that do not have a third person singular form ending in -(e)s. That is, we would not say *he cans, *he mays, *he musts, *he shalls,* and *he wills.* The reason for this peculiarity is that, historically, the present tense modal auxiliary forms were past tense forms and naturally, as past tenses, did not have present tense forms. These past tense forms replaced their corresponding present tense forms, and then a new past tense was created. Thus, for example, modern English *can* was historically a past tense form. *Can* became a present tense form, and then a new past tense form, *could,* filled the void. New past tenses were created for all of the modal auxiliaries except *must.* For some reason, when *must* became a present tense, no new past tense was created for it.

We now expand the rules for auxiliary to include modal auxiliaries.

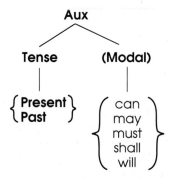

The parentheses ( ) around *modal* means that the element so marked is optional. In other words, English grammar does not require that a sentence contain a modal to be grammatical. There are no parentheses around tense because tense is obligatory: every grammatical sentence in English must contain a tense marker. Following is a sample derivation of a sentence containing a modal.

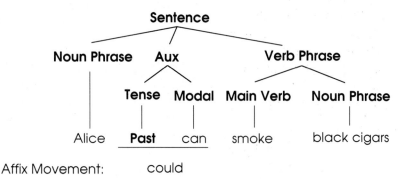

The affix movement rule attaches the tense marker (*Past* in this case) to the following verb, changing the infinitive modal *can* into the past tense form *could*:

> Alice could smoke black cigars.

There are several important points to make about the structure of this sentence. First, note that when we add a modal, the main verb *smoke* stays as an infinitive (i.e., it stays in its deep structure form). Nothing happens to the deep structure form of *smoke* because the tense marker is attached to the modal auxiliary verb *can*. Compare the two sentences:

1. Alice <u>smokes</u> black cigars.
2. Alice <u>can smoke</u> black cigars.

In sentence 1 the tense marker is attached to the main verb *smoke*. In sentence 2, the tense marker is attached to the modal auxiliary verb *can*. (Remember, in sentence 2, *can* is not an infinitive—it is the present tense surface form of the verb *can*).

Second, note that we can always predict exactly which verb will carry the tense marker—it is the first verb in the sequence. If there is a modal auxiliary in the deep structure, the tense marker—Present or Past—will attach to it, leaving the main verb unaffected. If there is no modal, the tense marker will attach to whatever verb comes first. In the case of sentence 1, the verb that comes first is the main verb *smoke*, and thus the tense marker attaches to it. In the case of sentence 2, the verb that comes first is the modal *can*, and thus the tense marker attaches to it, leaving the following verb (*smoke*) in its infinitive form. Put in more general terms, when we have a string of verbs, the only verb that is finite (i.e., carries a past or present tense marker) is the first verb. All following verbs will be nonfinite forms.

Third, note how the phrase structure and transformational rules interact to capture exactly how the English system works. In the deep structure (as produced by the phrase structure rules), tense is a prefix rather than the normal suffix. By building in the tense marker in the first position in the deep structure and by supplying the affix movement transformational rule, which attaches tense to whatever verb comes next, Chomsky guarantees that the rules will always work. Moreover, the rules capture a significant generalization about English—namely, there is only one tense marker per clause and it always attaches to the first verb. This is a good illustration of the way that a transformational grammar creates a set of artificial rules that replicate our intuitive knowledge about the structure of English sentences.

■ **Exercise 6.3. Modals**

Draw phrase structure trees and apply the affix movement rule to produce the following surface sentences (a few sentences without modals are included). (Answers to exercises are found on page 472.)

1. I might have a cold.
2. The garage should change the oil.
3. The fertilizer will increase the yield.
4. Bill brought the balloons.
5. Felix would like the movie.
6. Dorothy followed the Yellow Brick Road.
7. The book may provide an answer.
8. You must meet my Uncle Wilber.

9. A diamond can cut glass.

10. That may be the answer.

---

2. Perfect

The second optional element in the auxiliary system is the perfect. The perfect consists of two components: the helping verb *have* and a past participle affix (Past Part). Compare the following sentences:

Present:	Alice sees Fred.
Present Perfect:	Alice has seen Fred.
Past:	Alice saw Fred.
Past perfect:	Alice had seen Fred.

When we add the perfect, we make two additions, not one, to the sentence.

1. We add the helping verb *have* (in either its present or past form, depending on the tense marker), and

2. we change the form of the verb that follows *have* by adding to it a past participle marker; for example, in the preceding sentences, *see* was changed to *seen*. *Seen* is the past participle form of *see*. (You may find it helpful to review the discussion of past participle forms in Chapter 3.)

Following is how the perfect is built into the auxiliary (ignoring modals for the moment).

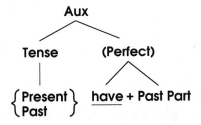

Note that *Perfect* is in parentheses because the perfect is an optional element—no sentence is required to have the perfect in order to be grammatical. The perfect is either present or past, depending on whether the tense marker is Present or Past. *Past Part* is an affix—a marker that is attached to the following verb by the affix movement rule. When it is attached to a verb, that verb will then be in the past participle form. Following are examples of derivations containing perfects.

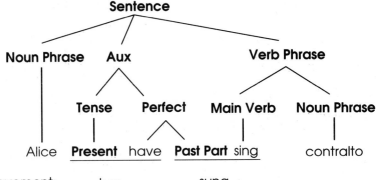

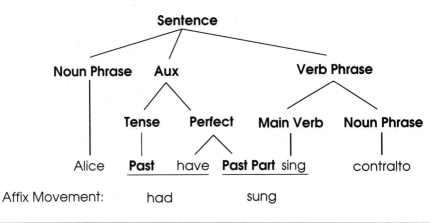

The affix movement rule now applies twice: it attaches the present tense marker to the following verb, *have*, producing *has* (*has* = *have* + Present), and it attaches the Past Part affix to the verb that follows it, *sing*, producing *sung* (*sung* = *sing* + Past Participle). Following is the same sentence with a past tense marker.

■ **Exercise 6.4. Perfect**

Draw phrase structure trees and apply the affix movement rule to produce the following surface sentences. (A few sentences without perfects are included.) (Answers to exercises are found on page 474.)

1. John has brushed his teeth.
2. John had brushed his teeth.
3. The conference has chosen a theme.
4. A student had reported the accident.
5. Leon has accepted his fate.
6. The ruling had established a precedent.
7. Portia faces life.
8. I have caught a fish.

9. We should limit the discussion.

10. They have attempted the impossible.

---

3. Progressive

The third optional element that can occur in the auxiliary is the progressive. Like the perfect, the progressive also consists of two parts. Compare the following sentences.

Present:	Alice <u>sings</u> contralto.
Present Progressive:	Alice <u>is singing</u> contralto.
Past:	Alice <u>sang</u> contralto.
Past Progressive:	Alice <u>was singing</u> contralto.

We have created the sentences in the progressive form by adding two elements.

1. the helping verb *be* (in the present or past form depending on which tense form was selected), and
2. the present participle marker (*-ing*), which is attached to the main verb *sing*.

You can probably guess how the progressive is built into the auxiliary system (ignoring modals and the perfect for the moment).

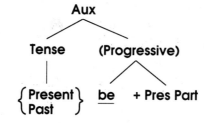

Following are some examples of derivations containing a progressive.

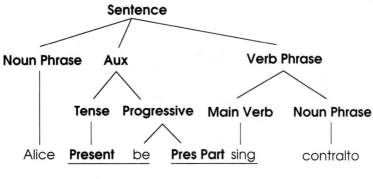

The affix movement rule applies twice: it attaches the present tense marker to the following verb, *be* in this case, and it attaches the present participle affix (*-ing*) to the following main verb, *sing* in this case, producing a present progressive, *singing*. This sentence is called a *present progressive* because it contains a present tense marker and the progressive. Following is the same sentence with a past tense marker.

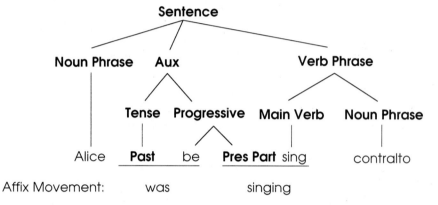

This sentence is called a *past progressive* because it contains a past tense marker and the progressive.

■ **Exercise 6.5. Progressive**

Draw phrase structure trees and apply the affix movement rule to produce the following surface sentences. (A few sentences without progressives are included.) (Answers to exercises are found on page 477.)

1. Sam is directing a play.
2. Sam was directing a play.
3. She is leading a discussion group.
4. I was painting the deck.
5. Garrick is organizing a dinner party.
6. You can identify the subject.
7. Holmes is a consulting detective.
8. The quartet was playing Mozart.
9. It had touched a nerve.
10. They were checking the records.

Let us briefly recapitulate. In transformational grammar, there are two components: a *phrase structure* component and a *transformational* component. The phrase structure component produces abstract grammatical structures called *deep structures*. The transformational component then converts these abstract structures to representations of actual sentences called *surface structures*. If only obligatory transformational rules are used, the surface structures are called *kernel* sentences. Optional transformational rules rearrange and combine deep structures to produce more complex, adultlike sentences.

The deep structure consists of three elements in this fixed order: (1) *noun phrase*, which is the source for subject nouns and pronouns, (2) *auxiliary*, which is the source for the tense marker and helping verbs, and (3) *verb phrase*. The verb phrase is the source for three subcomponents: (1) the *main verb*, (2) whatever the main verb requires to make a complete sentence—in all of the examples in this chapter, this element will be a *noun phrase*, which is the source for object nouns and pronouns, and (3) an optional element, *adverb*, which is the source for all optional adverbs and adverb phrases.

The auxiliary always begins with a *tense* marker. Tense refers solely to verb form, not meaning. Tense markers are either *present* or *past*— there is no finite future verb form in English. The tense marker and the two participle affixes (Pres Part and Past Part) are attached to whatever verb follows it by an obligatory transformational rule called the *affix movement* rule. Following the tense marker are sources for three optional helping verbs in the following order:

1. **Modal** (*can, may, must, shall,* and *will*)

2. **Perfect** (*have* plus a *past participle* marker; the past participle marker will be attached to the following verb by the affix movement rule)

3. **Progressive** (*be* plus a *present participle* marker; the present participle marker will be attached to the following main verb by the affix movement rule)

The fixed left-to-right order of the optional elements in the auxiliary is captured by the complete rule for the auxiliary.

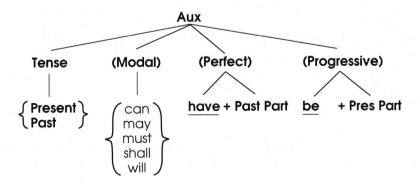

The affix movement rule attaches the tense marker to whatever verb immediately follows the tense marker. If there is a modal in the derivation of a particular sentence, then the modal will receive the tense marker. If there is no modal, the next element in line to receive the tense marker is the perfect helping verb *have*. If there is no perfect, then the next element is the progressive helping verb *be*. If there are no helping verbs in the auxiliary, then the tense marker attaches to the main verb, the first element in the verb phrase component, which immediately follows the auxiliary component. The application of the affix movement rule is necessary for the generation of all surface structures. In other words, the first verb (whether helping verb or main verb) in every sentence must carry a present or past tense marker.

Following are examples of all the different combinations of optional helping verbs (using *may* as the modal), first in the present tense and then in the past tense.

Present Tense

Present
Alice <u>sings</u> contralto.

Present + Modal
Alice <u>may sing</u> contralto.

Present + Perfect
Alice <u>has sung</u> contralto.

Present + Progressive
Alice <u>is singing</u> contralto.

Present + Modal + Perfect
Alice <u>may have sung</u> contralto.

Present + Modal + Progressive
Alice <u>may be singing</u> contralto.

Present + Perfect + Progressive
Alice <u>has been singing</u> contralto.

Present + Modal + Perfect + Progressive
Alice <u>may have been singing</u> contralto.

Past Tense

Past
Alice <u>sang</u> contralto.

Past + Modal
Alice <u>might sing</u> contralto.

Past + Perfect
Alice <u>had sung</u> contralto.

Past + Progressive
Alice was singing contralto.

Past + Modal + Perfect
Alice might have sung contralto.

Past + Modal + Progressive
Alice might be singing contralto.

Past + Perfect + Progressive
Alice had been singing contralto.

Past + Modal + Perfect + Progressive
Alice might have been singing contralto.

■ **Exercise 6.6. Order and names of auxiliary verbs**

Rewrite the auxiliary verbs in the correct order and name the auxiliary sequence. The first is done as an example. (Answers to exercises are found on page 479.)

1. Alice singing been have should contralto
   should have been singing   (Past modal perfect progressive)
2. We been have avoiding the issue
3. The tips touching be could
4. They been have examining the issue
5. I known have might
6. Leon have working been should in the kitchen
7. Everyone have finished will by now
8. Henry been visiting had his old mother
9. Leon collecting been might have bottle caps
10. The gift surprised have must them
11. He have ignored should the question
12. We participating have should been in the activities
13. Harry struggled had against fate
14. You afford can it
15. They been may have dancing
16. I had had the question before
17. Louise being was difficult

The affix movement rule applies to three elements in the phrase structure: tense (either present or past), the past participle from the perfect, and the present participle from the progressive. In transformational terminology, these three elements are collectively called *affixes*. Thus, the affix movement rule performs one function: it causes every affix in the deep structure to attach to whatever verb immediately follows that affix. The operation of the rule is automatic: in order for a grammatical surface structure to be produced, every affix in the deep structure must be attached to the verb that immediately follows it.

[Is it ever possible that an affix is *not* followed by a verb so that the affix movement rule cannot apply? Yes, under certain special circumstances, the tense marker can be separated from its following verb. When this situation arises, we make the affix movement rule apply by creating a dummy verb (bizarre as this may sound) for the tense marker to attach to. We discuss this strange, but very common, phenomenon in the following section.]

Following is a derivation for *Alice has been singing contralto*, a sentence that uses all three affixes.

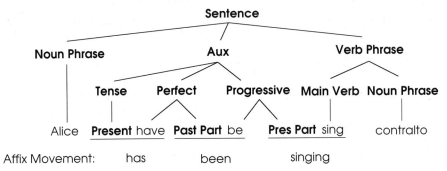

The affix movement rule applies three times.

1. It attaches the present tense marker to *have*,
2. it attaches the past participle to *be*, and
3. it attaches the present participle to the main verb *sing*.

Thus, despite their complete difference in form and meaning, the three affixes all follow the same rule: affixes attach to the verb that follows them.

Now let us look at a derivation that involves all three helping verbs: *Alice might have been singing contralto*.

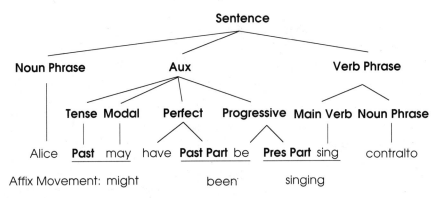

The affix movement rule again applies three times.

1. It attaches the past tense marker to the modal <u>may</u>,
2. it attaches the past participle to <u>be</u>, and
3. it attaches the present participle to the main verb <u>sing</u>.

The only difference between this derivation and the preceding one is that in this derivation the modal "captures" the tense marker so that no affix can be passed along to *have*, which stays as an infinitive.

If you think about the structure of the auxiliary and the function of the affix movement rule, you can see that, although there are many different combinations, the basic pattern is fairly simple: the first verb is finite (i.e., it carries the tense marker). All subsequent verbs are nonfinite; they are (1) an infinitive (if the verb follows a modal); (2) a past participle (if the verb follows *have*); or (3) a present participle (if the verb follows *be*). No other sequence or combination of forms is possible.

■ **Exercise 6.7. Auxiliary review**

Draw phrase structure trees and apply the affix movement rule to produce the following surface sentences. (Answers to exercises are found on page 480.)

1. We have been drawing trees.
2. The advertisement will attract a crowd.
3. The clutch engages the gears.
4. They have filed a motion.
5. The committee must approve the design.
6. He was a fool.
7. His claim is stretching the truth.
8. We should have warned them.
9. The Smiths would have been watching TV.
10. Godzilla might frighten the children.
11. Holmes was checking Lord Bumfrey's story.
12. Bugsy had acquired a large fortune.
13. They must have changed the combination.
14. Lady Smithers could take the pearls.
15. Leon loves Lilly.
16. Sir Desmond had had his answer.
17. The butler may have been polishing the silver.
18. The Legionnaires ordered clam juice.

"STRANDED" TENSE IN QUESTIONS AND NEGATIVE STATEMENTS

In this section we briefly examine the amazing behavior of tense in the formation of questions and negative statements. The purpose of this section is to reinforce the validity of Chomsky's innovative treatment of tense as a prefix in the deep structure. In this section we will see that tense can sometimes become separated from the rest of the auxiliary. In this case the tense marker is said to be "stranded." A stranded-tense marker is no longer followed by a verb. How can we pronounce or write a tense marker without a verb? We cannot. How does English solve this problem? By adding a dummy verb to the sentence—a verb that has no meaning at all, a verb whose only function is to carry the tense marker.

Questions

Compare the following kernel statements and their corresponding simple question forms.

Statement	Question
Alice may sing contralto.	May Alice sing contralto?
Alice had sung contralto.	Had Alice sung contralto?
Alice is singing contralto.	Is Alice singing contralto?

The rule for changing deep structures into simple questions seems easy enough: by applying a transformational rule to the deep structure, move the first verb (more accurately, the tense marker plus the first verb) to a position in front of the subject noun phrase. This is correct as far as it goes, but notice that all the examples contain helping verbs. Now see what happens when we try to apply this rule to deep structures that do not contain helping verbs.

Statement	Question
Alice sings contralto.	*Sings Alice contralto?
Alice sang contralto.	*Sang Alice contralto?

In earlier stages of English, questions of this type were grammatical. For example, following are some questions from Shakespeare's play *As You Like It*.

Know you where you are?
Called your worship?
Looks he as freshly as he did?

Change you color?

Speak you so gently?

Begin you to grow upon me?

For Shakespeare the preceding rule we developed for questions with helping verbs was valid for all sentences, even sentences without helping verbs. Shakespeare could form questions merely by moving the tense marker and first verb (whatever that verb was) to a position in front of the subject noun phrase.

In modern English the situation is much more complicated. We form these questions by using the verb *do*.

Statement	*Question*
Alice sings contralto.	<u>Does</u> Alice sing contralto?
Alice sang contralto.	<u>Did</u> Alice sing contralto?

By using transformational rules, we can create a rule system that captures a number of generalizations about how we form questions. The most important generalization we can make about simple questions in English is that they must begin with a verb. This generalization would predict that speakers of modern English would recognize the preceding sentences quoted from Shakespeare to be questions, even though they are not grammatically well-formed in modern English—a prediction that certainly seems correct.

A second generalization is that (with the exception of the questions with *do*) the verb that begins the question has been moved from its normal position following the subject noun phrase. The proof of this generalization may be found in the sentences that contain the perfect and the progressive.

	Statement	*Question*
Perfect:	Alice <u>had sung</u> contralto.	<u>Had</u> Alice <u>sung</u> contralto?
Progressive:	Alice <u>is singing</u> contralto.	<u>Is</u> Alice <u>singing</u> contralto?

Both the perfect and the progressive are two-part constructions. In the verb phrase of a sentence we cannot have the past participle *sung* unless it is immediately preceded by the helping verb *have* in some form—in the case of this sentence, *had*. Likewise, we cannot have the present participle *singing* unless it is immediately preceded by the helping verb *be* in some form—in the case of this sentence, *is*. The two preceding examples of questions, however, seem to violate this basic principle of English grammar because in each case we have a participle that is not directly preceded by its helping verb.

One possible conclusion we can draw is that questions have a profoundly different deep structure from their corresponding statements.

That is, for questions only, the auxiliary component puts the tense marker and first helping verb on the left of the subject noun phrase and the remainder of the auxiliary component on the right side of the noun phrase. This conclusion is both clumsy and counterintuitive. It seems much more natural to conclude that the deep structure formulation of the auxiliary of sentences is the same in questions as in statements, but that a transformational rule has *moved* the tense marker and the first helping verb from their normal position following the subject noun phrase to a position in front of the subject noun phrase.

The deep structure of each sentence contains all the information necessary to interpret the meaning of that sentence, including whether the sentence is to be interpreted as a statement or a question. If the deep structure indicates that a given sentence is to be interpreted as a question, then the deep structure triggers a *Question* transformation that alters the form of the deep structure to produce the correct surface structure for the question. For deep structures containing a helping verb, the Question transformation moves the tense marker and the first helping verb to a position in front of the subject noun phrase. The affix movement transformation will then apply, automatically producing the correct final surface forms. Following is how the question transformation will affect the example sentences containing a helping verb.

Deep:	Alice Pres may sing contralto
Question:	Pres may Alice sing contralto
Affix Mov:	May Alice sing contralto?
Deep:	Alice Past have Past Part sing contralto
Question:	Past have Alice Past Part sing contralto
Affix Mov:	Had Alice sung contralto?
Deep:	Alice Pres be Pres Part sing contralto
Question:	Pres be Alice Pres Part sing contralto
Affix Mov:	Is Alice singing contralto?

Now that we see how transformational grammar deals with the formation of questions that contain a helping verb, let us turn to questions that have *do* in the first position. We can make a generalization about these questions: the *do* carries the tense marker; for example, in the following sentence, the main verb stays in its deep structure infinitive form while the present or past tense marker is carried by *do*.

Present:	Does Alice sing contralto?
Past:	Did Alice sing contralto?

Regardless of how we deal with the origin of *do*, it is clear that the tense marker has moved away from its normal position to a position in front of the subject noun phrase. We can capture this generalization in a reformulation of the question transformation: if the tense marker is not followed by a helping verb, move the tense marker (by itself) to a position in front of the subject noun phrase. Following is how the question transformation will affect sentences without helping verbs.

Deep: Alice Pres sing contralto

Question: Pres Alice sing contralto

Deep: Alice Past sing contralto

Question: Past Alice sing contralto

We now have a *stranded* tense marker. A tense marker is stranded whenever the tense marker is not followed by a verb to which the tense marker can be attached by the affix movement transformation. Whenever (and for whatever reason) a tense marker is stranded, the verb *do* is inserted following the stranded tense marker. The *do* plays a grammatical role as a carrier of the tense marker, but it is void of any dictionary meaning. It is a semantically empty placeholder, as it were, filling a verb slot. Transformational grammar captures this generalization by creating the *do* through a transformational rule called *do support*. An automatic consequence of creating *do* by means of a transformational rule is that, by definition, the *do* cannot have any meaning because only those elements originating in the deep structure have meaning. Since the *do* does not exist in the deep structure, transformational theory predicts (correctly) that it can have form but no meaning. Following is how the *do* support rule will apply to the output of the question transformation to create a structure to which the affix movement will automatically apply.

Deep: Alice Pres sing contralto

Question: Pres Alice sing contralto

do support: Pres *do* Alice sing contralto

Affix Mov: Does Alice sing contralto?

Deep: Alice Past sing contralto

Question: Past Alice sing contralto

do support: Past *do* Alice sing contralto

Affix Mov: Did Alice sing contralto?

Let us briefly summarize about the formation of simple questions in English. There are two types of simple questions in English, depending on whether or not the question contains a helping verb. If the sentence contains a helping verb, the helping verb begins the question. If the sentence does not contain a helping verb, the verb *do* begins the question.

Transformational grammar captures these generalizations by two transformational rules: (1) the *question* transformation, and (2) the *do support* transformation. The question transformation is triggered by any deep structure that is to be interpreted as a question. The question transformation does one of two things according to the form of the deep structure sentence to which it applies.

1. If the tense marker is immediately followed by a helping verb (a modal, *have* from the perfect, or *be* from the progressive), then the rule moves both the tense marker and the following helping verb to a position in front of the subject noun phrase.

2. If the tense marker is *not* immediately followed by a helping verb (in other words, if it is followed by the main verb), then the rule moves the tense marker by itself to a position in front of the subject noun phrase. Placing the tense marker in this position has the effect of *stranding* the tense marker because the tense marker is not immediately followed by a verb to which it can be attached by the affix movement rule.

The *do* support rule applies whenever (and for whatever reason) a tense marker is stranded. The *do* support rule inserts the verb *do* into the sentence immediately following the stranded tense marker. Since the verb *do* is not generated in the deep structure, *do* can have no dictionary meaning; it is merely a placeholder. As a result of the *do* support transformational rule, the tense marker is now, as it were, "unstranded" so that the affix movement rule will automatically attach the tense marker to the verb *do*.

■ **Exercise 6.8. Questions**

Convert the following deep structures into questions following the format given above. Other sentences will go through one intermediate stage. An example of each question type is given. (Answers to exercises are found on page 484.)

1. *Deep:*   Leon Pres snore
   Question: Pres Leon snore
   do support: Pres do Leon snore
   Affix Mov: Does Leon snore?

2. *Deep:*   You Pres can give the answer
   Question: Pres can you give the answer
   Affix Mov: Can you give the answer?

3. *Deep:*   He Past justify his answer

4. *Deep:*   They Past wax the car

5. *Deep:* I Pres shall answer the phone
6. *Deep:* Your sister Pres want an ice-cream cone
7. *Deep:* You Past can wait here
8. *Deep:* They Past enlarge the prints
9. *Deep:* The witness Pres will invoke the 5th amendment
10. *Deep:* You Past look up the word in the dictionary
11. *Deep:* The flowers Pres bloom in the spring, tra-la
12. *Deep:* You Pres have Past Part overlook something
13. *Deep:* They Past have Past Part violate the country's airspace
14. *Deep:* You Pres have a quarter
15. *Deep:* They Past have a good time

Negative statements

Compare the following statements and their corresponding negatives.

Statement	Negative
Alice may sing contralto.	Alice may <u>not</u> sing contralto.
Alice had sung contralto.	Alice had <u>not</u> sung contralto.
Alice is singing contralto.	Alice is <u>not</u> singing contralto.

The rule for changing deep structures into negatives seems simple enough: insert *not* after the first verb. This is correct as far as it goes, but notice that all the examples contain auxiliary or helping verbs. See what happens when we try to apply this rule to deep structures that do not contain auxiliary verbs.

Statement	Negative
Alice sings contralto.	*Alice sings <u>not</u> contralto
Alice sang contralto.	*Alice sang <u>not</u> contralto

In earlier stages of English, negatives of this type were grammatical. For example, following are some negatives from Shakespeare's play *The Tempest*.

I feel not this deity in my bosom.

He misses not much.

I find not myself disposed to sleep.

Thou attend'st not.

Hang not on my garments.

For Shakespeare the rule was simple and uniform: insert *not* after whatever verb comes first, no matter whether the first verb is an auxiliary verb or the main verb itself.

In modern English we have two slightly different patterns for negation. In one pattern, the *not* occurs immediately after the first auxiliary verb. The other pattern requires that the *not* be used in conjunction with *do*. In transformational grammar, there is a negative marker in the deep structure of negative sentences, ensuring that the deep structure is given a negative interpretation. The negative marker is actually placed inside the sentence by the *not insertion* transformation. For sentences that contain a helping verb, the *not* insertion transformation puts *not* immediately after the first helping verb in the deep structure; for example, following is how the *not* insertion transformation (together with the automatic application of the affix movement transformation) would apply to the three example sentences containing helping verbs to produce grammatical surface structures.

Deep:	Alice Pres may sing contralto
not:	Alice Pres may not sing contralto
Affix Mov:	Alice may not sing contralto.
Deep	Alice Past have Past Part sing contralto
not:	Alice Past have not Past Part sing contralto
Affix Mov:	Alice had not sung contralto.
Deep:	Alice Pres be Pres Part sing contralto
not:	Alice Pres be not Pres Part sing contralto
Affix Mov:	Alice is not singing contralto.

Note that the *not* insertion transformation does not interfere with the normal application of the affix movement rule.

What generalization can we make about the pattern of negation that uses *do*? First, we know that *do* is used in sentences that do not have helping verbs. Second, we know that the *do* carries the tense marker, and that *do* is followed by *not*, as we can see in the following negative sentences.

Present:	Alice does not sing contralto.
Past:	Alice did not sing contralto.

Transformational grammar captures these generalizations by having a second version of the *not* insertion rule that places the *not* after the tense marker and before the main verb in the deep structure.

Deep:	Alice Pres sing contralto
not:	Alice Pres not sing contralto
Deep:	Alice Past sing contralto
not:	Alice Past not sing contralto

In deep structures of this type, the _not_ insertion rule places the _not_ between the tense marker and its following verb. In other words, the _not_ insertion rule has again stranded the tense marker. Whenever the tense marker is stranded (for whatever reason), the _do_ support rule is automatically applied, inserting the verb _do_ immediately after the tense marker. This rule, in turn, then permits the application of the affix movement rule.

Deep:	Alice Pres sing contralto
not:	Alice Pres not sing contralto
do support:	Alice Pres do not sing contralto
Affix Mov:	Alice does not sing contralto.
Deep:	Alice Past sing contralto
not:	Alice Past not sing contralto
do support:	Alice Past do not sing contralto
Affix Mov:	Alice did not sing contralto

Let us briefly summarize the formation of negatives in English. There are two types of negatives in English, depending on whether or not the sentence contains a helping verb. If the sentence contains a helping verb, the _not_ follows the first helping verb. If the sentence does not contain a helping verb, the negative sentence requires the use of _do_.

Transformational grammar captures these generalizations by one new transformational rule: the _not insertion_ transformation. This transformation is triggered by any deep structure that is to be interpreted as a negative. The _not_ insertion transformation does one of two things according to the form of the deep structure sentence to which it applies.

1. If the tense marker is immediately followed by a helping verb (a modal, _have_ from the perfect, or _be_ from the progressive), then the rule inserts _not_ immediately after the first helping verb.

2. If the tense marker is not followed immediately by a helping verb (in other words, if it is followed by the main verb), then the rule inserts the _not_ immediately after the tense marker and before the main verb. Placing the _not_ in this position has the effect of _stranding_ the tense marker because the tense marker is not immediately followed by a verb to which it can be attached by the affix movement rule.

   The _do_ support rule then applies automatically, inserting the verb _do_ into the sentence immediately following the stranded tense marker. Next, the affix movement rule will automatically attach the tense marker to the verb _do_.

One of the most striking features of transformational grammar is the power of a small number of transformational rules. In the preceding discussion we have seen two quite different constructions—questions and negatives—drawing on one transformation, the _do_ support rule, to explain in a simple and compelling way why English uses the otherwise mysterious _do_.

■ **Exercise 6.9. Negative statements**

Convert the following deep structures into negative statements following the preceding format given. An example of each type of negative is given. (Answers to exercises are found on page 485.)

1. *Deep:*   It Past rain
   not: It Past not rain
   do support: It Past do not rain
   Affix Mov: It did not rain.

2. *Deep:*   You Past shall laugh
   not: You Past shall not laugh
   Affix Mov: You should not laugh.

3. Deep: He Past accuse you of anything
4. Deep: That approach Pres will earn a penny
5. Deep: The contractor Past install a sprinkler system
6. Deep: Paul Pres like coffee
7. Deep: I Pres know all the answers
8. Deep: They Pres will arrive on time
9. Deep: The Congressman Past avoid the question
10. Deep: Leon Past have Past Part finish the exam yet
11. Deep: Scrooge Past contribute to the Christmas Fund
12. Deep: The piece Past fit into the puzzle
13. Deep: Watson Past blink an eye at Holmes's strange suggestion
14. Deep: You Past shall have Past Part compare their stories
15. Deep: We Pres be Pres Part go

PASSIVE

In traditional grammar, verbs are said to have _voice_. There are two voices: _active_ and _passive_. A verb is in the active voice when the subject of the verb is the performer of the action. A verb is in the passive voice when the subject of the verb is the recipient of the action. Compare the following sentences.

Active: John saw Mary.
Passive: Mary was seen by John.

In the active sentence, *saw* is in the active voice. Its subject, *John*, is the performer of the action; that is, John is the person doing the seeing. In the passive sentence, *seen* is in the passive voice. Its subject, *Mary*, is the recipient of the action; that is, Mary is not doing the seeing, John is. Mary is still the person being seen; that is, Mary is the recipient of the action of the verb.

In transformational terms, the passive is a transformation that completely reconfigures the sentence structure in the process of converting the deep structure into a surface form. The passive transformation does three things to the underlying deep structure.

1. It interchanges the subject and object noun phrases—the underlying object noun phrase moves to the position in front of the verb and the underlying subject noun phrase moves to the position after the verb,

2. it inserts *by* in front of the old subject noun phrase, making the old subject noun phrase into a prepositional phrase, and

3. it inserts the *passive auxiliary: be + Past Participle* as a final element in the auxiliary.

Following is how the passive sentence *Mary was seen by John* is derived.

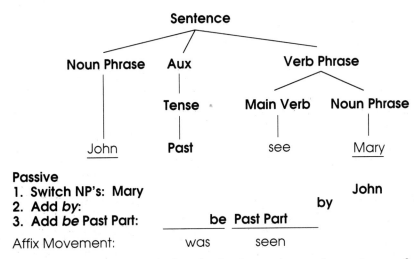

The deep structure underlies both the active and passive surface forms. The active, however, is a kernel sentence. That is, it is derived from the deep structure without any optional transformations. The passive transformation is a striking example of the extent to which an optional transformation can reshape the surface structure from its underlying deep structure origin. Nevertheless, the fact that the active and passive share a common deep structure means that they still have the same basic meaning—they are superficially different versions of the same basic sentence.

Since the passive auxiliary (*be* + past participle) always follows the other optional helping verbs in the auxiliary, it might seem reasonable to build the passive auxiliary into the deep structure as a fourth optional element in the auxiliary. However, there are many arguments against this approach. First, every verb in English can be used with the other three helping verbs, that is, every verb in English can be used with a modal, perfect, or progressive. But only transitive action verbs can be used with the passive auxiliary. Second, if we were to put the passive auxiliary into the deep structure, we would always be required to put *by* between the main verb and the following noun phrase, a requirement not shared with the modal, perfect, or progressive. Third, and perhaps most important of all, introducing the passive auxiliary by a transformational rule captures the paraphrase relationship between active and passive sentences—they are both derived from a single deep structure. If active and passive sentences were both produced in the deep structure, they would not be systematically related to each other because they would come from different (and by definition) unrelated sources, and hence would have different meanings. In fact, of course, the active and passive versions of a sentence mean the same thing—a fact that is captured by deriving them from the same underlying deep structure.

Note that we cannot draw a phrase structure tree for the passive surface form. Instead, we must draw a phrase structure tree diagram of the corresponding kernel surface form. The reason is simple: the deep structure represents the basic relations underlying the sentence *before any transformations are applied.*

We now examine passive sentences in which there are optional helping verbs.

Modal + Passive:	Mary can be seen by John.
Perfect + Passive:	Mary had been seen by John.
Progressive + Passive:	Mary was being watched by John.

The passive auxiliary *be* + *past participle* is the distinct signature of the passive transformation. Only a passive sentence has *be* as a helping verb followed by the main verb in the *past participle* form. (Remember, in the progressive, *be* will be followed by a verb in the *present participle* (*-ing*) form.)

Following are the transformational derivations for the preceding three passive sentences. The corresponding kernel sentences are given in parentheses to make the derivation easier to follow. Remember: we literally cannot draw a phrase structure tree for a passive sentence; we can only draw a phrase structure tree for the deep structure that underlies the passive sentence. The kernel is the surface form that most nearly corresponds to the deep structure.

> *Modal + Passive:*   Mary can be seen by John.
> *Kernel:*   John can see Mary.

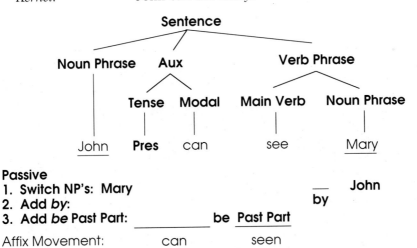

Passive
1. **Switch NP's:** Mary _____ John
2. **Add** *by:*   by
3. **Add** *be* **Past Part:** _____   be Past Part

Affix Movement: can   seen

Note that the present tense marker is attached to the modal *can*, so that the helping verb *be* from the passive transformation stays as an infinitive.

> *Perfect + Passive:*   Mary had been seen by John.
> *Kernel:*   John had seen Mary.

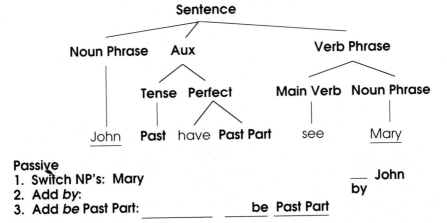

Passive
1. **Switch NP's:** Mary _____ John
2. **Add** *by:*   by
3. **Add** *be* **Past Part:** _____   be Past Part

Affix Movement: had   been   seen

There are two past participle markers (*been* and *seen*), the first derived from the perfect in the phrase structure component, and the second derived from the passive transformation.

Progressive + Passive: Mary was being watched by John.
Kernel: John was watching Mary

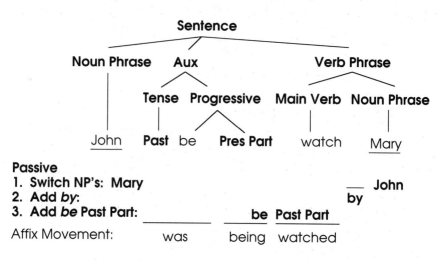

Passive
1. **Switch NP's: Mary** ————————————————— **John**
2. **Add** *by:*   **by**
3. **Add** *be* **Past Part:** ————————   **be Past Part** ————
Affix Movement: was   being   watched

■ **Exercise 6.10. Recognizing passives**

Most of the following sentences are passive. Rewrite the passive sentences into the corresponding active forms. (Answers to exercises are found on page 486.)

1. The book was reviewed by the committee.
2. His contributions were appreciated by everyone.
3. The Cabinet was informed by the President.
4. The total had been estimated by the committee.
5. The scientists had defined the problem.
6. The dog was being washed by the whole family.
7. The writers had been threatened by the editor.
8. Children must be accompanied by adults.
9. The gun was owned by a retired policeman.
10. Corla's embarrassing slip had been noticed by everyone.
11. The judge had granted the defendant's request.
12. We will be caught by them.
13. The accident could have been prevented by proper planning.
14. A microphone was recording the conversation.
15. The plan should be approved by the committee.

■ **Exercise 6.11. Deriving passives**
Draw phrase structure trees and apply the necessary transformational rules to derive the sentences in Exercise 10. Keep the noun phrases as units; that is, do not try to break them down. (Answers to exercises are found on page 487.)

THE ORDER OF TRANSFORMATIONAL RULES

We have now discussed, either formally or informally, the following six transformational rules (in alphabetical order).

Affix Movement
Dative Switch
Do Support
Not Insertion
Passive
Question

One of the remarkable insights from transformational grammar is that the order in which we apply the transformational rules is in a fixed sequence. That is, the output of one rule serves as the input to another rule. For example, we have already seen this kind of fixed sequence when we examined stranded tense markers. You recall that the tense marker was stranded as a result of either (a) the question transformation, which moved the tense marker away from the main verb, or (b) the *not* insertion rule, which placed *not* between the tense marker and the main verb. The tense marker was "unstranded" by the application of the *do* support transformation that inserted the verb *do* after the tense marker so that the affix movement rule could then apply. Implicit in this discussion is a fixed sequence of transformations.

1. Question/*Not* insertion
2. *Do* support
3. Affix Movement

In other words, the affix movement transformation could not apply until after the *do* had been inserted, and in turn, the *do* support transformation could be applied only if the tense had been stranded as a result of applying either the question transformation or the *not* insertion transformation.

The passive transformation must precede the question and *not* insertion transformations because the *be* that comes into existence as part of the passive transformation can take part in both the question and *not* insertion transformations. Compare the following sentences.

	Active	*Passive*
Statement:	John saw Mary.	Mary was seen by John.
Question:	Did John see Mary?	Was Mary seen by John?
Negative:	John did not see Mary.	Mary was not seen by John.

As you can see, the passive sentences form completely different questions and negatives because the passives contain a helping verb (*be* from the passive transformation) while the corresponding active sentences form their questions and negatives with *do* because there are no helping verbs in their sentences. Obviously, then, the question and *not* insertion transformations must follow the passive since they use the *be* that comes from the passive. The revised order for these transformations is as follows.

1. Passive
2. Question/*Not* insertion
3. *Do* support
4. Affix Movement

Finally, we can show that the passive must follow the dative switch transformation. The argument now is a little more difficult. Let us take the following deep structure.

John Past give Mary a present

If we apply the passive transformation, we get a perfectly grammatical sentence using the indirect object as the source for the new subject.

Mary was given a present by John.

However, we cannot apply a dative switch to this passive sentence because it is in the wrong form for the dative switch. Recall that the dative switch reverses the indirect and direct objects. The preceding passive sentence no longer has both a direct and indirect object, so the dative switch cannot be applied.

Let us now try the rules in the opposite order. Applying the dative switch to the preceding deep structure, we get the following sentence.

John gave a present to Mary.

The direct object noun phrase *a present*, which originally had been separated from the verb by the indirect object, has now been moved next to the verb. In this position, the passive transformation will take the direct object as the source for subject of the passive sentence.

A present was given to Mary by John.

This sentence, which is the result of applying first the dative switch and then the passive, is clearly one of the grammatical surface sentence forms of the deep structure *John* Past *give Mary a present*. However, if we perform the passive transformation before the dative switch, we cannot produce this sentence. Therefore, the only order of the two transformations that can correctly produce all the grammatical surface forms is first the dative switch and then the passive.

Following is the complete derivation of the sentence *A present was given to Mary by John*.

Kernel: John gave Mary a present.

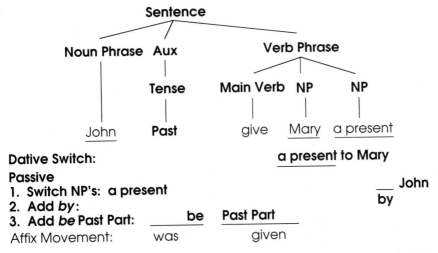

[Note that with two object noun phrases, the *Switch NP* rule is slightly different: the subject noun phrase in the deep structure is moved to a position at the end of the verb phrase.]

Since we know that the passive comes before the question and *not* insertion rule, we can now put all six rules in order.

1.   Dative Switch
2.   Passive
3.   Question/*Not* insertion*
4.   *Do* support
5.   Affix Movement

[* The arguments for the relative order of the question and *not* insertion rules are too complex to discuss here.]

As an example of the generative power of transformational grammar, following are the different surface sentences that can be created from a single deep structure by using just three transformations: the question, passive, and dative switch rule.

> *Deep Structure:*   John Past give Mary a present

1. *Kernel (no optional transformations):*   John gave Mary a present.
2. *Question:*   Did John give Mary a present?
3. *Passive:*   Mary was given a present by John.
4. *Passive + Question:*   Was Mary given a present by John?
5. *Dative:*   John gave a present to Mary.
6. *Dative + Passive:*   A present was given to Mary by John.
7. *Dative + Question:*   Did John give a present to Mary?
8. *Dative + Passive + Question:*   Was a present given to Mary by John?

SUMMARY

In this chapter we have explored what transformational grammar is and how it works. Transformational grammar is a set of rules capable of generating all of the grammatical sentences of English and describing their structure in a way that seems intuitively correct to native speakers of English.

Transformational grammar consists of a double set of rules. The first set is called the *phrase structure* rules. The phrase structure rules generate abstract grammatical structures, which, when words are attached, become abstract basic sentences called *deep structures*. Deep structures contain all the information necessary to interpret the meaning of sentences. Among the components of the deep structure are elements that indicate whether the deep structure is to be interpreted as a statement or a question, a positive sentence or a negative one.

A second set of rules, called *transformations*, converts the deep structures into representations of actual sentences, called *surface structures*. Transformations have the power to edit and and rearrange a deep structure, but they do not have the power to change the basic meaning of the surface structure from that determined by the deep structure underlying the surface structure. Transformations can chain together so that the output of one transformation becomes the input for a second transformation. This chaining effect allows a relatively few transformation rules to produce a large number of related surface structures from a single deep structure. Thus, from one deep structure, various transformations produce different surface structures that are paraphrases of each other. The surface structure that is the product of only obligatory transformations is called a *kernel* sentence. A kernel sentence is the surface structure that is closest in form to its underlying deep structure.

The operation of the two sets of rules was illustrated by a detailed discussion of Chomsky's innovative treatment of (1) tense and helping verbs and (2) the passive. In Chomsky's approach to tense and helping verbs, the Tense marker (either Present or Past) is the first (and sole) obligatory component of the Auxiliary (Aux). The other components of Aux are (in order) the following: Modal, Perfect, and Progressive. The structure of the Aux component guarantees that the Tense marker will always attach to whatever verb follows it and that the Modal, Perfect, and Progressive are always in the correct sequence. Additional justification for Chomsky's approach is found in the formation of questions and negative statements when the underlying deep structures do not contain helping verbs (i.e., verbs in the Aux component). In these sentences, the Tense marker is separated from the rest of the Aux. In this case, the Tense is said to be *stranded*. In order to form a grammatical surface structure, the stranded Tense marker must be attached to the dummy verb *do*, which is inserted into the sentence by a transformational rule.

The passive form of a sentence is derived from the deep structure by a family of three transformations. The first switches the subject and object NP's, the second adds *by* to the new object NP, and the third adds the passive auxiliary marker *be* + Past Part.

The final component of the chapter demonstrated that the transformational rules discussed in this chapter can be applied only in the following fixed relative sequence: (1) Dative Switch, (2) Passive, (3) Question/*Not* insertion, (4) *Do* support, and (5) Affix Movement.

■ Exercise 6.12. Applying multiple transformations on page 224

Following the format given on page 224, generate the corresponding eight surface forms from the following deep structures. (Answers to exercises are found on page 492.)

1. Sally Past tell the children a story
2. I Past find her an apartment
3. He Past may sell me Boardwalk

7

Sentence Combining

INTRODUCTION

In this chapter we examine the most important new approach to teaching grammar—sentence combining. The idea of encouraging students to write more complex sentences by teaching them to combine several simple sentences is not new. Shirley K. Rose (1983) traces sentence combining techniques back to textbooks written before the turn of the century. However, what is new is (1) a rationale for sentence combining derived from current theories of linguistics, and (2) a substantial body of research literature on the effectiveness of sentence combining as a teaching technique.

We discuss sentence combining from two perspectives: (1) the linguistic perspective on how sentence combining works, and (2) the pedagogical perspective on the classroom applications of sentence combining.

PART I: THE LINGUISTIC PERSPECTIVE

From the point of view of transformational grammar, sentence combining is the process of joining two deep structures to form a single surface structure. The least sophisticated way of joining the two deep structures is by *coordination*. In coordination, the two sentences are merely linked by a coordinating conjunction with little, if any, interaction between the sentences. A more sophisticated way of joining is by *embedding*. In the embedding process, a deep structure sentence is literally placed (embedded) inside another deep structure sentence. The embedded deep structure is then brought to the surface by a family of transformational rules that often permit a number of alternative surface forms. Thus, from one underlying embedded deep structure we may get a half dozen different variant surface forms, depending on which transformational rules have been applied. These various surface forms are related because they share a single common ancestor—the same embedded deep structure.

The great advantage of this approach is that superficially different but related surface forms—words, phrases, and clauses—are all brought together and treated as part of one process, rather than being treated as totally unrelated constructions, as they are in traditional schoolroom grammar. For example, in the process of *noun modification*, certain adjectives, certain adjective phrases, appositives, participles, participial phrases, and adjective clauses belong to the same family and are all derived from a common single source—an embedded deep structure sentence that modifies a noun. Grouping grammatical constructions by derivational process rather than by surface form enables us to connect grammar directly to the rhetorical choices that writers make among related surface forms.

In this section on the linguistic perspective, we will examine three sentence combining processes.

1. **noun modification.** deriving words, phrases, and clauses that modify nouns
2. **nominalization.** deriving phrases and clauses that replace nouns
3. **absolutes.** deriving a phrase that elaborates or explains the information in the main clause

These three types of sentence combining have been identified in the literature of sentence combining as being of special importance. The first two sentence combining processes, noun modification and nominalization, account for much of the growth in syntactic fluency that takes places during our school years (Hunt 1964). Use of the third sentence combining process, absolutes, was singled out in the highly influential work of Francis Christensen as one of the constructions that he considered to be characteristic of mature style (Christensen 1967, 1968).

NOUN MODIFICATION

In the transformational approach, a related family of noun modifiers including relative or adjective clauses, present and past participles and participial phrases, appositives, certain adjective phrases, and "true" adjectives are all derived from underlying deep structure sentences that say something about the nouns being modified. This underlying deep structure sentence is represented as being *embedded* inside the noun phrase in the following manner.

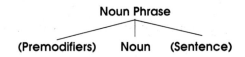

Noun Phrase

(Premodifiers)   **Noun**   **(Sentence)**

This phrase structure diagram indicates that a noun phrase consists of a noun, which may be preceded by premodifiers—articles, determiners, and certain types of adjectives—and may be followed by an embedded sentence. The term *embedded sentence* refers to a deep structure sentence that is placed inside another sentence; the embedded sentence can never come to the surface as an independent clause.

There is an important restriction on deep structure sentences that are embedded inside noun phrases: the embedded sentence must contain within it a noun that is the duplicate of the noun that the deep structure sentence modifies. This restriction guarantees that the embedded sentence says something about the noun being modified. If the embedded sentence does not contain within it a duplicate of the noun being modified, then no grammatical surface sentence can be produced, as in the following example.

> *They Past identify the person (the violin Past be a major com-
> ponent of the modern symphony
> orchestra)

Since the embedded sentence does not contain within it a duplicate of the noun *person*, the embedded sentence cannot produce a grammatical surface sentence. Following is an example of a valid embedded sentence.

> They Past identify the person (we Past see the *person*)

We can bring this embedded sentence to the surface as a relative clause.

> They identified the person (whom we saw)

Following is the complete deep structure diagram for the preceding sentence.

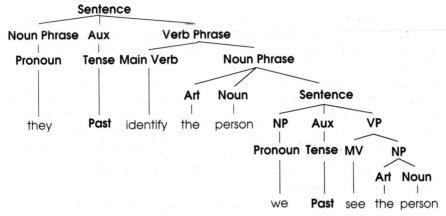

In the example, the embedded sentence contains within it the noun *person,* which is the duplicate of the noun that the embedded sentence is modifying.

Relative (adjective) clauses

Sentences that are embedded inside a noun phrase are converted into relative clauses by two transformational rules.

1. The *relative replacement rule (Rel Repl).* This rule replaces the duplicate noun with a relative pronoun. More accurately, the relative replacement rule replaces the entire noun phrase containing the duplicate noun with an appropriate relative pronoun.

2. The *wh- fronting rule* (so called because it applies to relative pronouns, many of which begin with the letters *wh-*). This rule moves the relative pronoun to the first position within the embedded sentence.

For example, following is how these two rules apply to the embedded sentence in the deep structure previously given.

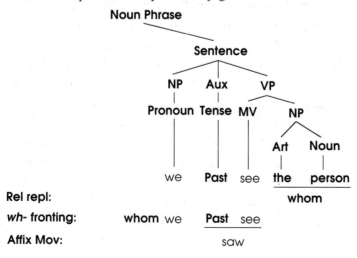

Note that the form of the relative pronoun (*whom* in this case) is determined by the function of the duplicate noun within the embedded sentence. In this sentence the relative pronoun replaces the object, so the relative pronoun is in the object form.

All the transformational rules that apply to the embedded sentence are executed before any transformational rules are applied to the main sentence. In other words, transformational rules work from the bottommost embedded sentence upwards to the main sentence. Accordingly, having completed all the applicable transformational rules in the embedded sentence, we then turn to the main sentence, where we apply affix movement to the main sentence to get the complete surface sentence consisting of a main clause, *They identified the person*, and the relative clause, *whom we saw*.

> They identified the person <u>whom we saw</u>

From this point on, we will not derive the main clause from its deep structure. Instead, for the sake of simplicity, the main clause in the examples will be given in its surface form.

In the following sentence, the relative pronoun replaces a duplicate noun playing the role of subject in the embedded sentence.

They identified the person	(the *person* Past strike us)
Rel Repl:	(who Past strike us)
Affix Mov:	(who struck us)

In the above sentence, *wh-* fronting does not apply because the relative pronoun is already in the first position within the embedded sentence.

In the following example, the duplicate noun is an object.

They identified the person	(the police Past find the *person*)
Rel Repl:	(the police Past find whom)
wh- fronting:	(whom the police Past find)
Affix Mov:	(whom the police found)

In the following example, the duplicate noun phrase is a possessive. In this case the possessive noun phrase (i.e., the possessive noun *mouse's* and its modifier *the*) is replaced by *whose*.

She saw the mouse	(the *mouse's* tail Past twitch)
Rel Repl:	(whose tail Past twitch)
Affix Mov:	(whose tail twitched)

In the preceding sentence, *wh-* fronting does not apply because the relative pronoun is already in the first position. If the *whose* is not in the first position, then it moves to the first position via *wh-* fronting, bringing the noun that it modifies along with it, as in the following example.

She saw the mouse   (she Past cut off the *mouse's* tail)
     Rel Repl: (she Past cut off whose tail)
   wh- fronting: (whose tail she Past cut off)
     Affix Mov: (whose tail she cut off)

In the following example, the duplicate noun phrase is the object of a preposition.

We saw the movie   (you Past complain about the *movie*)
     Rel repl: (you Past complain about that)
   wh- fronting: (that you Past complain about)
     Affix Mov: (that you complained about)

When the duplicate noun phrase is the object of a preposition, there is a second option—the preposition can be moved along with the relative pronoun to the first position of the embedded sentence:

We saw the movie   (you Past complain about the *movie*)
     Rel Repl: (you Past complain about which)
   wh- fronting: (about which you Past complain)
     Affix Mov: (about which you complained)

As an example of a derivation of a sentence containing a relative clause, following is the complete phrase structure tree and transformation rules for the sentence *They identified the person whom we saw.*

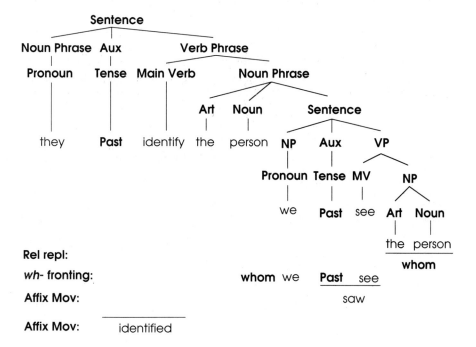

Note that there are two cycles of transformations: (1) transformations that apply to the embedded sentence, and (2) transformations that apply to the main sentence. The first cycle transforms the embedded sentence into a relative clause. The second cycle applies only the affix movement rule to the deep structure of the main sentence.

Let us briefly summarize. In transformational grammar, relative clauses are derived from deep structure sentences embedded inside a noun phrase. The embedded deep structure sentence must contain within it a duplicate of the noun that the embedded sentence modifies. This duplicate noun (along with its modifiers) [i.e., the entire noun phrase containing the duplicate noun] is replaced by a relative pronoun by means of the *relative pronoun replacement rule*. The form of the relative pronoun is determined by the function of the duplicate noun within the embedded deep structure sentence: if the duplicate noun plays the role of a subject, the relative pronoun will be *who* (ignoring for the moment the relative pronouns *that* and *which* since they do not change form); if it is an object or the object of a preposition, the relative pronoun will be *whom*; if it is possessive, the relative pronoun will be *whose*.

The relative pronoun is then moved to the first position within the embedded sentence (if it is not there already) by means of the *wh-fronting rule*. If the relative pronoun is the possessive *whose*, then the noun that *whose* modifies must move along with *whose* to the first position within the embedded sentence. If the relative pronoun is an object of a preposition, then we have an option: we can move the relative pronoun and leave the preposition behind, or in more formal English, we can move the preposition along with the relative pronoun.

Notice that the *wh- fronting* rule necessarily puts the relative pronoun directly next to the noun that the relative clause modifies. To see why this must be the case, recall that the embedded sentence that is the source of the relative clause is always the immediate next-door neighbor to the right of the noun. When the relative pronoun is moved to the first position within the embedded sentence by the *wh- fronting* rule, then the relative pronoun must be next to the noun. In other words, relative pronouns always immediately follow their antecedents.

All of the transformations pertaining to the embedded sentence are completed before any rules are applied to the main sentence. This sequence follows a general principle of transformational grammar: transformations apply first to the deep structure that is the most deeply embedded, then to the next most deeply embedded deep structure, and so on, until the topmost deep structure, the main sentence, is reached.

■ **Exercise 7.1. Forming relative clauses**

Convert the embedded sentences into relative clauses by applying the relative pronoun replacement, *wh- fronting* (if applicable), and affix movement rules. The first question is done as an example. (Answers to exercises are found on page 493.)

1. The editorial (I Past write the editorial) was well received

    Rel repl: The editorial (<u>I Past write that</u>) was well received

    wh- fronting: The editorial (<u>that I Past write</u>) was well received

    Affix Mov: The editorial (<u>that I wrote</u>) was well received

2. They took a risk (<u>the risk Past be totally unjustified</u>)
3. Alexander (<u>Alexander Past have a terrible day</u>) turned in early
4. I finally saw the bear (<u>we Past have Past Part see the bear's tracks earlier</u>)
5. The teacher changed the sentence (<u>we Past have trouble with the sentence</u>)
6. The Latin (<u>Latin Past be Past Part speak in the Middle Ages</u>) was "Church" Latin
7. We had a question about the route (<u>we Past have Past Part decide on route</u>)
8. My brother (<u>my brother's aim Past be unreliable</u>) broke a window
9. Leon's ballet (<u>he originally Past write the ballet for radio</u>) amused the critics
10. The lawyer found the discrepancy (<u>the discrepancy Past be in the witnesses' testimony</u>)
11. They found the horse (<u>the stranger Past have Past Part ride out of town on the horse</u>)
12. His belief was badly shaken by the events (<u>the events Past have Past Part take place</u>)

Reducing relative clauses

If the relative clause contains the verb *be* either as a main verb or an auxiliary verb, we have an additional option. By what we will call the *relative clause reduction rule (Rel Cl Red)*, we will delete (1) the relative pronoun, (2) the tense marker (Pres or Past), and (3) the verb *be* from the relative clause, thus reducing the relative clause to a phrase. Whatever follows the verb *be* is the sole survivor of the underlying relative clause. The relative clause reduction rule has the effect of cutting the relative clause in half; the first three elements—the relative pronoun, the tense marker, and the verb *be*—are deleted; whatever follows the verb *be* remains.

An easy way to visualize the relative clause reduction rule is to draw an imaginary line after the verb *be*. Everything on the left of that line is deleted; everything on the right of that line [which we will call (X)] stays: (relative pronoun + tense + *be* / X). Everything on the left of (/) is deleted; everything on the right (X) stays. (X) can be a number of different things. We will examine first the kinds of constructions created

(X) when *be* is used as a main verb, and then in a second section, we will examine the kinds of constructions created (X) when *be* is used as a helping verb.

***Be* used as a main verb.** *Be* as a main verb can be followed by three things: (1) a noun phrase (a predicate nominative in traditional terms), (2) an adjective (a predicate adjective in traditional terms), and (3) an adverb of place.

1. *be* + Noun Phrase. Following is an embedded sentence containing *be* followed by a noun phrase:

> Mr. Smith (Mr. Smith Pres be a pig farmer) bathes three times a day

The first step in turning this embedded sentence into a relative clause is to apply the relative replacement rule.

> *Rel repl:*   Mr. Smith (who Pres be a pig farmer) bathes three times a day

If we apply the affix movement rule to the preceding embedded sentence, we will create a relative clause surface structure.

> *Affix Mov:*   Mr. Smith (who is a pig farmer) bathes three times a day

However, before we apply the affix movement rule, we have another option: we may apply the *relative clause reduction rule (Rel Cl Red)*. This rule deletes *who* + Past + *be* from the relative clause, leaving behind (X), in this case a noun phrase.

> Mr. Smith (who Pres be / *a pig farmer*) bathes three
> times a day   (X)
>
> *Rel Cl Red:*   Mr. Smith (a pig farmer) bathes three times a day

As you can see, the relative clause reduction rule has deleted everything on the left of the imaginary line: *who Pres be / a pig farmer.* Everything on the right of the imaginary line is retained. In this sentence the material on the right of the line is the noun phrase *a pig farmer.* In traditional grammar, noun phrases of this type have a special name: they are *appositive phrases.* In a transformational grammar all appositives and appositive phrases are derived from relative clauses that contain *be* + a noun phrase. The relative clause reduction rule will delete everything from the relative clause except the noun phrase.

Following are some more examples of appositives and appositive phrases produced by the relative clause reduction rule.

> Holmes (who Past be / a consulting detective) lived
> on Baker Street
>
> *Rel Cl Red:*   Holmes (a consulting detective) lived on Baker
> Street

Holmes' confidant was Watson (who Past be / a medical doctor)

Rel Cl Red: Holmes' confidant was Watson (a medical doctor)

A bumbling policeman (who Past be / Inspector Lestrade) gave comic relief

Rel Cl Red: A bumbling policeman (Inspector Lestrade) gave comic relief

2. *be* + Adjective. Following is an embedded sentence containing *be* followed by an adjective.

Holmes was famous for his memory (his memory Past be remarkable)

The first step in turning the embedded sentence into a relative clause is to replace the duplicate noun and its modifiers with the appropriate relative pronoun.

Rel Repl: Holmes was famous for his memory (which Past be remarkable)

If we now apply the affix movement rule, we will produce a relative clause.

Affix Mov: Holmes was famous for his memory (which was remarkable)

However, before we apply the affix movement rule, we have another option: we can reduce the embedded sentence to an adjective by the relative clause reduction rule. This rule deletes *which* + Past + *be* from the embedded sentence, leaving behind (X): in this case, an adjective.

Holmes was famous for his memory (which Past be / remarkable)

Rel Cl Red: Holmes was famous for his memory (remarkable)

The surviving element from the relative clause is the adjective *remarkable*. In many languages (French, for example) adjectives often may follow the nouns that they modify. In English, however, we must apply an additional transformational rule, which we will call the *adjective switch rule (Adj Switch)*, to move the adjective in front of the noun it modifies.

Holmes was famous for his memory (remarkable)

Adj Switch: Holmes was famous for his (remarkable) memory

Following are some more examples of relative clauses reduced to modifying adjectives.

	I threw away the pizza (the pizza Past be soggy)
Rel Repl:	I threw away the pizza (which Past be / soggy)
Rel Cl Red:	I threw away the pizza (soggy)
Adj Switch:	I threw away the (soggy) pizza

	The bird (the bird Pres be early) gets the worm
Rel Repl:	The bird (that Pres be / early) gets the worm
Rel Cl Red:	The bird (early) gets the worm
Adj Switch:	The (early) bird gets the worm

	Throw the towels (the towels Pres be wet) in the sink
Rel Repl:	Throw the towels (that Pres be / wet) in the sink
Rel Cl Red:	Throw the towels (wet) in the sink
Adj Switch:	Throw the (wet) towels in the sink

3. *be* + **Adverb of place.** Following is an embedded sentence containing *be* followed by an adverb of place (usually, but not necessarily, an adverb prepositional phrase).

How much is that doggy (the doggy Pres be in the window)

The first step in turning the embedded sentence into a relative clause is to replace the duplicate noun and its modifiers with the appropriate relative pronoun.

> *Rel Repl:*   How much is that doggy (that Pres be in the window)

If we now applied the affix movement rule, we would produce a relative clause.

> *Affix Mov:*   How much is that doggy (that is in the window)

However, we again have the option of applying the relative clause reduction rule, which deletes *that* + Pres + *be* from the embedded sentence, leaving behind (X): in this case a prepositional phrase.

> How much is that doggy (that Pres be / in the window)

> *Rel Cl Red:*   How much is that doggy (in the window)

Notice that the prepositional phrase *in the window* is an adverb phrase in the deep structure but an adjective phrase in the surface structure because it modifies the noun *doggy*. This apparent contradiction is resolved when we consider the origin of this prepositional phrase. In the deep structure, the prepositional phrase is part of an embedded sentence modifying the noun *doggy*. When the relative clause reduction rule deletes everything from the embedded sentence except the prepositional phrase, the prepositional phrase, as it were, is the sole survivor of the embedded sentence and thus inherits the adjective function of the entire embedded sentence. Transformational rules affect the forms of structures, but not their functions. Thus, although the relative clause reduction rule deletes (redundant) information from the embedded sentence, it does not change the fact that whatever comes to the surface from the embedded modifying sentence still modifies the noun *doggy*.

Compare the prepositional phrase in the doggy sentence with the same prepositional phrase in the following sentence.

I looked in the window.

In this new sentence, the prepositional phrase *in the window* is not derived from an embedded sentence that modifies a noun; this prepositional phrase originates as an optional adverb phrase within the verb phrase.

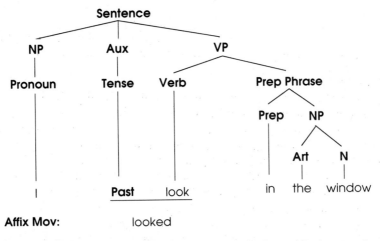

Now let us examine a few more instances of adjective phrases derived from embedded sentences containing adverb phrases of place, before we turn to a detailed examination of a sentence containing an ambiguous prepositional phrase. Following are three examples of adjective prepositional phrases.

	The castles (the castles Pres be in Wales) are breathtaking
Rel Repl:	The castles (which Pres be / in Wales) are breathtaking
Rel Cl Red:	The castles (in Wales) are breathtaking
	The mail (the mail Pres be on the desk) should be sorted
Rel Repl:	The mail (that Pres be / on the desk) should be sorted
Rel Cl Red:	The mail (on the desk) should be sorted

> I called the operator (the operator <u>Pres be in
> Chicago</u>)

Rel Repl: I called the operator (<u>who Pres be / in Chicago</u>)
Rel Cl Red: I called the operator (<u>in Chicago</u>)

As you recall from Chapter 3, prepositional phrases of place are often ambiguous: it is very difficult sometimes to tell whether a prepositional phrase of place should be interpreted as modifying the object noun or should be interpreted as modifying the verb. Consider the following sentence.

I found the boy <u>in the library</u>.

The prepositional phrase *in the library* is ambiguous. In one meaning, *in the library* is an adverb phrase that tells where the boy was found. We can paraphrase this sentence in the following way.

In the library, I found the boy.

In this meaning, *in the library* answers a typical adverb question.

Question: <u>Where</u> did you find the boy?
Answer: In the library.

We can represent this meaning of the sentence by the following phrase structure tree.

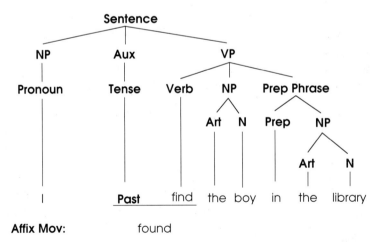

The prepositional phrase *in the library* is derived directly from the verb phrase, a point of origin that can only produce an adverb phrase. The adverb phrase has no grammatical connection with the noun phrase *the boy*; instead, the adverb phrase modifies the verb.

In the other meaning, *in the library* is an adjective phrase that tells *which* boy (of the many boys who were being looked for) was found.

We do not know where the boy from the library was found. He could have been found in the butler's pantry.

The adjective phrase comes from an embedded sentence that could be changed into a relative clause. This embedded sentence, however, is reduced to an adjective phrase. Following is the whole derivation.

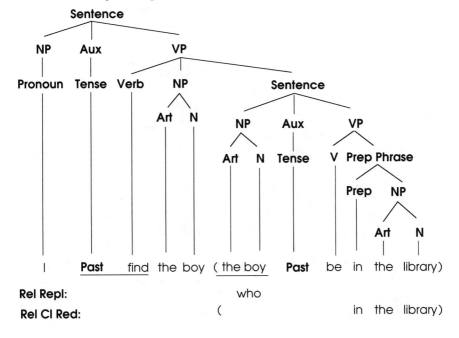

Rel Repl: who

Rel Cl Red: (in   the   library)

Affix Mov: found

Surface sentence: I found the boy **in the library.**

In the first derivation, the prepositional phrase *in the library* comes directly from the verb phrase as an adverb phrase. Even though the prepositional phrase is positioned next to the noun *boy*, the fact that it was not derived from the noun phrase source for *boy* means that *in the library* has no specific grammatical relation to *boy*.

In the second derivation, however, *in the library* comes from a deep structure sentence embedded inside the object noun phrase. This embedded sentence is the source of a relative clause that modifies *boy*. By the operation of the relative clause reduction rule, this embedded sentence is reduced to *in the library*. Any prepositional phrase whose ancestor was a sentence embedded in a noun phrase as a noun modifier must also be a noun modifier. Put the other way around, adjective phrases are derived from embedded sentences by the relative clause reduction rule.

By seeing how adjective phrases are derived from embedded sentences that are also the source for relative clauses, we now have a helpful test for distinguishing adjective and adverb phrases: if you can paraphrase the prepositional phrase as a relative clause, then the prepositional phrase must be an adjective phrase; if you cannot, then the prepositional phrase must be an adverb phrase.

The two different deep structure derivations for the ambiguous surface sentence *I found the boy in the library* are good illustrations of the power of transformational grammar. If the grammar of a surface sentence is ambiguous, then there must be as many different deep structures as there are structural meanings. We can explain the ambiguity of the surface form by tracing the different meanings back to their underlying deep structure origins where the differences in meaning will be embodied in differences of deep structure form.

This is exactly what we did with the ambiguous surface structure *I found the boy in the library*. We traced the adverb meaning back in the deep structure to an adverb origin within the verb phrase. We traced the adjective meaning back to a sentence embedded within the object noun phrase. If a surface structure exhibits structural (as opposed to word-level) ambiguity, then there must be exactly as many different deep structure *forms* as there are surface structure *meanings*.

Let us again stop and summarize. When a sentence embedded inside a noun phrase contains *be*, then we have an additional option besides creating a relative clause: after we have replaced the duplicate noun with the appropriate relative pronoun by the *relative replacement rule*, we may delete the relative pronoun, the tense marker, and the verb *be* by the *relative clause reduction rule*. This rule has the effect of cutting the embedded sentence in two; the first three elements—the relative pronoun, the tense marker, and the verb *be*—are deleted; whatever follows the verb *be* remains. So far we have examined embedded sentences in which *be* functions as the main verb. *Be* as a main verb can be followed by three things: (1) a noun phrase, (2) an adjective, and (3) an adverb of place.

Following is how the relative clause reduction rule applies to each of the elements (noun phrase, adjective, adverb of place) that can follow the verb *be*:

1. *Noun phrase:*

	I found the typewriter (the typewriter Past be an old Royal)
Rel Repl:	I found the typewriter (which Past be / an old Royal)
Rel Cl Red:	I found the typewriter (an old Royal)

The noun phrase, which is all that is left from the embedded sentence, is called an *appositive phrase* in traditional terms.

2. *Adjective:*

I found the typewriter (the typewriter Past be old)

Rel Repl: I found the typewriter (which Past be / old)

Rel Cl Red: I found the typewriter (old)

Adj Switch: I found the (old) typewriter

The adjective, which is all that is left from the embedded sentence, must be moved to a position in front of the noun it modifies by the adjective switch rule.

3. *Adverb of place:*

I found the typewriter (the typewriter Past be from school)

Rel Repl: I found the typewriter (which Past be / from school)

Rel Cl Red: I found the typewriter (from school)

The adverb of place, which is all that is left from the embedded modifying sentence, becomes an adjective phrase because it inherits the adjective function of its deep structure source.

■ **Exercise 7.2. Reducing embedded sentences with *be* as a main verb**

Applying the relative replacement, relative clause reduction, and (if appropriate) the adjective switch rules, reduce embedded sentences to appositives, adjectives, or adjective phrases. The first question is done as an example. (Answers to exercises are found on page 494.)

1. We travelled across Texas (Texas Pres be the largest state in America)

    Rel Repl: We travelled across Texas (which Pres be the largest state in America)

    Rel Cl Red: We travelled across Texas (the largest state in America)

2. Please get the book (the book Pres be on the top shelf)

3. The audience (the audience Past be strangely silent) began to take notice

4. With the money (the money Past be a gift from his parents) he bought a tuba

5. The jury ignored the story (the defendant Past give the story)

6. The soldiers (the soldiers Past be exhausted) returned to camp

7. Mike (Mike Pres be a bartender at a place (the place Pres be in town)) called me over

8. The heat (the heat Pres be intense) had broken all records

9. Baseball (baseball Pres be America's favorite sport) has been played for years
10. Adam (Adam Past come to the door first) is the oldest brother
11. They objected to delays (the delays Pres be costly and unnecessary)
12. Everyone appreciated the effort (you Past put in the effort)
13. The collectors recognized the value (the value Pres be obvious)

***Be* used as an auxiliary verb.** *Be* has two functions as an auxiliary verb: it is used (1) in forming the progressive, and (2) in forming the passive. In both cases the relative clause reduction rule functions in the same manner as it did when *be* was a main verb: the relative pronoun, tense marker, and *be* are deleted from the relative clause. The surviving portion of the relative clause remains as a modifying phrase. When *be* is used as a progressive, what results from the application of the relative clause reduction rule is either a *present participle* or a *present participial phrase*. When *be* is used as part of the passive, what results from the application of the relative clause reduction rule is either a *past participle* or *past participial phrase*.

1. Present participles and present participial phrases. The following embedded sentence contains the progressive auxiliary (*be* + Pres Part).

We saw a boy (the boy Past *be* Pres Part ride a unicycle)

The first step in creating a grammatical surface structure from the embedded sentence is to apply the relative replacement transformation.

Rel Repl: We saw a boy (who Past *be* Pres Part ride a unicycle)

If we apply affix movement to the embedded sentence, the resulting surface structure will be a relative clause.

Affix Mov: We saw a boy (who was riding a unicycle)

However, we have another alternative before we apply affix movement. Since the relative clause contains the verb *be*, we may apply the relative clause reduction rule, which will delete the relative pronoun, the tense marker, and the auxiliary verb *be*. The remaining portion of the embedded sentence, after the affix movement attaches the Pres Part marker to the following verb, is a present participle or present participial phrase.

We saw a boy (who Past be / Pres Part ride a unicycle)

Rel Cl Red: We saw a boy (Pres Part ride a unicycle)
Affix Mov: We saw a boy (riding a unicycle)

Note that the relative clause reduction rule now breaks apart the progressive auxiliary (*be* + Pres Part), deleting *be* along the the relative pronoun and the tense marker. The affix movement rule then attaches the Pres Part marker to the main verb in the normal manner. Since the main verb is now in the present participle form, the relative clause reduction rule has left behind a present participle verb (*riding*) and its object (*a unicycle*). In other words, the relative clause reduction rule has created a present participial phrase. Following are some more examples of this construction.

	The player (the player Past be Pres Part guard the center) fouled out
Rel Repl:	The player (who Past be / Pres Part guard the center) fouled out
Rel Cl Red:	The player (Pres Part guard the center) fouled out
Affix Mov:	The player (guarding the center) fouled out
	We cut down the tree (the tree Past be Pres Part tilt over the fence)
Rel Repl:	We cut down the tree (that Past be / Pres Part tilt over the fence)
Rel Cl Red:	We cut down the tree (Pres Part tilt over the fence)
Affix Mov:	We cut down the tree (tilting over the fence)
	The cat (the cat Past be Pres Part hide in the bushes) caught a bird
Rel Repl:	The cat (which Past be / Pres Part hide in the bushes) caught a bird
Rel Cl Red:	The cat (Pres Part hide in the bushes) caught a bird
Affix Mov:	The cat (hiding in the bushes) caught a bird

It is possible to move a participial phrase that modifies a subject noun to a position in front of the noun it modifies. For instance, we can readily move the present participial phrase in the following example from its position after the subject noun phrase to a position in front of the subject noun phrase.

The professor, cleverly diagraming the sentences, enlightened her grateful students.

Cleverly diagraming the sentences, the professor enlightened her grateful students.

When the subject is a pronoun, moving the participial phrase in front of the subject is virtually obligatory. For example, compare the following two versions.

She, cleverly diagraming the sentences, enlightened her grateful students.

Cleverly diagraming the sentences, she enlightened her grateful students.

While the first sentence may not be ungrammatical, it is certainly stilted. We would all prefer the version that moved the participial phrase to a position in front of the subject pronoun.

If the relative clause contains an intransitive verb and no modifiers, the relative clause reduction rule will produce a participle. In that case, we must treat the participle like an adjective and move it in front of the noun by the adjective switch rule, as in the following examples.

	They finally replaced the neon tube (the neon tube Past be Pres Part flicker)
Rel Repl:	They finally replaced the neon tube (that Past be / Pres Part flicker)
Rel Cl Red:	They finally replaced the neon tube (Pres Part flicker)
Affix Mov:	They finally replaced the neon tube (flickering)
Adj Switch:	They finally replaced the (flickering) neon tube
	Holmes found the revolver (the revolver Past be Pres Part smoke)
Rel Repl:	Holmes found the revolver (which Past be / Pres Part smoke)
Rel Cl Red:	Holmes found the revolver (Pres Part smoke)
Affix Mov:	Holmes found the revolver (smoking)
Adj Switch:	Holmes found the (smoking) revolver
	They anxiously watched the clouds (the clouds Past be Pres Part threaten)
Rel Repl:	They anxiously watched the clouds (that Past be / Pres Part threaten)
Rel Cl Red:	They anxiously watched the clouds (Pres Part threaten)
Affix Mov:	They anxiously watched the clouds (threatening)
Adj Switch:	They anxiously watched the (threatening) clouds

■ **Exercise 7.3. Present participles and present participial phrases**

Turn the embedded sentences into present participles or present participial phrases. The first question is done as an example. (Answers to exercises are found on page 495.)

1. Gabriela (Gabriela Past be Pres Part exploit her advantage) rushed the net

   Rel Repl: Gabriela (who Past be Pres Part exploit her advantage) rushed the net

   Rel Cl Red: Gabriela (Pres Part exploit her advantage) rushed the net

   Affix Mov: Gabriela (exploiting her advantage) rushed the net

2. The judge (the judge Past be Pres Part uphold the dignity of the court) called for order

3. Watson (Watson Past be Pres Part nurse a severe headcold) reluctantly followed Holmes into the wet sewer

4. The crowd (the crowd Past be Pres Part cheer) spilled out of the stadium

5. The sheriff (the sheriff Past be Pres Part check his pistols) turned to face the angry mob

6. I was sourly greeted by a clerk (the clerk Past be Pres Part complain)

7. The driver (the driver Past be Pres Part look at his map) nearly missed the freeway exit

8. The kids (the kids Past be Pres Part risk life and limb) climbed up the cliff

9. The conductor (the conductor Past be Pres Part bow to the audience) motioned for the soloists to rise

10. The ghost (the ghost Past be Pres Part manifest herself as a Rockette) appeared in the hallway again

11. The senator glared at the audience (the audience Past be Pres Part snicker)

---

2. Past participles and past participial phrases. Past participles and past participial phrases are formed in a manner very similar to present participles and present participial phrases—with one important difference: the relative clause that is the source for the past participle and past participial phrase *must be in the passive voice*. The passive transformation supplies *be* as a helping verb. The *be* then permits the application of the relative clause reduction rule. In the following sentence the embedded sentence is in a deep structure form.

The game (the storm Past delay the game) will be replayed later

One way that we can bring the embedded sentence to the surface is by converting it into a relative clause by applying the relative replacement and affix movement rules.

> *Rel repl:* The game (that the storm Past delay) will be
> replayed later
>
> *Affix Mov:* The game (that the storm delayed) will be replayed
> later

However, we have another option. Before we convert the embedded sentence into a relative clause, we can turn it into a passive.

> *Passive:* The game (the game Past be Past Part delay by the
> storm) will be replayed later

[*Note:* From now on, we will condense the three steps of the passive transformation into one operation.]

The passive embedded sentence can now be turned into a relative clause.

> *Rel repl:* The game (that Past be Past Part delay by the storm)
> will be replayed later
>
> *Affix Mov:* The game (that was delayed by the storm) will be
> replayed later

However, since the passive transformation has added the helping verb *be* to the embedded sentence, we can now exploit a further option before we apply the affix movement rule to create a relative clause: we can apply the relative clause reduction rule and reduce the embedded sentence to a phrase.

> *Rel Repl:* The game (that Past be / Past Part delay by the
> storm) will be replayed later
>
> *Rel Cl Red:* The game (Past Part delay by the storm) will be
> replayed later
>
> *Affix Mov:* The game (delayed by the storm) will be replayed
> later

All past participles and past participial phrases are produced by the following cycle of rules.

1. The *passive rule* transforms the embedded sentence into a passive.
2. The *relative pronoun replacement rule* (*Rel Repl*) replaces the subject of the passive sentence with the appropriate relative pronoun.
3. The *relative clause reduction rule* (*Rel Cl Red*) deletes the relative pronoun, the tense marker, and the verb *be*. (Recall that the *be* was inserted into the embedded sentence by the passive transformation.)
4. The *affix movement rule* attaches the past participle marker (also created by the passive transformation) to the main verb of the embedded sentence.

Following are some more examples of embedded deep structures first turned into passive relative clauses and then reduced to participial phrases.

The glass (the blow Past shatter the glass) cut two people

Passive: The glass (the glass Past be Past Part shatter by the blow) cut two people

Rel Repl: The glass (which Past be / Past Part shatter by the blow) cut two people

Rel Cl Red: The glass (Past Part shatter by the blow) cut two people

Affix Mov: The glass (shattered by the blow) cut two people

The movie (countless commercials Past interrupt the movie) quickly became boring

Passive: The movie (the movie Past be Past Part interrupt by countless commercials) quickly became boring

Rel Repl: The movie (which Past be / Past Part interrupt by countless commercials) quickly became boring

Rel Cl Red: The movie (Past Part interrupt by countless commercials) quickly became boring

Affix Mov: The movie (interrupted by countless commercials) quickly became boring

We watched a movie (somebody Past edit the movie for television)

Passive: We watched a movie (the movie Past be Past Part edit for television)

[*Note:* The phrase *by somebody* has been deleted— see below.]

Rel Repl: We watched a movie (that Past be / Past Part edit for television)

Rel Cl Red: We watched a movie (Past Part edit for television)

Affix Mov: We watched a movie (edited for television)

When the *by* phrase in a passive sentence contains an indefinite pronoun (e.g., *somebody* or *something*) or an object of *by* that is clear from context, the entire *by* + noun phrase construction may be deleted by a transformation called (not surprisingly) the *by deletion rule (by Del)*. If there are no modifiers in the embedded sentence, the relative clause reduction rule and affix movement rule will then reduce the embedded sentence to a *past participle*. In this case, we must treat the past participle like an adjective and move it in front of the noun by the adjective switch rule, as in the following example.

	They finally replaced the neon tube (somebody Past break the neon tube)
Passive & by Del:	They finally replaced the neon tube (the neon tube Past be Past Part break)
Rel Repl:	They finally replaced the neon tube (that Past be / Past Part break)
Rel Cl Red:	They finally replaced the neon tube (Past Part break)
Affix Mov:	They finally replaced the neon tube (broken)
Adj Switch:	They finally replaced the (broken) neon tube

As you may have noticed, this treatment of past participles is parallel to the treatment of present participles in the previous section, the main difference being that present participles are derived from underlying active sentences with a progressive rather than from passive sentences. Recall, for example, the derivation of the sentence *They finally replaced the (flickering) neon tube*.

Following are some more examples of past participles used as adjectives.

	The crowd (something Past disappoint the crowd) left the stadium
Passive & by Del:	The crowd (the crowd Past be Past Part disappoint) left the stadium
Rel Repl:	The crowd (which Past be / Past Part disappoint) left the stadium
Rel Cl Red:	The crowd (Past Part disappoint) left the stadium
Affix Mov:	The crowd (disappointed) left the stadium
Adj Switch:	The (disappointed) crowd left the stadium

	The editor withdrew the article (someone Past criticize the article
Passive & by Del:	The editor withdrew the article (the article Past be Past Part criticize)
Rel Repl:	The editor withdrew the article (that Past be / Past Part criticize)
Rel Cl Red:	The editor withdrew the article (Past Part criticize)
Affix Mov:	The editor withdrew the article (criticized)
Adj Switch:	The editor withdrew the (criticized) article

	I bandaged my knee (something Past scratch my knee)
Passive: & by Del:	I bandaged my knee (my knee Past be Past Part scratch)
Rel Repl:	I bandaged my knee (which Past be / Past Part scratch)
Rel Cl Red:	I bandaged my knee (Past Part scratch)
Affix Mov:	I bandaged my knee (scratched)
Adj Switch:	I bandaged my (scratched) knee

Let us briefly recap how past participles and past participial phrases arc formed. When an embedded sentence is transformed into a passive by the *passive*, one component of the new passive sentence is the passive auxiliary (*be* + Past Part). After the duplicate noun and its modifiers (the new subject of the passive sentence) have been replaced by a relative pronoun through the *relative replacement rule*, we then have an option. We can either (1) apply the *affix movement rule* and create a relative clause, or (2) apply the *relative clause reduction rule* and create a past participle or past participial phrase. The relative clause reduction rule deletes the relative pronoun, the tense marker (Pres or Past), and the helping verb *be*. (The *be*, you recall, was introduced as part of the passive transformation.) What remains of the relative clause (assuming application of the *affix movement rule*, which attaches the Past Part marker to the main verb) is a past participle or a past participial phrase. If a past participle remains, then it is treated like an adjective; that is, it is moved in front of the noun it modifies by the *adjective switch rule*.

■ **Exercise 7.4. Past participles and past participial phrases**

Turn the embedded sentences into passives, then reduce the passive to a past participle or past participial phrase. If the embedded contains an indefinite pronoun, delete the *by* phrase to produce a past participle. The first question is done as an example. (Answers to exercises are found on page 497.)

1. We bought the VCR (*Consumer Reports* Past recommend the VCR)

   Passive: We bought the VCR (the VCR Past be Past Part recommend by *Consumer Reports*)

   Rel Repl: We bought the VCR (that Past be Past Part recommend by *Consumer Reports*)

   Rel Cl Red: We bought the VCR (Past Part recommend by *Consumer Reports*)

   Affix Movement: We bought the VCR (recommended by *Consumer Reports*)

2. They lived in a miserable apartment (incompetent builders Past construct the apartment)
3. John (the wind Past bother John) missed the target completely
4. Captain Midnight received a message (somebody Past hide the message)
5. Leon (the group Past exclude Leon) finally went home
6. Aunt Sally (the news Past depress Aunt Sally) unplugged the radio
7. We collected the tents (something Past damage the tents)
8. Near the village there is a fort (Crusaders Past build the fort in the 14th century)

9. The movement (<u>somebody Past discredit the movement</u>) eventually collapsed

10. Marcia (<u>every paper in the country Past interview Marcia</u>) began to hit the talk shows

---

Let us now summarize the entire noun modification process. With the exception of premodifiers—articles, numbers, and some adjectives— all noun modifiers come from sentences embedded inside the noun phrase following the nouns they modify. These embedded sentences can always come to the surface as relative clauses by means of the *relative replacement rule (Rel Repl)*, the *wh- fronting rule* (if applicable), and the *affix movement rule (Affix Mov)*.

However, if the embedded sentences contain the verb *be*, then the embedded sentences can be reduced to various other types of modifying phrases or even to single word modifiers depending on (1) the role of *be* (main verb or auxiliary verb), and (2) the function of the words that follow *be*. The key point, though, is that all these different types of modifiers are derived from the same embedded sentence that is also the source of relative (adjective) clauses, and all (including relative clauses) have undergone the relative replacement rule.

The embedded sentence is reduced to modifying phrases or single word adjectives or participles by one rule: the *relative clause reduction Rule (Rel Cl Red)*, which deletes (1) the relative pronoun, (2) the tense marker (Past or Present), and (3) the verb *be*. The type of modifier that results from the operation of this rule depends on what followed the verb *be*, that is, on what was not deleted from the embedded sentence.

If *be* was the main verb in the embedded sentence, there are three possible types of structures that will have survived the operation of the relative clause reduction rule: (1) noun phrases, (2) adjectives, and (3) prepositional phrases of place. The noun phrase has become an *appositive*. The adjective must be moved to a position in front of the noun it modifies by the *adjective switch rule (Adj Switch)*. The prepositional phrase of place has become an *adjective phrase* following the noun it modifies.

If *be* was a helping verb, the relative clause reduction rule will leave behind a participle marker (either Pres Part or Past Part) and the entire verb phrase from the embedded sentence. The participle markers have different origins.

☐ Pres Part comes from the progressive auxiliary (*be* + Pres Part).

☐ Past Part is derived from the passive auxiliary (*be* + Past Part) from the application of the *passive* transformation to the embedded sentence before any other rules were applied.

The participle markers (Pres Part and Past Part) are automatically attached to the following verb by the *affix movement rule*. If the Pres Part was attached to a transitive verb or to an intransitive verb modified by one or more adverbs or adverb phrases, the resulting structure is a *present participial phrase*. If the Pres Part was attached to an intransitive verb with no modifiers, the resulting structure is a *present participle*.

If the Past Part was attached to a verb which is modified by one or more adverbs or adverb phrases, the resulting structure is a *past participial phrase*. If the Past Part was attached to a verb with no modifiers (a situation possible only if the *by deletion rule* has been applied to the passive sentence), the resulting structure is a *past participle*.

Both present and past participles must be moved to a position in front of the noun that they modify by the *Adjective Switch Rule (Adj Switch)*.

A schematic presentation of the preceding information may help keep it organized.

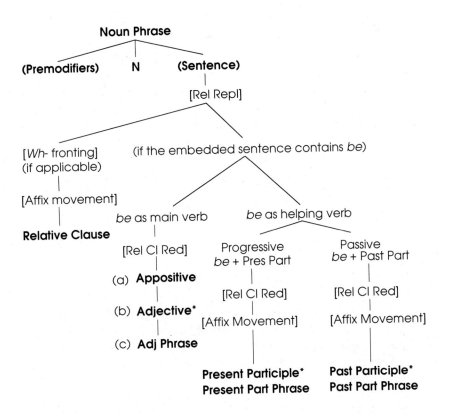

Noun Phrase

(Premodifiers)   **N**   **(Sentence)**

[Rel Repl]

[*Wh-* fronting]   (if the embedded sentence contains *be*)
(if applicable)

[Affix movement]

Relative Clause   *be* as main verb   *be* as helping verb

[Rel Cl Red]   Progressive   Passive
   be + Pres Part   *be* + Past Part

(a) **Appositive**

   [Rel Cl Red]   [Rel Cl Red]

(b) **Adjective***

   [Affix Movement]   [Affix Movement]

(c) **Adj Phrase**

Present Participle*   **Past Participle***
Present Part Phrase   **Past Part Phrase**

* Must undergo [Adjective Switch]

■ **Exercise 7.5. Review of noun modification**

Turn the embedded sentences into as many forms of noun modification as possible. Label your answers. The first question is done as an example. (Answers to exercises are found on page 499.)

1. We diagramed the sentence (the teacher Past put the sentence on the board)

   Rel Clause: We diagramed the sentence that the teacher put on the board.

   Rel Clause (Passive): We diagramed the sentence that was put on the board by the teacher.

   Past Part Phrase (Passive): We diagramed the sentence put on the board by the teacher.

2. The steps (the steps Past be in the back yard) needed to be fixed

3. Yelling at the referee was a foul (the foul Past be certain)

4. The people (the people Past be Pres Part come through the door) were dressed in costumes (the costumes Past be outlandish)

5. The road (someone Past oil the road) was much better than before

6. The picture (the picture Past be a seascape (the seascape Past be bright)) was perfect for my office

7. Holmes (Holmes Past learn little from the butler) turned his attention to the footprints

8. We followed the trail (someone Past mark the trail)

9. Again Watson heard the noise (the noise Past be a tapping (the tapping Past be mysterious) under the floorboards)

10. The bike (the bike Past be Pres Part speed hopelessly out of control) left the path and jumped the curb (the curb Past be steep)

11. Lestrade (Lestrade Past be Pres Part grow increasingly uneasy at Holmes's explanation (Holmes's explanation Past be strange)) turned to Watson in frustration

NOMINALIZATION

Nominalization is the second of the three sentence combining processes that we are examining. *Nominalization* is the name in transformational grammar for the process by which embedded sentences take the role of nouns. These embedded sentences come to the surface as noun clauses or noun phrases, the latter including verbal phrases.

Unlike relative clauses, which can modify any common noun, nominalizations are very restricted. They can be used only in sentences where an *abstract noun* can be used. Some abstract nouns are *outcome, plan, idea, goal, thought, reason*. The other main types of nouns are *concrete* (e.g., *brick, footstool, desk, house, sand, flower*) and *animate* (e.g., *people, boy, girl, child, cow, fish, elk*). *Human* nouns are a major subcategory of animate nouns.

The noun *outcome* is a good test word for abstract nouns because *outcome* is compatible with nearly any verb that will accept an abstract noun. For example, (taking the noun clause *that John rebutted the speaker* as an example of a nominalization) a nominalization can be used as a subject in the following sentence because the verb *surprise* will accept an abstract noun as a subject.

The <u>outcome</u>   surprised us.

<u>That John rebutted the speaker</u> surprised us.

The same noun clause can be used as an object in the following sentence because the verb *discover* will accept an abstract noun as an object.

We discovered   the <u>outcome</u>.

We discovered <u>that John rebutted the speaker.</u>

Many verbs will not accept an abstract noun. For example, the verb *applaud* requires a human subject, and the verb *surprise* ('strike with amazement') requires a human object. When we try to use the noun clause *that John rebutted the speaker* with these two verbs, the result is ungrammatical.

*<u>That John rebutted the speaker</u> applauded the performance.

*The event surprised <u>that John rebutted the speaker.</u>

When a noun clause is used with a verb that requires a concrete noun, the results are even more outlandish.

*<u>That John rebutted the speaker</u> tipped over.

*The fisherman hooked his line on <u>that John rebutted the speaker.</u>

We can show that the verbs in the preceding four example sentences do not accept abstract nouns by replacing the noun clauses with the abstract test noun *outcome*.

*The <u>outcome</u> applauded the performance.

*The event surprised the <u>outcome</u>.

*The <u>outcome</u> tipped over.

*The fisherman hooked his line on the <u>outcome</u>.

In transformational grammar, nominalizations—noun clauses, verbals that function as nouns, and certain noun phrases—are derived from full underlying sentences that replace abstract nouns. Compare the deep structure source for relative (adjective) clauses with the source for nominalizations.

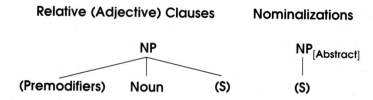

A relative clause comes from a sentence embedded inside a noun phrase; moreover, the embedded sentence is bound by two important restrictions: (1) the embedded sentence must follow the head noun of the noun phrase, and (2) the embedded sentence must contain within it a noun that is a duplicate of the head noun.

A nominalization, on the other hand, is an embedded sentence that plays the role of an entire noun phrase; it replaces, as it were, the noun phrase. Unlike the embedded sentence that is the source of a relative clause, there are no restrictions on the internal structure of the embedded sentence that is the source of a nominalization.

Nominalizations can come to the surface in one of two ways.

☐ as *noun clauses*
☐ as *noun phrases*

The difference between the two different nominalization surface forms is what happens to the *tense* marker. In the derivation of noun clauses, the tense marker is attached to the following verb as usual, creating a finite verb (a verb in the present or past tense). In the derivation of noun phrases, on the other hand, the tense marker is deleted, so the resulting surface structure has no finite verb and is, therefore, by definition, a phrase rather than a clause.

There are two types of *noun clauses*.

☐ *that* type (Example: I know *that you are right*)
☐ *wh-* type (Example: I know *who you are*)

For an explanation of this terminology, see the discussion of noun clauses in Chapter 4.

There are three types of *noun phrases*, depending on what replaces the tense marker in the embedded sentence.

☐ The tense marker is replaced by a present participle marker (Pres Part), creating a *gerund* or *gerund phrase*, one type of verbal phrase. (Example: I hate *being late*.)

☐ The tense marker is replaced by *to*, creating an *infinitive* or *infinitive phrase*, another type of verbal phrase. (Example: I hate *to be late*.)

☐ The tense marker and the main verb are both replaced by an abstract noun. This type of phrase, which has no conventional name in traditional grammar, is called here an *abstract noun phrase* (Example: The paper announced *the Senate's ratification of the treaty*.)

The following diagram summarizes the various ways in which nominalizations can come to the surface.

Nominalization Types

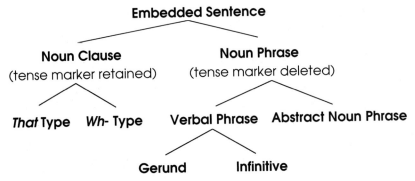

Taking *John* Past *refuse the offer* as the embedded sentence, we can produce the following nominalized surface forms.

Noun Clause:
   That Type: that John refused the offer
   Wh- Type: what John refused; who refused the offer
Noun Phrase:
   Verbal:
      Gerund: (John's) refusing the offer
      Infinitive: (for John) to refuse the offer
      Abstract NP: (John's) refusal of the offer

In the following sections, we discuss the nominalization processes by which embedded sentences are transformed into surface forms.

Noun clauses

Noun clauses retain the tense marker of the underlying full sentence, thus preserving a full subject-verb relationship.

That type noun clauses are formed by merely adding the introductory words *that, if,* or *whether (or not)* to the underlying sentence. Consider the following example.

<u>(John Past rebut the speaker)</u> surprised us

From the underlying sentence we can produce a *that* type noun clause by adding *that* and applying the necessary affix movement rule.

<u>(*that* John rebutted the speaker)</u> surprised us

Following are examples with *if* and *whether (or not)*, the other two introductory words for *that* type noun clauses.

A good fisherman always knows (<u>*if* he has a bite</u>)

I don't know (<u>*whether or not* we will finish painting before dark</u>)

Wh- type noun clauses are more complicated. The *wh-* word must appear in the underlying sentence as a noun or an adverb. The *wh-* word is then moved to the first position within its clause by our old friend *wh- fronting*, which was used in the previous section to move relative pronouns to the first position in relative clauses. Here *wh- fronting* will move a somewhat different group of *wh-* words (interrogative pronouns and adverbs) to the first position of the embedded sentence.

Following are some examples of *wh-* type noun clauses with the *wh-* word playing various noun roles inside the embedded sentence. *Wh- fronting* moves the *wh-* word to the first position in the embedded sentence if the *wh-* word is not the subject (and thus already in the first position).

Subject:	(*whoever said that*) was pulling your leg
Object:	(you want *whatever*) is OK with me
wh- fronting:	(<u>*whatever* you want</u>) is OK with me
Predicate Nominative:	(it is *whatever*) looks good to me
wh- fronting:	(*whatever* it is) looks good to me
Object of Preposition:	(<u>he told me about *what*</u>) is none of your business
wh- fronting:	(<u>*what* he told me about</u>) is none of your business

Following are examples of *wh-* words playing various adverb roles inside the noun clause:

Time:	(you are ready *whenever*) is fine
wh- fronting:	(<u>*whenever* you are ready</u>) is fine
Place:	(the best food is *where*) will be his destination
wh- fronting:	(<u>*where* the best food is</u>) will be his destination
Manner:	(you get away with so much *how*) is beyond me
wh- fronting:	(<u>*how* you get away with so much</u>) is beyond me
Reason:	I don't know (there's no sun up in the sky *why*)
wh- fronting:	I don't know (*why* there's no sun up in the sky)

■ Exercise 7.6. *That* and *wh-* type noun clauses

Turn the embedded sentences into noun clauses. [Ignore affix movement.] If the embedded sentence contains a *wh-* word, use *wh- fronting;* otherwise, add *that* or *whether* as appropriate. The first two questions are done as examples. (Answers to exercises are found on page 500.)

1. (we go to the ball game) depends on the weather
   (*whether* we go to the ball) game depends on the weather
2. I finally found (I was looking for what)
   wh- fronting: I finally found (what I was looking for)
3. The computer keeps track of (you log on or off whenever)
4. (you said whatever about our problems) made quite an impression on them
5. (you were not hurt worse) is a miracle
6. We want to know (they cannot finish their jobs on time why)
7. Can you tell me (I can get to the train station how)
8. The question is (who will clean this mess up)
9. (we will win) is a foregone conclusion
10. They were asked about (they wanted what for dinner)
11. (you decide whatever) is OK with me
12. (there is a will where), there is a way
13. We wondered (the game would start on time)
14. I don't understand (you put up with all that why)
15. I know (you know (he knows))
16. He knew (I was right about (the Giants won the pennant when))

Noun phrases

In this type of nominalization the tense from the underlying full sentence is not preserved, and thus the embedded sentence is reduced to a noun phrase. There are two main types of noun phrases derived from embedded sentences: *verbal phrases* and what we call *abstract noun phrases.*

1. Verbal Phrases. In creating verbal phrases, the *tense replacement rule (Tense Repl)* replaces the tense marker in the embedded sentence with either (1) the present participle marker (Pres Part) or (2) the infinitive marker *to.* In the first case, the application of the tense replacement rule will lead to the creation of a gerund or gerund phrase. In the second case, the application of the tense replacement rule will lead to the creation of an infinitive or infinitive phrase. We examine each type of replacement in turn.

Gerunds and gerund phrases. In this type of reduction, three transformational rules apply to the embedded sentence.

1. The *tense replacement rule* replaces the tense marker in the embedded sentence with the present participle marker (Pres Part).
2. The *affix movement rule* attaches the present participle marker (Pres Part) to the following verb, creating a gerund.
3. The *subject rule* does one of two things.
   a. It changes the subject of the embedded sentence to its corresponding possessive form; for example, it changes *Fred* to *Fred's; I* to *my; they* to *their, we* to *our, she* to *her,* etc., or
   b. it deletes the subject of the embedded sentence if the subject can be understood from context.
   We indicate the two different functions of the subject rule (deleting the subject or retaining the subject as a possessive) by putting the possessive form of the subject in parentheses.

Following are some derivations that show the changes from underlying embedded sentences to gerund phrases.

	(John Past rebut the speaker) surprised everyone
Tense Repl:	(John Pres Part rebut the speaker) surprised everyone
Affix Mov:	(John rebutting the speaker) surprised everyone
Subject:	((John's) rebutting the speaker) surprised everyone

	(she Past be so quick) pleased the coaches
Tense Repl:	(she Pres Part be so quick) pleased the coaches
Affix Mov:	(she being so quick) pleased the coaches
Subject:	((her) being so quick) pleased the coaches

	(we Pres have Past Part win the election) was clear
Tense Repl:	(we Pres Part have Past Part win the election) was clear
Affix Mov:	(we having won the election) was clear
Subject:	((our) having won the election) was clear

When the gerund phrase is derived from a sentence embedded in the position of an object, the subject rule can delete the subject only if the subject of the embedded sentence is identical with the subject of the main sentence. If the subject of the embedded sentence is not identical with the subject of the main sentence, then the subject of the embedded sentence must be retained.

Following is an example where the subject of the embedded sentence is identical with the subject of the main sentence.

	They reported (they Past see the accident)
Tense Repl:	They reported (they Pres Part see the accident)
Affix Mov:	They reported (they seeing the accident)
Subject:	They reported ((their) seeing the accident)

The subject rule allows two possible surface forms for the embedded sentence.

Subject retained as possessive:	They reported (their seeing the accident)
Subject deleted:	They reported (seeing the accident)

As we would expect, the two surface forms are paraphrases of each other because they are derived from the same deep structure.

Following now is an example where the subject of the embedded sentence is different from the subject of the main sentence.

	They reported (Ralph Past see the accident)
Tense Repl:	They reported (Ralph Pres Part see the accident)
Affix Mov:	They reported (Ralph seeing the accident)
Subject:	They reported (Ralph's seeing the accident)

The subject rule allows only possible surface forms for the embedded sentence.

Subject retained as possessive:	They reported (Ralph's seeing the accident)

If, in violation of the subject rule, we deleted the subject from the embedded sentence, we would produce the following gerund phrase.

*They reported (seeing the accident)

The only possible interpretation of this surface sentence is that *they* (not *Ralph*) saw the accident. The sentence is ungrammatical in its intended meaning (that *Ralph*, not *they*, saw the accident). The only possible interpretation of this surface structure (that *they* saw the accident) cannot properly be traced back to the actual deep structure (*Ralph Past see the accident*). In other words, a transformational derivation is grammatical only if the surface structure conveys the meaning inherent in the deep structure. Consider the two sentences together.

*They reported (<u>Ralph Past see the accident</u>)
*They reported (<u>seeing the accident</u>)

We can see clearly that the second example is not a grammatical surface structure derivation from the deep structure of the first.

If the verb in the embedded sentence is intransitive (and has no modifiers), and if we delete the subject, we are left with nothing but the gerund; that is, we have derived a gerund as opposed to a gerund phrase. Following is a sample derivation of a gerund.

	(someone Past drive) puts babies to sleep
Tense Repl:	(someone Pres Part drive) puts babies to sleep
Affix Mov:	(someone driving) puts babies to sleep
Subject:	(driving) puts babies to sleep

■ **Exercise 7.7. Gerunds and gerund phrases**

Reduce the embedded sentences to gerunds and/or gerund phrases by the tense replacement, affix movement, and subject rules. The first question is done as an example. (Answers to exercises are found on page 501.)

1. (<u>Napoleon Past retreat from Moscow</u>) was an unparalleled disaster

    Tense Repl: (<u>Napoleon Pres Part retreat from Moscow</u>) was an unparalleled disaster

    Affix Mov: (<u>Napoleon retreating from Moscow</u>) was an unparalleled disaster

    Subject: ((Napoleon's) retreating from Moscow) was an unparalleled disaster

2. (<u>the flowers Past burst into sudden bloom</u>) made it seem like spring in the kitchen

3. Our trip was nearly ruined by (<u>Leon Past have Past Part lose the map</u>)

4. (<u>Watson Pres assist Holmes in his investigation</u>) is a necessary, but artificial, plot device

5. (<u>the wind Past be from the north</u>) forced the Admiral to return to port

6. (<u>the children Past have Past Part eat earlier</u>) made our meal more pleasant

7. We resented (<u>they Past object to the proposal</u>) very much

8. The recruits practiced (<u>they Past salute</u>) all afternoon

9. (<u>we Past be always anxious about the time</u>) prevented us from really enjoying ourselves

10. (I Pres diet) is not much fun
11. He appreciated (she Past fix dinner for a change)
12. He appreciated (he Past fix dinner for a change)

Infinitives and infinitive phrases. The process of forming infinitives and infinitive phrases is similar to the process of forming gerunds and gerund phrases. Fundamental to both processes is the deletion of the tense marker in the embedded sentence by the *tense replacement rule*. The difference between gerunds and gerund phrases on the one hand and infinitives and infinitive phrases on the other is the nature of the element that is inserted into the embedded sentence in place of the tense marker. When the tense replacement rule replaces the tense marker with a present participle marker, the resulting surface structure will be a present participle (a gerund) or a present participial phrase (a gerund phrase). However, when the tense replacement rule replaces the tense marker with *to*, the resulting surface structure will be an infinitive or infinitive phrase. If the verb in the embedded sentence is intransitive and has no modifiers, the resulting structure is an infinitive; in all other cases, the resulting structure is an infinitive phrase.

The *subject rule* plays essentially the same role with infinitives and infinitive phrases as it does with gerunds and gerund phrases: it either retains the subject of the embedded sentence or deletes the subject if the subject is clear from context. With infinitives and infinitive phrases, however, the subject rule behaves somewhat differently when the embedded sentence plays the role of subject in the main sentence than the subject rule does when the embedded sentence plays the role of object in the main sentence. [Unlike gerunds and gerund phrases, infinitives and infinitive phrases cannot play the role of an object of a preposition in the main sentence.]

When the embedded sentence plays the role of a subject in the main sentence (or predicate nominative), the subject rule does one of two things.

1. It changes the subject of the embedded sentence to a prepositional phrase beginning with *for*; for example, it changes *Fred* to *for Fred; I* to *for me; she* to *for her*, etc., or
2. it deletes the subject of the embedded sentence if the subject can be understood from context.

We will indicate the two different functions of the subject rule (retaining the subject as part of a prepositional phrase or deleting the subject) by putting the prepositional phrase in parentheses.

Following are some example derivations of infinitives and infinitive phrases playing the role of subject in the main sentence (with the optional prepositional phrase in parentheses).

	(John Past rebut the speaker) surprised us
Tense Repl:	(John to rebut the speaker) surprised us
Subject:	((for John) to rebut the speaker) surprised us

	(she Past be so quick) impressed the coaches
Tense Repl:	(she to be so quick) impressed the coaches
Subject:	((for her) to be so quick) impressed the coaches

	(I Past snore loudly) was unheard of
Tense Repl:	(I to snore) was unheard of
Subject:	((for me) to snore loudly) was unheard of

Following are some examples of infinitive phrases playing the role of predicate nominative. The subject rule deletes the subject of the embedded sentence if it can be understood from context.

	My only alternative was (I Past resign my position)
Tense Repl:	My only alternative was (I to resign my position)
Tense:	My only alternative was (to resign my position)

If the subject of the embedded sentence cannot be understood from context, it must be retained as the object of *for*.

	Kafka's last request was (a friend Past burn his works)
Tense Repl:	Kafka's last request was (a friend to burn his works)
Tense:	Kafka's last request was (for a friend to burn his works)

An infinitive (as opposed to an infinitive phrase) is derived from an unmodified intransitive verb with the subject deleted.

	(I Past sleep) seemed out of the question
Tense Repl:	(I to sleep) seemed out of the question
Subject:	(to sleep) seemed out of the question

When an infinitive or infinitive phrase plays the role of an object in the main sentence, the rules governing what happens to the subject of the embedded sentence are quite complex. For most verbs that will permit an infinitive or infinitive phrase as an object, what happens to the subject of the embedded sentence is determined by whether or not it is identical with the subject of the main sentence. There are two possibilities.

1. If the subject of the embedded sentence is different from the subject of the main sentence, then the embedded subject must be retained. In this case, the subject transformation does nothing to the deep structure. [That is, unlike the retained subject when the embedded sentence is used as the subject of the main sentence, the preposition *for* is not added, but if a pronoun is used, the pronoun must be changed to the object form.]
2. If the subject of the embedded sentence is the same as the subject of the main sentence, then the embedded subject must be deleted.

Following are examples of both possibilities.

1. Embedded subject different from subject of main sentence

I wanted (he Past do the dishes)

| *Tense Repl:* | I wanted (he to do the dishes) |
| *Subject:* | I wanted (him to do the dishes) |

The subject of the embedded sentence (*he*) is different from the subject of the main sentence (*I*); therefore, the subject of the embedded sentence is retained, but it is changed to its object form (*him*).

2. Embedded subject the same as subject of main sentence

I wanted (I Past do the dishes)

| *Tense Repl:* | I wanted (I to do the dishes) |
| *Subject:* | I wanted (to do the dishes) |

The subject of the embedded sentence (*I*) is the same as the subject of the main sentence (*I*); therefore, the subject of the embedded sentence must be deleted.

Another class of verbs has an infinitive or infinitive phrase after a direct object.

John persuaded Mary to do the dishes.

In this example, who is going to do the dishes—John or Mary? Clearly, Mary is. Thus, in the deep structure, *Mary* is the subject of the embedded sentence. Following is how we could represent the derivation of this sentence.

John persuaded Mary (Mary Past do the dishes)

| *Tense Repl:* | John persuaded Mary (Mary to do the dishes) |
| *Subject:* | John persuaded Mary (to do the dishes) |

As expected, the subject transformation deletes the subject of the embedded sentence. However, sentences of this type differ from the more common *want* type in that the subject transformation deletes the subject of the embedded sentence when it is the same as the *object* of the main sentence—not the subject as was the case with *want* type verbs.

Now, you may ask, how do we know that there are two *Mary*s in the deep structure and not just one? Wouldn't it be simpler to posit a deep structure like the one above for the verb *want*, where the entire embedded sentence is the object?

John persuaded (Mary Past do the dishes)

There are several arguments against this deep structure, the simplest and most persuasive being the fact that we can readily make the main sentence into a passive.

Mary was persuaded to do the dishes by John.

The noun phrase *Mary* can only become the subject of a passive sentence if it was the object of the verb *persuade* in the deep structure. But we know that *Mary* is the subject of the verb *do* in the embedded sentence. Since one and the same noun phrase cannot be simultaneously the object of a verb in the main sentence and the subject of an embedded sentence, there must be two different *Mary*s—one the object of *persuade* in the main sentence, and the other the subject of the verb *do* in the embedded sentence.

There is an important restriction on the deep structure of sentences of this type: the subject of the embedded sentence must the same as the object of the main sentence. If we made the subject of the embedded sentence different from the object of the main sentence, we would produce an ungrammatical surface structure:

John persuaded Mary (Fred Past do the dishes)
Tense Repl: John persuaded Mary (Fred to do the dishes)
Subject: *John persuaded Mary (Fred to do the dishes)

If we deleted *Fred* from the embedded sentence, we would produce a surface structure that was ungrammatical in the intended meaning.

*John persuaded Mary (to do the dishes)

The only possible interpretation of this surface structure is that Mary did the dishes, not Fred—a meaning incompatible with the deep structure.

Let us summarize what we have discovered about using infinitives and infinitive phrases as objects in the main sentence. First, and most important, we have discovered that there are very complex rules governing the relation of the subject of the embedded sentence to the main sentence.

Some verbs, like *want*, will permit embedded sentences to have subjects that are different from the subject of the main sentence (i.e., the subject of *want*). If the embedded subject is not the same as the subject of the main sentence, the embedded subject must be retained in the surface sentence (in its object form if it is a pronoun); if the embedded subject is the same as the subject of the main sentence, the embedded subject must be deleted.

Some verbs, like *persuade*, have a quite different relation to the embedded sentence. For verbs in the class, the embedded sentence follows a direct object. The subject of the embedded sentence must be identical to the direct object, and the embedded subject must then be deleted.

For all these different verb classes, however, the subject rule plays essentially the same role: it retains the embedded subject if the verb in the main sentence will permit the embedded subject to be different from the nouns in the main sentence (e.g., *want*); it deletes the embedded subject if it is identical with a noun in the main sentence (e.g., *decide* and *want*).

Note the many points of similarity between the formation of infinitives and infinitive phrases on the one hand and gerunds and gerund phrases on the other.

- [ ] Both come from underlying sentences embedded in the position of abstract noun phrases.
- [ ] Both use the tense replacement rule to replace the tense markers of the embedded sentences with elements that create nonfinite verbs: in the case of gerunds and gerund phrases, the tense marker is replaced with a present participle marker; in the case of infinitives and infinitive phrases, the tense marker is replaced with *to*.
- [ ] When the embedded sentence plays the role of subject of the main sentence, both can either retain the subject of the embedded sentence (in a non-subject surface form) or can delete it if it is clear from context.
- [ ] When the embedded sentence plays the role of object of the main verb, both have more complex rules that delete the subject of the embedded sentence if it is identical with a noun in the main sentence and retain the subject of the embedded sentence if it is not identical with a noun in the main sentence.
- [ ] Finally, the two types of constructions are often interchangeable with little, if any, difference in meaning. For example, from the following deep structure we can produce either a gerund or an infinitive phrase.

Deep structure:	I love (I Pres eat pizza)
Gerund phrase:	
Tense Repl:	I love (I Pres Part eat pizza)
Affix Mov:	I love (I eating pizza)
Subject:	I love (eating pizza)
Infinitive phrase:	
Tense Repl:	I love (I to eat pizza)
Subject:	I love (to eat pizza)

The preceding pair of sentences demonstrates the ability of transformational grammar to capture significant generalizations about our perception of language. The sentences *I love eating pizza* and *I love to eat pizza* have surface structures that seem to be substantially different. Yet speakers of English know that, despite their apparent differences, the two sentences are really superficial variants of one basic sentence. Transformational grammar is able to relate them in a way that captures both their difference in form (surface structures) and their sameness in basic meaning (deep structure). The sentences share a single deep structure origin. They are derived by essentially the same set of transformational rules with but a single difference in the operation of one rule, the tense replacement rule.

■ **Exercise 7.8. Infinitives and infinitive phrases**

Reduce the embedded sentences to infinitives and/or infinitive phrases by the *tense replacement rule, affix movement rule* (if needed), and *subject rule*. The first question is done as an example. (Answers to exercises are found on page 502.)

1. (the company Past forbid smoking on the job) was not something that overjoyed everyone

   Tense Repl: (the company to forbid smoking on the job) was not something that overjoyed everyone

   Subject: ((for the company) to forbid smoking on the job) was not something that overjoyed everyone

2. (the weatherman Past predict snow) seemed absurd at the time

3. (the runner Pres hesitate between first and second) is a sign of poor coaching

4. John offered (John Past resign)

5. (they Past leave without saying goodbye) was really rude

6. (he Past wash the dishes without making a fuss) was a real switch

7. (the company Past redesign the front entrance) was surprisingly expensive

8. Kafka wanted (a friend Past burn his works)

9. The plan was (Fred Past impersonate the Secretary of State)

10. (he Past have Past Part return our call so promptly) came as a real surprise

11. We decided (we Past go out for dinner)

12. Mary asked John (John Past pass her the potato salad)

13. I want (I Pres be alone)

2. Abstract noun phrases. In this type of reduction, the main verb in the embedded sentence is replaced by an abstract noun. Since there is no longer any verb in the embedded sentence, the tense marker is deleted. As in the formation of gerunds and gerund phrases, the subject of the embedded sentence is either deleted or retained as a possessive. Following are the steps in the derivation of this type of noun phrase.

1. The main verb is changed into an etymologically related abstract noun (i.e., into an abstract noun that is in the same word family as the verb) and the tense marker is deleted by the *Abstract Noun Rule (Ab Noun)*. If there is no such related abstract noun, then this rule cannot be applied and an abstract noun phrase cannot be derived.
2. As in gerund phrases, the subject of the verb may be either (a) retained as a possessive, or (b) deleted if it is clear from context (in which case the article *the* is automatically added). We indicate the option of retaining the subject by putting the possessive in parentheses.

Following is an example derivation.

(John Past resign) came as a complete surprise
Ab Noun: (John resignation) came as a complete surprise
Subject: ((John's) resignation) came as a complete surprise

In this example, the verb *resign* has been transformed into the corresponding abstract noun *resignation* and the tense marker has been deleted by the abstract noun rule, and the subject *John* has been transformed into the possessive form *John's*. If we had chosen to delete the subject altogether, the surface form of the sentence would be as follows.

(the resignation) came as a complete surprise

There is one additional wrinkle: if the verb in the embedded sentence is transitive, the corresponding abstract noun must be followed by a preposition—usually *of*. Following are some examples of abstract noun phrases derived from embedded sentences with transitive verbs.

We were pleased by (John Past refuse the offer)
Ab Noun: We were pleased by (John refusal of the offer)
Subject: We were pleased by ((John's) refusal of the offer)

The accident delayed (I Past complete the assignment)
Ab Noun: The accident delayed (I completion of the assignment)
Subject: The accident delayed ((my) completion of the assignment)

	Cassandra foretold (the Greeks Past destroy Troy)
Ab Noun:	Cassandra foretold (the Greeks destruction of Troy)
Subject:	Cassandra foretold ((the Greeks') destruction of Troy)

	(George Past announce his retirement) caught us by surprise
Ab Noun:	(George announcement of his retirement) caught us by surprise
Subject:	((George's) announcement of his retirement) caught us by surprise

	The editor supported (the reporter Past expose the incident)
Ab Noun:	The editor supported (the reporter exposure of the incident)
Subject:	The editor supported ((the reporter's) exposure of the incident)

The relation between the verb in the embedded sentence and the form of the abstract noun is quite unpredictable. In just the preceding examples above, we encountered four different suffixes that changed the verb into an abstract noun: *-tion (resign/resignation; complete/completion; destroy/destruction); -al (refuse/refusal); -ment (announce/announcement);* and *-ure (expose/exposure).* Not only is there no fixed way to change verbs into abstract nouns; many verbs do not have a corresponding abstract noun form at all, and thus, unlike verbals, this type of reduction is not always possible. For example, compare the following underlying sentences.

(the company Past publish her book) surprised her

(the company Past print her book) surprised her

The verb *publish* happens to have the corresponding abstract noun form *publication.* Accordingly, we can reduce this sentence to an abstract noun phrase.

	(the company Past publish her book) surprised her
Ab Noun:	(the company publication of her book) surprised her
Subject:	((the company's) publication of her book) surprised her

However, the very similar verb *print* does not happen to have a corresponding abstract noun form, and thus there is no grammatical surface structure with an abstract noun phrase.

*(the company's printification of her book) surprised her

As one would expect, the two verbal forms of *print* do exist.

> *Gerund phrase:*   (the company's printing her book) surprised
> her
>
> *Infinitive phrase:*   (for the company to print her book) surprised
> her

Notice that the retained subject for both the gerund form and the abstract noun form is a possessive. In a way, the gerund *printing* plays the role of the abstract noun form of the verb *print*. Thus it follows that we can optionally add to the gerund form the *of* that appears when we change a verb into an abstract noun.

> (the company's printing (of) her book) surprised her

■ Exercise 7.9. Abstract noun phrases

Reduce the embedded sentences to abstract noun phrases by *abstract noun* and *subject* rules. The first question is done as an example. (Answers to exercises are found on page 504.)

1. The city was shocked by (the reporter Past expose the scheme)

   > *Ab Noun:*   The city was shocked by (the reporter exposure of
   > the scheme)
   >
   > *Subject:*   The city was shocked by ((the reporter's) exposure
   > of the scheme)

2. (she Past conceive the idea) astonished the critics
3. (we Pres calculate the net present benefit) is included in our project proposal
4. Everyone was painfully aware of (Harry Past refuse to face reality)
5. The press was caught off guard by (the government suddenly Past impose martial law) [Note what happens to the adverb *suddenly* when the verb it modifies is changed into an abstract noun.]
6. (the farmers Past employ migrant workers) was a common practice in the small farming community
7. Once we entered the door (we Past disrupt the gathering) was immediately apparent
8. (they immediately Past recover the stolen bonds) was naturally the primary concern of the insurance company
9. The city council approved (the company Past expand its plant in Easton)
10. The Mayor expected (Leon Past retract his statement)
11. (Sir Mortimer despicably Past seduce Lady Cravencroft) filled the readers with foreboding

---

■ **Exercise 7.10. Review of nominalizations**

Transform each of the following embedded sentences into as many nominalized surface forms (noun clause, gerund, infinitive, abstract noun phrase) as possible. The first question is done as an example. (Answers to exercises are found on page 505.)

1. (John Past investigate the incident) surprised us

   Noun clause: (that John investigated the incident) surprised us

   Gerund: (John's investigating (of) the incident) surprised us

   Infinitive: (for John to investigate the incident) surprised us

   Ab Noun phrase: (John's investigation of the incident) surprised us

2. (Leon Past reject the bottle caps) was an unexpected development
3. We all noticed (he Past behave strangely)
4. (the test Past be on verbals) upset all the students
5. There was quite a debate about (the company Past exploit the shoreline)
6. A likely outcome was (the legislature Past create new districts)
7. (they Past disrupt the elections) was reported by the newspaper
8. We had grown used to (the truck Past have a loud muffler)
9. After yet another truly appalling meal, Lady Crumhorn decided (Lady Crumhorn Past give the cook her notice)
10. (the court Past reverse the decision) was expected at any time
11. (you Past forgive your enemies) will drive them crazy
12. I tried (I Past start the engine)
13. We asked the professor (the professor Past postpone the test)
14. (Holmes Past demonstrate how the crime was committed) astonished Inspector Lestrade

---

ABSOLUTES

The final sentence combining process we examine creates a construction called an *absolute*. An absolute is a sophisticated construction rarely encountered in young or inexperienced writers. An absolute enables us to add substantial amounts of information to the main clause while still staying within the bounds of a single sentence. Following is an example of a sentence that has been extended by no less than four parallel absolutes.

The office was in chaos—telephones ringing, papers scattered on the floor, empty coffee cups everywhere, and the staff punchy with exhaustion.

By examining the preceding four absolute phrases and their underlying deep structures, we can gain some insight into how these absolutes are created:

1. telephones ringing
   Deep structure: telephones Past be Pres Part ring
2. papers scattered on the floor
   Deep structure: papers Past be Past Part scatter on the floor
3. empty coffee cups everywhere
   Deep structure: empty coffee cups Past be everywhere
4. the staff punchy with exhaustion
   Deep structure: the staff Past be punchy with exhaustion

As you can see, the four deep structures all contain the verb *be*, two as a main verb (examples 3 and 4) and two as a helping verb (examples 1 and 2). The four surface structures were formed by deleting both the tense marker and the verb *be*. The resulting structure is an absolute. It retains from the deep structure the original subject and whatever followed the verb *be*. If the verb *be* was an auxiliary, then the subject will be followed by a participle marker—either (a) a present participle marker (Pres Part) if the *be* was part of the progressive auxiliary (*be* + Pres Part), or (b) a past participle marker (Past Part) if the *be* was part of the passive auxiliary (*be* + Past Part). The participle marker will be attached automatically to the following verb by the affix movement rule.

We call the rule that deletes the tense marker and the verb *be* the *Absolute Deletion Rule (Absol Del)*. This rule is similar to the relative clause reduction in that both rules delete the tense and the verb *be*. Recall, however, that the relative clause reduction rule also deleted the relative pronoun subject from the embedded sentence. Thus, absolutes differ from reduced relative clauses in that *absolutes always retain their deep structure subjects*. Following are some examples of absolutes.

| | (the program Pres be over) I turned the TV off |
| *Absol Del:* | (the program over) I turned the TV off |

	The quarrel ended as usual (Ralph Pres be angry) and (Alice Pres be Pres Part cry)
Absol Del:	The quarrel ended as usual (Ralph angry) and (Alice Pres Part cry)
Affix Mov:	The quarrel ended as usual (Ralph angry) and (Alice crying)

> We were on our way again (the car Pres be Past Part
> repair)

Absol Del: We were on our way again (the car Past Part repair)

Affix Mov: We were on our way again (the car repaired)

> (a fresh breeze Past be Pres Part spring up) we
> launched the boat

Absol Del: (a fresh breeze Pres Part spring up) we launched the
> boat

Affix Mov: (a fresh breeze springing up) we launched the boat

> (the money Past be on the table) the betting began in
> earnest

Absol Del: (the money on the table) the betting began in earnest

It is especially easy to confuse an absolute with a present participial phrase if the absoloute contains a possessive pronoun that refers to a noun in the main sentence. Following is an example of such a sentence.

> The ship began turning in a large circle (its rudder
> Past be Past Part jam by the collision)

Absol Del: The ship began turning in a large circle (its rudder
> Past Part jam by the collision)

Affix Mov: The ship began turning in a large circle (its rudder
> jammed by the collision)

The possessive pronoun *its* in the embedded sentence refers to the noun *ship* in the main sentence. This semantic connection, however, does not constitute a grammatical connection; thus, the embedded sentence is an absolute.

This same embedded sentence could play the role of a noun modifier if it were embedded within the appropriate noun phrase of the main sentence and underwent the relative replacement rule.

> The ship (the ship's rudder Past be Past Part jam by
> the collision) began turning in a large circle

Rel Repl: The ship (whose rudder Past be Past Part jam by the
> collision) began turning in a large circle

Affix Mov: The ship (whose rudder was jammed by the collision)
> began turning in a large circle

As you can see, the embedded sentence is now a relative clause modifying *ship*. The embedded sentence cannot be reduced to a participial phrase by the relative clause reduction rule (even though it contains the verb *be*) because the *wh-* word (*whose*) is a possessive—embedded sentences can be reduced to participial phrases only when the *wh-* word is the subject of the embedded sentence. [Recall that the relative clause reduction rule applies to the sequence (relative pronoun + tense marker + *be*). This sequence exists only when the relative pronoun is the subject of the embedded sentence.]

Some key points of differences between the absolute and relative clause are the following:

1. The relative clause contains a relative pronoun; the absolute does not;
2. the relative clause is embedded following the noun it modifies; the absolute is outside the boundary of the main sentence—an absolute can never be inside the main sentence; and
3. the absolute has lost its tense marker; the relative clause still retains its tense marker.

There is a second way of forming absolutes by means of the *tense replacement rule (Tense Repl)*. The tense replacment rule replaces the tense marker with the present participle marker, which the affix movement rule then attaches to the following verb. Following is an example of an absolute formed in this manner.

(the captain Past see our signal) the ship put about

Tense Repl: (the captain Pres Part see our signal) the ship put about

Affix Mov: (the captain seeing our signal) the ship put about

As you recall, the tense replacement rule was used to create gerunds and gerund phrases by replacing the tense marker in an embedded sentence with a present participle marker (Pres Part). Why does the same rule now produce an absolute rather than a gerund or gerund phrase?

There are two reasons. First, and most important, it is the role of the embedded sentence in the deep structure that determines the function of the surface structure derived from the embedded sentence; the transformational rules affect only the form of the surface structure. The tense replacement rule applies to deep structure sentences that are embedded in totally different ways. The embedded sentence that is the source for gerunds and gerund phrases is embedded as a noun phrase and plays the role of a noun phrase. The embedded sentences that are the sources for absolutes are not noun phrases; in fact they are not inside the main sentence at all, but are "modifiers" of the main sentence as a whole.

(S absolute **)** **(S** absolute **)** ... **S (S** absolute **)** **(S** absolute **)** ...

Each of these deep structure sentences ($S_{absolute}$) is earmarked to undergo the transformations that reduce each of them to absolute phrases.

The second reason is that the transformations that convert embedded sentences to particular types of surface structures are a package deal. In order for a sentence embedded as a noun phrase to be reduced to a gerund or gerund phrase, there are *two* special transformations that must be applied (assuming the automatic application of affix movement): (1) the tense replacement rule, and (2) the subject rule. The latter transformation is obligatory. That is, once the tense marker in a sentence embedded as a noun phrase has undergone tense replacement, the original subject of the embedded sentence *must* be either deleted or changed to a non-subject form (a possessive in the case of gerunds and gerund phrases). The original subject cannot stay in its deep structure form. In the derivation of absolutes, however, the tense replacement rule cannot be followed by the subject rule. In other words, the subject of the embedded sentence *must not* be deleted; in an absolute, the subject must be retained in its original deep structure form.

Following are some more examples of absolutes generated by the tense replacement rule.

	(the children Past need some supplies) I stopped off at the store
Tense Repl:	(the children Pres Part need some supplies) I stopped off at the store
Affix Mov:	(the children needing some supplies) I stopped off at the store
	(the committee Pres lack a quorum) the chair adjourned the meeting
Tense Repl:	(the committee Pres Part lack a quorum) the chair adjourned the meeting
Affix Mov:	(the committee lacking a quorum) the chair adjourned the meeting
	We drafted an answer (the reporter's question Past deserve a reply)
Tense Repl:	We drafted an answer (the reporter's question Pres Part deserve a reply)
Affix Mov:	We drafted an answer (the reporter's question deserving a reply)

The production of absolutes by means of the tense replacement rule or absolute deletion rule introduces an interesting stylistic option: there is nothing to prohibit either of these rules from also applying to embedded sentences that contain the verb *be*. That is, for embedded sentences that contain *be*, we now have two routes by which we can produce an absolute: we can use either (1) the absolute deletion rule, which forms an absolute by deleting the tense marker and the verb *be*, or (2) the tense replacement rule, which forms an absolute by replacing the tense marker with a present participle marker (the latter then requiring the use of affix movement to attach the present participle marker to the verb *be*). Following is an example of both methods of forming absolutes applied to the same embedded sentence.

(the dishes Past be Past Part finish) we all turned in

1. *Absol Del:* (the dishes Past Part finish) we all turned in

  Affix Mov: (the dishes finished) we all turned in

2. *Tense Repl:* (the dishes Pres Part be Past Part finish) we all turned in

  Affix Mov: (the dishes being finished) we all turned in

Following are the two different absolutes.

(the dishes finished) we all turned in

(the dishes being finished) we all turned in

As we would predict from the fact that these two different versions shared a single common deep structure ancestor, the two absolutes have the same basic meaning. The different transformational routes have produced surface structures that are paraphrases of one another; they are literally superficial variants. Following are some more examples of embedded sentences containing *be*. In version (a), the tense marker and *be* are deleted by the absolute deletion rule; in version (b), the tense marker is replaced by a Pres Part marker by the tense replacement rule.

(a) (the captain Past be below) the first mate took the helm

Absol Del: (the captain below) the first mate took the helm

(b) (the captain Past be below) the first mate took the helm

Tense Repl: (the captain Pres Part be below) the first mate took the helm

Affix Mov: (the captain being below) the first mate took the helm

(a) I answered the phone (the secretary Past be out of the office)

Absol Del: I answered the phone (the secretary out of the office)

(b)   I answered the phone (the secretary Past be out of the office)

Tense Repl: I answered the phone (the secretary Pres Part be out of the office)

Affix Mov: I answered the phone (the secretary being out of the office)

Absolutes are always set off from the main sentence by either a comma or a dash. Absolutes are never punctuated with semicolons or periods because the absolutes would then be punctuated as though they were independent sentences. Punctuating them in this manner would make them sentence fragments.

■ **Exercise 7.11. Absolutes**

Reduce the embedded sentences to absolute phrases. If both ways of forming an absolute apply to *be* in the embedded sentence, show both derivations. The first question is done as an example. (Answers to exercises are found on page 506.)

1. (our power Past be Past Part cut off) we went out to dinner

   (a) *Absol Del:*   (our power Past Part cut off) we went out to dinner
       Affix Mov: (our power cut off) we went out to dinner
   (b) *Tense Repl:*   (our power Pres Part be Past Part cut off) we went out to dinner
       Affix Mov: (our power being cut off) we went out to dinner

2. The court announced its decision (two justices Past dissent)

3. (the game Past be out of reach) the crowd began to leave

4. (Karen Past have Past Part compile the names) we began to address the envelopes

5. (their noise Past disturb the neighbors) they received many complaints

6. They fell into formation (their uniforms Past be stiff with starch) (their shoes Past be Past Part polish) (their brass Past gleam)

7. The car went into the ditch (its wheels still Past spin)

8. They waited patiently (legs Past be Past Part cross) (arms Past be Past Part fold) (eyes Past be Past Part close) (faces Past be utterly blank)

9. (their passports Past have Past Part be Past Part check) the passengers were allowed to go

10. (the scaling ladders Past be in position) the attack on the walls began

11. (no other issues Past be Past Part present) the meeting was adjourned.

REVIEW

In this unit on the linguistic perspective of sentence combining, we have examined three different ways in which deep structure sentences can be embedded within main sentences: (1) by noun modification, (2) by nominalization, and (3) by constructing absolutes. At least one version of each of these three processes has created an *-ing* form of the main verb in the embedded sentence. For example, compare the following sentences, each containing the *-ing* form of the verb *apply* in a different function.

1. Each person <u>applying</u> for a job must complete this form.
2. Each person's <u>applying</u> for a job took forever.
3. Each person <u>applying</u> for a job, the line went around the block.

In sentence 1, *applying* is part of a *present participial phrase.*

In sentence 2, *applying* is part of a *gerund phrase.*

In sentence 3, *applying* is part of an *absolute phrase.*

If all three types of sentence embedding produce the same *-ing* surface structure, how can we tell the different types of surface structures apart? The answer is that we can tell them apart because they have distinctly different relations to their main sentences. They have different relations to the main sentence precisely because they inherit the relations their source underlying embedded sentences have to their main sentences. You might think of this as a manifestation of a "like father, like son" relationship between deep structure (father) and surface structure (son). In other words, the role surface structures play is determined by the role that their underlying source sentences (deep structures) play. Thus, despite the similarity of the surface forms, the three uses of *applying* reflect three completely different underlying relationships between the *applying* phrases and their main clauses.

As a way of reviewing these three relationships, our discussion examines how each of these three sentences is derived from its deep structure, and then focuses on the ways that the three different types of surface structures can be recognized.

1. Present participial phrases

Following is the derivation of sentence 1.

Each person (<u>each person Pres be Pres Part apply for a job</u>) must complete this form

Rel Repl: Each person (<u>who Pres be Pres Part apply for a job</u>) must complete this form

Rel Cl Red: Each person (<u>Pres Part apply for a job</u>) must complete this form

Affix Mov: Each person (<u>applying for a job</u>) must complete this form

A present participial phrase can always be recognized by paraphrasing the present participial phrase as a relative clause, that is, by restoring the relative pronoun and the tense marker. For example, sentence 1 can be paraphrased as follows.

Each person (*who is* applying for a job) must complete this form

Every present participial phrase has a corresponding relative clause. When we attempt to expand the other two uses of *applying* to relative clauses, the results are ungrammatical.

2. *Gerund:*   *Each person's <u>who is</u> applying for a job took forever.

3. *Absolute:*   *Each person <u>who is</u> applying for a job, the line went around the block.

2. Gerund phrases

Following is the derivation of sentence 2.

                (each person Past apply for a job) took forever

Tense Repl: (each person Pres Part apply for a job) took forever

Affix Mov: (each person applying for a job) took forever

Subject: (each person's applying for a job) took forever

Since gerund phrases are used in place of abstract noun phrases, they can always be identified by replacing the gerund phrase with *it*. For example, in sentence 2 we can replace the gerund phrase with *it*.

<u>Each person's applying for a job</u> took forever.
            It

When we attempt to replace the other two uses of *applying* with *it*, the result is ungrammatical because they do not play the role of a noun phrase in their main sentences.

1. *Relative:*   <u>Each person applying for a job</u> must complete this
                          *It
              form.

3. *Absolute:*   <u>Each person applying for a job</u>, the line went
                        *It
              around the block.

Another very useful tip-off for recognizing gerund phrases is that the preserved subject is always in a possessive form. Thus, in sentence 2 the retained subject is the possessive noun *person's*. (Remember, though, that subjects of embedded sentences are often deleted when they are clear from context. This test can still be used if you restore the subject.)

3. Absolutes

Following is the derivation for sentence 3.

(each person Past <u>apply for a job</u>) the line went around the block

Tense Repl: (each person Pres Part <u>apply for a job</u>) the line went around the block

Affix Mov: (each person <u>applying for a job</u>) the line went around the block

Since absolutes are not grammatically linked to the main clause, absolute phrases can be recognized by the fact that they are always set off from the main sentence by a comma or a dash (but note that nonrestrictive present participial phrases can also be set off with commas). They are called *absolutes* because one meaning of the word absolute is "complete in itself, independent." It might help you to remember what an absolute is if you remember that they are "absolutely" grammatically independent of the main clause. While there is no positive test for identifying absolutes, they can always be recognized by the fact that they fail the tests for present participial phrases and gerund phrases.

An absolute can always be distinguished from a present participial phrase by the fact that an absolute cannot be expanded to a relative clause.

*Each person <u>who is</u> applying for a job, the line went around the block.

The basic difference between absolutes and present participial phrases is that present participial phrases modify a specific noun in the main clause and, accordingly, underlying the participial phrase there must be a duplicate of the noun in the main clause that the present participial phrase is modifying—that is, there must be a relative pronoun. Absolute phrases, on the other hand, do not modify any single noun in the main clause. In a way, absolute phrases modify the whole main clause rather than a specific word within the clause.

Absolutes can always be distinguished from gerund phrases by the fact that absolutes cannot be replaced with an *it*.

<u>Each person applying for a job</u>, the line went around the block.
*It

■ **Exercise 7.12. Distinguishing present participial, gerund, and absolute phrases**

Underline and identify the present participial, gerund, and absolute phrases in the following sentences. (Answers to exercises are found on page 508.)

1. The plant, having already manufactured a similar product, was an obvious choice for the contract.
2. The plant's having already manufactured a similar product was an advantage.
3. The plant having manufactured a similar product, we bid for the contract.
4. Holmes' becoming suspicious of the blind beggar was the turning point in the case.
5. Holmes, becoming suspicious of the blind beggar, immediately gave chase.
6. Holmes becoming suspicious of the blind beggar, Watson began to make inquiries about him.
7. The alarm sounding, the firemen quickly donned their gear.
8. The alarm, sounding throughout the building, aroused the firemen.
9. The alarm's sounding aroused the firemen.
10. The plan's attaining quick success was our only hope.
11. Attaining quick success, the plan changed everything.
12. The plan attaining quick success, we immediately sought out a tax shelter.
13. The elderly man hesitating at the door slipped into the room unnoticed.
14. The elderly man's hesitating at the door went unnoticed.
15. The elderly man hesitating at the door, the waiter bustled forward.

■ **Exercise 7.13. Identifying absolute, participial, and gerund phrases.**

Underline and identify the absolutes, participial phrases, and gerunds in the following sentences. (Answers to exercises are found on page 508.)

1. The President's authorizing the appointment caused considerable controversy.
2. The agreement assuring future cooperation has been accepted by all parties.
3. The SEC has been in the news a lot lately, insider trading being on TV every night.
4. Unexpected developments delayed our announcing our decision.
5. The reporters investigating the story were criticized for spreading groundless rumors.
6. Students transferring from other institutions often lose credits in the process.
7. The experiment resolving the question, the researchers began writing up their project.

8. Anticipating the questions is half the battle in dealing with reporters.

9. Revenues exceeding expectations, the company declared a dividend.

10. The key to the company's succeeding was constantly incorporating new ideas without losing contact with the dealers.

11. Reserving judgment for the moment, Ronald turned to other matters demanding his attention.

12. The spokesman having admitted the government's continuing involvement, Congress called for an investigation of all activities relating to the sale.

13. Making a good impression on his date was Leon's motivation for sending her the singing telegram.

PART II: THE PEDAGOGICAL PERSPECTIVE

The modern classroom use of sentence combining has grown out of the work of many different people—each person with his own particular interests and frame of reference. [See Mellon (1979) for a discussion of the history of sentence combining.] Since no one deliberately set out to create the modern version of sentence combining, its evolution has followed a tortuous pathway. The following discussion of the pedagogical use of sentence combining is essentially historical. It describes the contributions of the major people in the field in chronological order. Without this historical frame of reference the modern approach is difficult to understand.

The historical approach also emphasizes that there have been different approaches to sentence combining that have never been fully reconciled. Moreover, it is still unclear how sentence combining best fits into the overall English curriculum. Chapter 8 discusses some of these larger issues.

KELLOGG HUNT

Without a doubt the modern approach to sentence combining stems from the work of Kellogg Hunt. In 1964 Hunt completed a developmental study of various grammatical structures in the writing of fourth, eighth, and twelfth graders (Hunt 1964). Hunt's study won the prestigious National Council of Teachers of English (NCTE) research award for significant contribution to the teaching of English, and his study was published by them in 1965 as NCTE Research Report No. 3.

Hunt's landmark study did two things: (1) it established a new unit for measuring writing maturity—the *T-unit,* and (2) it demonstrated that from a statistical standpoint the growth in T-unit length from fourth grade writers to twelfth grade writers (and beyond to professional adult writers) was largely due to significant changes in the frequency of a relatively small number of grammatical constructions. In other words, syntactic maturity is a function of the frequency of these grammatical constructions. Let us examine both aspects of Hunt's study in more detail.

T-units. Earlier research on the development of writing was plagued by the lack of any standard measure by which different writers could be uniformly compared. The most obvious unit, the sentence, is limited by the fact that younger and less able writers are not able to punctuate very well. For example, in Hunt's study one fourth grader had an astonishingly high average sentence length of 72 words for two essays. The writer achieved this precocious feat by the simple mechanism of using no periods in his essays. Conversely, another writer might have a very low average number of words per sentence because he or she uses too many periods, creating innumerable fragments.

The alternative to accepting the writer's punctuation is for the researcher to "correct" it. The difficulty with the researcher's doing this is that the new punctuation is a creation of the researcher and that the researcher is then investigating the researcher's own writing rather than what the writer wrote. Also, the researcher's punctuation is subjective; no one else will necessarily agree with it. Hunt illustrates this problem by referring to a passage in C. C. Fries's *Structure of English* (Fries 1952) that, Fries claims, English teachers will cut into from three to nine sentences depending on the taste of the individual.

Hunt's T-unit avoids the problem of subjectivity because T-unit division follows a simple two-step procedure that ensures that the same passage will always be divided up in the same way no matter who is doing the analysis (provided, of course, that the users interpret the meaning of the passage in the same way).

- ☐ Divide the passage into the smallest units that could be punctuated as independent sentences. Hunt called these units *minimal terminal units*, or T-units, for short.
- ☐ Do not create any sentence fragments elsewhere by your T-unit divisions.

Hunt illustrates the procedure with the following passage written by a fourth grader (only the spelling has been corrected).

> *I like the movie we saw about Moby Dick the white whale the captain said if you can kill the white whale Moby Dick I will give this gold to the one that can do it and it is worth sixteen dollars they tried and tried but while they were trying they killed a whale and used the oil for the lamps they almost caught the white whale* (1965, 20)

The first possible T-unit (minimal terminal unit) is

I like the movie/

If we were to make a T-unit division here, we would violate the second step in the procedure by creating the following fragment.

we saw about Moby Dick the white whale/

Thus the first correct T-unit is the following.

I like the movie we saw about Moby Dick the white whale/

Following is how the entire passage would be divided up into six T-units (/) following the two-step procedure.

I like the movie we saw about Moby Dick the white whale/
the captain said if you can kill the white whale Moby Dick I will give this
gold to the one that can do it/
and it is worth sixteen dollars/
they tried and tried/
but while they were trying they killed a whale and used the oil for the lamps/
they almost caught the white whale/

Note the following.

☐ T-units are allowed to begin with coordinating conjunctions; for example, *and it is worth sixteen dollars.*

☐ T-units may contain understood words; for example, *they tried and tried* [to kill the whale]. However, a T-unit must contain a subject and a finite verb.

■ **Exercise 7.14. T-units**

The following passages were written by ninth graders. The passages have been slightly edited and corrected, but they are punctuated exactly as they were written. Divide the passages into T-units. (Answers to exercises are found on page 509.)

Passage 1

I'm going to tell you how to play and live the game of Dungeons and Dragons. You must find your way through maze. Slay dragons and unknown foes. You will find yourself a new role of another person. Here are some of the characters that you might play the Swordsman, War Lord, Sorcerer and Wizard. To gain in this game you must collect spells gold and jewels from the maze. Before you start to play Dungeons and Dragons you should buy a Dungeons and Dragons playing guide which costs $11.95. Then you can start it with mazes which cost $5.50 a maze. Now I think you are ready to play have fun may your spells be many and your adventures be great.

Passage 2

Twister comes in a box about a foot long. The game has the instructions on the box it has a long plastic sheet with different colors such as green, yellow, blue, and red. The first thing you do is take out the plastic sheet and spread it across the floor now take out the spinner you might have to put it together after you have done that you have four squares with the spinner in the middle each square has something left foot red, yellow, blue, and green each square has the same colors the second square would have left hand and the same amount of colors in that square the third square would have right foot and the fourth square would have right hand. Now you are ready to play twister. You can play all by yourself you can have three people playing the game and you can have four people playing too. Now you are ready to play you need a friend or a parent to referee the game you and your partner get anywhere on the sheet now have your friend or parent spin say it lands on right foot green you and your partner put your foot on the green you keep doing this until your partner falls out of the game and this means you have won the game.

Passage 3

You deal five cards to each player, then the dealer will ask you if you want to trade any number of cards. For the ones that don't follow a number right after the other card.

After all the players have traded. You start the bidding. After all the players have quit, because the bid went too high. You show them your cards. You may have won or someone else has. It all depends on the cards.

The mean (average) number of words per T-unit is determined by dividing the total number of words by the number of T-units. For example, in the passage about Moby Dick quoted from Hunt there are 68 words and six T-units. Thus the mean (average) number of words per T-unit is 68 words divided by six T-units: 68/6 = 11.3 words per T-unit.

Hunt's study of average fourth, eighth, and twelfth graders and professional adult writers revealed the following mean number of words per T-unit (1965, 56):

Grade:	4	8	12	Professional adult
T-unit length:	8.6	11.5	14.4	20.3

The increase in T-unit length across the four groups of writers is statistically significant at the .01 level (a relatively high level of confidence which means that there is less than one chance in a hundred of these results' being accidental). Using these mean T-unit lengths as grade level norms, we see that the fourth grade author of the Moby Dick passage, despite his inability to punctuate, is writing at close to a typical 8th grade level.

What accounts for the growth in T-unit length?

Hunt established that there was a statistically significant growth in mean T-unit length from fourth to eighth to twelfth grade and beyond to professional adult writers. As Hunt puts it, there is a "clear indication that T-unit length is somehow tied closely to maturity" (1964, 141).

The next step in his study was to identify those grammatical structures that most directly contribute to this growth in mean T-unit length. Since a T-unit is an independent clause that can be expanded only by (1) adding subordinate clauses (adverb, adjective, or noun clauses) to the main clause or by (2) lengthening clauses (both main and subordinate) by adding nonclausal words and phrases (i.e., adjectives and adverbs modifiers plus nominalizations), Hunt's task was to determine the relative contribution of each of these two options (adding more clauses and lengthening clauses by adding nonclause words and phrases) to the growth of T-unit length over time as writers mature.

1. Frequency of clauses. Adjective clauses were the only type of clause to show substantial gain in frequency of use over time—eighth graders used twice as many per T-unit as fourth graders did, and twelfth graders used nearly twice (1.8) as many as eighth graders—whereas adverb clauses and noun clauses showed only modest gains.

2. Adding nonclause words and phrases. Nonclausal adverbs did not increase over time; in fact, some categories (e.g., adverbs that modified verbs) actually declined over time. However, the other two types of nonclauses—adjectives and nominalizations—showed substantial gains over time.

Adjective constructions of all types increased in frequency over time with adjective prepositional phrases and various kinds of participles and participial phrases produced by reducing relative clauses showing substantial growth.

Nonclause nominalizations (i.e., gerunds, infinitives, and other types of reduced sentences) showed substantial growth—twelfth graders, for example, used over three times as many nominalizations per T-unit as fourth graders did. This increase in nominalizations is all the more striking because there was not a corresponding increase in the frequency of whole, unreduced noun clauses.

In summary, what Hunt found in his study was that the significant increase in T-unit length from fourth to eighth to twelfth graders could be largely attributed to three specific areas of grammar: (1) an increase in the frequency of use of adjective clauses, (2) an increase in the frequency of use of certain nonclause adjective constructions (most of which are derived from adjective clauses), and (3) an increase in the frequency of use of nonclause nominalizations. Moreover, the growth in these three specific areas extended to professional adult writers, who showed significant growth in these same areas as compared with twelfth graders.

Hunt illustrates the process of syntactic maturity with the following passage (1965,144-5).

> 1. *The sailor finally came on deck.*
> 2. *He was tall.*
> 3. *He was rather ugly.*
> 4. *He had a limp.*
> 5. *He had offered them the prize.*

As the passage stands, it consists of five T-units with an average length of 4.6 words. Not even a fourth grader would write in this elementary a manner. A skilled fourth grader might reduce several of the sentences to nonclause structures and combine them as follows.

> 1. *The sailor finally came on deck.*
> 2. *He was tall and rather ugly and had a limp.*
> 3. *He had offered them the prize.*

This version contains three T-units with an average word length of 7.3, which is above the fourth-grade average of 6.6 words per T-unit.

A twelfth grader might consolidate all of these T-units together to produce a single sentence.

> *The tall, rather ugly sailor with a limp, who had offered them the prize, finally came on deck.*

This sentence is now 18 words long, longer than the 14.4 word average for twelfth graders.

Hunt concludes that as we grow older, we are able to express ourselves with increasing succinctness and economy by consolidating a number of simple sentences into more complex constructions that "squeeze out" redundancies. The two main techniques we rely on for this consolidation are two of the processes we examined in the first part of this chapter: (1) noun modification, the process of adding relative clauses and sentences reduced to various types of phrases that modify nouns (e.g., participial phrases and appositives), and (2) nominalization, the process of replacing abstract noun phrases with embedded sentences and sentences reduced to various types of noun phrases (e.g., verbals and abstract noun phrases).

In the final section of his study, "Implications for the Curriculum," Hunt says:

> *This study suggests a kind of sentence-building program that probably has never been produced. . . . The aim would be to widen the student's span of grammatical attention and concern. The method would be for him to reduce independent clauses to subordinate clauses and nonclauses, consolidating them with adjoining clauses and T-units. He could work up to structures of considerable depth and complexity comparable to those exhibited by twelfth graders and superior adults.* (1965, 157)

Hunt (1970) published a follow-up study based not on an analysis of writing samples, but on the analysis of revisions of a passage written in kernel sentences. (The passage, developed by Roy O'Donnell, has become quite well-known in the literature and is often referred to simply as the "aluminum" test.) Following is the passage along with the actual directions used in the research project. Do it as an exercise.

■ **Exercise 7.15. Hunt/O'Donnell's** *Aluminum* **test**

Aluminum

Directions: Read the passage all the way through. You will notice that the sentences are short and choppy. Study the passage and then rewrite it in a better way. You may combine sentences, change the order of words, and omit words that are repeated too many times. But try not to leave out any of the information.

> *Aluminum is a metal. It is abundant. It has many uses. It comes from bauxite. Bauxite is an ore. Bauxite looks like clay. Bauxite contains aluminum. It contains several other substances. Workmen extract these other substances from the bauxite. They grind the bauxite. They put it in tanks. Pressure is in the tanks. The other substances form a mass. They remove the mass. They use filters. A liquid remains. They put it through several other processes. It finally yields a chemical. The chemical is powdery. It is white. The chemical is alumina. It is a mixture. It contains aluminum. It contains oxygen. Workmen separate the aluminum from the oxygen. They use electricity. They finally produce a metal. The metal is light. It has a luster. The luster is bright. The luster is silvery. This metal comes in many forms.* (1970, 11–12)

■ **Exercise 7.16. T-unit analysis of** *Aluminum* **test**

Now divide your revision into T-units, count the number of words in your revision, and divide this number by the number of T-units to get the mean (average) number of words per T-unit.

This controlled passage enabled Hunt to compare the way that children of various grade levels and skilled adults consolidate kernel sentences. Hunt found, for example, that T-unit length increased both with age and with ability level within the same grade. Following are his findings for T-unit length by grade (1970, 20).

G4	*G6*	*G8*	*G10*	*G12*	*Skilled adults*
5.42	6.84	9.84	10.44	11.30	14.78

Your mean word per T-unit score probably was in the 11–15 range.

The growth in T-unit length was a result of older writers' increasing ability to consolidate multiple kernel sentences into more complex surface sentences. One way Hunt measured the degree of sentence combining was to count the number of sentences that were embedded into each main clause (1970, 28).

G4	G6	G8	G10	G12	Skilled adults
0.13	0.6	1.4	1.8	2.2	4.1

In other words, a fourth grader was able to embed a second reduced sentence inside a main clause in only one sentence out of eight (13%) whereas skilled adults, on the average, embedded four reduced sentences inside each main clause. Hunt observes:

> One can scarcely escape the conclusion that as writers mature they take advantage of more and more opportunities for consolidating sentences. No doubt, diminishing returns would set in at some point along the line if [consolidation were] carried to too great an extreme, but the evidence presented for skilled adults indicates that the point of diminishing returns is so far in advance of the point reached by school children that curriculum makers need not worry about this matter.   (1970, 53)

JOHN MELLON

In 1962 Mellon, then a student at Harvard, developed "sentence-embedding problems" as a component in a transformational grammar curriculum he developed as part of a graduate seminar. Mellon credits a colleague, Patrick Hodgkin, at Culver Military Academy, where Mellon had previously taught, as the inspiration for the "sentence-embedding" technique.

In 1964 Mellon realized that his "sentence-embedding problems" were remarkably similar to the kind of sentence building program that Hunt had proposed in his research project.

In 1965 Mellon received a federal grant to test the hypothesis that "practice in transformational sentence-combining would enhance the normal growth of syntactic fluency" (Mellon 1969, 28). The research project was an academic-year study of the effect of teaching transformational grammar (both through formal instruction in the concepts of transformational grammar and through practice with sentence combining transformations, with an emphasis on the latter) on the writing ability of seventh-grade students. Mellon concentrated his sentence combining exercises on the structures that Hunt found to account for the bulk of syntactic growth—adjectives (both relative clauses and non-clause adjective phrases) and nominalizations.

The results of the study, published as *Transformational Sentence-Combining: A Method for Enhancing the Development of Syntactic Fluency in English Composition* (NCTE 1969), were quite striking. In every area that Mellon measured, there was statistically significant growth. Moreover, drawing on the norms of eighth graders established by

Hunt's study, Mellon was able to show that his students had achieved an accelerated growth in syntactic maturity of three "years" during the course of the experiment. In other words, according to Hunt's norms, Mellon's seventh graders were writing like tenth graders at the end of the year. Mellon's group also showed statistically significant gains over two control groups that did not study transformational grammar or practice sentence combining.

Mellon's major contribution was to seize upon sentence combining as an effective vehicle for teaching how simple sentences are combined (and then reduced) to form more mature sentences and to demonstrate in a carefully designed empirical study how effective this approach can be in improving student writing—something that eighty years of research on the effects of traditional grammar had never been able to do.

FRANK O'HARE

O'Hare, in his *Sentence Combining: Improving Student Writing without Formal Grammar Instruction* (NCTE 1973), reported on his study, which in many respects replicated Mellon's but with the crucial difference that O'Hare removed sentence combining from the context of formal grammar teaching. O'Hare's version of sentence combining is not embedded in a systematic presentation of transformational grammar, although the actual machinery of sentence combining is not very different from Mellon's. Where Mellon uses terms that have been technically defined in transformational grammar (like "T infinitive") to cue specific sentence combining operations, O'Hare uses comparable nontechnical terms ("FOR + TO"). While the Mellon and O'Hare studies were not greatly different in what they were investigating, the O'Hare study had a profound impact on the teaching of English by moving sentence combining out of the forbidding arena of technical linguistics and into the mainstream of composition teaching. In other words, English teachers could reap the developmental benefits of sentence combining without having to teach a class in transformational grammar as a necessary prerequisite.

WILLIAM STRONG

William Strong in his 1973 textbook *Sentence Combining: A Composing Book* (Strong 1973) continued the movement away from linguistics and toward rhetoric by presenting sentence combining exercises in a discourse block with no directions (or "cues") that tell the student which specific transformational operation to employ in the combining process. Uncued sentence combining exercises—exercises in which the student is free to combine the sentences in whatever way the student considers to be rhetorically effective—are in an "open" (as opposed to "cued") format. In open-format sentence combining exercises, the focus is on the rhetorical effect of one choice over another choice rather than on the linguistic mechanisms employed in combining the sentences. The sentence combining exercises that you have encountered in this book would be considered "cued" because you were directed to produce a surface sentence of a specific grammatical type.

FRANCIS CHRISTENSEN

In an article in *English Journal* entitled "The Problem of Defining a Mature Style" (Christensen 1968), Francis Christensen challenged Hunt's definition of mature style. For Christensen, a genuinely mature style is a stylistically effective style, not just a statistical norm. He was concerned that Hunt's approach appeared to equate length (words per T-unit) with quality—that longer sentences are inherently more mature than shorter sentences. In particular he was concerned that Hunt and Mellon encouraged students to lengthen T-units by nominalizations.

> *The very hallmark of jargon is the long noun phrase—the long noun phrase as subject and the long noun phrase as complement, the two coupled by a minimal verb. One of the hardest things to learn in learning to write well is how to keep the noun phrases short. The skillful writer is the writer who has learned how to keep them short.* (1968, 575)

Christensen then argued that good writers lengthen sentences by what he called *free modifiers* as opposed to *bound modifiers*.

> *Bound modifiers are word modifiers. They are close or limiting or restrictive modifiers. They are, in a sense, obligatory, and, being obligatory, they do not give the writer the freedom of choice that rhetoric demands. Free modifiers, on the other hand, are modifiers not of words but of constructions, from which they are set off by junctures or punctuation. Grammatically, they are loose or additive or nonessential or nonrestrictive. The constructions used are prepositional phrases; relative and subordinate clauses; noun, verb, adjective, and adverbial phrases or clusters; and, one of the most important, verbid clauses or absolutes.* (1968, 576–7)

Christensen, in his influential *Notes Toward a New Rhetoric* (Christensen 1967), described this kind of mature sentence as a *cumulative sentence*. A cumulative sentence has a relatively simple main clause, which is elaborated or commented on by free modifiers. Following is an example of a cumulative sentence that Christensen gave in *Notes* (1967, 9).

> *He dipped his hands in the bichloride solution and shook them,*
>   *a quick shake, (Noun Cluster)*
>   *fingers down, (Absolute)*
>   *like the fingers of a pianist above the keys. (Prep Phrase)*
>   Sinclair Lewis

Here, three free modifiers (a noun cluster, an absolute, and a chain of prepositional phrases) elaborate the main clause.

In "The Problem of Defining a Mature Style" Christensen characterized the features of what he considered to be a mature style.

> *1. A mature style will have a relatively high frequency of free modifiers, especially in the final position. The frequency of free noun, verb, and adjective phrases and of verbid clauses* [absolutes] *will be high.*
>
> *2. Such a style will have also a relatively high frequency of structures of coordination within the T-unit—what might be called intra-T-unit coordination* [i.e., compound free modifiers as opposed to compound main clauses]. (1968, 579)

Christensen's concept of the cumulative sentence and his criticism of "bigger is better" T-units have had a considerable impact on the development of sentence combining materials. One consequence has been an increasing emphasis on sentence combining exercises that produce what Christensen called free modifiers and a de-emphasis on nominalization exercises. Another consequence has been an increased emphasis on classroom discussion of the relative rhetorical effectiveness of alternative solutions to sentence combining problems rather than sentence combining exercises as isolated pencil and paper activities as ends in themselves.

The past two decades have seen an explosion of research on the effectiveness of sentence combining. Probably the single best known study was conducted in 1976 by Max Morenberg, Donald Daiker, and Andrew Kerek (Daiker, Kerek, and Morenberg 1978) in the freshman writing program at Miami University. Their work is important because it was an unusually large and well conducted study. The experimental freshman composition sections used William Strong's *Sentence Combining: A Composing Book*, which contained 90 "open" (uncued) sentence combining exercises, leading to cumulative sentences with participles and absolutes. Strong's book was supplemented with additional material on appositives, infinitives, complex prepositional phrases, and parallel constructions. Class discussion emphasized the rhetorical reasons for choosing one solution over another.

The experimental sections (the sections that used sentence combining) showed a statistically significant growth in both words per clause and words per T-unit, while the control sections showed no significant gain. However, the most striking feature of this study was an analytic rating of experimental and control essays that rated the essays from the experimental sections as significantly superior to the control section essays in five of six categories (ideas, supporting details, voice, sentence structure, and diction/usage). The results of the analytic rating are particularly important because one common criticism of evaluating sentence combining solely on the basis of increased words per clause or

T-unit has been that while the measurement of the growth may be statistically reliable, the growth itself is so slight in absolute terms that it is invisible to anyone but statisticians. In other words, growth in words per T-unit may be statistically real but inconsequential for practical purposes. The analytic rating showed that sentence combining can foster visible improvement in the areas that composition courses have traditionally valued.

In recent years sentence combining has been studied and evaluated by literally hundreds of research projects—more than any teaching technique in the language arts field. In his *Research on Written Composition* (Hillocks 1986), George Hillocks, Jr., reviews the major research literature on sentence combining (141–151). He comments:

> *The overwhelming majority of these studies have been positive, with about 60 percent of them reporting that work in sentence combining, from as low as grade 2 through the adult level, results in significant advances (at least at p ≤ .05) on measures of syntactic maturity. Thirty percent of the reports have recorded some improvement at a nonsignificant level or at a level which was not tested for significance. Only 10 percent of the reports have been negative, showing either no significant differences or mixed results.*
>
> *More important, many studies have shown significant gains in quality for students engaged in sentence combining, gains which appear to be concomitants of increased T-unit and clause length.* (142–43)

The evidence that sentence combining can bring about a significant qualitative and quantitative gain in student writing now appears unquestionable. However, it is not clear how long lasting these gains are. Hillocks (145) reports mixed findings from the relatively small number of studies that have investigated the persistence of qualitative and quantitative gains achieved through sentence combining. Some studies have found that both the qualitative and quantitative gains persisted over a period of several months, while other studies have been negative. Twenty-eight months after their major 1978 study, Daiker, Kerek, and Morenberg conducted a follow-up of their experimental (sentence combining) and control groups (non-sentence combining). They found that while the experimental groups did not lose what they had gained (i.e., they did not regress), the experimental groups were no longer statistically different from the control groups. In other words, the control groups had caught up to the experimental groups, so that the relative advantage that the experimental group had originally obtained over the control group had disappeared over time (Kerek, Daiker, and Morenberg 1980).

Whatever future research tells us about the long-term effects of sentence combining, there is, nevertheless, no doubt that it has an immediate and measurable effect on writing. Exactly what and how sentence combining affects writing has been extensively debated. Some have even called sentence combining a practice in search of a theory. Mellon in his influential essay "Issues in the Theory and Practice of Sentence Combining: A Twenty Year Perspective" (Mellon 1979) argues that one of the most important aspects of sentence combining is that it helps developing writers look at the *way* they say something as an object of analysis, discussion, and improvement in its own right. Mellon calls this ability to examine the form of one's own writing *decentering*:

> A new skill, the skill of decentering, emerges during the junior high grades, allowing students (a) to regard their written words as external realities, hence craftable artifacts, and (b) to stop and re-start the flow of language without losing their thought and intention. . . .
>
> Sentence combining practice can trigger the onset of decentering, teach the operations of surface-structure sentence combining, and exercise the student in the manipulation of these operations in ways that facilitate their subsequent use in actual writing. (21)

In his article "How Sentence Combining Works," Strong (1985) argues along the same lines. Strong gives four reasons why sentence combining succeeds:

1. Sentence combining is a vehicle for students to teach themselves about basic grammar and mechanics through observing how sentences go together.

2. Sentence combining improves *automaticity*, "making the processing of print so natural, so unselfconscious, so deeply ingrained in neural machinery, that decoding and transcription per se become virtually irrelevant. . . . Automaticity, once again, is what enables us to concentrate on meaning" (339). Strong argues that poor writers have to spend so much effort in translating their ideas into written form that they have little opportunity to focus on meaning and larger rhetorical considerations. Sentence combining provides critical practice in helping writers hold sentences in their heads for editing, rethinking, and transcribing into a written form—to "hear" their sentences as their audience will.

3. Sentence combining extends developing writers' use of more sophisticated transformations that they do not use in their spoken language.

4. Through whole discourse exercises, sentence combining can effectively introduce skill-deficient writers to the "pattern" of different discourse modes—by, for example, extending a comparison/contrast or narrative, or by providing additional support for a proposition or counterarguments for a piece of persuasive writing.

In an invaluable booklet on the classroom use of sentence combining, *Creative Approaches to Sentence Combining*, Strong (1986) summarizes what he considers the key assumptions that underlie the sentence combining [SC] approach:

1. SC is not real writing. However cleverly devised they may be, exercises are no substitute for naturalistic (real writing) experiences in which students create personal meanings. SC is a skill-building adjunct to a language/composition program, not a busywork curriculum.

2. SC is not a model of the composing process. Most SC pertains to revision and editing, not invention or drafting. Moreover, real writing evolves from invented or discovered meanings, not given ones. SC *can* serve as a writing springboard, when students enter an exercise imaginatively.

3. SC exercises come in two basic varieties: cued (or signaled) and open (usually whole-discourse) exercises. Cued problems are useful for teaching target transformations, while open exercises help teach stylistic decision making in a large prose context.

4. SC is one approach to improved syntactic fluency—namely, better control and maturity in sentence construction. However, the aim of SC is to make good sentences, not merely long ones. Students should be taught that clarity counts—and that brevity has force.

5. SC instruction assumes that mistakes are a natural, inevitable, and desirable part of language learning. Mistakes provide feedback. The point is to learn from errors, not practice them. Usage workshops are a regular part of SC, with students sharing and comparing solutions to problem sentences.

6. SC instruction should move from oral rehearsal to written transcription. In transferring power from their primary language system (speaking) to the secondary system (writing), students develop inner speech, a physiological prerequisite for composing. SC helps develop automaticity and syntactic control.

7. SC can be used to teach virtually any language/composition concept inductively. Active/passive voice, sentence variety, transitions, parallel structure, free modifiers, paragraph organization, cohesion—all can be approached through SC exercises. Even literary appreciation can be taught with SC.

8. SC requires that teachers model editing and decision-making skills with students. Students should be encouraged to give reasons for their stylistic decisions. Mindless combining—without instructional focus or follow-up work—will soon prove boring to a class. Too much SC ruins its appeal.

9. SC is mainly a synthetic process, not an analytic one. Sooner or later, however, analysis plays a role—as in the decombining of overly complex texts. Teachers should share their viewpoints, not impose them as gospel. Rhetorical contexts for SC help achieve analytic aims.

10. SC works best when done two or three times a week for short periods, when students use exercises as springboards for journals or controlled writing, when teachers and students monitor problem sentences, and when transfer is made to real writing—either through
decombined student drafts or marginal notations.   (22)

SUMMARY

This chapter discusses sentence combining from two perspectives: the
linguistic and the pedagogical. From the linguistic perspective, sentence
combining is the process of *embedding*, the placing of one deep structure
inside another deep structure. In this chapter we examined three different types of embedding: (1) *noun modification*, deriving words, phrases, and clauses that modify nouns, (2) *nominalization*, deriving phrases
and clauses that replace nouns; and (3) *absolutes*, deriving phrases that
elaborate or explain main clauses.

In noun modification, a sentence is embedded inside the noun phrase.
This embedded sentence can come to the surface as a relative clause.
However, if the embedded sentence contains the verb *be*, the embedded
sentence can be reduced to a phrase by deleting the relative pronoun,
the tense marker, and the verb *be*. The type of phrase thus created
depends on what follows the verb *be* in the deep structure of the embedded sentence. If *be* is followed by a noun phrase, an appositive phrase is
created. If *be* is followed by a predicate adjective, a modifying adjective
is created. If *be* is followed by an adverb of place, an adjective phrase
is created. If *be* is part of the progressive auxiliary, a present participle or present participial phrase is created. If *be* is part of the passive
auxiliary, a past participle or past participial phrase is created.

In nominalization, an embedded sentence replaces an abstract noun
phrase. The embedded sentence can come to the surface in either of
two ways: as a noun clause (if the tense marker from the embedded
sentence is retained) or as a noun phrase (if the tense marker from
the embedded sentence is deleted). There are three different types of
noun phrases, depending on the fate of the tense marker. If the tense
marker is replaced by a present participle, a gerund or gerund phrase is
created. If the tense marker is replaced by *to*, an infinitive or infinitive
phrase is created. If the tense marker is deleted and the verb replaced
by an etymologically related noun, an abstract noun phrase is created.

In creating an absolute, a deep structure sentence is reduced to a
phrase by replacing the tense marker with a present participle marker.
The resulting surface structure retains both the subject noun phrase
and the entire verb phrase, though, of course, there no longer is a finite
verb. If the deep structure contains the verb *be*, a second option also
exists: the tense marker and the verb *be* are both deleted, creating a

surface structure consisting of the subject noun phrase and whatever follows the verb *be* in the underlying deep structure.

From the pedagogical perspective, sentence combining is a classroom technique used to help students write more sophisticated sentences by combining multiple simple (kernel or near kernel) sentences. A review of sentence combining research showed that about 60 percent of studies that used sentence combining in the classroom found a statistically significant increase in measures of syntactic maturity in students' writing (as measured by increase in number of words per clause or per T-unit). Many of these studies also showed significant gains in the quality of the the students' writing.

Several researchers have offered explanations for how sentence combining improves students' writing. Mellon suggested that sentence combining enables students to gain the skill of *decentering*: the ability to look at their writing as an object of analysis, discussion, and improvement. Strong suggested that sentence combining succeeds for four reasons: (1) it is a vehicle for students to teach themselves about basic grammar and mechanics; (2) it improves *automaticity*, the process of holding sentences in writers' heads for editing, rethinking, and transcribing into actual written form; (3) it extends developing writers' use of more sophisticated transformations than they use in their spoken language; and (4) it provides whole discourse exercises for teaching students different discourse modes.

8

Grammar in the Classroom

INTRODUCTION

This chapter is concerned with two issues. In Part I, as background, we discuss the role of grammar in the secondary classroom. The key point here is that since there is no longer a consensus on how grammar should be taught (or even if it should be taught at all), individual teachers must develop their own strategy for teaching grammar. In Part II, we discuss our options for teaching grammar more effectively. The discussion in this section centers around the two rationales for teaching grammar: (1) that grammar is valuable for its own sake, and (2) that grammar helps students write better. The main points made in Part II are the following.

☐ Traditional grammar can be taught much more effectively if it is free to incorporate new insights from modern grammars.

☐ Those aspects of grammar that directly relate to teaching writing are the best way to introduce the formal study of grammar for its own sake.

☐ Sentence combining is an effective vehicle for teaching both traditional and transformational grammar.

333

PART I: THE ROLE
OF GRAMMAR IN THE SECONDARY CLASSROOM

Since at least the beginning of this century, grammar has been one of the three major components of the English curriculum (along with composition and literature). The main justification for teaching grammar has been that grammar plays an important (some say critical) role in teaching composition, particularly in helping students deal with problems of mechanics.

Beginning in the 1950s and 1960s, however, a number of factors conspired to de-emphasize the importance of grammar in teaching composition. First, and probably most important, was a shift within the teaching profession concerning the goals and methods of teaching composition. Probably reflecting the spirit of the times, the teaching of writing was made more relevant to student needs. There has been a general shift in emphasis away from writing as a letter-perfect final product and onto the writing process. There has been a much greater emphasis on expressive and creative writing with a corresponding de-emphasis on formal correctness for its own sake (thus also de-emphasizing the contribution of grammar). Second, a growing body of research has questioned the effectiveness of grammar teaching in helping students control mechanical error. Third, the development of structural linguistics provided a new and competing approach to grammar that has severely undercut the hitherto unchallenged status of schoolroom traditional grammar (and by extension, the application of traditional grammar to teaching writing).

The most influential attack on the value of teaching traditional grammar appeared in an NCTE publication *Research in Written Composition* (1963) by Richard Braddock, Richard Lloyd-Jones, and Lowell Schoer. For many schools, this widely quoted statement legitimized the abandonment of traditional grammar teaching:

> *In view of the widespread agreement of research studies based upon many types of students and teachers, the conclusion can be stated in strong and unqualified terms: the teaching of formal grammar has a negligible or, because it usually displaces some instruction and practice in composition, even a harmful effect on improvement in writing.* (37–8)

As one would expect, such a radical break with a tradition for teaching grammar that stretches back to the eighteenth century engendered enormous controversy within the secondary schools. As a result we now have a situation in which buildings in the same district and even English teachers inside the same building profoundly disagree on how grammar should be taught and even on whether it should be taught at all. Since this controversy is one that all English teachers are necessarily caught up in, it is important that new teachers understand something about the nature of the conflict and the effect that it has had on the English classroom.

What are the key issues and why are they so difficult to resolve? On the face of it, the key issue is simple to state: should secondary schools teach grammar? Obviously, though, this is only the surface of the real issues. Underlying the question are many larger issues, among them: what is grammar, how does it work, how does a knowledge of grammar relate to problems of writing and to matters of style? We begin by discussing the meaning of the term *grammar*.

Hartwell (1985), in his widely quoted article "Grammar, Grammars, and the Teaching of Grammar," distinguishes between no less than five different meanings of the term *grammar* (109–111):

Grammar 1: Our internal, unconscious rule system. The grammar that we have in our heads.
Grammar 2: The scientific analysis of grammar. The linguist's model of Grammar 1.
Grammar 3: Usage. What people mean when they say that someone doesn't use very good grammar.
Grammar 4: The schoolroom version of traditional grammar. The grammar that is found in secondary textbooks.
Grammar 5: Stylistic grammar. The use of grammar for the purpose of teaching style. Among the approaches included here would be sentence combining.

The conflict is really three-cornered. One camp, reflecting the viewpoint of Braddock, Lloyd-Jones, and Schoer, sees no reason for teaching grammar (of any type) either for its own sake or because of its supposed contribution to teaching composition. A second camp adheres to the conventional reasons for teaching schoolroom traditional grammar, Grammar 4. A third camp also believes in teaching grammar, but rejects Grammar 4; this group would teach some form of Grammar 2 instead.

The debate between the second camp, advocates of Grammar 4, and the third camp, advocates of Grammar 2, has been long and acrimonious. The hostile positions of the adversaries and the lack of a viable middle ground between the positions has caused school systems to swing from one extreme to another. The debate has centered around two issues: should grammars be prescriptive or descriptive, and the role of grammar in dealing with student writing error.

For advocates of Grammar 4, grammar plays a prescriptive role. English, like any living language, is perceived to be in a constant state of flux. Without the normative influence of Grammar 4, English speakers would be free to use the language in any way they saw fit. Not only would there then be a collapse of standards of correctness; there would eventually be such a growth of colloquialisms and idiosyncratic grammatical constructions that English would no longer be our shared language. [This is not just speculation. Such collapses have indeed taken place. For example, after the collapse of the Roman Empire, the shared common language of the Empire, Latin, broke down into mutually unintelligible local dialects.] On the other hand, advocates of Grammar 2 see language as a resilient, living organism that has survived quite well for thousands of years without the guidance of grammarians. Therefore, the role of grammar is to describe the language as it is in all its richness and diversity, not to prescribe what some remote "experts" think it should be.

The advocates of Grammar 4 see Grammar 4 playing an absolutely essential role in dealing with mechanical error. Anyone who has corrected a set of high school essays does not need to be convinced that the control of mechanical error in writing is a serious problem for a substantial number of students. Advocates of Grammar 4 believe that the source of the error is the students' lack of understanding of the rules of Grammar 4. The errors are errors precisely because they violate the rules of Grammar 4. If students truly controlled Grammar 4, they would not make mechanical errors. Thus, giving students a knowledge of Grammar 4 is a critical step in helping them deal with their own mechanical errors.

Advocates of Grammar 2 deny the premise that errors are caused by a lack of knowledge of the rules of Grammar 4. They believe that errors have a number of causes; for example: conflicts between the students' dialect and the dialect of the standard language; conflicts between the spoken language and the conventions of writing; and students' simplifying or overgeneralizing the complex patterns of the standard dialect. Since none of these causes is rooted in a conscious knowledge of Grammar 4, the study of Grammar 4 will not address them. Since advocates of Grammar 2 are essentially *descriptive* (as opposed to *prescriptive*) in their orientation, they have been relatively little concerned with the problems of student writing error. Advocates of Grammar 4, with some justification, argue that advocates of Grammar 2 have tended to sweep the problem of writing error under the rug by either ignoring its significance or by defining it away as a conflict of equally valid dialects.

In the 1950s and 1960s, schoolroom traditional grammar, Grammar 4, was ridiculed by structural linguists as being unscientific and invalid. To a certain extent the schoolroom traditional grammar curriculum was replaced by a grammar curriculum based on structural linguistics, a form of Grammar 2. The development of this alternative grammar curriculum was a major achievement because it entailed both the development of classroom materials and the creation of retraining programs for in-service teachers (both accomplished with a level of federal funding that we can only dream about now).

However, just as these efforts were beginning to bear fruit, transformational grammar burst onto the scene. Transformational linguists in their turn were quick to ridicule structural linguistics (and by extension, the curriculum based on structural linguistics) as being unscientific and invalid. The language curriculums based on structural linguistics—still embroiled in endless controversy with traditionally oriented teachers and now cut off from support from the discipline of linguistics—quietly faded away, so that today (except for a few areas of the country that had especially strong curriculum centers and a high level of in-state support) they are now almost forgotten.

For most school districts, this was one revolution too many. Caught between the criticisms of schoolroom traditional grammar on the one hand and the instability of competing modern linguistic theories on the other, many school districts said, "a plague on both your houses," and, following Braddock, Lloyd-Jones, and Schoer's advice, abandoned the systematic teaching of grammar altogether. [Typically, however, school districts did not follow Braddock et al. in replacing grammar with more writing; instead, they replaced grammar with the study of literature.] The result is that two decades of students have now passed through the public school system with a minimal acquaintance with the formal study of grammar unless it was acquired through the study of a foreign language.

In the 1980s we have seen the pendulum swing back toward a greater concern with the quality of student writing and with the study of grammar. Many school districts have returned to the teaching of traditional grammar, though they differ greatly on the extent of their commitment. Some schools teach the whole canon of traditional grammar including diagraming. Other schools do little beyond spasmodically teaching traditional terms for parts of speech. Many schools fall between these extremes. They teach part of speech terminology, the major sentence relationships (e.g., subject, verb, direct object, indirect object), and the basic clause types, but do not teach diagraming.

PART II: TEACHING GRAMMAR MORE EFFECTIVELY

In order to teach any subject effectively, we must be very clear what it is that we are teaching and why we are teaching it. Up until the 1950s, the answers to these two questions were clearcut: traditional grammar (Hartwell's Grammar 4) was the only grammar available in the secondary classroom and it was taught for two reasons: (1) for its own sake—a knowledge of basic grammatical terminology and concepts was expected of every literate person, and (2) for its practical application to writing—a knowledge of Grammar 4 was thought to play an important role in learning to write correctly.

However, as was discussed in the previous section, there is no longer today any consensus in the secondary English profession on what grammar is or why grammar (however defined) should be taught. When there is no consensus, the natural tendency (not unreasonably) is to keep on doing whatever you have been doing and wait for something to turn up. Thus those teachers and school districts that have maintained a tradition of teaching traditional grammar continue to teach Warriner's as though nothing had happened in the past 30 years. Those teachers and school districts that have abandoned teaching grammar in the past will continue to ignore it. The majority of teachers and school districts, though, continue to vacillate ineffectually between the two extremes, teaching some grammar in a piecemeal fashion one year and dropping it the next.

Since a clear consensus on teaching grammar is lacking, individual teachers must develop their own strategy for dealing with grammar. I believe that the extreme strategy of abandoning grammar altogether does our students a disservice for two reasons. First, language is such an important part of our lives that students do need to know something about how it works. That is, grammar is legitimate as a topic of study in its own right. Second, as Mellon (1979) argues, students need to be able to look at their own writing as an external reality that they can evaluate at arm's length, as it were, and see how it will appear to someone else. Without this ability, students cannot really see their words as "craftable artifacts" that can be improved by revision or that can be monitored for surface error. The study of grammar plays an important role in developing students' ability to look at their language as an artifact.

Let us now examine in more detail each of these two rationales for picking a grammar for use in secondary schools—that the study of grammar is valuable for its own sake and that a knowledge of grammar helps students learn to write better.

TEACHING GRAMMAR FOR ITS OWN SAKE

The first rationale for teaching grammar, that it is valuable for its own sake, has tended to be overshadowed by its pedagogical applications. For example, as you may recall from Chapter 5, the study of English grammar was started in British schools in the seventeenth century not for its own sake but for the purpose of teaching the terms and concepts that would be needed for teaching Latin grammar. In the nineteenth century, the study of grammar was primarily justified on totally different pedagogical grounds—that the rigor of the study of grammar developed the mind. In American schools in the late nineteenth and the twentieth centuries, grammar has primarily been justified in terms of teaching writing.

However, studying grammar is an intellectually valid curricular goal, whether grammar has immediate practical applications or not. After all, if direct practical application were the sole consideration in choosing subjects in the secondary curriculum, the only subjects taught would be vocational education, home economics, and driver education. Certainly, no one could defend chemistry, physics, biology, or literature on the grounds of their immediate practical applications. For example, we do not reject the teaching of biology on the grounds that such knowledge cannot be proven to make our bodies work better.

We can make a strong case for teaching Grammar 2, here defined as classical transformational grammar, in the secondary classroom. The study of English grammar at the university level is totally dominated by transformational grammar (in its various guises). Transformational grammar has become an important academic discipline in its own right. In the past two decades there have been literally thousands of books, PhD dissertations, and journal articles about English grammar from the transformational point of view. While controversial theories abound, there is no controversy about the level of factual knowledge about English grammar that has been attained since the publication of *Syntactic Structures* in 1957: what we know today is a quantum leap beyond what was known then. Moreover, transformational grammar has had a great impact on the surrounding fields of psychology, sociology, and philosophy as well as on more remote fields such as information science and neurology.

If this is the case, shouldn't we follow the lead of the universities and teach classical transformational grammar beginning in the primary grades and continuing in the secondary classroom as a subject matter in its own right? I think it would be wonderful if we could. However, I do not think it very likely that we will be able to for a number of reasons that cluster in two areas: first, problems arising from the volatile nature of transformational grammar, and second, problems arising in the classroom.

The first problem arises from the fact that transformational grammar is still a very young discipline. While the study of grammar is one of mankind's older recorded intellectual activities, transformational grammar is a new field in the sense that it has approached the study of language from such a novel perspective that linguists today are sailing on totally uncharted waters. Young disciplines like transformational grammar are exciting, but they are volatile. Since its founding in the late 1950s, transformational grammar has undergone at least four major changes. For example, several of the important aspects of "classical" transformational grammar have been rejected by some theoreticians (including Chomsky himself).

Such rapid change means that there is little consensus on which form of transformational grammar should be taught, or even what transformational grammar is. And if experts disagree, what can nonexperts be expected to do? The high level of disagreement among professionals in the field has discouraged the development of pedagogical materials at the secondary level because secondary textbook publishers are not going to commit themselves to a new approach to grammar unless it is supported by a broad consensus.

The second problem arises when we attempt to teach transformational grammar in the classroom. Despite the lack of consensus among transformational grammarians, some schools, attracted by the intellectual achievements of transformational grammar and by its powerful analyses of English, have successfully incorporated transformational grammar into their language curriculum. Nevertheless, teachers who attempt to teach transformational grammar (especially ones who are on their own) face a number of practical problems in using transformational grammar in the classroom.

☐ Teaching a form of grammar that does not purport to improve writing subjects the teacher to constant demands for justification, not only from parents but from students and fellow teachers because the conventional wisdom is that grammar is taught because it helps students write better. Unfortunately, the strongest argument in favor of transformational grammar, intellectual validity, is an argument that even those who are supportive of new approaches will find bewildering at best.

☐ The fact that most students fail to learn schoolroom traditional grammar is considered to be the fault of the student. Teachers are thus protected by an expected norm of student failure. However, if a teacher departs from the conventional curriculum, then that teacher assumes responsibility for student success. In other words, it is the students' fault if they do not learn traditional grammar, but it is the teacher's fault if they do not learn transformational grammar.

☐ Traditional grammar has been used in English classrooms for generations. Parents, administrators, and English teachers themselves studied traditional grammar. It is what you do in an English class. Even the fact that students do so poorly with traditional grammar is not seen as a reason for questioning the importance of traditional grammar because that failure is already built into the system as an expected norm. There is even a perverse opposite argument: the fact that students do so poorly with traditional grammar shows that they need to spend even more time working on it. Teaching traditional grammar conforms to conventional wisdom: you never have to justify why you are doing it. If you teach transformational grammar, on the other hand, the burden of justification is completely on you.

☐ Traditional grammar provides a prebuilt curriculum; that is, there is a well-established content and an order in which that content is taught. When a teacher undertakes transformational grammar, the teacher must create a rationale for both the content and the sequence. While this is stimulating to a point, it also takes an enormous amount of time—a scarce commodity for all teachers.

☐ Traditional grammar instruction has a well-established support system of handbooks, student learning aids, packaged teaching materials, workbooks (with answers for the teacher), ditto masters, and the like. The teacher can draw on this vast array of materials to use in the classroom, thus removing much of the day-to-day burden of providing materials for the students. Very little comparable support material exists for transformational grammar, and consequently the teacher is required to spend a great deal of time developing classroom exercises from scratch. As a practical matter, nearly all systematic attempts to teach a transformational curriculum have been dependent on the support of a university curriculum center.

☐ Hypothetically one could skirt the problem of insufficient support materials by emphasizing the discovery aspect of transformational grammar. Indeed, one of the great advantages of transformational grammar is that it lends itself to a discovery- or inquiry-oriented curriculum. However, this open-ended approach shifts the burden away from materials and onto the teacher. In order to succeed in any inquiry-oriented approach, the teacher would need to have a solid knowledge of (1) the theory of transformational grammar, (2) how it analyzes the major areas of English syntax, and (3) how to make such an approach work in the classroom.

A single introductory course in transformational grammar (let alone the few chapters in this book) is not adequate preparation either in transformational theory or in its analysis of English syntax. Imagine how difficult it would be to conduct a comparable inquiry-oriented approach in a field such as mathematics or biology with only a single introductory-level course. Moreover, the knowledge of how to make such an approach actually work in the classroom does not even yet exist in any codified manner—except for sentence combining.

In summary, successful implementation of a transformational grammar curriculum in the secondary classroom (desirable as that goal may be) requires a body of support materials, well-trained teachers, and a highly supportive administration that encourages innovative curriculum development projects. This is not to say that such curriculum projects have not been successful. But the beginning teacher should be aware that the stringent conditions for the success of such undertakings are rarely met, and that in the absence of these conditions, even herculean efforts of individual teachers usually end in frustration.

If a self-contained, disciplinary teaching of classical transformational grammar in the secondary classroom is a nonstarter for a variety of practical reasons, what are our alternatives?

For me, a return to Grammar 4, schoolroom traditional grammar as it has conventionally been taught, is not a viable alternative. Some teachers, of course, have succeeded wonderfully in teaching Grammar 4. However, for most students in most classrooms, the study of Grammar 4 has not been successful. The very fact that all standard secondary English textbooks repeat the same grammar material at each grade level tacitly acknowledges that no one really expects students to understand Grammar 4. In a kind of inoculation theory of education, Grammar 4 is repeated each year in the hope that this time it will "take." Most students have an extremely negative attitude toward schoolroom traditional grammar, rooted, I believe, in their frustration in not being able to understand it or to use it with much success in dealing with their own writing problems.

The problem that students have encountered with Grammar 4 is not in the concepts of grammar per se. The problem, I believe, is primarily in the conventional pedagogy for teaching the terminology and concepts of traditional grammar. The conventional pedagogy is completely dependent on students' ability to understand the formal, abstract definitions of the terms and concepts. However, many students find the definitions hard to understand and thus very difficult to use in practice. Part of the problem is that the definitions presuppose that students already have a high level of conscious knowledge about grammar and an ability to manipulate that conscious knowledge. Robert DeBeaugrande (1984) describes the problem in these terms:

> As long as school grammar is couched in vague or technical terms, it is not 'basic' enough to help students with genuine literacy problems, and we will achieve very little by going 'back' to it. Such grammar is like a ladder with the lower rungs taken out: the real beginner can't get anywhere. Students who don't happen to figure out by themselves, through lengthy induction, what the basic terms mean, won't profit much from grammatical instruction. If school grammar succeeded in past times, the student population was much narrower and more uniform than what we have today; it was much easier to rely on hidden presuppositions about things we couldn't explain very well. (359)

Grammar is essentially a technical vocabulary for talking about language. In Grammar 4 this vocabulary is taught by means of abstract, formal definitions. These definitions are usually based on the meaning of the terms being defined; for example, a noun is defined as "a word used to name a person, place, thing, or idea." The problem with this definition is not that it is wrong. The problem is that the definition presupposes knowledge of the thing being defined. In other words, unless the student already knows what a noun is, the student cannot use the definition correctly.

To cite an example used in Chapter 1, the word *blue* is the name of a color, and by the terms of the definition ought, therefore, to be a noun. The definition of noun in Grammar 4 is not a tool that can be easily used to test words to see if they are nouns. The definition only really makes sense if you already know how to recognize nouns. As DeBeaugrande (1984) points out, this kind of definition effectively cuts the beginning student out of the loop: if the student does not already intuitively recognize nouns, the formal definition is too broad to be helpful.

In order to teach traditional grammar successfully to the majority of our students, we need to reach students at their level. I think that to some extent the problems that most students have with Grammar 4 spring from our Latinate tradition for teaching English grammar. If we were to teach Latin grammar to our students, their knowledge would be restricted to the rules that we taught them. On the other hand, when we teach English grammar, our students have an enormous intuitive knowledge of English to draw upon. However, our tradition for teaching English grammar treats students as though they were learning a foreign language. When we study a second language, our problem is to turn our conscious knowledge of the rules we have been taught into intuitive language behavior, that is, into unconscious knowledge. When we study our own native language, the problem is the reverse: we already have an unconscious, intuitive knowledge of the language, but we have no conscious knowledge of the rules. From this point of view, the conventional pedagogy of Grammar 4 is backwards: it teaches English grammar to native speakers of English as though English were a foreign language to them. Instead, we need to capitalize on our students' intuitive knowledge of English. We can lead students to a conscious understanding of English grammar by helping them tap into their unconscious knowledge.

The methodology used in the first four chapters of this book is based on the premise that students can use their intuitive knowledge of English to help them consciously define the technical vocabulary of traditional grammar. For example, speakers of English intuitively know how to use nouns. By raising their intuitive knowledge of how nouns are used to a conscious level, students can determine if a word is a noun by seeing if they can use it as a noun. Rather than identifying a noun by appealing to the abstract definition of a noun, students can identify a noun by tapping into their own knowledge to see if the word is used in ways that are characteristic of nouns. In Chapter 1 of this book, for example, common nouns are identified (a) by their form (e.g., common nouns can be made plural and possessive), (b) by words that occur with common nouns (e.g., common nouns can be used after *the*), and (c) by words that can substitute for nouns (e.g., *it* and *they* can substitute for singular and plural common nouns, respectively). The advantage of this approach is that it builds on knowledge that students already possess. It empowers students to identify parts of speech and other grammatical concepts on their own.

However, this approach can work only if students consciously know which features are the critical ones for making identifications. Although it may seem strange to put it this way, the problem that native speakers of a language have is that they know the answers, but they do not know the questions. In other words, to tap into their unconscious knowledge of English, they must consciously know what structural paraphrase tests to use in identifying a given part of speech or grammatical construction. The goal of the methodology used in the first four chapters is to give students the conscious knowledge of exactly which structural features to use.

Following are the major structural paraphrase tests that were used in the first four chapters, together with references to the exercises that reinforced the tests.

1. Common nouns: the use of plural and possessive paraphrases, the "tip off" word *the*, and the substitution of *it*. Ch 1, Ex 1.3. Identifying common nouns, on page 15.

2. Predicate adjectives: "tip off" word *very*, comparative/superlative paraphrase, paraphrase as modifying adjective, adverb in *-ly*. Ch 1, Ex 1.12. Identifying predicate adjectives, on page 38.

3. Verbs: paraphrase as past or future. Ch 1, Ex 1.19. Testing for verbs, on page 55.

4. Adverbs that modify verbs: paraphrase as adverb question. Ch 1, Ex 1.20. Identifying adverbs that modify verbs, on page 58.

5. Complete sentences/fragments: expanding fragments into complete sentences. Ch 2, Ex 2.1. Recognizing fragments and complete sentences, on page 73.

6. Subjects: paraphrasing subject noun phrase with pronouns. Ch 2, Ex 2.2. Identifying subjects, on page 75.

7. Normal sentence word order/complete predicates: moving introductory elements into normal sentence-final position. Ch 2, Ex 2.3. Putting sentences into normal order and identifying complete predicates, on page 77.

8. Indirect object: paraphrasing with *to/for*. Ch 2, Ex 2.5. Identifying objects, on page 82.

9. Adjective/adverb phrases: substitution tests that distinguish adjective and adverb phrases. Ch 3, Ex 3.5. Identifying prepositional phrases, on page 111.

It is important to remember that the structural paraphrase tests used in the first four chapters do not contradict the traditional definitions. The tests supplement the traditional definitions. The tests are most useful for those students who have difficulty with the abstractness of the traditional definitions. An interesting twist is that once students have gained conscious control over the structural paraphrase tests and have sufficient experience using them, then the traditional definitions may come to make sense to them.

By borrowing methodologies from structural linguistics for teaching parts of speech we have created a slightly different kind of traditional grammar—a slightly less traditional, traditional grammar, as it were. In order to distinguish this version of traditional grammar from schoolroom traditional grammar (Hartwell's Grammar 4), let us call this new version *revised traditional grammar* (which we will now designate as Grammar 4a). Revised traditional grammar, Grammar 4a, is not profoundly different from schoolroom traditional grammar except that it is free to incorporate grammatical concepts from structural linguistics where appropriate and to use techniques from structural and transformational grammar in order to help students use their intuitive knowledge of English to gain a better grasp of traditional terms and concepts.

So far we have augmented the methodology of schoolroom traditional grammar, Grammar 4, with pedagogical techniques borrowed from structural linguistics. We have not suggested any changes in the actual *content* of schoolroom traditional grammar. However, there are three areas associated with the verb in which insights from structural linguistics and transformational grammar would be very helpful to students.

- ☐ a description of phrasal verbs. Phrasal verbs are verb + preposition constructions that form new verbs; for example, *turn on* in the sentence *John turned on the light*. There are literally thousands of phrasal verbs in English. To ignore them is to ignore a major part of English vocabulary.
- ☐ a broader definition of the term *complement*. The term *complement* should pertain to any construction required by a verb, not just to nouns and predicate adjectives; for example, the verb *put* requires an adverb of place after the object. When we put something, we must put it somewhere. Broadening the definition of complement is important because we want students to be able to strip complex sentences down to their most basic form. We

need to help them distinguish between what is required in a sentence (subject + verb + complement) and what is added on as an option.

☐ a clearer treatment of tense. Students would find the whole concept of *tense* much clearer if we were to adopt Chomsky's treatment of the Auxiliary [Tense + (Modal) + (Perfect) + (Progressive)]. Several widely used traditional secondary textbook series have, in fact, incorporated Chomsky's approach to the Auxiliary quite successfully.

The first four chapters of this book are an attempt to create a revised traditional grammar. The content (including the terminology and the sequence of presentation of topics) in the first four chapters is exactly what teachers will encounter in schoolroom traditional grammar textbooks. In that respect, the first four chapters are utterly conventional. However, what is not at all conventional is the methodology by which that content is taught. In other words, the book teaches traditional content by nontraditional methods.

If you are in a school where you are expected to teach traditional grammar, the methodology introduced in the first four chapters is a very effective supplement to any standard traditional grammar textbook. Using structural paraphrase tests will give your students a sense of being in control of grammatical terms and concepts. Moreover, you can introduce this methodology without contradicting any of the standard definitions.

Following are some practical suggestions for teaching traditional grammar that you may find helpful.

☐ Do not spend too much time on part of speech identification. Sometimes teachers feel that unless students can completely master parts of speech in Chapter 1, they cannot go on to the sentence and its parts in Chapter 2. I think this is a mistake for several reasons. First, we are really more interested in students' developing a sense for how sentences are built. Part of speech identification is a means to that larger goal; it is not fully an end in itself. Second, students need information from the whole sentence in order to determine parts of speech. For example, one of the keys we use for identifying nouns is by first finding the words that play the role of subject or object; these words are nouns because they play roles that only nouns can play. Third, some parts of speech are difficult to recognize or define at the word level. For example, it is nearly impossible to talk about prepositions without first talking about the larger unit of the prepositional phrase. Sometimes students are caught in a kind of Catch-22 situation in which their failure to succeed in word-level part of speech identification prohibits them from moving on to sentence-level exercises, and yet the sentence-level information may be critical in their ability to recognize parts of speech.

☐ The verb is the heart of the sentence. No sentence can be formed without a verb—the only possible one word sentences are imperative verbs. The verb has both semantic and grammatical links to the subject and the complement. Thus, rather than beginning part of speech identification with nouns, it may be more effective to begin with the verb. Also, by beginning with the verb, we are connecting parts of speech with sentence structure.

☐ Verbal phrases are very difficult for students. Since both traditional sentence diagraming and sentence combining analyze verbal phrases as reduced clauses, students may find it easier to deal with verbal phrases *after* you have already taught clauses and can then show how verbals can be paraphrased as full clauses.

Let us summarize what we have said about the rationale of teaching grammar for its own sake. The conventional pedagogy of schoolroom traditional grammar, Grammar 4, has not been successful with many students. One way of making traditional grammar more accessible to students is to introduce insights from more modern grammars, creating a slightly different version of schoolroom traditional grammar that we have named *revised traditional grammar,* Grammar 4a. The suggested revisions are primarily in the methodology by which the traditional content is taught. The main pedagogical innovation is to teach the traditional terms and concepts by drawing on students' intuitive ability to paraphrase words and sentences through a number of different structural paraphrase tests. This chapter also advocated augmenting the content of Grammar 4 with three insights from structural linguistics and transformational grammar: phrasal verbs, a broader definition of *complement*, and Chomsky's treatment of tense.

TEACHING GRAMMAR
AS A WAY OF HELPING STUDENTS WRITE BETTER

The second rationale for teaching grammar is that a knowledge of grammar helps students write better. In this section we first review the research literature on the causes and treatment of student writing error and then turn to the larger question of the relation between grammar and writing.

1. Student writing error

Since the early twentieth century, the most common justification for teaching grammar in the classroom has been that students require a conscious knowledge of grammar to control mechanical error in their own writing; that is, that correctness in language is the result of conforming to a set of consciously learned grammar rules. Accordingly, mechanical errors in writing result from violating these rules. Therefore, the traditional classroom remedy has been to teach the relevant rules of Grammar 4 through explanation and classroom activities, usually workbooks. Even schools that are reluctant to teach a full grammar curriculum often feel obliged to teach the rules of Grammar 4 in a piecemeal manner in order to respond to the problems of mechanical error. [For the remainder of this chapter, we use the term *error* to mean the common errors of *punctuation* (omitted apostrophe, run-on sentence, sentence fragment, comma splice, comma omitted with a coordinating conjunction that joins two independent clauses, and comma faults) and *grammar* (subject-verb agreement, faulty parallelism, misplaced modifier, dangling modifier, and pronoun agreement error).]

Now, how effective is this strategy? A number of research studies going back to the first decade of this century have investigated the effectiveness of teaching the rules of traditional grammar as a method for reducing mechanical error in student writing. Not one of these many studies ever found evidence that the strategy worked. That is, not one study found a positive correlation between the study of traditional grammar and a measurable reduction of mechanical error. [See Hartwell (1985) for an extensive review of the research studies on the relation of traditional grammar and error.] In other words, students who studied Grammar 4 did not improve their control over mechanical error in any way that could be detected by the researchers. Moreover, researchers and teachers alike have often noted that even those students who did seem to gain control over mechanical error in structured exercises were unable to transfer that learning to reducing that same type of error in their own writing.

Some of the early studies on the relationship of traditional grammar and error reduction were not so well controlled or documented as comparable studies would be today. [See Kolln (1981) for a critical review of this older research literature.] Nevertheless, there have been a number of well designed and conducted modern studies that have reached the same conclusion. The best known modern study was conducted in New Zealand (Elley et al. 1976). This study has attracted considerable attention because it was unusually large (248 students in eight matched classes), covered a relatively long span of time (3 years), and was carefully designed and controlled.

The study compared three language programs: (1) a traditional grammar program (P. R. Smart's *Let's Learn English*), (2) the transformational grammar strand from the Oregon Curriculum, and (3) the rhetoric and literature strands from the Oregon Curriculum. The transformational grammar strand was very linguistically oriented and made no attempt to relate grammar to either writing problems or questions of style. The rhetoric and literature strand did not deal with grammar at all.

The study was particularly concerned with the effect that these three different programs—traditional grammar, linguistically oriented transformational grammar, and no grammar at all—would have on student writing. The researchers compared students' writing in eleven areas, including English usage, spelling, essay mechanics, essay style, essay structure, and essay content. They found that there was no major difference in the writing of students among the three different groups. In other words, students wrote the same whether they had had three years of traditional grammar, linguistically-oriented transformational grammar, or no grammar at all.

Can we then conclude from this study that it is proven that teaching grammar (either Grammar 2 or Grammar 4) does not reduce error in student writing? Not at all. First, negative studies never prove negative generalizations. The fact that this well designed study found no correlation between teaching grammar and reduction of mechanical error does not mean that, in fact, there was no correlation even for these students. There may have been a correlation, but the methodology was not sufficiently sensitive to detect it. Second, the fact that the particular approaches used in teaching grammar in this study failed to correlate with a reduction in error says nothing about the success or failure we can expect from other approaches to teaching grammar. What this and other studies do show, however, is that those who maintain that we *must* teach Grammar 4 in order to enable students to reduce mechanical error lack empirical support for such a strong stance.

In recent years, researchers have begun to study mechanical error as a phenomenon in its own right. While this research is still in its infancy, it has already revolutionized our thinking about error. The landmark study of writing error is Mina P. Shaughnessy's *Errors and Expectations* (1977). This book deals with the severe writing problems of nontraditional students who entered the City University of New York through an open admissions policy. The book, based on an error analysis of 4,000 placement exams, is remarkable both for its pioneering exploration of the causes and treatment of writing error and for the respect that the author has for these writers. Following is her overview of her approach:

> I have reached the persuasion that underlies this book—namely that B[asic] W[riting] students write the way they do, not because they are slow or non-verbal, indifferent to or incapable of academic excellence, but because they are beginners and must, like all beginners, learn by making mistakes. These they make aplenty and for such a variety of reasons that the inexperienced teacher is almost certain to see nothing but a chaos of error when he first encounters their papers. Yet a closer look will reveal very little that is random or 'illogical' in what they have written. And the keys to their development as writers

often lie hidden in the very features of their writing that English teachers have been trained to brush aside with a marginal code letter or a scribbled injunction to 'Proofread!' Such [teacher] strategies ram at the doors of their incompetence while the keys that would open them lie in view. (5)

Three ideas about the causes of error are implicit in this statement.

1. Basic writers, even though they are native speakers of English, do not command the special forms and conventions of written English, which are sufficiently different from oral language to constitute a separate dialect. In this sense, basic writers exhibit some of the behavior of learners of a second language.

2. Errors are not random or accidental but are the result of the writers' learning strategy.

3. Errors are a necessary part of the learning strategy. That is, basic writers make errors of a certain type as a necessary consequence of their learning process. These errors, then, are a sign of development and progress.

Each of these ideas has been the inspiration of subsequent research on the causes of error, and they serve as a convenient way to summarize much current thinking about error.

1. Learning to write standard English is like acquiring a new dialect. There are three ways in which learning to write is like acquiring a new dialect.

☐ The written language rejects many grammatical features of spoken dialects.

Rightly or wrongly, the written language is not as tolerant of dialect variation as the spoken language is. Some examples of features that are common in some spoken dialects but nonstandard in written English are certain verb forms (e.g., *I seen him*) and certain ways of forming negatives (e.g., *ain't* and double negatives). Even though we recognize that from a linguistic perspective these nonstandard forms are legitimate in their own right (in fact many of them were grammatical in earlier stages of the English language), it is nonetheless a fact of life that these forms are unacceptable in modern written English. For many basic writers, acquiring a new set of written forms to replace what seem to be perfectly serviceable equivalents in the spoken language is a substantial task. It means replacing language that seems normal and comfortable with language that seems artificial, stilted, and even alien.

☐ The written language is a special form of encoding the spoken language.

Let us set aside differences among various spoken dialects and instead compare standard spoken English with its written counterpart. The sheer mechanics of converting the standard spoken language to its written equivalent requires mastering a number of conventions. For example, we all know without instruction how to pronounce English words, but we all have to learn, more or less painfully, how to spell them.

The written language is not related to the spoken language in an exact one-to-one manner. There are features in the spoken language that have no exact equivalent in the written language and vice versa. These discrepancies pose problems for all of us, but for basic writers these differences are formidable. Many of the common grammar and punctuation errors of basic writers can be traced to these discrepancies between the written and spoken language. First we will examine some errors that result from distinctions made in the spoken language but not made in the written language, and then we will examine errors that result from the reverse situation: distinctions made in the written language but not made in the spoken language.

In the spoken language we rely heavily on intonation to group together grammatically related units—words, phrases, and clauses. To a certain extent, intonation features in the spoken language are paralleled by punctuation marks in the written language. For example, the falling pitch that signals the end of a sentence in spoken English is reflected by the period at the end of a written sentence, and the rising pitch that signals a question is reflected by the question mark.

However, a major problem for basic writers is that pauses in the middle of spoken sentences only partly correspond to commas. It is true that commas correspond to pauses in the spoken language, but the reverse is not true—not every pause is written as a comma. The discrepancy results from the fact that the rules of English pronunciation establish certain points within a sentence as natural pausing points. These points are between the major syntactic units—between subject and verb, verb and object, object and adverbs. Pausing between these units (called *phrase units* by phoneticians) for breath or to plan ahead is normal and is not usually noticed by the hearer. It is entirely natural for basic writers, laboriously writing out sentences word by painful word, to stop and regroup at these pause points and then to put in a comma to reflect the pause. This misuse of the comma is especially common when the subject is followed by a long prepositional phrase or adjective clause because we need to pause for breath there, with the result that the comma separates the subject from the predicate. For example, the following sentence contains a typical comma error of this type.

*The idea that I have presented in this paper, is summarized in the following quote.

No matter how strange the comma looks, it correctly identifies a major pause point in the sentence, and when read aloud, the sentence—with its lengthy pause between subject and verb—sounds perfectly normal.

This problem with comma punctuation is sometimes inadvertently worsened by a teacher who has too strongly equated pauses and commas and who has also (quite correctly) encouraged basic writers to read their work aloud. When basic writers do exactly what the teacher has recommended, they will read their work aloud, note the pause between subject and verb, and put in a comma.

A teacher unaware of the source of this comma error may conclude that basic writers who make this mistake have made the comma error because they do not know grammar. That is, basic writers do not know that they have separated the subject from the verb by the comma, and thus they must not know what subjects and verbs are. The teacher may then attempt to deal with the problem by reviewing basic subject and verb identification. Since, however, the teacher's attempt at correcting the error has nothing to do with the actual cause of the error—the students' equating pauses with commas—the grammar exercises will not help the writers deal with the problem. Although the writers may get better at identifying subjects and verbs in workbook exercises (a skill that has its own validity), they will still make the same comma error in their writing because the treatment they received bore no real relation to the cause of their problem.

Conversely, many errors of basic writers can be traced to distinctions made in the written language that do not have anything corresponding to them in the spoken language. A simple example is the need to distinguish consciously in the written language between common and proper nouns because of the need to capitalize the latter. There is nothing in our pronunciation of proper nouns that corresponds to a capital letter.

A major problem for all basic writers (and for some otherwise skillful writers) is the use of the apostrophe to distinguish the possessive -s from the plural -s in writing. For example, we use the apostrophe in the phrase *the teacher's pencil* to indicate that the -s in *teacher's* is a possessive form rather than a plural form. In the spoken language, of course, the two forms are pronounced identically. Thus, when we use an -s form in writing nouns, we must consciously decide which grammatical function the -s plays (possessive or plural) and then punctuate accordingly. This conscious distinction between the two different uses of -s is not necessary in the spoken language. Clearly, a major part of the problem is that since spoken language does not distinguish between the two functions of -s, our ear does not guide us in deciding when to use or not use an apostrophe in written English; we must learn the distinction consciously.

☐ Written English requires a larger vocabulary and more complex constructions than spoken English.

Our written language is much more complex than our spoken language. When we write, we use a whole range of abstract words that we would feel self-conscious about using in spoken language. Basic writers do not control these abstract words very well. In addition to misusing the meaning of abstract words, basic writers make the much more disorienting error of incorrectly deriving abstract words from other parts of speech. Here are some examples from Shaughnessy of this error:

> He is headed in a <u>destructional</u> way.
> There should always <u>be preparance</u> in any occupation....
> The loser would be the Chinese people, who <u>resemblance</u> the Godfather.
> (190)

One of Shaughnessy's many valuable observations about the basic writers she studied is that they are emotionally and cognitively adults with complex ideas that they are trying to communicate; they are not content to express adult ideas in third-grade language. Consequently, basic writers attempt complex structures that they cannot always control. For example, subject-verb agreement errors often occur when the subject is separated from its verb by a modifying prepositional phrase or adjective clause. In these cases, the writers have made the verb agree with the nearest noun rather than with the actual subject noun. Consider, for example, the subject-verb error in the following sentence.

*A <u>group are</u> anchored in the harbor.

This error is unlikely to occur, and if it did, the writer would probably note it and correct it. But look at the longer, related sentence.

*A <u>group</u> of single-masted fishing boats <u>are</u> anchored in the harbor.

When the subject is separated from the verb, a subject-verb agreement error is much more likely to be made and, once made, more likely to go unnoticed by the writer for two reasons: (1) the apparent noun-verb sequence *boats are* does not catch our eye as looking wrong, and (2) there is a conflict between the topic of the sentence, *boats*, and the grammatical subject, *group*. In most sentences the topic and the grammatical subject are identical. However, in the preceding example, the subject is the semantically empty word *group*. In our short term memory of the sentence, we tend to replace the low semantic content word *group* with the high semantic content word *boats*. If someone were to ask us to recall this sentence a few moments after we had read it, we would likely recall that the subject was *boats*, not *group*. Accordingly, in lengthy or complex sentences, we tend to make the verb agree with the semantic topic rather than the semantically empty grammatical subject.

A teacher who is unfamiliar with the cause of this error might conclude that this basic writer does not know fundamental grammar and set the student to work doing remedial exercises. While such exercises are not harmful, it is questionable how helpful they actually are for this type of student because they do not address the real problem—a sentence that is so long and complex that the basic writer loses track of the sentence's structure and takes as the subject the topic noun nearest to the verb. The very fact that the exercises are remedial will only provide the student with practice on relatively simple sentences. However, this writer does not have trouble with subject-verb agreement in simple sentences; he or she has trouble in complex, adultlike sentences. In other words, the problem is in the writer's inability to cope with the complexity of the adult sentences he or she attempts to write, not in the childlike sentences presented in remedial grammar exercises. Such mismatches between the complexity of the error and the simplicity of the remediation help explain why there is sometimes such poor transfer from grammar exercises to the writer's own work.

2. Errors are the result of a deliberate strategy. Obviously, basic writers do not deliberately choose to produce errors. However, they consciously and unconsciously employ strategies (rules), some of which have errors as side effects. Basic writers, like first- and second-language learners, are not passive. Errors are not always random events that happen unpredictably through the writers' ignorance or inadvertency; errors often result from rules that learners have hypothesized. For the most part, this kind of error results from the overgeneralization of a tentative rule. We have seen an example of this overgeneralization when basic writers equate commas with pauses. Many times this rule—when there is a pause, put in a comma—will result in the correct use of commas, but sometimes (e.g., between subject and verb), the strategy leads basic writers to put commas in the wrong places.

Sometimes basic writers will grimly persevere with an obviously inadequate strategy (which even they can see is clearly not working) because it is the only reed they can cling to. For them to do otherwise would mean abandoning themselves to hopeless chaos and confusion. Sometimes basic writers will do the opposite: drop one strategy in the middle of an essay in favor of the totally reverse strategy. A not uncommon example of this reversal is a paper in which the writer will put in commas at every possible juncture in the first half of the essay, and then in the second half revert to the opposite "if in doubt, leave them out" strategy and use no commas at all.

Muddled as they are, basic writers are not passive. Their strategies are their best attempts to make sense of what they are doing. If they had a better strategy, they would use it. Any strategy, even a poor one, is better than no strategy. Consequently, when we provide negative feedback or suggestions based on abstract (even arcane) grammatical terminology, we are not meeting their needs for practical, workable strategies that they can incorporate into their own systems.

3. Errors are necessary. We know from studies of how children acquire their first language and how both children and adults acquire a second language that language learning takes place through a kind of trial-and-error strategy in which broad generalizations (rules) are successively refined and narrowed. For example, children acquiring the rules for the pronunciation of the past tense forms of English verbs begin with a general rule that attaches a dental sound (/t/ or /d/) to the stem of the verb. The children's rule (erroneously) causes them to treat verbs whose stems end in a /t/ or /d/ sound (such as *part* and *fade*) as already being in the past tense. Only later are they able to revise their rule to produce the correct past tense forms for these verbs. Even then, children will overgeneralize the rules to irregular verbs, producing such forms as *hitted* and *singed*. Eventually, of course, children will recognize that these verbs are irregular and exempt them from the regular rules for forming the past tense.

These errors are not random. Such past tense forms as *runned* and *singed* are evidence that children are working out the system for forming the past tense. These forms reflect what we might call "intermediate" rule systems. In order for children to reach a final rule system compatible with the adult system, they have to work their way through the intermediate stages. Thus the errors that these intermediate rules produce reflect necessary stages in the learning process. It is not that errors cause improvement; the errors are a necessary byproduct of various stages in the development of an adultlike rule system. Learning cannot take place without the intermediate rule systems and the errors that they unavoidably create.

A disproportionate emphasis on grammatical error (to the exclusion of other aspects of writing) gives students the message that good writing is nothing but error-free writing. While certainly control of error is part of good writing, it should not be the sole consideration at every step of the writing process. A disproportionate emphasis on error has two unintended consequences: (1) it discourages teacher and students alike from taking the content of student writing seriously, and (2) it encourages students to write considerably below their ability level because they can more easily control less sophisticated language. We want high school students to write like adults, not to retreat to a fifth-grade comfort zone where they can write without error.

Evidence from second language learners and from basic writers indicates that these learners employ the same strategy of rule formation: overgeneralization followed by intermediate stages of adjustment until the adult rule system is reached. Thus, the errors that basic writers make reflect intermediate and probably necessary stages in their development of the rules of mature writing. Consider how counterproductive it would be if we reacted to children's errors in learning to speak in the same way that we react to students' errors in learning to write.

The modern perspective on the causes of error provides us with many insights on how classroom teachers can address the problems of writing error. For many basic writers, the main cause of writing error is that learning written English is like learning a new dialect. We can assist basic writers by drawing on what we know about the comparable learning process of second-language learning and children learning their first language.

From studies of first- and second-language acquisition, we know that the absolutely fundamental condition for acquiring a language is the learner's meaningful exposure to it. If the written language is tantamount to a special dialect, then those learners who read a great deal are already immersed in it meaningfully, and conversely those learners who seldom read have had little (if any) meaningful exposure to it. Thus, expecting poor readers to write well is asking them to make bricks without straw.

The other way that students gain meaningful exposure is by doing a great deal of writing in as supportive an environment as possible. Fortunately many schools have adopted process-oriented writing programs that break writing down into several stages—brainstorming, idea drafting, audience drafting, and finally surface editing. Other related techniques, such as keeping daily journals and peer editing groups, have also proven effective.

A problem with some conventional classrooms that approach writing as mere error avoidance is that teachers are then compelled to scrutinize all the writing of students in order to catch and correct any errors. There are two problems with this approach. First, it implies that error-free writing is good writing. Being error-free may be a necessary condition for good writing, but it is not a sufficient condition. Moreover, the nearly exclusive emphasis on error avoidance devalues the content of what is written. Students are led to believe that it does not make any difference what they write as long as it is written without mechanical error. Students can hardly expect to develop any sensitivity to effective writing when we ourselves place no value on it in our evaluation of their work.

Second, if teachers feel that they must correct every word that their students write, they have placed themselves in an impossible position. They have two choices: (1) they can continue to give writing assignments to their 150 students and then destroy their own personal and professional lives in keeping up with the paper flow, or (2) they can stop giving writing assignments altogether and instead pass out workbooks and ditto sheets. [An insidious corollary to error avoidance is that we can reduce student writing error to zero by not having them write at all.]

Often teachers seem to hold a tacit notion that grammatical errors are like bad habits. Unless errors are corrected, the errors will become established patterns, which will be more difficult to eradicate later. We know from research in both children's acquisition of their first language and in adults' acquisition of a second language that this model of error is simplistic. Language is more than merely a set of habits. Errors disappear when learners are able to make better hypotheses. If we are afraid to let students make errors, we have cut them off from the trial-and-error experiences they need to form the tacit hypotheses that will enable them to correct their own errors. We are not really interested in prohibiting our students from making errors but in having them develop their own techniques for dealing with their errors.

Learners cannot make better hypotheses without more meaningful exposure to the language or dialect they want to acquire. Exposure to mature writing is an absolute precondition for writing maturely. Only through direct reading experience can students acquire the features of the written language that differ from the spoken language: (1) the standard language forms, (2) the different ways the written language encodes the spoken language, and (3) the abstract vocabulary and complex constructions of the written language.

In addition to providing a good reading program, the teacher can provide a number of other activities to assist basic writers. However, training or special exercises can never by themselves compensate for lack of extensive exposure to the language that we want our students to write. The following suggestions, then, are supplements to a good reading program.

Teaching standard language forms. Nonstandard forms jump out of the page so vividly, and we react to them so strongly, that we can easily be misled about both their frequency and the relative ease with which basic writers can bring them under control. The number of nonstandard forms, mostly verbs, that basic writers use is in fact very small. These nonstandard verb forms are essentially vocabulary differences between written and spoken English, and, as such, they can be relatively easily isolated and treated.

Nevertheless, two major problems can exist with students who speak black English: (1) their spoken dialect may appear to be significantly different from standard English, and (2) black students can be concerned with maintaining their dialect as a part of their social and cultural identity. Although a full discussion of black English is outside the scope of this chapter, some general observations may be helpful. First, the differences between black English and standard English are real, but they are much less significant than they first appear because we tend to notice differences, not similarities. In fact, the differences in rules are small in comparison with the number of rules that are shared. In transformational terms, the differences are mostly in surface form: the deep structures are largely identical, but the way they are realized as surface forms may be quite different from their realization in standard English.

We can respond to the second issue—the desire of many black students to maintain their dialect for social and cultural reasons—with some common sense and good will. We must recognize that all of us have the right to our own language. Putting people down for the way they talk is unacceptable behavior, even for English teachers. I think we need to draw a distinction between the freedom of the spoken language and the normalization of the written language.

Standard written English does not preserve differences among spoken dialects—excepting, of course, deliberate attempts to reflect the spoken language in stories and plays. There is no such thing as a standard written male or female English or a standard written black English. It is even difficult to tell American from British writers, except for a relatively small number of spelling and vocabulary differences. We all write a common standard English. Most people will accept the validity of a standardized written language. And most students will accept the validity of English teachers' correcting their written language because the students realize that written English is a second dialect, which must be learned. However, these same students might not accept correction of their spoken language. [Farr and Daniels' *Language Diversity and Writing Instruction* (1986) provides a helpful overview of the issues and gives practical suggestions for improving the teaching of writing to high school students who are native speakers of nonstandard English dialects.]

Teaching differences between the written and spoken language. Some basic writing students write fewer than a thousand words in their entire career in the secondary grades. It is hard to become good at something if we never do it. The first chapter of Shaughnessy deals with the handwriting problems of basic writers. She documents how difficult it is for many adult basic writing students just to control the movement of a pencil across a piece of paper. Thus, an often overlooked problem of basic writers is their poor control of the mechanical process of writing.

Poor writing control interferes with the writer's ability to look beyond the immediate word being written, often causing the writer to lose completely the train of thought and to make various mistakes in linking distant parts of the sentence together: for example, forgetting that the sentence began with a subordinating conjunction and thus punctuating a dependent clause as though it were an independent clause; making a subject-verb agreement error when the verb is separated from the subject; and forgetting the exact forms of the verb when attempting to use parallel constructions (so that, for example, an infinitive is made parallel to a finite verb). In all these cases, basic writers (unconsciously) understand how the rules work; they are just not able to monitor the final sentence form because they must focus their attention on the physical production of the sentence. What appears as a grammar problem may be rooted in handwriting.

Some exercises that have proven helpful in gaining control over handwriting problems are verbatim copying of models of good prose and taking dictation—both surprisingly effective, but all too seldom used. Another type of exercise is nonstop writing, or freewriting, an activity in which the student is instructed to write continuously for a certain number of minutes without raising the pencil from the paper, except to separate one word from the next. If the student hits a block, he or she is instructed to recopy the previous sentence until continuation becomes possible.

2. The relation of grammar and writing

The well-known New Zealand study (Elley et al. 1976) showed that if we teach grammar (either schoolroom traditional grammar, Grammar 4, or transformational grammar, Grammar 2) for its own sake, it has no measurable impact on student writing. The main point from the New Zealand study is that we get exactly what we pay for. That is, if we teach grammar in isolation from writing, students learn grammar that is not connected to writing. Students will connect grammar with writing only if we explicitly link the two.

Following are some important links that we can make between grammar and writing.

☐ Basic grammar terminology.
Grammar terminology (e.g., *noun, verb, prepositional phrase, sentence, subject, object, phrase, clause*) is a very convenient vocabulary for talking about all aspects of writing. If students feel comfortable with grammar terminology, then the teacher is able to talk to students (and students talk to each other) about writing with a shared vocabulary—an obvious advantage.

☐ Key grammatical concepts.
Mina Shaughnessy (1977, 130–137) states that the failure of basic writers to understand the following four grammatical concepts underlies most common grammatical and punctuation errors: (1) the sentence, (2) inflection—the system of inflectional suffixes in the major part of speech classes—(3) tense, and (4) agreement—both subject-verb agreement and the agreement of pronouns with their antecedents. She argues that time spent on students' mastering these four grammatical concepts is well worthwhile.

☐ Monitoring for errors.

One of the major themes of this book has been that students have a vast unconscious knowledge of their language that they can tap into in order to help themselves monitor their own writing for correctness. However, the structural paraphrase techniques that deal with specific errors of punctuation and grammar require students to have a conscious awareness of grammatical structure. Without this awareness, students cannot use the tests.

Following are the types of errors of punctuation and grammar that have been addressed by means of structural paraphrase techniques (along with a reference to the exercise that teaches the paraphrase technique).

1. Apostrophe error: Ch 1, Ex 1.6. Using apostrophes, on page 23.

2. Subject/object error in compound prepositions: Ch 1, Ex 1.10. Pronoun case, on page 32.

3. Sexist pronouns: Ch 1, Ex 1.11. Eliminating sexist pronouns, on page 36.

4. Punctuating coordinate adjectives: Ch 1, Ex 1.15. Punctuating adjectives, page 45.

5. Subject-verb agreement: Ch 2, Ex 2.4. Checking for nearest-noun subject-verb agreement error, on page 78.

6. Dangling participle: Ch 3, Ex 3.12. Dangling participles, on page 127.

7. *Who/whom*: Ch 4, Ex 4.2. Distinguishing between *who/whom*, on page 152.

8. Punctuating subordinating conjunctions and conjunctive adverbs: Ch 4, Ex 4.6, on page 168.

☐ Sentence combining.

A great deal of error can be traced to students' attempting more complex constructions. [Diaute (1981) gives strong empirical support for the connection between error and sentence complexity.] For example, the nearest-noun type of subject-verb error is a direct result of lengthy subject noun phrases that separate the verb from the subject. Conversely, absence of error may reflect simplicity of sentence structure rather than mastery of grammatical conventions. For example, students who never attempt to combine multiple deep structures will not have trouble with run-ons or comma splices—not because they have mastered run-ons and comma splices, but because they are not yet sophisticated enough to write complex sentences that engender the problem.

The most important and widely used modern technique for improving basic writers' ability to control more complex structures is, of course, sentence combining. Sentence combining offers two quite different advantages for dealing with error.

First, for the student, sentence combining improves *automaticity*. Automaticity, you recall, is Strong's term for "making the processing of print so natural, so unselfconscious, so deeply ingrained in neural machinery, that decoding and transcription per se become virtually irrelevant" (1985, 339). We hypothesize that if students are able to use more complex structures with greater automaticity, they would be better able to monitor for error. The implicit model here is that we only have a certain amount of mental "processing space" available to us at any moment in time. If we must struggle to control the combination of multiple deep structures, we have little "processing space" available for the more mundane task of monitoring for error. By making the production of complex sentences more automatic, "processing space" could then be available to monitor for error.

Second, for the teacher, sentence combining proves an effective vehicle for teaching students about certain punctuation errors that result from the production of more complex sentences. Following are some examples of punctuation errors that have been addressed by sentence combining exercises in this book.

1. Commas omitted with coordinating conjunctions joining two independent clauses: Ch 1, Ex 1.25. Commas with coordinating conjunctions, on page 64.
2. Punctuating restrictive and nonrestrictive clauses: Ch 4, Ex 4.3. Recognizing restrictive and nonrestrictive adjective clauses, on page 157.
3. Punctuating introductory adverb clauses: Ch 4, Ex 4.5. Recognizing and punctuating adverb clauses that modify verbs, on page 164.

Hartwell's Grammar 5, stylistic grammar, is the use of grammar specifically for the purpose of teaching style. Sentence combining is the one grammar-based approach to writing that has strong empirical support for improving the quality of writing (not just mechanical correctness) independent of any theory of grammar. Although historically sentence combining is an outgrowth of classical transformational grammar, it really is a process or procedure rather than a theory of grammar in its own right. As a process or procedure it is a natural bridge between the study of language and the study of style.

From a linguistic perspective, sentence combining focuses on a relatively small number of transformational rules that embed one sentence in another. Sentence combining exercises give students kernel or near-kernel sentences as input. The kernel sentences serve as proxies for deep structures. Thus, the entire focus of sentence combining is on the transformation of given deep structures (as represented by their kernel forms) into their various surface structure forms. The embedding transformational rules that are at the heart of sentence combining are noun-centered—(a) noun modification rules (the rules that create relative clauses, adjectives, and various types of phrases), and (b) nominalization rules (the rules that create noun clauses and verbals). These two types of embedding rules have several very important characteristics.

First, as we saw in our discussion of Kellogg Hunt's work in Part II of Chapter 7, these two types of embedding rules play a major role in the level of syntactic fluency. As children mature from childhood to young adulthood, their gain in syntactic fluency (as defined by number of words per T-unit) is largely attributable to their increased use of these two types of embedding transformation. These two types of embedding rules are thus especially important in our linguistic and stylistic development.

Second, these two types of embedding rules (plus the rules for creating absolutes) give us a great deal of choice among alternative surface structures. Consequently, these rules provide an especially important vehicle for raising rhetorical and stylistic questions. Grammar provides users of a language with options; rhetorical and stylistic considerations govern the choices among those options. In transformational terms, the transformational component of grammar describes the different surface forms that can be derived from one deep structure; rhetorical and stylistic considerations govern the selection of the one surface structure (from among the many grammatically permitted surface structure paraphrases) that is the most effective for a particular audience. Perhaps the single greatest advantage of sentence combining is here: it allows students to consciously test and debate which alternative combination of surface structures is the most effective. Since all the students engaged in a particular sentence combining exercise have identical starting points (the same kernel sentences, i.e., the same meaning), they can then profitably compare solutions (combinations of surface structures). Part One in Daiker, Kerek, and Morenberg's *The Writer's Options* (1986) is an excellent example of how sentence combining can be used to teach stylistic options.

CONCLUSION

I think that we need to rethink our whole approach to teaching grammar in the classroom. I believe that we have come at it from the wrong end. We have tried to teach grammar for its own sake—either schoolroom traditional grammar, Grammar 4, or some form of Grammar 2, either structural linguistics or transformational grammar—with little regard for the relation of grammar to writing. As a result, we have not been able to help our students connect grammar to their own writing. I think we have an opportunity to be much more successful by going about it the other way: deal first with those areas of grammar that have direct applications to teaching writing, and only then move into grammar for its own sake. I suggest that we begin with applied grammar and use it as a springboard into teaching grammar for its own sake. The applied grammar is very much like Hartwell's Grammar 5, sentence combining, though I would include within Grammar 5 the structural paraphrase techniques summarized previously in this chapter.

I think that pedagogically it makes much more sense to students if we begin with those aspects of grammar that directly relate to writing—both to problems of error and to matters of style. Grammar then grows directly out of student writing rather than being a self-contained body of knowledge taught with the vague promise that it will somehow be useful someday.

Sentence combining is a particularly important bridge between writing and grammar because it is so flexible. It has the great advantage of allowing the individual teacher to choose how much or how little formal grammar to build into it. The teacher can focus primarily on questions of rhetoric and style with minimal use of grammatical terms and concepts, or the teacher can use the sentence combining process as a springboard for describing the transformational rules required to combine simple sentences. Sentence combining's flexibility permits the teacher to move back and forth between style and grammar as the teacher sees the need. Sentence combining is a natural bridge into the formal study of grammar—both traditional grammar and transformational grammar.

In traditional grammar, sentence combining is a particularly effective method for teaching certain types of phrases and clauses. The basis of sentence combining is that certain complex structures within the main clause are derived from full underlying sentences. Interestingly, this is also the approach implicit in traditional diagraming. For example, the diagrams of verbals, verbal phrases, participles, participial phrases, and all dependent clauses reflect the fact that these constructions are derived from complete sentences. Sentence combining is a natural first step in helping students to recognize these constructions and in teaching how to diagram them.

Following are the constructions in the first four chapters that were introduced by sentence combining, together with a reference to the appropriate exercise.

1. Appositives/appositive phrases: Ch 3, Ex 3.7. Recognizing appositives and appositive phrases, on page 115.
2. Participles/participial phrases: Ch 3, Ex 3.10. Recognizing participles and participial phrases, on page 123.
3. Gerunds/gerund phrases: Ch 3, Ex 3.13. Recognizing gerunds and gerund phrases, on page 131.
4. Infinitives/infinitive phrases: Ch 3, Ex 3.15. Recognizing infinitives and infinitive phrases, on page 137.
5. Relative clauses: Ch 4, Ex 4.1. Forming relative clauses, on page 151.
6. *That* type noun clauses: Ch 4, Ex 4.8. Recognizing *that* type noun clauses, on page 173.
7. *wh-* type noun clauses: Ch 4, Ex 4.9. Recognizing *wh-* type noun clauses, on page 176.

In transformational grammar, sentence combining is a vehicle that a linguistically sophisticated teacher can use to introduce concepts from the modern study of grammar without having to undertake a whole new curriculum. As we saw in Part I of Chapter 7, the actual transformational rules governing the sentence combining processes of noun modification and nominalization are (relatively) simple. That is, there are a small number of transformational rules involved in each type of embedding process, the operation of each rule can be described in a straightforward manner, the rules operate with few exceptions, and the rules govern a rich variety of surface sentence types. In other words, the transformational rules underlying these sentence combining processes lend themselves well to classroom teaching of classical transformational grammar. Through a study of these rules, students can gain an important insight into how transformational grammar describes our intuitive linguistic rule system.

SUMMARY

This chapter is concerned with two main issues: (1) the role of grammar in the secondary classroom, and (2) how to teach grammar more effectively. The first issue, the role of grammar in the secondary classroom, depends, in turn, on what we believe grammar is and why we believe it should be taught. An important first step in defining this issue is Hartwell's distinction between five different meanings of the term *grammar*: grammar 1, native speaker's internal rule system; grammar 2, linguists' analysis of grammar; grammar 3, usage; grammar 4, schoolroom traditional grammar; and grammar 5, stylistic grammar. Since the 1950s in the United States, there has been an ongoing debate between the advocates of grammar 2 and grammar 4. This debate has been so acrimonious and inconclusive that it has led many schools to abandon the systematic teaching of grammar altogether. Any resolution of this conflict between types of grammar hinges on why we want to teach grammar in the first place.

Historically, American schools have had two rationales for teaching grammar: for its own sake, and as a tool for teaching writing. In terms of the first rationale, teaching grammar as a legitimate subject of study in its own right would seem to lead schools toward grammar 2. After all, the study of grammar 2, particularly classical transformational grammar, has produced a quantum leap in our understanding of language in general and English grammar in particular. However, a host of practical considerations—the lack of consensus within the field of linguistics, the extensive technical training that would be required of teachers, and the lack of support materials for classroom use—all conspire to make teaching grammar 2 in the secondary classroom a difficult proposition.

Returning to a completely conventional form of grammar 4, schoolroom traditional grammar, is not a viable alternative because, as DeBeaugrande puts it, school grammar is not basic enough to reach our students. The alternative Chapter 8 offers is to revise traditional grammar by incorporating insights from structural linguistics and transformational grammar. The suggested revisions are primarily in methodology—drawing on students' intuitive ability to identify grammatical components through the use of paraphrase tests—and in augmenting the traditional grammatical analysis of verbs with phrasal verbs, a broader definition of complement, and Chomsky's treatment of tense.

The second rationale American schools have had for teaching grammar is as a tool for teaching writing—especially for helping students deal with problems of mechanical error. Before addressing the larger issue of the relation of grammar and writing, the chapter reviews the research literature on the relation of grammar and writing. Extensive research has failed to find a positive correlation between students' conscious knowledge of grammar and their ability to write. However, in recent years research has begun to examine error as a phenomenon in its own right, leading to the following observations about error: (1) the written form of English is sufficiently different from the form spoken by many students as to constitute a separate dialect that must be acquired in ways similar to acquiring a second language; (2) writers' errors are not random or accidental, but are the result of writers' learning strategy; and (3) writers' errors are a necessary part of the learning strategy. A detailed examination of students' actual errors provides insight into the causes of the errors and suggests specific strategies for helping students deal with certain errors in more effective ways.

In many ways, however, the most important implication of the research on grammar and writing is that teaching grammar in isolation from writing has little effect on students' ability to deal with error. Students will connect grammar with writing only if we explicitly link the two. The chapter discusses four important links between grammar and writing that can be made in the classroom: (1) teaching basic grammar terminology as a useful shared vocabulary for talking about grammar and writing; (2) teaching key grammatical concepts (the sentence, inflection, tense, agreement) that underlie most written error; (3) teaching students practical techniques for monitoring error in their own writing; and (4) teaching sentence combining as a unique bridge between grammar and writing.

The chapter's main conclusion is that teaching grammar in isolation from writing is a mistake. A better alternative is to teach those areas of grammar that have direct practical application to teaching writing. The paraphrase techniques presented in the first four chapters are helpful tools for giving students a conscious understanding of key grammatical concepts as well as tools for monitoring certain types of error. Sentence combining is a second important technique. Sentence combining not only provides an important vehicle for teaching phrases and clauses; it also allows the teacher to move back and forth along a continuum with writing (questions of style and rhetoric) at one end and grammar at the other end.

Suggested
Further Readings

Traditional grammar

Donald W. Emery. 1961. *Sentence Analysis*. New York: Holt, Rinehart and Winston.

This widely available booklet gives a clear discussion of sentence diagraming with many examples. It gives diagraming conventions for constructions not discussed in Chapters 1–4 of this text.

T. R. Neuburger. 1989. *Foundation: Building Sentence Skills*. 3rd ed. Boston: Houghton Mifflin.

This is a combination grammar book and workbook. It provides clear explanations of traditional grammatical concepts and has many pages of exercises illustrating each point. This book is an excellent source for supplementary exercises or to give to students who need extra help. It uses a simple marking system in place of diagraming that many teachers have found useful.

Sidney Greenbaum. 1989. *A College Grammar of English*. New York: Longman.

An excellent overview of the major features of English grammar in the tradition of the descriptive grammars of Sweet and Jespersen. It supplements traditional grammar with some aspects of structural linguistics and transformational grammar.

Structural linguistics

Leonard Bloomfield. 1933. *Language*. New York: Henry Holt.

This book defined the field of structural linguistics. Even though the book is now over fifty years old, it is a lucid, intelligent discussion of language that can still be read with great profit.

Transformational grammar

1. General introduction to classical transformational grammar

Neil Smith and Deirdre Wilson. 1979. *Modern Linguistics: The Results of Chomsky's Revolution*. Bloomington, Indiana: Indiana University Press.

This is an excellent broad overview of classical transformational grammar. It is intended for a nonspecialist audience. It is a literate and perceptive book.

367

2. Introductory linguistics textbooks

Adrian Akmajian, Richard A. Demers, and Robert M. Harnish. 1984. *Linguistics: An Introduction to Language and Communication*. 2nd ed. Cambridge, Mass.: The MIT Press.

Edward Finegan and Niko Besnier. 1989. *Language: Its Structure and Use*. San Diego, Cal.: Harcourt Brace Jovanovich.

Victoria Fromkin and Robert Rodman. 1988. *An Introduction to Language*. 4th ed. New York: Holt, Rinehart and Winston.

All three textbooks survey the field of linguistics. They contain brief, nontechnical introductions to classical transformational grammar. The chapter in Finegan and Besnier is especially good.

3. Introductory classical transformational grammar textbooks of English

Noel Burton-Roberts. 1986. *Analysing Sentences: An Introduction to English Syntax*. London: Longman.

Richard Veit. 1986. *Discovering English Grammar*. Boston: Houghton Mifflin.

Both books are introductory level texts that approach English grammar from the classical transformational standpoint. If you have read Chapters 6 and 7 in this book, you can follow either of these books. The Burton-Roberts text is more concerned with English than with presenting a linguistic theory while the Veit text has a heavy emphasis on the machinery of phrase structure rules.

4. Advanced treatment of English syntax from a classical transformational perspective

James D. McCawley. 1988. *The Syntactic Phenomena of English*. 2 vols. Chicago.: University of Chicago Press.

This two-volume work surveys the main features of English grammar with an emphasis on the role of transformations. It contains detailed discussions of the research literature.

Modern ("post-classical") transformational grammar

1. English grammar textbooks incorporating a modern transformational perspective

C. L. Baker. 1989. *English Syntax*. Cambridge, Mass.: The MIT Press.

Jeffrey P. Kaplan. 1989. *English Grammar: Principles and Facts*. Englewood Cliffs, New Jersey: Prentice Hall.

Both textbooks draw on a somewhat eclectic blend of modern and classical theory to describe English syntax. Although neither book focuses on linguistic theory per se, both books depart radically from the conventional topics and explanations of classical transformational grammar under the influence of modern transformational theory.

2. Introductions to modern transformational grammar

Andrew Radford. 1981. *Transformational Syntax*. Cambridge (England): Cambridge University Press.

This is the most accessible introduction to modern transformational theory. It develops the basis for modern transformational theory by a careful and well-supported analysis of English syntax.

3. General introduction to modern transformational grammar

V. J. Cook. 1988. *Chomsky's Universal Grammar*. Oxford: Basil Blackwell.

An excellent introduction to the major components of modern transformational theory. Technical, but unusually well written and surprisingly easy to follow.

Reference grammar

Randolph Quirk, Sidney Greenbaum, Geoffrey Leech, and Jan Svartvik. 1985. *A Comprehensive Grammar of the English Language*. London: Longman.

No institutional library should be without this 1,799-page reference work, which offers an encyclopedic description and analysis of the features of English grammar. While it is not written within any one theoretical framework, it draws heavily on the vast corpus of transformational research on English of the past two decades. Its bibliography alone runs twenty-three pages.

History of grammar teaching

Dennis E. Baron. 1982. *Grammar and Good Taste: Reforming the American Language*. New Haven, Conn.: Yale University Press.

A highly readable history of American attitudes about language and grammar teaching. Chapter 6 contains a good discussion of the origin of grammar teaching in the seventeenth and eighteenth centuries.

Role of grammar

Patrick Hartwell. 1985. Grammar, Grammars, and the Teaching of Grammar. *College English* 47: 105–127.

This article contains a comprehensive review of literature on the grammar wars. His discussion of the five different meanings of the term 'grammar' helps clarify many issues.

Martha Kolln. 1981. Closing the Books on Alchemy. *College Composition and Communication* 32: 139–151.

This article contains an excellent statement of the reasons for teaching grammar; it also contains a good bibliography.

Grammar and composition

David Bartholomae. 1980. The Study of Error. *College Composition and Communication* 31: 253–269.

An important article in both the theory of error and the practice of remediation.

Journal of Basic Writing. Instructional Resource Center, The City University of New York, 535 East 80th Street, New York, NY 10021.

This is a journal in the Mina Shaughnessy tradition that deals with the problems of basic writers. All institutional libraries should subscribe to this publication.

Donald A. McQuade, editor. 1986. *The Territory of Language: Linguistics, Stylistics, and the Teaching of Composition*. Carbondale, Ill.: Southern Illinois University Press

This anthology contains a number of important articles on grammar and composition. Many of the articles contain extensive bibliographies on grammar and composition.

Mina P. Shaughnessy. 1977. *Errors and Expectations: A Guide for the Teacher of Basic Writing*. New York: Oxford University Press.
> The foundation stone of modern work on grammar and composition. This book should be in the personal library of every English teacher.

Grammar and literature

Elizabeth Closs Traugott and Mary Louise Pratt. 1980. *Linguistics for Students of Literature*. New York: Harcourt Brace Jovanovich.
> Chapter 4 gives an excellent introduction to classical transformational grammar and then relates transformational grammar to the analysis of literature.

Sentence combining

Donald A. Daiker, Andrew Kerek, and Max Morenberg, editors. 1979. *Sentence Combining and the Teaching of Writing: Selected Papers from the Miami University Conference*. Conway, Ark.: L & S Books. Also available as ED 259 393.

————. 1985. *Sentence Combining: A Rhetorical Perspective*. Carbondale, Ill.: Southern Illinois University Press.
> These two anthologies contain articles of major importance and provide extensive bibliographies on sentence combining.

Donald A. Daiker, Andrew Kerek, and Max Morenberg. 1986. *The Writer's Options: Combining to Composing*. 3rd ed. New York: Harper & Row.
> This is the most widely used sentence combining book on the college market. Part one contains nine units that use sentence combining to teach mechanics and style in a most effective manner. The book is designed for beginning college students, but it has been used very successfully with senior high school students.

William Strong. 1986. *Creative Approaches to Sentence Combining*. Urbana, Ill.: ERIC Clearinghouse on Teaching and Communication Skills and the National Council of Teachers of English.
> This booklet has two parts: a section that summarizes the theory and research on sentence combining, and a section on how to do sentence combining in the classroom. This book is an absolute must for all those who want to use sentence combining in their classrooms.

————. 1983. *Sentence Combining: A Composing Book*. New York: Random House.

————. 1984. *Sentence Combining in Action* Series. New York: Random House.
> These Random House publications are probably the most successful secondary level sentence combining books currently available.

Works Cited

Braddock, Richard, et al. 1963. *Research in Written Composition*. Urbana, Ill.: NCTE.

Christensen, Francis. 1967. *Notes toward a New Rhetoric*. New York: Harper & Row.

——. 1968. The Problem of Defining a Mature Style. *English Journal* 57 : 575–79.

Chomsky, Carol. 1969. *The Acquisition of Syntax in Children from 5 to 10*. Cambridge, Mass.: MIT Press

Chomsky, Noam. 1957. *Syntactic Structures*. 'sGravenhage: Mouton.

——. 1965. *Aspects of the Theory of Syntax*. Cambridge, Mass.: MIT Press.

Daiker, Donald A.; Kerek, Andrew; and Morenberg, Max. 1986. *The Writer's Options: Combining to Composing*. 3d ed. New York: Harper & Row.

——. 1978. Sentence Combining at the College Level: An Experimental Study. *Research in the Teaching of English* 12 : 245–56.

DeBeaugrande, Robert. 1984. Forward to the Basics: Getting Down to Grammar. *College Composition and Communication* 35 : 358–67.

Diaute, Collete. 1981. Psycholinguistic Foundations of the Writing Process. *Research in the Teaching of English* 15 : 5–22.

Elley, W. B. et al. 1976. The Role of Grammar in a Secondary School English Curriculum. *Research in the Teaching of English* 10 : 5–21.

Fries, Charles C. 1927. *The Teaching of the English Language*. New York: Thomas Nelson and Sons.

——. 1927. The Rules of the Common School Grammars. *PMLA* 42.

——. 1952. *The Structure of English: An Introduction to the Constructions of English Sentences*. New York: Harcourt, Brace and World.

Hartwell, Patrick. 1985. Grammar, Grammars, and the Teaching of Grammar. *College English* 47 : 105–127.

Hillocks, George, Jr. 1986. *Research on Written Composition: New Directions for Teaching*. Urbana, Ill.: ERIC Clearinghouse on Reading and Communication Skills and the National Conference on Research in English.

Hunt, Kellogg W. 1964. *Differences in Grammatical Structures Written at Three Grade Levels, the structures to be analyzed by transformational methods*. Cooperative Research Project, No. 1998. ED 003 322. Tallahassee: Florida State University.

————. 1965. *Grammatical Structures Written at Three Grade Levels*. NCTE Research Report, No. 3. Urbana, Ill.: NCTE

————. 1970. *Syntactic Maturity in Schoolchildren and Adults*. Monographs of the Society for Research in Child Development, No. 134. Chicago: University of Chicago Press.

Jespersen, Jens Otto Harry. 1922. *Language, its Nature, Development, and Origin*. London: G. Allen.

————. 1924. *The Philosophy of Grammar*. London: G. Allen and Unwin.

————. 1933. *Essentials of English Grammar*. New York: Henry Holt.

Kerek, Andrew; Daiker, Donald A.; and Morenberg, Max 1980. Sentence Combining and College Composition. *Perceptual and Motor Skills* 51 : 1059–1157.

Kolln, Martha. 1981. Closing the Books on Alchemy. *College Composition and Communication* 32 : 139–151.

————. 1984. *Language and Composition*. New York: Macmillan.

Leonard, Sterling A. 1962. *The Doctrine of Correctness in English Usage 1700–1800*. New York: Russell and Russell.

Lyman, Rollo L. 1921. *English Grammar in American Schools Before 1850*. Washington, D.C.: U.S. Office of Education Bulletin No. 12.

Mellon, John C. 1969. *Transformational Sentence-Combining: A Method for Enhancing the Development of Syntactic Fluency in English Composition*. NCTE Research Report No. 10. Urbana, Ill.: NCTE.

————. 1979. Issues in the Theory and Practice of Sentence Combining: A Twenty-Year Perspective. In *Sentence Combining and the Teaching of Writing*, edited by Donald A. Daiker, Andrew Kerek, and Max Morenberg. Conway, Arkansas: L & S Books.

O'Hare, Frank. 1973. *Sentence Combining: Improving Student Writing without Formal Grammar Instruction*. NCTE Research Report No. 15. Urbana, Ill.: NCTE.

Pooley, Robert C. 1957. *Teaching English Grammar*. New York: Appleton-Century-Crofts.

Quirk, Randolph; Greenbaum, Sidney; Leech, Geoffrey; and Svartvik, Jan. 1985. *A Comprehensive Grammar of the English Language*. London: Longman.

Rose, Shirley K. 1983. Down from the Haymow: One Hundred Years of Sentence-Combining. *College English* 45 : 483–91.

Ross, John R. 1968. *Constraints on Variables in Syntax*. Mimeo. Bloomington: Indiana University Linguistics Club.

Shaughnessy, Mina P. 1977. *Errors and Expectations: A Guide for the Teacher of Basic Writing*. New York: Oxford University Press.

Strong, William. 1973. *Sentence Combining: A Composing Book*. New York: Random House.

————. 1985. How Sentence Combining Works. In *Sentence Combining: A Rhetorical Perspective*, edited by Donald A. Daiker, Andrew Kerek, and Max Morenberg. Carbondale, Ill.: Southern Illinois University Press.

————. 1986. *Creative Approaches to Sentence Combining*. Urbana, Ill.: ERIC Clearinghouse on Reading and Communication Skills and NCTE.

Sweet, Henry. 1891. *A New English Grammar, Logical and Historical*. Oxford: Clarendon Press.

Answers to Exercises

CHAPTER 1 PARTS OF SPEECH

■ Exercise 1.1. Identifying proper nouns (page 8)

2. <u>Henry</u> is an army officer stationed in <u>Greenland</u>.
3. They live in <u>Maryland</u>, just outside <u>Washington, DC</u>.
4. <u>Democrats</u> will have a hard time in the <u>West</u> this year.
5. <u>Lodi</u> is west of here.
6. My brother will be going back to school next fall.
7. The <u>Sierra Club</u> is an environmental organization.
8. The statues date from the early fifteenth century.
9. <u>Norman Smith</u>, chairman of the board of <u>Caltex Corporation</u>, will speak.
10. There is always a spring storm in the northern plains.
11. I am majoring in secular humanism.
12. Next month we change to daylight saving time.
13. The secretary of state has his office in <u>Foggy Bottom</u>.
14. For more information on our program, please contact the <u>Department of Planning</u>.
15. He hoped to get on the staff of a museum that specialized in classical and medieval art.
16. He is a student of the <u>New Deal</u> and the <u>War on Poverty</u>.
17. We are taking a class in late eighteenth century and early romantic poets.

■ **Exercise 1.2. Identifying mass/uncountable nouns (page 11)**

2. There is a huge deposit of <u>copper</u> in Arizona.
   *deposit of a copper; *deposits of coppers

3. It is very difficult to eliminate <u>smoke</u> completely.
   *eliminate a smoke; *eliminate smokes

4. It is made of <u>iron</u>.
   *made of an iron; *made of irons

5. I need to press some clothes. Are you done with the iron?
   Iron is countable.

6. I didn't like his talk to the club at all.
   Talk is countable.

7. All that <u>talk</u> amounts to very little.
   *a talk amounts to very little; *talks amount to very little

8. <u>Lightning</u> struck a tree in Easton.
   *a lightning struck a tree; *lightnings struck a tree

9. I love <u>music</u>.
   *a music; *musics

10. The applicant for the job has a great deal of <u>experience</u>.
    *a great deal of an experience; *a great deal of experiences

11. <u>Photography</u> is obviously not his strength.
    *a photography is not his strength; *photographies are not his strength
    (*Strength* is countable: photography is not a strength; (they) are not his strengths.)

12. The <u>applause</u> must have overwhelmed him.
    *an applause; *applauses

13. <u>Dust</u> gets into my contact lenses.
    *a dust; *dusts

14. They were doing <u>research</u> on comets.
    *a research on comets; *researches on comets

15. We finally got some <u>sunshine</u>.
    *got a sunshine; *got some sunshines

16. Cast your <u>bread</u> upon the <u>water</u>.
    *cast a bread; *cast your breads;
    *upon a water; *upon the waters (grammatical in earlier English)

17. The lamb is too hot to eat. (a trick question—two answers)
    1. <u>lamb</u> (meat on the table) *a lamb is too hot (for us) to eat; *lambs are too hot (for us) to eat
    2. <u>lamb</u> (living animal) countable

■ Exercise 1.3. Identifying common nouns (page 15)

2. A <u>merger</u> may be against the law.
   (1) mergers; (2) the merger; (3) it may be against the law
3. They would not pay any attention to a <u>warning</u>.
   (1) warnings; (2) the warning; (3) pay any attention to it
4. Clear <u>formulation</u> of the problem is essential.
   (1) formulations . . . are; (2) the formulation; (3) it is essential
5. The instrument measures <u>velocity</u>.
   (1) velocities; (2) the velocity; (3) the instrument measures it
6. They registered a <u>protest</u> against the decision.
   (1) protests; (2) the protest; (3) they registered it
7. I was attracted by an unusual <u>texture</u>.
   (1) by unusual textures; (2) the unusual texture; (3) I was attracted by it
8. We recorded a <u>discontinuity</u>.
   (1) discontinuities; (2) the discontinuity; (3) we recorded it
9. <u>Departure</u> is always a sad occasion.
   (1) departures are; (2) ?the departure; (3) it is always a sad occasion
10. The problem was discovered after a quick <u>inspection</u>.
    (1) quick inspections; (2) the quick inspection; (3) . . . discovered after it
11. A <u>stitch</u> in time saves nine.
    (1) stitches . . . save; (2) the stitch; (3) it saves nine
    (Comment: Any change of a fixed phrase sounds somewhat strange.)
12. It is hard to catch an <u>error</u> of that type.
    (1) errors; (2) the error; (3) it is hard to catch it
13. An <u>assistant</u> came to the door.
    (1) assistants; (2) the assistant; (3) he/she came to the door
14. <u>Slavery</u> was common in the classical world.
    (1) *slaveries were; (2) *the slavery; (3) it was common . . .
15. We had <u>fish</u> for dinner last night.
    (1) fish (plural—like *deer*); (2) the fish; (3) we had it for dinner . . .
16. We all admired a <u>drawing</u> he got in Rome.
    (1) drawings; (2) the drawing; (3) we all admired it
17. He was considered to be singularly lacking in <u>insight</u>.
    (1) insights; (2) *the insight; (3) . . . lacking in it

■ Exercise 1.4. Identifying nouns (page 16)

1. <u>Chicago</u> is known as the windy <u>city</u> for obvious <u>reasons</u>.
2. <u>Mass</u> is a technical <u>concept</u> in <u>physics</u>.
3. A good <u>plumber</u> can fix any <u>sink</u> ever made.
4. A <u>pound</u> of <u>hamburger</u> will not feed us.
5. We loved the <u>south</u> of <u>France</u>.
6. He is always looking for <u>grants</u>.

7. The good <u>fairy</u> granted her <u>wish</u>.
8. <u>Economists</u> issued dire <u>predictions</u> at regular <u>intervals</u>.
9. <u>Profits</u> were heading south.
   (south is not a noun: (1) *southes; (2) *profits were heading the south; (3) *profits were heading it)
10. The <u>army</u> steadily advanced on <u>Moscow</u>.
11. He forgot to telephone his <u>office</u>.
12. What he lacked in <u>intelligence</u> he made up for in <u>courage</u>.
13. <u>Garth</u> used <u>knives</u> and <u>forks</u> in strange new <u>ways</u>.
14. His <u>interpretation</u> of the <u>act</u> was upheld by the <u>court</u>.
15. His <u>trip</u> to <u>Dallas</u> was an unmitigated <u>disaster</u>.
16. His <u>fastball</u> quickly became feared by every <u>batter</u> in the <u>league</u>.
17. <u>Henry</u> could write <u>essays</u> as fast as he could <u>talk</u>.
18. <u>Garrick</u> is a <u>demon</u> at <u>Trivial Pursuit</u>.

■ **Exercise 1.5. Spelling possessive nouns (page 19)**

2. fly: fly's; flies; flies'
3. Price: Price's; Prices; Prices'
4. man: man's; men; men's
5. Marx: Marx's; Marxes; Marxes'
6. Smith: Smith's; Smiths; Smiths'
7. Hopkins: Hopkins' or Hopkins's; Hopkinses; Hopkinses'
8. puppy: puppy's; puppies; puppies'
9. George: George's; Georges; Georges'
10. Gibbons: Gibbons' or Gibbons's; Gibbonses; Gibbonses'
11. Holmes: Holmes' or Holmes's; Holmeses; Holmeses'
12. Dobbs: Dobbs' or Dobbs's; Dobbses; Dobbses'
13. woman: woman's; women; women's
14. Robins: Robins' or Robins's; Robinses; Robinses'
15. Kris: Kris's; Krises; Krises'
16. Davis: Davis' or Davis's; Davises; Davises'
17. boss: boss's; bosses; bosses'

■ **Exercise 1.6. Using apostrophes (page 23)**

2. Revised: *today's society*
   <u>have</u> test: **Today has a society.*
   <u>whose</u> test: **whose society? *its society*
   <u>of</u> test: *the society of today*
3. Revised: *the player's head*
   <u>have</u> test: *The player has a head.*
   <u>whose</u> test: *whose head? his/her head*
   <u>of</u> test: *the head of the player*

4. Revised: *the devil's helper / the devils' helper*
   have test: *The devil has a helper. / The devils have a helper.*
   whose test: *whose helper? his/her/its/their helper*
   of test: *the helper of the devil(s)*

5. Revised: *every child's life*
   have test: *Every child has a life.*
   whose test: *whose life? his/her life*
   of test: *the life of every child*

6. Revised: *a person's height*
   have test: *?A person has height.*
   whose test: *whose height? his/her height*
   of test: *the height of a person*

7. Revised: *favorite team's shirt*
   have test: *Favorite team has a shirt.*
   whose test: *whose shirt? their shirt*
   of test: *the shirt of the favorite team*

8. Revised: *the fighter's hands / the fighters' hands*
   have test: *The fighter has hands. / The fighters have hands.*
   whose test: *whose hands? his/her/their hands*
   of test: *the hands of the fighter(s)*

9. Revised: *the skier's weight / the skiers' weight*
   have test: *?The skier has weight.*
   whose test: *whose weight? his/her/their weight*
   of test: *the weight of the skier(s)*

10. Revised: *the state's rule / the states' rule*
   have test: *The state has a rule. / The states have a rule.*
   whose test: *whose rule? its/their rule*
   of test: *the rule of the state(s)*

11. Revised: *the guard's defender / the guards' defender*
   have test: *The guard has a defender. / The guards have a defender.*
   whose test: *whose defender? his/her/their defender*
   of test: *the defender of the guard(s)*

12. Revised: *a woman's world*
   have test: **A woman has a world.*
   whose test: *whose world? her world*
   of test: *the world of a woman*

13. Revised: *another team's word*
   have test: *Another team has a word.*
   whose test: *whose word? its/their word*
   of test: *the word of another team*

14. Revised: *the umpire's decision / the umpires' decision*
   have test: *The umpire has a decision. / The umpires have a decision.*
   whose test: *whose decision? his/her/their decision*
   of test: *the decision of the umpire(s)*

15. Revised: *the body's major muscles*
   have test: *The body has major muscles.*
   whose test: *whose major muscles? its muscles*
   of test: *the major muscles of the body*

■ **Exercise 1.7. Personal pronoun terminology (page 27)**

[Note: some answers with other genders are also correct.]

2. Excuse ___me___ , that coat is ___mine___ .

　　　　　1-Sg-Obj　　　　　　　　　1-Sg-Poss

3. ___He/She___ gave ___them___ the book back.

　　3-Sg-Sub　　　　3-Pl-Obj

4. ___We___ saw ___you___ at the movie last night.

　　1-Pl-Sub　　　2-Pl-Obj

5. The cat left ___it___ on the porch.

　　　　　　　　3-Sg-Obj

6. Give ___them___ to ___me___ .

　　　3-Pl-Obj　　　1-Sg-Obj

7. ___It___ is ___yours___ .

　3-Sg-Sub　　2-Sg-Pos

8. What is ___mine___ is ___mine___ ; what is ___yours___ is ___mine___ too.

　　　　1-Sg-Pos　　　1-Sg-Pos　　　　　2-Sg-Pos　　　1-Sg-Pos

9. ___He/She___ gave ___him/her___ the brush-off.

　　3-Sg-Sub　　　3-Sg-Pos

10. ___We___ sold ___them___ to ___him/her___ .

　　1-Pl-Sub　　　3-Pl-Obj　　　3-Sg-Obj

11. ___It___ is ___I___ .

　3-Sg-Sub　　1-Sg-Sub

■ **Exercise 1.8. Using pronoun terminology (page 30)**

[Note: There are many possible correct answers.]

2. ___Who___ are ___you___ ?

　　?　　　　　P

3. ___He___ injured ___himself___ while playing chess.

　　P　　　　　　R

4. ___This___ is a better buy than ___that___ .

　　D　　　　　　　　　　　　D

5. ___Everybody___ knows ___his___ name. ___He___ is the Lone Ranger.

　　I　　　　　　　P　　　　　　P

6. ___I___ never told ___you___ ___that___ .

　P　　　　　　P　　　D

7. ___What___ can ___they___ tell ___us___ about ___it___ ?

　　?　　　　P　　　　P　　　　　P

8. ___That___ is not what ___we___ meant.

　　D　　　　　　　P

9. ___All___ of the third graders were worried about the calculus test.

　　I

10. If ___they___ are not careful, ___they___ will cut ___themselves___.
 P (they) · P (they) · R (themselves)

11. Well, ___what___ do ___you___ know about ___that___?
 ? (what) · P (you) · D (that)

12. ___What___ delightful place is ___this___?
 ? (What) · D (this)

■ **Exercise 1.9. Identifying pronouns (page 30)**

2. What do you know about that?
 ? (What) · P (you) · D (that)

3. One for all and all for one.
 I (One) · I (all) · I (all) · I (one)

4. What can I do for you?
 ? (What) · P (I) · P (you)

5. That is the last thing I would do.
 D (That) · P (I)

6. Who asked him to come?
 ? (Who) · P (him)

7. Nobody knows the trouble I have seen.
 I (Nobody) · P (I)

8. That contraption will never get off the ground, Wilbur.

9. Can we get you anything at the store?
 P (we) · P (you) · I (anything)

10. Another victory like that and we are done for.
 D (that) · P (we)

11. Would you like another?
 P (you) · I (another)

12. He is a friend of her sister.
 P (He)

13. She is a friend of ours.
 P (She) · P (ours)

14. Someone took all of the clean cups.
 I (Someone) · I (all)

15. Your logic is impeccable but despicable.

16. Many are called, but few are chosen.
 I (Many) · I (few)

■ **Exercise 1.10. Pronoun case (page 32)**

3. John and me want to be partners.
 We

 Revision: John and I want to be partners.

4. I hope that Fred and I can learn to get along with each other.
 OK · we

5. After <u>Alice and him</u> called, we had to change our dinner plans.
   they
   Revision: After Alice and he called, we had to change our dinner plans.

6. Above <u>Dorrie and I</u> was an ornate, carved ceiling.
   us
   Revision: Above Dorrie and me was an ornate, carved ceiling.

7. The reason we are late is that <u>Harvey and me</u> got lost.
   we
   Revision: The reason we are late is that Harvey and I got lost.

8. The gift was originally intended for <u>Sally and she</u>.
   them
   Revision: The gift was originally intended for Sally and her.

   OK
9. Our visitors went with <u>Alfred and me</u> to the movies.
   us

10. The outcome of the case surprised both <u>Holmes and I</u>.
    us
    Revision: The outcome of the case surprised both Holmes and me.

11. Louise answered the phone because <u>Joel and me</u> had already left.
    we
    Revision: Louise answered the phone because Joel and I had already left.

    OK
12. Ludwig proudly announced that <u>Gretchen and he</u> had been selected.
    they

13. Only <u>Fred and me</u> would have been home at the time.
    we
    Revision: Only Fred and I would have been home at the time.

14. Why did Mr. Smith ask <u>you and I</u> to leave?
    us
    Revision: Why did Mr. Smith ask you and me to leave?

15. Near <u>Holmes and I</u> was the dark tower that we had seen earlier.
    us
    Revision: Near Holmes and me was the dark tower that we had seen earlier.

■ **Exercise 1.11. Eliminating sexist pronouns (page 36)**
[Other answers are possible.]

2. Native speakers of a language instantly understand whatever is said to them.
3. Successful politicians always remember the names of their constituents.
4. The people in the next office were letting their phone ring.
5. When people don't look at you when they are talking, we tend not to trust them.
6. Experts are people who charge you for listening to them.
7. People are known by the company they keep.

8. They all had to put their two cents in.
9. The members of the group indicated their first choice.
10. Agents who are in charge of the case will make their determination.
11. When patients are in pain, they need immediate attention.
12. We all have our weaknesses.
13. Procrastinators are people who never finish their work on time.
14. If students want to get good grades, they must study hard.
15. Customers always get their way.
16. All the members of the task force had completed their assignment.

■ **Exercise 1.12. Identifying predicate adjectives (page 38)**

2. Her entry into the water was <u>graceful</u>.
   1. Her entry into the water was very graceful.
   2. more graceful; most graceful
   3. a graceful entry
   4. gracefully
3. His sense of humor is <u>strange</u>.
   1. His sense of humor is very strange.
   2. stranger; strangest
   3. a strange sense of humor
   4. strangely
4. The attack was <u>unprovoked</u>.
   1. The attack was quite unprovoked.
   2. more unprovoked; most unprovoked
   3. an unprovoked attack
   4. ?unprovokedly
5. The investigation of the incident seemed <u>thorough</u>.
   1. The investigation of the incident seemed very thorough.
   2. more thorough; most thorough
   3. a thorough investigation
   4. thoroughly
6. His gestures were often <u>dramatic</u>.
   1. His gestures were often very dramatic.
   2. more dramatic; most dramatic
   3. dramatic gestures
   4. dramatically
7. The approach to the problem seems <u>practical</u>.
   1. The approach to the problem seems very practical.
   2. more practical; most practical
   3. a practical approach
   4. practically
8. The children were <u>disappointed</u>.
   1. The children were very disappointed.
   2. more disappointed; most disappointed

3. disappointed children
4. disappointedly

9. The society has been <u>active</u> for many years.
    1. The society has been very active for many years.
    2. more active; most active
    3. active society
    4. actively

10. At that altitude the air becomes <u>thin</u>.
    1. At that altitude the air becomes very thin.
    2. thinner; thinnest
    3. thin air
    4. thinly

11. The proposal was <u>interesting</u>.
    1. The proposal was very interesting.
    2. more interesting; most interesting
    3. an interesting proposal
    4. interestingly

12. The kids were playing football.
    No predicate adjective in this sentence

13. The issue was <u>dead</u>.
    1. The issue was quite dead. ?The issue was very dead.
    2. deader; deadest
    3. a dead issue
    4. deadly (comment: *Deadly* can be used either as an adverb or an adjective. In the phrase *deadly earnest* it is used as an adverb.)

14. The issue was <u>deadly</u>.
    1. The issue was quite deadly. The issue was very deadly.
    2. more deadly; most deadly
    3. a deadly issue
    4. No corresponding adverb with *-ly*

15. The students were resting.
    No predicate adjective in this sentence
    1. *The students were very/quite resting.
    2. *more resting; *most resting
    3. resting students (comment: This is grammatical, but *resting* here is a participle rather than an adjective.)
    4. *restingly

■ **Exercise 1.13. Recognizing modifying adjective classes (page 40)**

   1   3   4   6
2. a huge old wood ship

   1 2   3   7
3. the first primitive European societies

   1   3   4   5
4. some sensitive new pink tissue

5. Sir Roderick's valuable red feather cape
   $\overset{1}{}\quad\overset{3}{}\quad\overset{5}{}\quad\overset{6}{}$

6. that evil old stone idol
   $\overset{1}{}\quad\overset{3}{}\quad\overset{4}{}\quad\overset{6}{}$

7. its popular new satin finish
   $\overset{1}{}\quad\overset{3}{}\quad\overset{4}{}\quad\overset{6}{}$

8. our innovative new continental design
   $\overset{1}{}\quad\overset{3}{}\quad\overset{4}{}\quad\overset{7}{}$

9. the entire urban population
   $\overset{1}{}\quad\overset{2}{}\quad\overset{7}{}$

10. several broken wooden crates
    $\overset{2}{}\quad\overset{3}{}\quad\overset{6}{}$

11. these frightening new technical problems
    $\overset{1}{}\quad\overset{3}{}\quad\overset{4}{}\quad\overset{7}{}$

12. our hot sausage pizza
    $\overset{1}{}\quad\overset{3}{}\quad\overset{6}{}$

13. the third annual German dinner
    $\overset{1}{}\quad\overset{2}{}\quad\overset{3}{}\quad\overset{7}{}$

14. our two massive old oak desks
    $\overset{1}{}\quad\overset{2}{}\quad\overset{3}{}\quad\overset{4}{}\quad\overset{6}{}$

15. the first known European explorers
    $\overset{1}{}\quad\overset{2}{}\quad\overset{3}{}\quad\overset{7}{}$

16. my only clean white cotton shirt
    $\overset{1}{}\quad\overset{2}{}\quad\overset{3}{}\quad\overset{5}{}\quad\overset{6}{}$

■ **Exercise 1.14. Identifying adjectives (page 43)**

2. His first book was about early rural development in England.
   (A A ... A A)

3. The first subject was only of academic interest.
   (A A ... A)

4. The next proud owner of a new portable hot tub will be announced soon.
   (A A A ... A A A)

5. Finally, the bathtub was clean.
   (A ... PA)

6. Eighteenth-century Latin grammar is the source of modern grammar.
   (A A ... A ... A)

7. His new coat was in a sorry state after the thunderstorm.
   (A A ... A A ... A)

8. The semi-liquid steel is poured out in a continuous mass.
   (A A ... A A)

9. The questions seemed odd.
   (A ... PA)

10. A successful swindler often has polite manners.
    (A A ... A)

11. They selected an accurate new machine.
    (A A A)

12. The hand-made wool suit looked expensive.
    (A A A ... PA)

         A   A   A   A   A
⌐ 13. The dark stranger was a rough, tough hombre.

        A   A   PA
   14. His incoherent explanation was unsatisfactory.

        A   A   A   PA
   15. The possible junior partnership sounded promising.

              A   A   A
⅛ 16. Often the early bird gets the worms.

       A   A   PA
ꝗ 17. A word to the wise is sufficient.

       A   A   A   A   A
   18. His insulting behavior almost created a major diplomatic incident.

■ **Exercise 1.15. Punctuating adjectives (page 45)**

1. The young lad had a cheerful, happy smile for everyone.
2. As far as I am concerned, he is a regular old crook.
3. Dracula had an ordinary, normal childhood.
4. He answered the detective's questions in halting, accented English.
5. His suggestion provided an effective, convenient solution.
6. He was a proper English butler of the old school.
7. He was a difficult, contrary, obstinate child.
8. She decided that her basic black dress was appropriate.
9. Lady Mortlock's heart was smitten by the tall dark stranger.
10. It is a dangerous, dirty job, but someone has to do it.
11. We all noticed her delicate, smooth complexion.
12. She toyed with her beautiful new pearls.
13. Holmes fixed the cabbie with a remarkably steady, cold eye.
14. Alexander had a terrible, horrible, no-good, very bad day.
15. Lady Dedlock was hopelessly attracted by the lawyer's sophisticated, witty conversation.
16. The mysterious dark shape had been seen in the abbey again.
17. The original American musical was changed into a British novel.
18. Unfortunately, we attended a disorganized, sloppy, unprofessional performance.

■ **Exercise 1.16. Identifying adjectives and adverbs that modify adjectives (page 47)**

                                                    Adv
2. The thought of a day in the country was an extremely good idea.

                                   Adv
3. Their unorthodox proposal brought a very swift response.

                        Adv
4. They bought a quite beautiful old print of a square-rigged ship.

5. No one expects the Spanish Inquisition!

6. The mad professor had struck again.

7. The new bargaining agreement was easily ratified.
   (Comment: *Ratified* is the main verb, not a predicate adjective.)

8. Their first trip across the Atlantic Ocean was a terrifying experience.
   (Comment: *Atlantic Ocean* could be treated as a compound noun.)

9. The public's reaction to the work was a definitely cold one.
   _{Adv}

10. The government attempted a surprisingly bold diplomatic initiative.
    _{Adv}

11. The profusely grateful clients thanked Holmes.
    _{Adv}

12. The surprising new claim was given a thoroughly demanding test.
    _{Adv}

13. I didn't think the idea seemed very funny at all.
    _{Adv}

14. In spite of his undoubtedly heroic efforts, Watson didn't have a clue.
    _{Adv}

15. Donald memorized tediously long lists of Anglo-Saxon kings.
    _{Adv}
    (Comment: *Anglo-Saxon kings* could also be a compound.)

16. The perpetually damp British summer weather became depressing.
    _{Adv}

17. A successful mystery writer makes us miss the clearly obvious facts.
    _{Adv}

18. In a well-known early story, Holmes was completely outwitted by an
    apparently naive young woman.
    _{Adv}

■ **Exercise 1.17. Recognizing forms of *be* (page 49)**

2. __They__ __were__ in very bad shape.
     Subject   3rd-Pl-Past

3. __I__ __am__ not your sweet baboo!
     Subject   1st-Sg-Pres

4. __You__ __are__ a menace to the public.
     Subject   2nd-Sg-Pres

5. __They__ __were__ such good friends.
     Subject   3rd-Pl-Past

6. __I__ __was__ an only child.
     Subject   1st-Sg-Past

7. __They__ __are__ absolutely mistaken about that!
     Subject   3rd-Pl-Pres

8. __You__ __were__ in such a hurry to finish.
     Subject   2nd-Pl-Past

9. $\underset{\text{Subject}}{\underline{\text{He/She/It}}}$ $\underset{\text{3rd-Sg-Past}}{\underline{\text{was}}}$ a pain in the neck.

10. $\underset{\text{Subject}}{\underline{\text{I}}}$ $\underset{\text{1st-Sg-Pres}}{\underline{\text{am}}}$ able to leap tall buildings at a single bound.

11. $\underset{\text{Subject}}{\underline{\text{You}}}$ $\underset{\text{2nd-Sg-Past}}{\underline{\text{were}}}$ sixteen.

■ Exercise 1.18. Identifying action and linking verbs (page 52)

2. Mr. Brown <u>confirmed</u>[A] his reservation.

3. Mr. Brown <u>grew</u>[L] angry at the delay.

4. The noise in the room <u>was</u>[L] absolutely overwhelming.

5. The Feds <u>stimulate</u>[A] the economy through the interest rate.

6. I <u>am</u>[L] not an alarmist!

7. Dr. Rodgers <u>classified</u>[A] the specimens by chemical composition.

8. His categories <u>seem</u>[L] correct to me.

9. The engineers <u>initiated</u>[A] the process.

10. It <u>gets</u>[L] worse every day.

11. Next, <u>soften</u>[A] the butter.

12. The visitors <u>looked</u>[L] grateful.

13. The visitors <u>looked</u>[A] around gratefully.
   (Comment: In 12, *grateful* (adjective) describes the visitors; in 13, *gratefully* (adverb) describes what the visitors did—the manner in which they "looked around.")

14. I <u>went</u>[A] first.

15. She <u>gazed</u>[A] out the windows.

16. The ideas <u>seem</u>[L] OK to me.

17. Leon <u>gets</u>[L] upset easily.

18. They <u>recruit</u>[A] string players from the nearby colleges.

■ **Exercise 1.19. Testing for verbs (page 55)**

2. They score more points in the second half.
   Past: They scored . . .
   will: They will score . . .

3. Critics characterize his plots as simplistic.
   Past: Critics characterized . . .
   will: Critics will characterize . . .

4. My fingers become stiff in cold weather.
   Past: My fingers became . . .
   will: My fingers will become . . .

5. The rules generate a number of sentences.
   Past: The rules generated . . .
   will: The rules will generate . . .

6. The cookies look strange.
   Past: The cookies looked . . .
   will: The cookies will look . . .

7. South-bound trains usually depart from Platform 2.
   Past: South-bound trains usually departed . . .
   will: South-bound trains usually will depart . . .

8. Red wines generally improve with age.
   Past: Red wines generally improved . . .
   will: Red wines generally will improve . . .

9. Time and tide wait for no man.
   Past: Time and tide waited . . .
   will: Time and tide will wait . . .

10. They meet our requirements.
    Past: They met . . .
    will: They will meet . . .

11. The aches and pains persist for several days.
    Past: The aches and pains persisted . . .
    will: The aches and pains will persist . . .

12. They are strange bedfellows.
    Past: They were . . .
    will: They will be . . .

13. Crop rotation and good tilling reduce soil loss.
    Past: Crop rotation and good tilling reduced . . .
    will: Crop rotation and good tilling will reduce . . .

14. They reproduce like rabbits.
    Past: They reproduced . . .
    will: They will reproduce . . .

15. The salesmen exaggerate.
    Past: The salesmen exaggerated.
    will: The salesmen will exaggerate.

16. The wines go with the food very well.
    Past: The wines went . . .
    will: The wines will go . . .
17. Grammarians classify words by part of speech categories.
    Past: Grammarians classified . . .
    will: Grammarians will classify . . .

■ **Exercise 1.20. Identifying adverbs that modify verbs (page 58)**

2. The vet had examined the horse recently.
   Q: When did the vet examine the horse? A: recently
3. The ants crawled everywhere.
   Q: Where did the ants crawl? A: everywhere
4. The children were plainly dressed.
   Q: How were the children dressed? A: plainly
5. The pilot looked down.
   Q: Where did the pilot look? A: down
6. He quickly unzipped the tent flap.
   Q: How did he unzip the tent flap? A: quickly
7. She answered the questions correctly.
   Q: How did she answer the questions? A: correctly
8. The operator will return your call immediately.
   Q: When (or How soon) will the operator return your call? A: immediately
9. Gradually they became accustomed to the altitude.
   Q: When (or How soon) did they become accustomed to the altitude?
   A: gradually
10. Recently we sent you a letter.
    Q: When did we send you a letter? A: recently
11. I played badly today.
    Q: How did I play today? A: badly
    Q: When did I play badly? A: today
12. We rarely watch TV.
    • Q: How often do we watch TV? A: rarely
13. Leon invariably sleeps through his 8 o'clock class.
    Q: How often/When does Leon sleep through his 8 o'clock class?
    A: invariably
14. She told the story effectively.
    Q: How did she tell the story? A: effectively
15. It had to happen eventually.
    Q: When did it have to happen? A: eventually
16. I left my glasses somewhere.
    Q: Where did I leave my glasses? A: somewhere
17. There will be a full moon tonight.
    Q: When will there be a full moon? A: tonight

■ **Exercise 1.21. Identifying adverbs that modify adjectives and adverbs (page 59)**

                    Adj
2. Fred is <u>dreadfully</u> serious about the whole business.

          Adj
3. You are <u>quite</u> right.

                   Adj
4. The down-payment was <u>unusually</u> large.

               Adv
5. We will be done <u>pretty</u> soon.

        Adj
6. We were <u>nearly</u> ready.

             Adj
7. He was at that <u>terribly</u> awkward age.

            Adv
8. We played <u>surprisingly</u> well.

            Adj
9. It was a <u>remarkably</u> strong performance.

       Adv
10. She talks <u>so</u> softly.

          Adj
11. They are <u>seldom</u> ready.

              Adj
12. Cinderella has become <u>dreadfully</u> fat in her old age.

          Adj
13. The dog was <u>strangely</u> silent.

           Adv
14. They didn't want it <u>that</u> badly.

             Adv
15. The changes have occured <u>somewhat</u> irregularly.

         Adj
16. Lestrade was <u>entirely</u> correct in his opinion.

         Adv
17. Harvard fought <u>rather</u> fiercely.

■ **Exercise 1.22. Identifying adverbs (page 60)**

1. The swampy camp was <u>constantly</u> infested with <u>savagely</u> stinging bugs.
2. They are <u>very</u> suspicious of <u>unusually</u> glib strangers.
3. I went <u>home</u> <u>early</u>.
4. We saw that program <u>just</u> <u>recently</u>.
5. They <u>usually</u> come to see us <u>afterwards</u>.
6. <u>Comparatively</u> few speakers have done <u>so</u> <u>well</u> <u>here</u>.
7. They have <u>often</u> been working on the road <u>lately</u>.
8. <u>Recently</u> he has been tardy <u>less</u> <u>often</u>.

9. <u>Nearly</u> every company had <u>already</u> issued its final report.

10. The <u>disgustingly</u> dirty water <u>eventually</u> evaporated.

11. The two events were <u>very</u> <u>closely</u> related.

12. It is <u>necessarily</u> true.

13. Boy Scouts are <u>almost</u> <u>always</u> prepared.

14. He <u>usually</u> gives me <u>too</u> many green beans.

15. They were <u>very</u> sorry about the unfortunate accident.

16. <u>Invariably</u> Aunt Harriet gets <u>slightly</u> embarrassed.

17. The coins were <u>nearly</u> <u>equally</u> divided.

18. John came <u>home</u> <u>Thursday</u>.

19. She smiled <u>very</u> <u>sweetly</u>.

■ **Exercise 1.23. Review: Identifying nouns, verbs, adjectives, and adverbs (page 60)**

    Adj   N   V   Adv
1. The airplane landed smoothly.

    Adj   N   V   Adj   N
2. The Constitution protects free speech.

    N   Adv   V   Adj Adj   N
3. Sarah always makes a good impression.

    N   V   Adv   Adj
4. Dracula is always polite.

    Adj   N   V   Adj   Adj   N
5. The Count appreciated his neighborly attitude.

    Adj   N   Adv   V   Adj Adj   N
6. The cleaner nearly ruined my new sweater.

    Adj Adj   N   V Adj   N   Adv
7. A new conductor led the orchestra today.

    Adj   Adj Adj   N   V Adj Adj   N
8. Unfortunately, the tuba player had a bad cold.

    N   Adv   V   Adj   Adj   N
9. Holmes carefully examined the pocket's contents.

    Adj   Adv   Adj   N   V   Adj   N   Adv
10. The unusually dry summer threatened many crops here.

    Adj   Adj   N   V   Adv   Adj
11. The rookie cop seemed very embarrassed.

    Adj   N   Adv   V   Adj   Adj   N
12. The explorers eventually chose the northern route.

    Adj   N   V   Adj   N
13. Artificial intelligence studies formal systems.

    Adj   N   V   Adj   Adj   N   Adj
14. The class passed the history examination easily.

    Adj   Adj   Adj   N   V   Adj   N
15. The first seven questions were the hardest.

    N   V   N   Adv
16. Leon enjoys debating now.

      Adj   N   V   Adj Adj   N
17. The Boy Scouts helped the old lady. (*Boy Scouts* is a noun compound)

      Adj   Adj   N   V Adj Adj   N
18. Every dark cloud has a silver lining.

■ **Exercise 1.24. Identifying prepositional phrases (page 62)**

1. He answered the reporter's questions during the flight.
2. The typewriters in the library were repaired over Christmas.
3. I walked by the window in the kitchen.
4. Except for the ending, I like your idea about the poem.
5. Certain words in a sentence function as modifiers.
6. I haven't had a minute to myself since breakfast.
7. Holmes placed a nasty problem in front of Inspector Lestrade.
8. The car in the lot behind the building was finished as of noon.
9. John's uncooperative attitude toward the project is part of the problem.
10. A friend of mine received an award for his writing.
11. You must come and see us during your vacation.
12. We ended on good terms in spite of our differences.
13. According to the butler, she had been in the library at the time.
14. Everybody but me solved the crime within the required time.
15. Under the cover of darkness, we crossed the field without incident.
16. Holmes examined the cloak with the red trim on the bottom.
17. Holmes examined the cloak with his powerful hand lens.
18. There is a tavern in the town.

■ **Exercise 1.25. Commas with coordinating conjunctions (page 64)**

2. a. The performers dazzled the crowd, and they amazed the critics.
   b. The performers dazzled the crowd and amazed the critics.
3. a. The editor compiled a list of typographical errors, and he/she sent them to the grateful author.
   a. The editor compiled a list of typographical errors and sent them to the grateful author.
4. a. The workers stacked the crates in the warehouse, and they labeled them according to their contents.
   b. The workers stacked the crates in the warehouse and labeled them according to their contents.
5. a. The candidate invoked the names of the founding fathers, and he/she promised to follow in their footsteps.
   b. The candidate invoked the names of the founding fathers and promised to follow in their footsteps.
6. a. The Boy Scouts synchronized their watches, and they oriented their maps.
   b. The Boy Scouts synchronized their watches and oriented their maps.

7. a. The astrologer forecast the future of the stock market, and he called his broker.

   b. The astrologer forecast the future of the stock market and called his broker.

8. a. Dripping wet, Leon got out of the shower, and he answered the phone for the third time.

   b. Dripping wet, Leon got out of the shower and answered the phone for the third time.

9. a. A couple in a brand-new BMW wheeled into the filling station, and they paid for their gas with nickels and dimes.

   b. A couple in a brand-new BMW wheeled into the filling station and paid for their gas with nickels and dimes.

10. a. Glinda took off the witch's ruby slippers, and she gave them to Dorothy.

    b. Glinda took off the witch's ruby slippers and gave them to Dorothy.

11. a. Holmes sent a wire to Scotland Yard, and he told Watson to pack his service revolver.

    b. Holmes sent a wire to Scotland Yard and told Watson to pack his service revolver.

■ **Exercise 1.26. Identifying conjunctions (page 66)**

3. This is (either) very good cheese (or) very bad meat.

4. I'm sure that he is right, (yet) I can't help worrying about it.

5. We waved (and) signaled, (but) no waiter would pay any attention to us.

6. We got into the car (and) drove to the station.

7. Did you want coffee, tea, (or) milk?

8. Holmes fooled (not only) Watson (but also) Inspector Lestrade.

9. Thanks to careful planning (and) more than our share of good luck, we were successful.

10. John (neither) smokes (nor) watches daytime soaps.

11. (Either) you give me my money back, (or) I'll hold my breath.

12. Henry jumped to his feet (and) ran to the door.

13. Unfortunately, I am (neither) rich (nor) famous.

14. Mary planned the wedding, (and) her mother made up the guest list.

15. He is (either) a fool (or) a knave.

16. They had better hurry, (for) the game is about to start.

17. I saved my money (and) bought (both) a rod (and) a new reel.

■ Exercise 1.27. Review I. Identifying parts of speech (page 68)

   Adj   Adj   N   V   Adv   Adj   Prep P
1. The overall effect was quite disappointing for us.

   Adj Adj   N   Adv   V   N   C   N
2. The new mystery completely baffled Holmes and Watson.

    Adv   Adj   Adj   N   V   Adj Adj   N
3. Almost all professional writers keep a daily journal.

   Adj   N   Adv   V   Adj Adj   Adj   N   Prep Adj   N
4. The FDA carefully evaluated the new French drug in their labs.

   Adj   N   V Adj   Adj   Adj   N   Adv
5. The Sun Belt had a massive population growth recently.

    Adj   Adj   N   V   Adv   Adj
6. Good entry-level positions are usually scarce.

    Adj   Adj   N   Adv V Prep Adj Adj   Adj   N
7. These old flashbulbs often fail at the worst possible time.

   Adj   Adj   N   V   Adv   Adj
8. The young witness was visibly nervous.

       N   V   Adj   Adj   N   Prep Adj   N
9. Holmes located the missing bullet in the wainscot.

    Adj   N   Adv   V   Adv Adj   Adj   N   C   N
10. The agency often hired too many consulting firms and experts.

    I   N   V   Adj N   Adv   Adv
11. Oh, Jason missed the bus again today.

      N   V   Adj Adj   N   Adv
12. Scientists discovered a new particle recently.

   Adj   N   C   N   V   Adv   Adj   Adv
13. Shelf space and storage are always limited here.

   Adj   N   V   Adj Adv   Adj   N   Prep Adj   N
14. The commission expected a more favorable outcome from the hearing.

     N   Adv   V   N   Adv   Prep Adj   N   Prep
15. Holmes always quizzed Watson unmercifully about the methods of

     Adj   N
scientific deduction.

   Adj   N   V   Adv   Adj Prep P
16. The slope seemed terribly steep to me.

    N   V   Adj   Adj   N   C   N
17. Godzilla ordered the poached fish and artichokes.

■ Exercise 1.28. Review II: Identifying parts of speech (page 69)

      V   Adj   N
1. Diagram this sentence.

   P   V   Adj N   Prep Adj   Adj   N
2. I found a map in the glove compartment.

     N   V   Prep Adj   N   Prep   N   Adv Adv
3. Fred went to a college out of state last year.

     N   V   N   Adj   N
4. Sally sold Sarah some sandwiches.

```
     P    V     Adj   Prep  Adj    N
5. We were happy about the decision.
```

```
    N   C  P    V     Adj   N   Prep Adj    N
6. John and I finished the project  in  the library.
```

```
       I    Adj   N   Prep Adj   N    V   Adv    Adj
7. Nonsense, the paint  on  that bench is perfectly dry.
```

```
   Adj    N   Prep Adj Adj   N     V  N
8. The answer  to  the first question is 42.
```

```
      V    Adj   N    C  Adj   Adj      N
9. Underline the subject and the simple predicate.
```

```
    Adj  Adj    N     V  Adj Adj    N     Prep Adj  N  Prep      N
10. The young blonde found  a  nice apartment  in  the city  for  King Kong.
```

```
    Adj  N  Prep Adj   N     Adv     V   Adj Adj   C   Adj     Adj      N
11. The kid  at  the counter finally bought  a  liver and onion ice-cream cone.
```

```
     P    V     Adv     Adj   Prep Adj  N  Prep Adj N
12. They were completely wrong about the size  of  the lot.
```

```
     Adj        N     Prep   Adj    N   V   Adv    Adv     Adj
13. Holmes's deductions  in  criminal cases are almost always accurate.
```

```
    V   P  Adj   N    I
14. Give me  a  coke, please.
```

```
   Adj   Adj    N     V   Adj  N
15. A rolling stone gathers no moss.
```

```
   Prep Adj   Adj     N     Prep  P  Adj   N    V   Adv  Adv    Adj
16. In  a  complex society like ours, the issues are often very confusing.
```

```
     N    V    Prep Adj Adj    N    C    V   Prep Adj   N
17. Jones singled  in  the first inning and walked  in  the third.
```

CHAPTER 2. SENTENCE

■ **Exercise 2.1. Recognizing fragments and complete sentences (page 73)**
[Many possible answers]

2. Whatever you want is OK with me.
3. We were completely confused about the situation. c
4. The runner was safe at home.
5. You can be sure of that. c
6. What he said was OK by me.
7. As soon as you can, give me a call.
8. I lost my bubble gum on top of old smoky.
9. That was correct, more or less.
10. Get it to me by noon, if not sooner.
11. Your message was understood.
12. There is not a chance that Tampa Bay will win.

13. When the Christmas rush is over, I am going to take it easy.

14. I couldn't believe it. C

15. After you called about the package from the mail room, I got the strangest message from the head office.

16. If it's OK with you, it is OK with me.

■ **Exercise 2.2. Identifying subjects (page 75)**

2. The modern art (world) was shocked by Fred's use of bananas.
   It

3. The (unions) in this area have traditionally opposed open shops.
   They

4. The (program) has been canceled.
   It

5. An (announcement) of a major new project will be made this week.
   It

6. Naturally, the major (sources) for his story are a closely guarded secret.
   They

7. The proposed new industry (standards) are likely to be controversial.
   They

8. The economic (conditions) of the country depend on the balance of trade.
   They

9. The so-called (window of opportunity) for the launch is this month.
   It

10. The (dock) and the (buildings) near the river have become quite valuable.
    They

11. The (secretary), the (treasurer), and the (vice-president) are flying to Brazil.
    They

12. A (stitch) in time usually saves nine.
    It

13. The (tax rate) for purchases made after March 1 has been lowered.
    It

14. As always, the (list) of suspects in her new novel is overwhelming.
    It

15. Several large cold (fronts) from Canada will affect our weather.
    They

16. Increasingly, the (internationalization) of trade in commodities makes us an eco-
    It
    nomic global village.

■ **Exercise 2.3. Putting sentence into normal order and identifying complete predicates (page 77)**

2. Close the door on your way out. (Comment: *you* is the implied subject.)
3. You may have trouble adjusting the focus at first.
4. Mary Ann managed to get the car door open by using a coat hook.
5. Call me as soon as you get there.
6. The cashier noticed the missing bills late in the day.
7. I have several appointments this afternoon.
8. He shoved the oranges into the back of the refrigerator today.
9. He put the canoe into the water gracefully and with no wasted motions.
10. You should eat your soup with a spoon under most circumstances.
11. You were contacted by one of our sales staff recently.
12. They heard the mysterious tapping at the window again.
13. Holmes pulled out his service revolver with a flourish.
14. King Arthur has been having doubts about his marriage recently.
15. The sun is shining somewhere.
16. Change the subject if he starts talking about his snail collection.
17. You would be right most of the time.

■ **Exercise 2.4. Checking for nearest noun subject-verb agreement error (page 78)**

2. The answers for the problems in the first section is on page 312.
   a. *They is on page 312. b. *Answers is on page 312.
3. Only one finalist out of several hundred contenders are selected.
   a. *He/She are selected. b. *Finalist are selected.
4. Plans belonging to the city planning department is public property.
   a. *They is public property. b. *Plans is public property.
5. Three mistakes in a row means that you are out.
   a. *They means that you are out. b. *Mistakes means that you are out.
6. Parking in the marked spaces are forbidden by city ordinance.
   a. *It are forbidden by city ordinance. b. *Parking are forbidden . . .
7. The persons seated in the back row needs to move forward.
   a. *They needs to move forward. b. *Persons needs to move forward.
8. The number of accidents caused by drunk drivers increase at night.
   a. *It increase at night. b. *Number increase at night.
9. One of these three classes are required for your major.
   a. *It are required for your major. b. *One are required . . .
10. The heavy fall rain in the mountains have washed a lot of soil away.
    a. *It have washed a lot of soil away. b. *Rain have washed a lot . . .
11. The boxes in the back of the trailer goes in the storage room.
    a. *They goes in the storage room. b. *Boxes goes in the storage . . .

12. The luggage belonging to the transit passengers are now available.
    a. *It are now available. b. ^Luggage are now available.
13. The radio shown in their new catalogs were just what we wanted.
    a. *It were just what we wanted. b. *Radio were just what . . .
14. The experts that we polled at the university has confirmed our opinion.
    a. *They has confirmed our opinion. b. *Experts has confirmed . . .
15. Parking in the downtown lots over night are prohibited.
    a. *It are prohibited. b. *Parking are prohibited.
16. Pain in the joints of the fingers and toes signal arthritis.
    a. *It signal arthritis. b. *Pain signal arthritis.

■ **Exercise 2.5. Identifying objects (page 82)**

2. Babar ruled the <u>land</u> of the elephants.
   (DO above "land")

3. The elephants befriended young <u>Tarzan</u>.
   (DO above "Tarzan")

4. Leon displayed a surprising <u>knowledge</u> of the situation.
   (DO above "knowledge")

5. Stark terror concentrates the <u>mind</u> wonderfully.
   (DO above "mind")

6. She parked my <u>car</u> on the street.
   (DO above "car")

7. Garrick sold <u>me</u> <u>Boardwalk</u>.
   (IO above "me", DO above "Boardwalk")
   Paraphrase: Garrick sold Boardwalk to me.

8. Igor began the <u>operation</u> confidently.
   (DO above "operation")

9. You cannot alter the <u>situation</u>.
   (DO above "situation")

10. Holmes always solved the <u>mystery</u>.
    (DO above "mystery")

11. He finally told <u>me</u> the <u>answer</u>.
    (IO above "me", DO above "answer")
    Paraphrase: He finally told the answer to me.

12. The investigation confirmed Holmes's worst <u>suspicion</u>.
    (DO above "suspicion")

13. We drew <u>Anne</u> a <u>picture</u>.
    (IO above "Anne", DO above "picture")
    Paraphrase: We drew a picture for Anne.

14. The farmer killed a <u>duckling</u> for us.
    (DO above "duckling")

15. The wizard granted <u>them</u> three <u>wishes</u>.
    (IO above "them", DO above "wishes")
    Paraphrase: The wizard granted three wishes to them.

■ **Exercise 2.6. Identifying subject complements (page 85)**

2. Thanks to his grammar teacher, Leon became a better <u>person</u>.
   Pred Nom

3. The new patient was in a dangerous coma.

4. Hearing the news, the general grew <u>angry</u>.
   Pred Adj

5. Aunt Sally was there on time.

6. His home brew tasted just <u>awful</u>.
   Pred Adj

7. The queen was in the parlor, eating bread and honey.

8. The cat acted <u>crazy</u>.
   Pred Adj

9. I am <u>mad</u> at myself for saying that.
   Pred Adj

10. Rudolph remained a <u>private</u> for several more months.
    Pred Nom

11. I answered their questions.

12. Later that year, Lady Windermere fell <u>ill</u>.
    Pred Adj

13. The answer to the meaning of life was <u>42</u>.
    Pred Nom

14. At first the idea sounded <u>crazy</u> to me.
    Pred Adj

15. The winner of the contest was in a state of shock.

16. Louise looked <u>angry</u>.
    Pred Adj

17. Louise looked angrily at the rude waiter.

■ **Exercise 2.7. Identifying complement types (page 86)**

2. These sentences are <u>rich</u> in subject-verb agreements.
   Link Sub Comp

3. We completed the first <u>portion</u> of the test in good time.
   Trans   *DO*

4. The post office returned the <u>package</u> to Marty.
   Trans   *DO*

5. Cinderella was in a foul mood that day.
   Link

6. Alice bought <u>Fred</u> a new dish <u>towel</u> for Father's Day.
   Trans   *IO*   *DO*

7. I smell <u>smoke</u>.
   Trans   *DO*

               Link Sub Comp
8. My dog smells awful.

             Trans   IO   DO
9. The agent sold them the replacement parts.

                  Link Sub Comp
10. Today, Leon turned 30.

       Link
11. Fred is never on time.

                           Trans   DO
12. With a satisfied look, Aunt Sally fit the last piece into the puzzle.

               Trans   DO
13. Everyone likes chocolate cake.

                   Trans   DO
14. Apparently no one noticed the incident in Lady Crumhorn's drawing room.

                      Trans   DO
15. With deep regret, Charles declined a second helping.

                 Link   Sub Comp
16. Leon eventually became a famous and beloved grammarian.

             Link Sub Comp
17. The tenor sounded flat to me.

■ Exercise 2.8. Classifying sentences by purpose (page 88)

1. What do you know about that? Interrogative
2. It seems pretty simple to me. Declarative
3. That's what you think! Exclamatory
4. Holmes warned Watson to stay back. Declarative
5. To get the mean, total the data and divide by the number of observations. Imperative
6. Is everything all right here? Interrogative
7. His mission was to seek out and destroy the enemy. Declarative
8. I did not order a bottle of Chateau Yquem with my chili dog! Exclamatory
9. He asked if I could come in this afternoon. Declarative
10. Can you come in this afternoon? Interrogative
11. Publish or perish. Imperative
12. The very existence of Bertha's Kitty Boutique was at stake! Exclamatory
13. He tends to get excited about little things. Declarative
14. Blend in the cream cheese until smooth. Imperative
15. We will soon be home. Declarative
16. Remember where you are. Imperative
17. The total far exceeded our most optimistic projections! Exclamatory
18. Has the cat got your tongue? Interrogative
19. Return to headquarters at once! Imperative

■ **Exercise 2.9. Diagramming the basic sentence: I (page 92)**

1. The Eagle has landed.

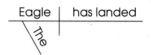

2. They lowered the lifeboats.

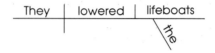

3. Fred always split his infinitives.

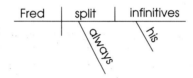

4. The room was a mess.

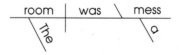

5. They are playing our song.

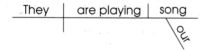

6. He became a legend.

7. Most politicians kiss babies and shake hands.

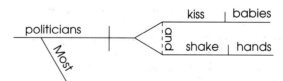

8. We went home and changed our clothes.

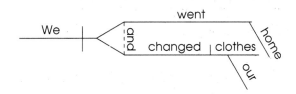

9. The sketch was not very funny.

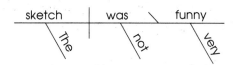

10. They sought a long-range solution.

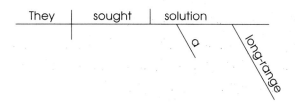

11. Usually, he is a very good little dog.

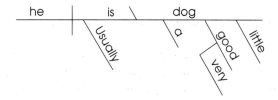

12. He tapped the glass and cleared his throat loudly.

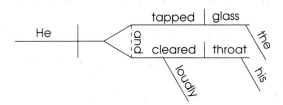

13. Joan and I sanded the old desk yesterday.

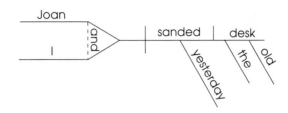

14. The residents were constantly complaining.

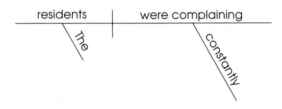

15. The play was at an old theater.

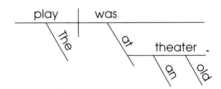

16. I made Fred a sandwich.

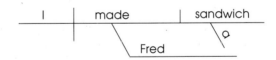

17. Are you coming?

18. What is the answer?

■ **Exercise 2.10. Diagramming the basic sentence: II (page 93)**

1. The Count politely took a small bite.

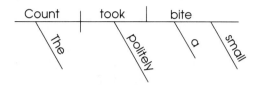

2. The plumber flooded the basement and the garage.

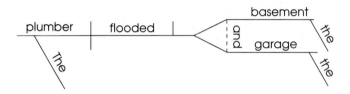

3. Lady Grenville graciously greeted the humble peasants.

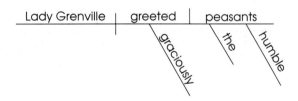

4. She found Anne an apartment.

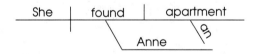

5. A policeman's lot is not a happy one.

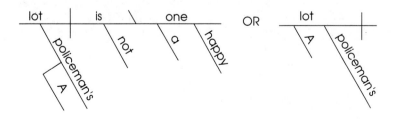

6. I had a terribly bad cold recently.

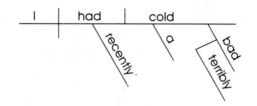

7. Williams rounded first and took second base.

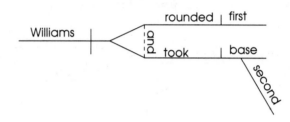

8. Wasn't the rainy landscape gloomy and depressing?

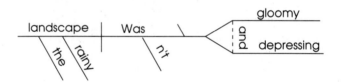

9. They explored the constantly changing desert.

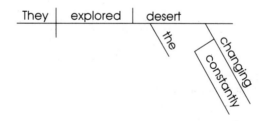

10. Tarzan and Jane loathe bananas.

11. Did you take your pills?

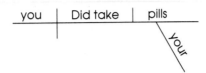

12. The mysterious red stain was there again.

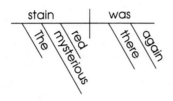

13. The dog gave Holmes an idea.

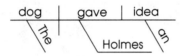

14. The office resembled a movie set.

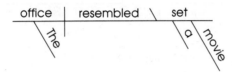

15. What is the matter?

16. Naturally, he had wanted a full-time job and reasonable pay.

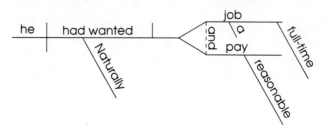

17. The boss promised me a promotion yesterday.

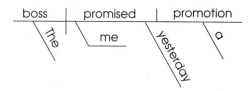

18. Where are you going now?

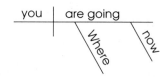

19. Tell me the truth!

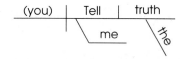

CHAPTER 3 PHRASES

■ **Exercise 3.1. Identifying noun phrases I (page 97)**

2. Unfortunately, <u>many of the voters</u> opposed <u>the new tax measures</u>.
                they   them

3. <u>The elk in this area</u> are protected.
       They

4. <u>The wet children</u> dried <u>their hands</u> energetically.
          They   them

5. <u>A little girl in the front row</u> easily guessed <u>the answer</u>.
         She   it

6. <u>Complex mathematical expressions</u> defined <u>the object's path</u> correctly.
               They   it

7. <u>The group of volunteers</u> finally painted <u>the old barn</u>.
      It/They   it

8. <u>These lights</u> always attract <u>some bugs</u>.
      They   them

9. <u>That tree branch</u> just snagged <u>my pants</u>.
      It   them

10. <u>Some girls in local costumes</u> performed <u>a dance</u>.
      They   it

11. The cold wind was killing most of the new plants.
<u> </u>   It   them

11\. The cold <u>wind</u> was killing <u>most of the new plants</u>.
             It   them

12\. <u>Several guest speakers</u> made <u>excellent presentations</u> last night.
            They   them

13\. <u>The black prongs</u> cover <u>the small holes in the base plate</u>.
          They   them

14\. <u>The students</u> had to use <u>absentee ballots</u>.
        They   them

15\. <u>The police</u> have established <u>the owner of the stolen car</u>.
      They   it/him/her

16\. In his dream <u>the old man</u> saw <u>a long flight of stairs</u>.
               he   it

17\. In English, <u>modifying adjectives</u> almost always precede <u>their nouns</u>.
                 they   them

■ **Exercise 3.2. Identifying noun phrases II (page 98)**

2. The (chairman) of the committee ruled the (motion) invalid.

3. A (few) of the members protested his (ruling).

4. However, the (chairman) could cite (all) of the by-laws.

5. All the (motions) confused the poor (secretary) no end.

6. Finally, (several) of the members got (Robert's Rules of Order) out.

7. The (organization) thanked the (members) of the committee.

8. (Most) of us would never undergo that (kind) of pressure again.

9. The (laundry) didn't remove the (stain) on my tablecloth.

10. A (few) of us have never paid income (tax).

11. The rank-and-file union (members) met yesterday.

12. The (outcome) of the case confirmed my worst (suspicions).

13. A (phrase) is a (group) of related words.

14. Soon (many) of the bored children quit the (game).

15. The fastest (runners) on the team could not steal second (base).

16. (All) of the commentators predicted the (results) of the election.

17. Beethoven's (symphonies) completely dominated the next (generation) of composers.

■ **Exercise 3.3. Verb and verb phrase names (page 103)**

2. The senator's aides <u>are denying</u> the statement.
   Pres progressive

3. They <u>will have finished</u> by now.
   Future perfect

4. The doctor <u>prescribed</u> aspirin.
   Past

5. I <u>will be</u> busy all afternoon.
   Future

6. We <u>interrupt</u> this program for an important message.
   Present

7. I <u>am</u> already <u>working</u> on it.
   Pres progressive

8. They <u>will have invested</u> a fortune on it by then.
   Future perfect

9. He <u>had</u> nearly <u>wrecked</u> the turntable.
   Past perfect

10. He <u>will have been sleeping</u> all afternoon.
    Future perfect progressive

11. That <u>tasted</u> just awful.
    Past

12. He <u>has</u> certainly <u>been</u> persistent in his efforts.
    Pres Perfect

13. The secretary <u>informed</u> the chairman.
    Past

14. He <u>will</u> probably <u>argue</u> against the measure.
    Future

15. Lady Lockridge <u>will have collected</u> all the insurance.
    Future perfect

16. Watson <u>was considering</u> an alternative plan.
    Past progressive

17. This <u>is</u> silly.
    Pres

■ **Exercise 3.4. Diagraming verb phrases (page 104)**

1.

2.

3.

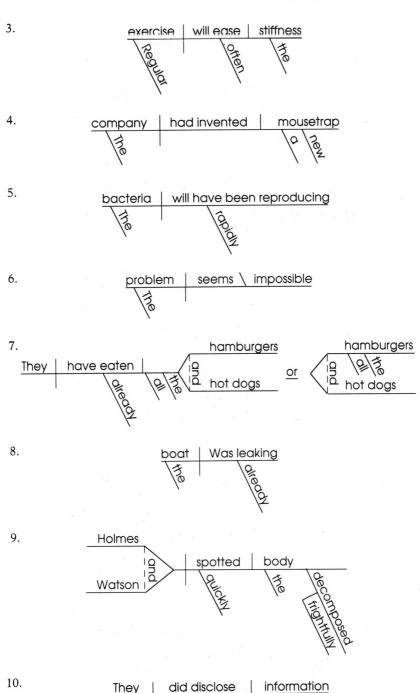

4.

5.

6.

7.

8.

9.

10.

11.

They | were \ people
nice
such

12. Frankenstein | has been coloring | eggs   or   Easter eggs
today   his   Easter   his

13.

They | are splitting | infinitives
always   their

14.

Holmes | calculated | odds
rapidly   the

15.

he | Has   aged

16.

events | had discouraged | him
The   naturally

17.

quiz | will be \ one
Tomorrow's   a   nasty

18.

John   watching | game
        and | have been | and   the
Ralph   painting | deck
                                                      the

■ **Exercise 3.5. Identifying prepositional phrases (page 111)**

3. I think that he overplayed the part <u>of the tough reporter</u>. [Adj]
   I think that he overplayed it.

4. We bought an old cabin <u>in the mountains</u>. [Adj]
   We bought it.

5. He is an Englishman <u>in spite of all temptations</u>. [Adv]
   In spite of all temptations he is an Englishman.

6. We finally found substitutes <u>for our injured players</u>. [Adj]
   We finally found them.

7. He has attended City College <u>for the last few weeks</u>. [Adv]
   For the last few weeks he has attended City College.

8. The drug store <u>in River City</u> carries them. [Adj]
   It carries them.

9. The prosecutor <u>in the case</u> convinced the jury <u>without much difficulty</u>. [Adj] [Adv]
   Without much difficulty he/she convinced the jury.

10. I just stood there shaking <u>after the accident</u>. [Adv]
    After the accident I just stood there shaking.

11. I still trusted him despite <u>all the evidence</u> <u>against him</u>. [Adv] [Adj]
    Despite it I still trusted him.

12. Everybody <u>in town</u> has seen the movie <u>at the Palace</u>. [Adj] [Adj]
    He/She has seen it (or They have seen it).

13. The company was acquired <u>within a week</u>. [Adv]
    Within a week the company was acquired.

14. They will issue new stock <u>in the company</u> <u>as of the first</u>. [Adj] [Adv]
    As of the first they will issue it.

15. The Division mounted an all-out attack <u>without air support</u> <u>at dawn</u>. [Adj] [Adv]
    At dawn the Division mounted it.

16. I fell asleep during <u>the program</u> <u>about whales</u>. [Adv] [Adj]
    During it I fell asleep.

■ **Exercise 3.6. Diagraming prepositional phrases (page 113)**

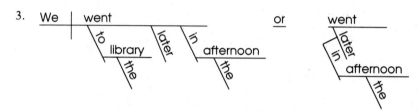

1.

2.

3.

4.

5.

6.

7.

8.

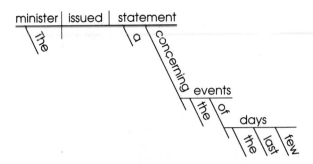

9.

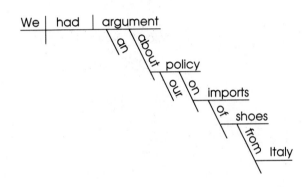

10.

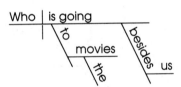

11.

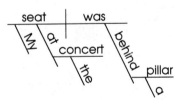

12.

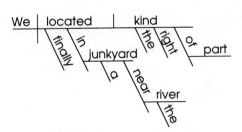

13.

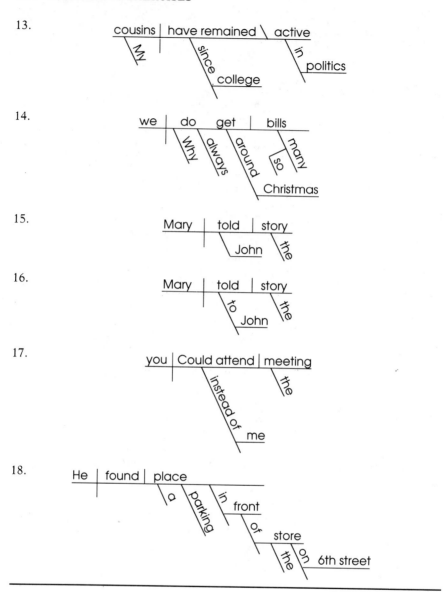

14.

15.

16.

17.

18.

■ **Exercise 3.7. Recognizing appositives and appositive phrases (page 115)**

2. Dorothy saw her old enemy, the Wicked Witch of the West.

3. The Pacific Ocean, the earth's largest body of water, was unknown to the ancient world.

4. Export processing zones, managed industrial parks, specialize in light manufacturing.

5. The answer to the question, 42, came as a complete surprise.

6. PDQ Bach, an imaginary son of JS Bach, composed *The Stoned Guest*.

7. Watson, a slightly comic figure, is the perfect foil for Holmes.

8. My grandfather, a man with firm convictions, refused to get electric lights.

9. Calvin Coolidge, the 30th President of the United States, was known as "Silent Cal."

10. The theater, one of the old movie palaces, was undergoing renovation.

11. She finally got around to taking the test, a multiple choice examination on philosophy.

12. They elected Leon, a person who could hardly spell his own name, class secretary.

■ **Exercise 3.8. Diagraming appositives and appositive phrases (page 117)**

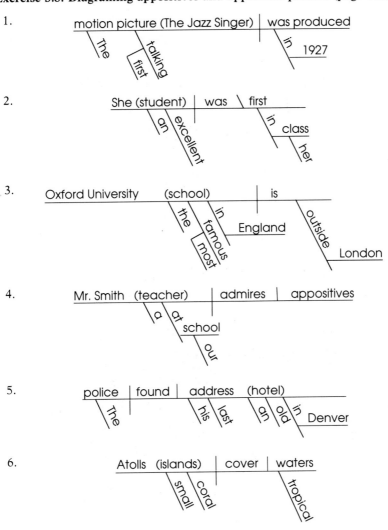

7.

Homer (poet) | was \ blind
the / Greek

8.

children | loved | tortillas (type)
The / a \ of pancake
cornmeal

9.

Holmes | noticed | man (soldier)
the / a \ in clothing
civilian

10.

Oakridge (street) | will take | you
the / first \ after Main / there

11.

Nematodes (worms) | attack | roots
microscopic / the \ of plants
cotton

12.

player | got | points (score)
The / first / 12,000 / a \ high \ in game
this

13.

Noel Coward | wrote | Private Lives (play)
in 1930 / his \ best-known

14.

15.

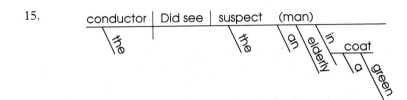

16.

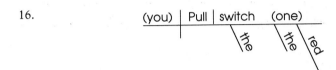

17.

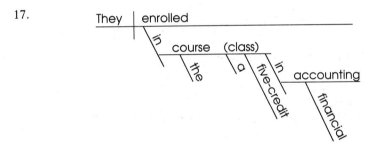

18.

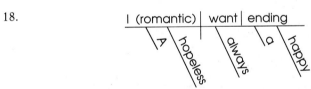

■ **Exercise 3.9. Nonfinite verb forms (page 119)**

2. chose   1. to choose   2. choosing   3. have chosen

3. came   1. to come   2. coming   3. have come

4. protested   1. to protest   2. protesting   3. have protested

5. saw   1. to see   2. seeing   3. have seen

6. faded   1. to fade   2. fading   3. have faded

7. bought   1. to buy   2. buying   3. have bought

8. fulfilled   1. to fulfill   2. fulfilling   3. have fulfilled

9. ran   1. to run   2. running   3. have run

10. substituted   1. to substitute   2. substituting   3. have substituted

11. dug   1. to dig   2. digging   3. have dug
12. conceded   1. to concede   2. conceding   3. have conceded
13. dreamed   1. to dream   2. dreaming   3. have dreamed
14. spent   1. to spend   2. spending   3. have spent
15. inquired   1. to inquire   2. inquiring   3. have inquired
16. split   1. to split   2. splitting   3. have split
17. sold   1. to sell   2. selling   3. have sold
18. cut   1. to cut   2. cutting   3. have cut

■ **Exercise 3.10. Recognizing participles and participial phrases (page 123)**

[Note: In most cases the participial phrase can be used either in front of or following the noun it modifies.]

2. Greeted with warm applause by the audience, the conductor stepped to the podium.
3. The teller, noticing his strange behavior, called the manager over.
4. (Being) pulled by two wreckers, the truck finally began to inch forward.
5. The event, having been mentioned on several news programs, was soon the talk of the town.
6. Trying to set a new record, Leon climbed to the top of the flagpole.
7. (Being) endlessly bothered by pigeons, Leon gave up in disgust.
8. Grabbing the picnic basket and table cloth, they ran for shelter.
9. (Being) ridiculed by his neighbors, Leon took up gardening.
10. John, forsaking all others, married Marcia.
11. Expressing a great interest in worm farming, the salesman engaged Uncle Ralph in conversation.
12. Being fed by hand, the calf soon gained its weight back.

■ **Exercise 3.11. Diagraming participles and participal phrases (page 125)**

1.

2.

3.

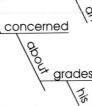

4.

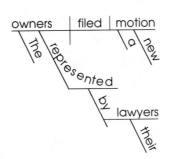

5.

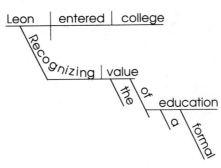

6.

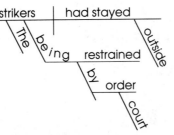

7.

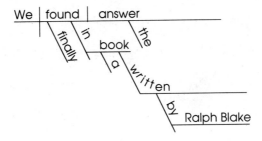

8.

9.

10.

11.

12.

13.

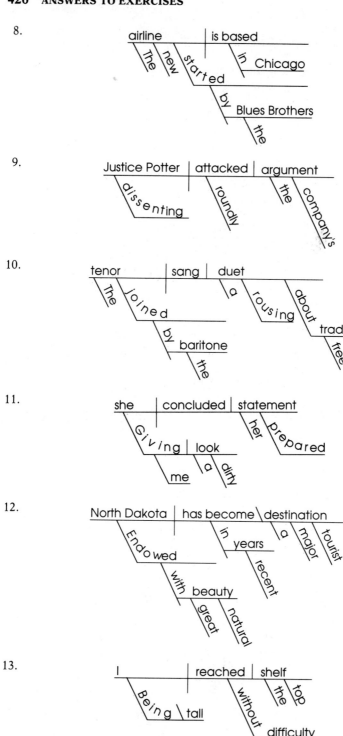

14.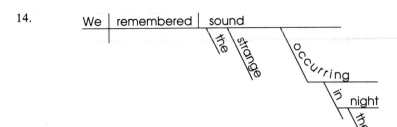

15.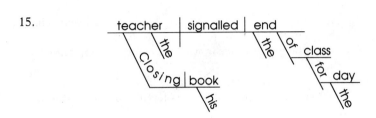

16.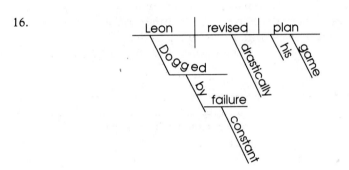

17.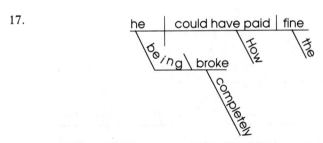

18.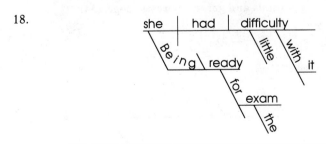

■ **Exercise 3.12. Dangling participles (page 127)**
[Note: many possible answers]

2. I began sorting through my books, which were piled on the floor.
3. When I detoured through my old neighborhood, our house looked the same as ever.
4. Having matured, I now enjoy the Flintstones.   OK
5. Being old Dodger fans, we were pleased with the outcome of the game.
6. Don, who was once considered only an average player, has improved his game enormously.
7. There was excitement in the air because we were hoping for a league championship.
8. Disappointed by the unexpected defeat, we, nevertheless, applauded the team's efforts.   OK
9. Working for old Mr. Green, we learned the value of a good day's work.
10. Finishing in 2 hours and 37 minutes, John was terrifically successful in his first marathon.
11. When I finished with my term paper, we went out for a pizza.
12. Shining in the sun, the water looked very inviting.   OK
13. Running across the plowed field, I twisted my ankle.
14. You cannot easily tell these artificial flowers made from a new plastic from real ones.
15. Warped and twisted from the heat, my records were ruined.

■ **Exercise 3.13. Recognizing gerunds and gerund phrases (page 131)**

2. Protecting the President is their main job.
3. They tried adjusting the starter.
4. They talked about going out for a hamburger.
5. Being sorry isn't enough.
6. I didn't think about being caught in traffic.
7. Being always late got him into a lot of trouble.
8. They managed to avoid working in the student union.
9. She was interested in studying classical Greek.
10. Rejecting the plan prohibits developing the idea further.
11. Avoiding taking a stand against the proposal attracted wide attention.

■ **Exercise 3.14. Diagraming gerunds and gerund phrases (page 134)**

1.

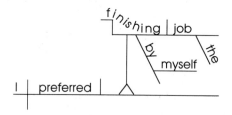

2.

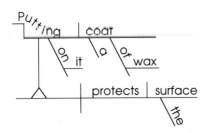

3.

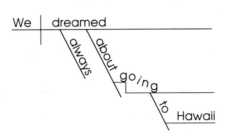

4.

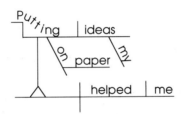

5.

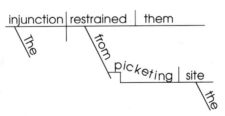

6.

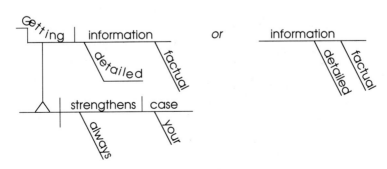

7.

8.

9.

10.

11.

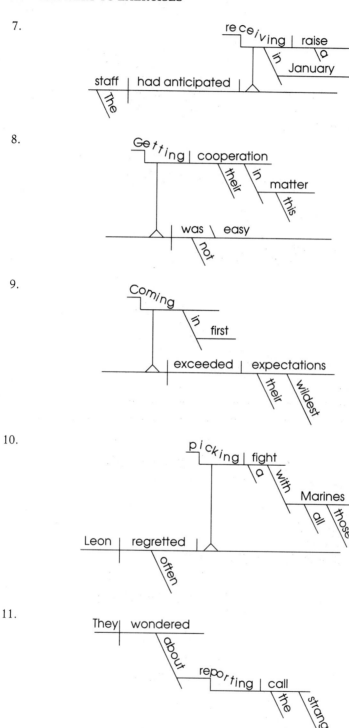

12.

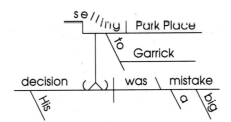

13.

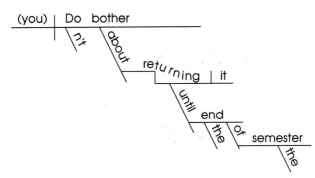

14.

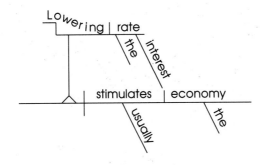

15.

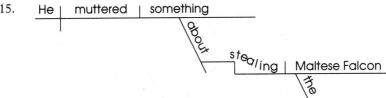

16.

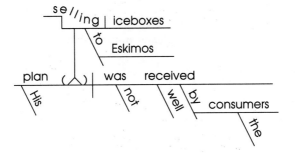

17.

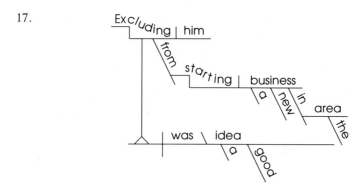

18.

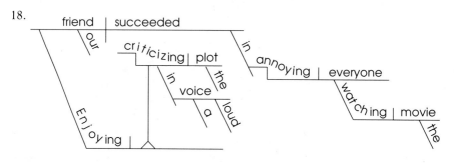

■ **Exercise 3.15. Recognizing infinitives and infinitive phrases (page 137)**

2. She expected to win the election.
3. We will manage to make a profit somehow.
4. His best opportunity was to lead spades.
5. To keep on smoking is very foolish of you.
6. Everybody managed to get the cans open, except you.
7. The idea was to get the place cleaned up before lunch.
8. To come in first was beyond our wildest expectation.
9. He claimed to want to preserve the American way of life.
10. To miss an inch is to miss a mile.

■ **Exercise 3.16. Diagraming infinitives and infinitive phrases (page 139)**

1.

2.

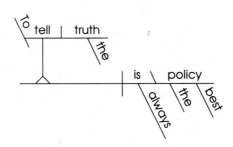

3.

4.

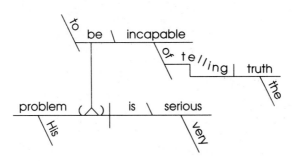

5.

6.

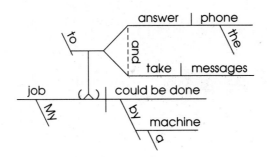

7.

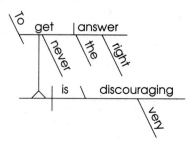

8.

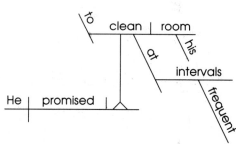

9.

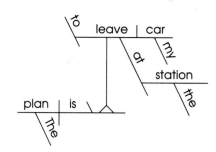

10.

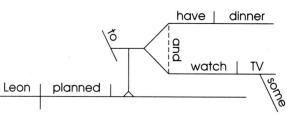

11.

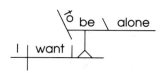

12.

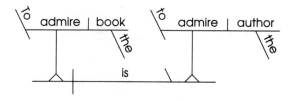

13.

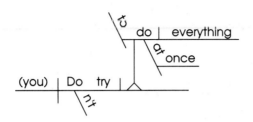

14.

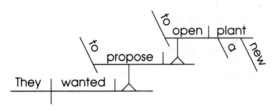

15.

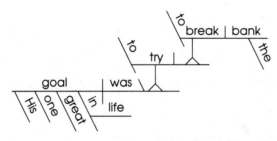

16.

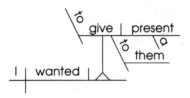

17.

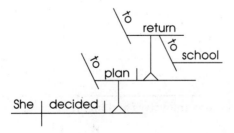

18.

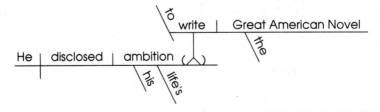

■ **Exercise 3.17. Identifying uses of infinitives and infinitive phrases (page 142)**

                     Adj

2. Will you have a chance <u>to get away</u> this weekend?

               Adv

3. I went home early <u>to get some work done today</u>.

         Adv

4. Are you ready <u>to go home now</u>?

   Adv

5. <u>To get to Broadway</u>, turn left at the next light.

          Noun

6. <u>To lessen the impact of the decision</u> was important to them.

           Adv

7. We were all sorry <u>to see the outcome</u>.

     Adj   Adj

8. It was a time <u>to live</u> and a time <u>to die</u>.

         Adv

9. Weren't you sad <u>to leave home</u>?

                Adv

10. They scanned the entire structure <u>to locate any defects</u>.

     Noun

11. <u>To be elected on the first ballot</u> would be a great victory.

           Adj

12. That was not the time <u>to make your move</u>.

        Noun

13. They decided <u>not to unload the furniture</u> after all.
    (Comment: Compare with *They did not decide to unload the furniture after all.*)

    Adv

14. <u>To take such a chance at this stage of the game</u>, you must be very sure of yourself.

15. He wouldn't listen to anyone.
    (Comment: *to anyone* is a prepositional phrase—no verb.)

         Noun

16. Luckily, the conductor refused <u>to be distracted by the noise</u> backstage.

    Noun

17. They tried <u>to sell the picture to a museum</u>.

■ **Exercise 3.18. Diagraming infinitives and infinitive phrases (page 143)**

1.

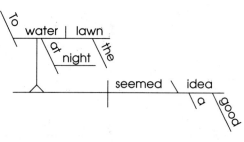

2.

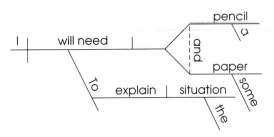

3.

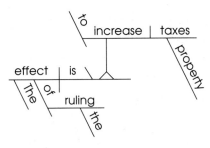

4.

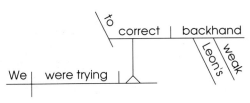

5.

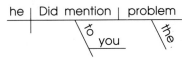

6.

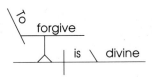

7.

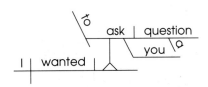

8.

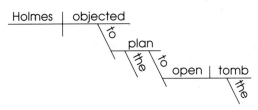

9.

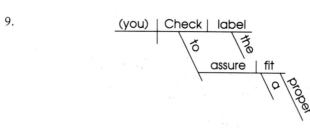

10.

11.

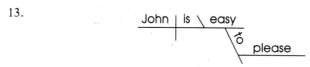

12.

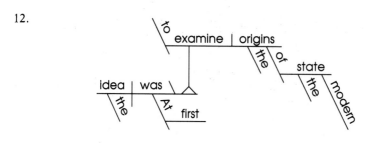

13.

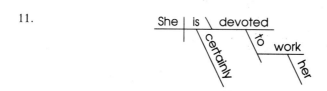

14.

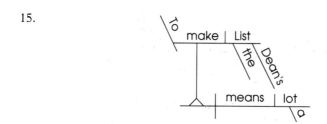

15.

16.

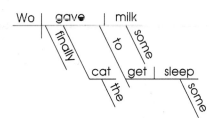

17.

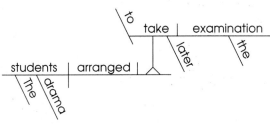

18.

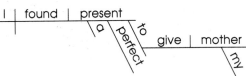

■ Exercise 3.19. Review I (page 143)

1.

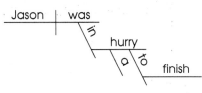

2.

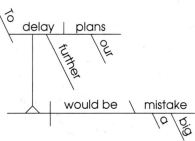

3.

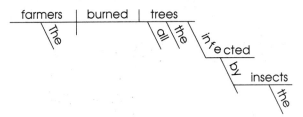

4.

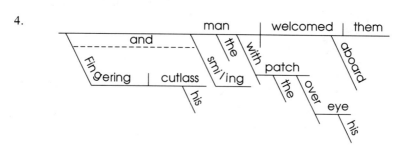

5.

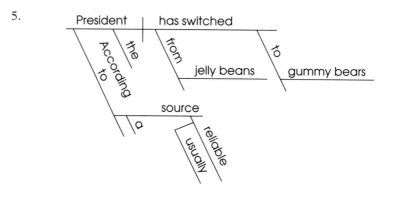

6.

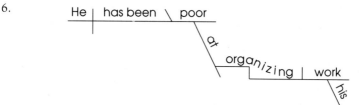

7.

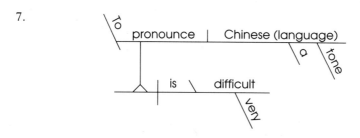

8.

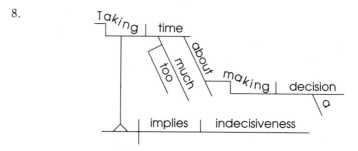

9.

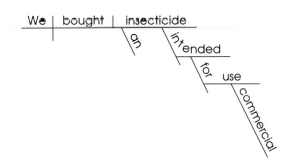

10.

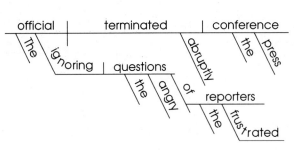

11.

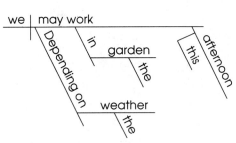

12.

13.

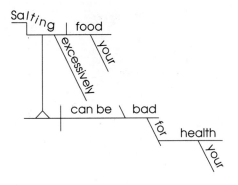

14.

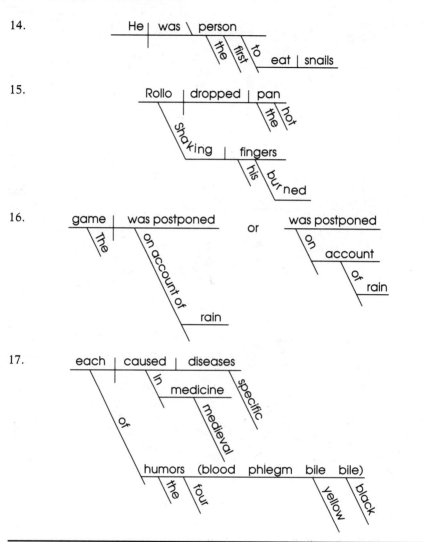

15.

16.

17.

Exercise 3.20. Review II (page 144)

1.

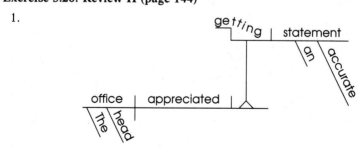

2.

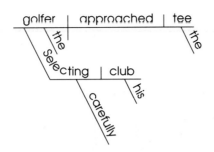

3.

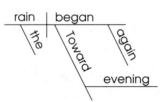

4.

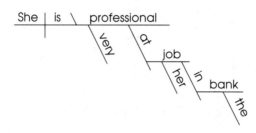

5.

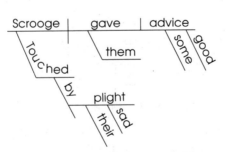

6.

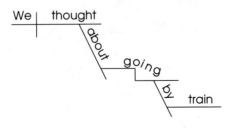

7.

8.

9.

10.

11.

12.

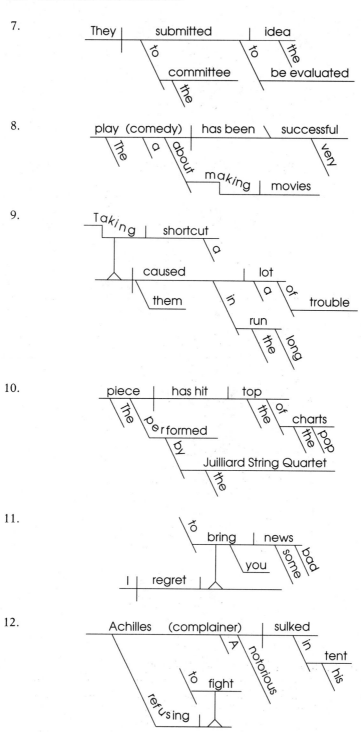

13.

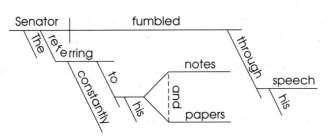

14.

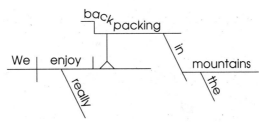

15.

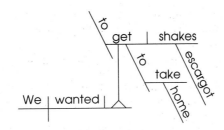

16.

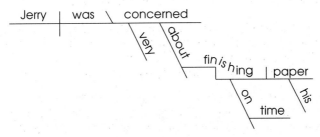

17.

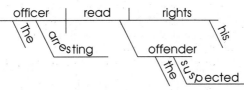

18.

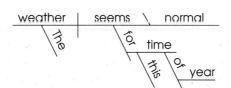

CHAPTER 4   CLAUSES

■ **Exercise 4.1. Forming relative clauses (page 151)**

2. They welcomed the visitors (they had long anticipated the visitors' arrival).

   Step 1:   They welcomed the visitors (they had long anticipated <u>whose arrival</u>).

   Step 2:   They welcomed the visitors <u>whose arrival</u> they had long anticipated.

3. My uncle finally found the letter (the IRS had sent him the letter).

   Step 1:   My uncle finally found the letter (the IRS had sent him <u>that/which</u>).

   Step 2:   My uncle finally found the letter <u>that/which</u> the IRS had sent him.
   My uncle finally found the letter <u>the IRS</u> had sent him.

4. The soup (we had the soup last night) is in the icebox on the bottom shelf.

   Step 1:   The soup (we had <u>that/which</u> last night) is in the icebox on the bottom shelf.

   Step 2:   The soup <u>that/which</u> we had last night in in the icebox on the bottom shelf.
   The soup we had last night is in the icebox on the bottom shelf.

5. The scientists hoped to unify the theories (the theories had been developed over the past decade).

   Step 1:   The scientists hoped to unify the theories (<u>that/which</u> had been developed over the past decade).

6. The treaty (Congress had been debating the treaty's fate for months) was finally approved in a voice vote.

   Step 1:   The treaty (Congress had been debating <u>whose</u> fate for months) was finally approved in a voice vote.

   Step 2:   The treaty <u>whose</u> fate Congress had been debating for months was finally approved in a voice vote.

7. The company returned the parts (the parts' design had proven so unsatisfactory).

   Step 1:   The company returned the parts (<u>whose</u> design had proven so unsatisfactory).

8. I finally passed the exam (I was worried about the exam).

   Step 1:   I finally passed the exam (I was worried about <u>that/which</u>).

   Step 2:   I finally passed the exam <u>that/which</u> I was worried about.
   I finally passed the exam I was worried about.

   Step 1:   I finally passed the exam (I was worried <u>about which</u>).

   Step 2:   I finally passed the exam <u>about which</u> I was worried.

9. The story was based on documents (the government has just declassified the documents).

   Step 1:   The story was based on documents (the government has just declassified that/which).

   Step 2:   The story was based on documents that/which the government has just declassified.

   The story was based on documents the government has just declassified.

10. I found the book (the poem was taken from the book).

    Step 1:   I found the book (the poem was taken from that/which).

    Step 2:   I found the book that/which the poem was taken from.

    I found the book the poem was taken from.

    Step 1:   I found the book (the poem was taken from which).

    Step 2:   I found the book from which the poem was taken.

11. The objects (I found the objects in the attic) turned out to be worth several hundred dollars.

    Step 1:   The objects (I found that/which is in the attic) turned out to be worth several hundred dollars.

    Step 2:   The objects that/which I found in the attic turned out to be worth several hundred dollars.

    The objects I found in the attic turned out to be worth several hundred dollars.

12. They were in an old trunk (the trunk had belonged to my grandfather).

    Step 1:   They were in an old trunk (that/which had belonged to my grandfather).

■ **Exercise 4.2. Distinguishing between <u>who</u> and <u>whom</u> (page 152)**

                                       OK
3. In class we studied the Anglo-Saxons who originally came from Germany.

   Test: In class we studied the Anglo-Saxons. <u>They</u> originally came from Germany. they = who

                                       OK
4. The king met with the bishops who had previously opposed his policies.

   Test: The king met with the bishops. <u>They</u> had previously opposed his policies. they = who

                                       whom
5. Donald became a wealthy banker who everyone envied for his amusing anecdotes about the International Monetary Fund.

   Test: Donald became a wealthy banker. Everyone envied <u>him</u> for his amusing anecdotes about the International Monetary Fund.

   him = whom

                                       whom
6. The company employed a shipping clerk who I greatly admired.

   Test: The company employed a shipping clerk. I greatly admired <u>him</u>.

   him = whom

7. The voters summarily rejected the candidates who the party had nominated at the convention. [whom, above "who"]

   Test: The voters summarily rejected the candidates. The party had nominated <u>them</u> at the convention. them = whom

8. The story had been filed by a correspondent who the bureau chief had personally selected because of his knowledge of the language. [whom, above "who"]

   Test: The story had been filed by a correspondent. The bureau chief had personally selected <u>him</u> because of his knowledge of the language. him = whom

9. The plot revolved around a rural sheriff who had a strange tendency for driving police cars off cliffs at high speeds. [OK, above "who"]

   Test: The plot revolved around a rural sheriff. <u>He</u> had a strange tendency for driving police cars off cliffs at high speeds. he = who

10. Lady Lockheart graciously acknowledged the peasants who were allowed to watch their betters at play. [OK, above "who"]

    Test: Lady Lockheart graciously acknowledged the peasants. <u>They</u> were allowed to watch their betters at play. they = who

11. The manager called in the pitcher who the team had acquired in a trade with Tacoma the week before. [whom, above "who"]

    Test: The manager called in the pitcher. The team had acquired <u>him</u> in a trade with Tacoma the week before. him = whom

12. The long-suffering patient finally turned on the dentist who had ridiculed his brushing habits. [OK, above "who"]

    Test: The long-suffering patient finally turned on the dentist. <u>He</u> had ridiculed his brushing habits. he = who

---

■ **Exercise 4.3. Recognizing restrictive and nonrestrictive adjective clauses (page 157)**

2. His carelessness caused an accident that/which should never have happened.

3. The people whose party we attended are old friends of ours.

4. We settled on the wording of Section 13b, which had previously been in dispute.

5. They identified the person who won the lottery yesterday.

6. The first proposal that/which we submitted was rejected by the committee.

7. The night sky was lit by the moon, which was just rising over the hills.

8. Napoleon, who was actually from Corsica, became a French patriot.

9. Holmes found the driver who had mysteriously vanished on the night of the murder.

10. I bumped into my boss, who was also doing some last minute shopping.

11. Charles, whose error caused all the trouble to begin with, finally found his mistake.

12. We got the item that/which you had asked about.

■ **Exercise 4.4. Diagraming adjective clauses (page 159)**

1.

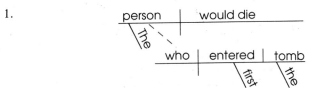

2.

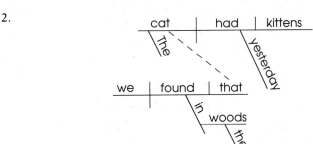

3.

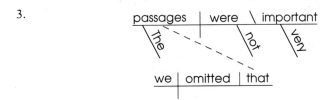

4.

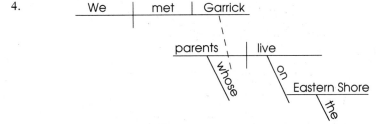

5.

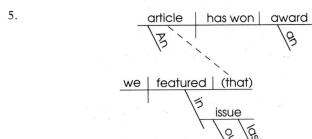

6.

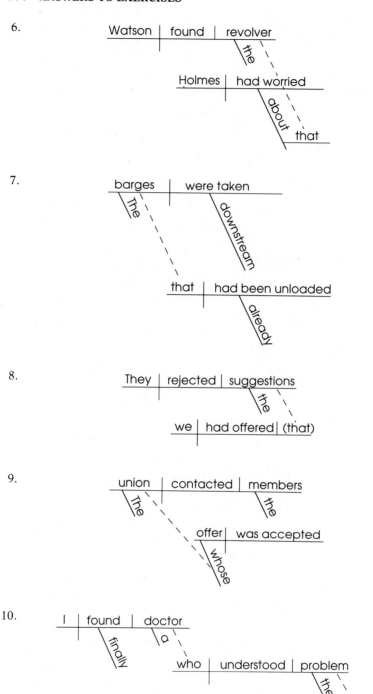

7.

8.

9.

10.

11.

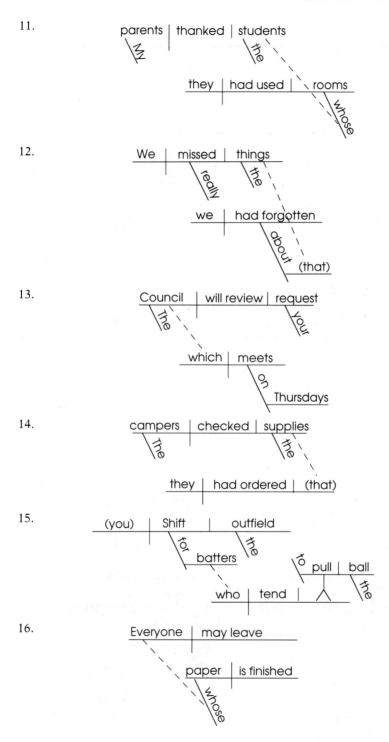

12.

13.

14.

15.

16.

17.

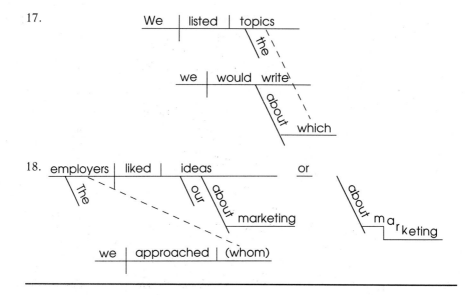

18.

Exercise 4.5. Recognizing and punctuating adverb clauses that modify verbs (page 164)

[Note: different subordinating conjunctions are also correct.]

2. a. We will cut your phone off unless you pay your bill.
   b. Unless you pay your bill, we will cut your phone off.
3. a. I am still gaining weight, although I have been eating nothing but carrot sticks.
   b. Although I have been eating nothing but carrot sticks, I am still gaining weight.
4. a. I bought my roommate a new ribbon because I use her typewriter all the time.
   b. Because I use her typewriter all the time, I bought my roommate a new ribbon.
5. a. I couldn't write my paper before I found all the references.
   b. Before I found all the references, I couldn't write my paper.
6. a. They were stripping off the old wallpaper as though their lives depended on it.
   b. As though their lives depended on it, they were stripping off the old wallpaper.
7. a. The dog followed him wherever he went.
   b. Wherever he went, the dog followed him.
8. a. The coaches review the films each week before they decide which plays to prepare.
   b. Before they decide which plays to prepare, the coaches review the films each week.
9. a. I liked the movie after all, although I hate to admit it.
   b. Although I hate to admit it, I liked the movie after all.

10. a. He dehydrated because he does not drink enough water while running.

    b. Because he does not drink enough water while running, he dehydrated.

11. a. Watson tried to behave as though he was not wearing the most ridiculous disguise.

    b. Adverb of manner clause cannot be moved to first position.

■ **Exercise 4.6. Distinguishing subordinating conjunctions and conjunctive adverbs (page 168)**

                    Sub Conj
2. I was upset because I had damaged the arm on my turntable.

   Sub Conj: Because I had damaged the arm on my turntable, I was upset.

   Conj Adv: *I was upset; I had, because, damaged the arm on my turntable.

              *I was upset; I had damaged the arm on my turntable, because.

                  Sub Conj
3. We are ready to leave unless there is something else you need to do.

   Sub Conj: Unless there is something else you need to do, we are ready to leave.

   Conj Adv: *We are ready to leave; there is, unless, something else you need to do.

   Conj Adv: *We are ready to leave; there is something else you need to do, unless.

                          Conj Adv
4. The experiment had been affected by the accident; therefore, we had to start all over again.

   Sub Conj: *Therefore we had to start all over again, the experiment had been affected by the accident.

   Conj Adv: The experiment had been affected by the accident; we, therefore, had to start all over again.

              The experiment had been affected by the accident; we had to start all over again, therefore.

                  Sub Conj
5. Aunt Sally has been depressed since she was badly beaten at Monopoly.

   Sub Conj: Since she was badly beaten at Monopoly, Aunt Sally has been depressed.

   Conj Adv: *Aunt Sally has been depressed; she was, since, badly beaten at Monopoly.

              Aunt Sally has been depressed; she was badly beaten at Monopoly, since.

                Conj Adv
6. She passed Go; nevertheless, she was forced to sell her railroads.

   Sub Conj: *Nevertheless she was forced to sell her railroads, she passed Go.

   Conj Adv: She passed Go; she was, nevertheless, forced to sell her railroads.

              She passed Go; she was forced to sell her railroads, nevertheless.

Sub Conj

7. The doctor was called to testify inasmuch as she took the X-rays.

Sub Conj: Inasmuch as she took the X-rays, the doctor was called to testify.

Conj Adv: *The doctor was called to testify; she, inasmuch as, took the X-rays.

                *The doctor was called to testify; she took the X-rays, inasmuch as.

Conj Adv

8. The general was not able to consolidate his forces; thus, he lost a unique opportunity to defeat the opposition.

Sub Conj: *Thus he lost a unique opportunity to defeat the opposition, the general was not able to consolidate his forces.

Conj Adv: The general was not able to consolidate his forces; he, thus, lost a unique opportunity to defeat the opposition.

                ?The general was not able to consolidate his forces; he lost a unique opportunity to defeat the opposition, thus.

Sub Conj

9. We stayed up to watch the program, even though it was getting pretty late.

Sub Conj: Even though it was getting pretty late, we stayed up to watch the program.

Conj Adv: *We stayed up to watch the program; it was, even though, getting pretty late.

                *We stayed up to watch the program; it was getting pretty late, even though.

Conj Adv

10. The program was filmed near our school; consequently, we recognized many of the settings.

Sub Conj: *Consequently we recognized many of the settings, the program was filmed near our school.

Conj Adv: The program was filmed near our school; we, consequently, recognized many of the settings.

                The program was filmed near our school; we recognized many of the settings, consequently.

Sub Conj

11. The kids decided to sleep on the porch as the night was quite warm.

Sub Conj: As the night was quite warm, the kids decided to sleep on the porch.

Conj Adv: *The kids decided to sleep on the porch; the night, as, was quite warm.

                *The kids decided to sleep on the porch; the night was quite warm, as.

Conj Adv

12. The company offered compensation; nevertheless, we went to court.

Sub Conj: *Nevertheless we went to court, the company offered compensation.

Conj Adv: The company offered compensation; we, nevertheless, went to court.

                The company offered compensation; we went to court, nevertheless.

■ **Exercise 4.7. Diagraming adverb clauses (page 170)**

1.

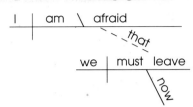

2.

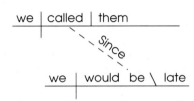

3.

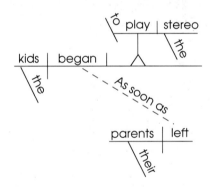

4.

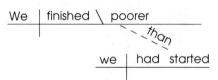

5.

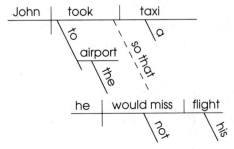

6.

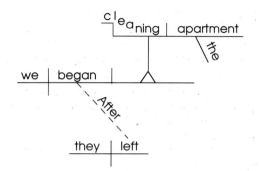

7.

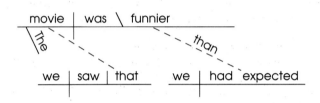

8.

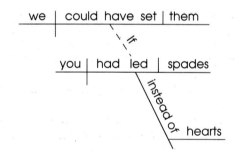

9.

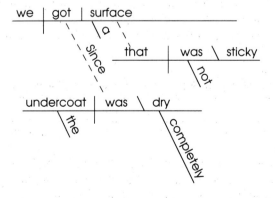

10.

11.

12.

13.

14.

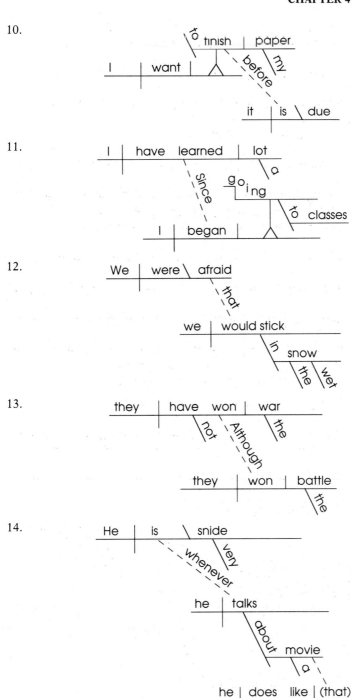

15.

16.

17.

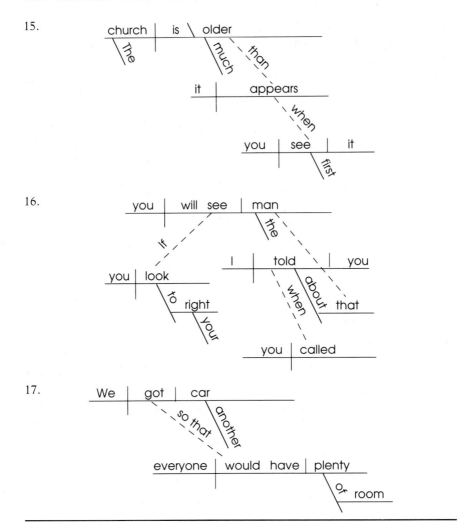

■ **Exercise 4.8. Recognizing *that*-type noun clauses (page 173)**

2. Lady Smyth suspected that something was afoot.
3. That the idea was endorsed by the President quickly squelched the opposition.
4. The motion, that fattening desserts should be banned from the mess hall, passed without a dissenting vote.
5. The idea was that Leon would collect thousands of bottle caps.
6. They argued about whether Dorothy should take her ruby slippers.
7. That he was no friend of mine was apparent to everyone.
8. They should tell us if they are planning on coming with us tonight.

9. The question is whether or not he can be trusted.
10. That he could diagram 100 sentences in 10 minutes strained credulity.
11. That she is nearly always correct shows that she is well prepared.

■ **Exercise 4.9. Recognizing *wh*-type noun clauses (page 176)**

2. Where we went wrong is painfully obvious to us now.
3. We finally reached an important decision about what we should have for lunch.
4. We finally agreed on when we should pick up the van.
5. What affects the price of gold does not necessarily affect the value of the dollar.
6. Everyone asked why they did it.
7. You are what you eat.
8. Leon agonized over where he should keep all those stupid bottle caps.
9. Whose telephone call it is is none of your business.
10. He would not tell me who he was.
11. How you stand depends on where you sit.

■ **Exercise 4.10. Diagraming noun clauses (page 178)**

1.

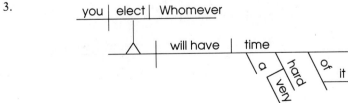

2.

3.

4.

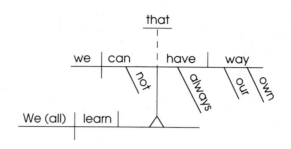

5.

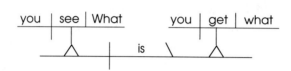

6.

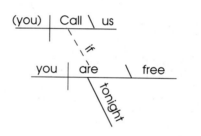

7.

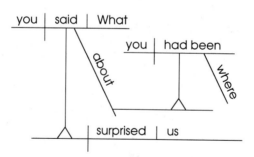

8.

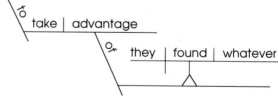

9.

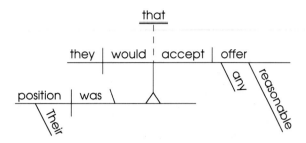

10.

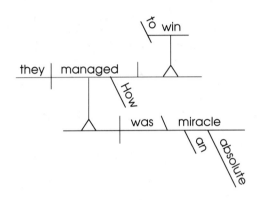

11.

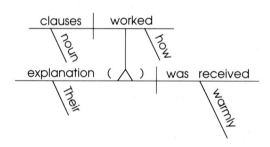

12.

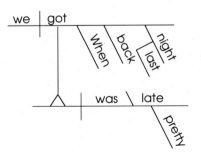

13.

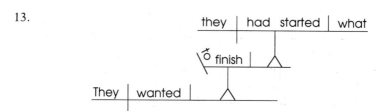

14.

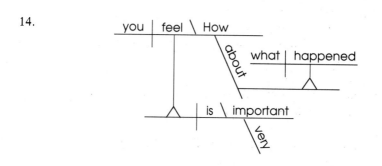

15.

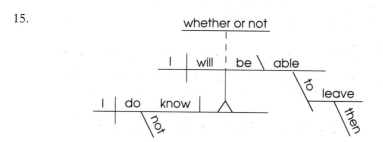

16.

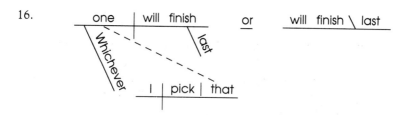

17.

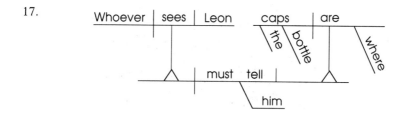

18.

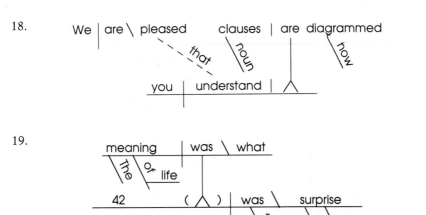

19.

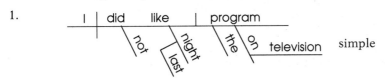

■ **Exercise 4.11. Diagraming and classifying sentences by structure (page 181)**

1.

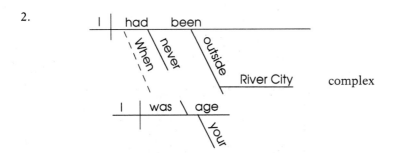

simple

2.

complex

3.

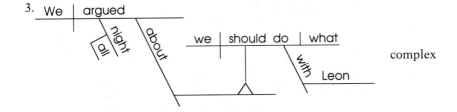

complex

4.

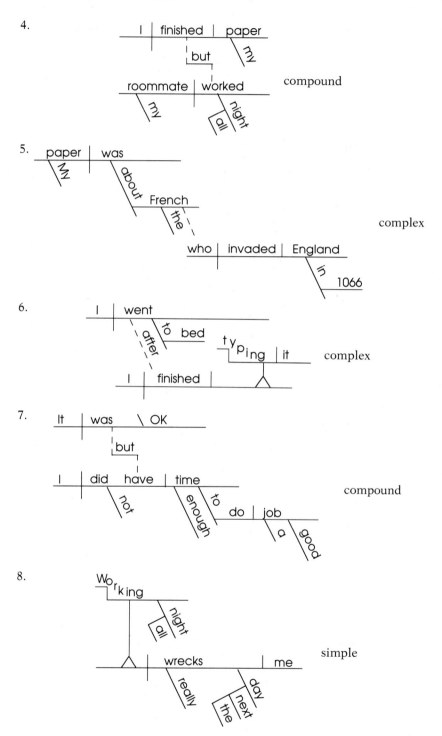

compound

5.

complex

6.

complex

7.

compound

8.

simple

9.

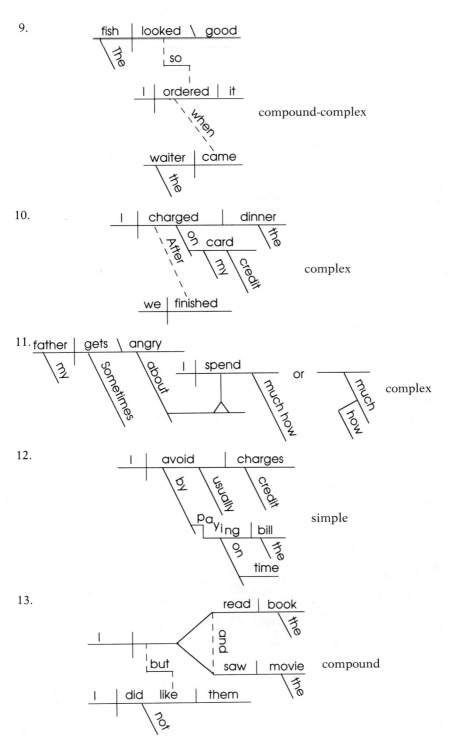

compound-complex

10.

complex

11.

complex

12.

simple

13.

compound

14.

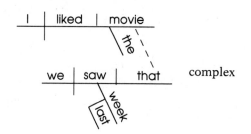

complex

15.

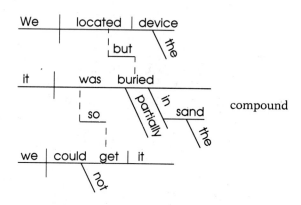

compound

16.

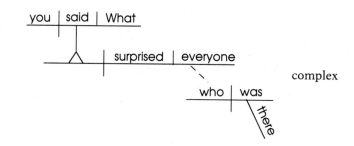

complex

17.

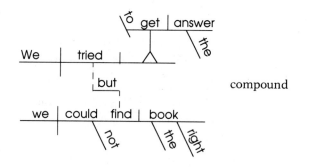

compound

18.

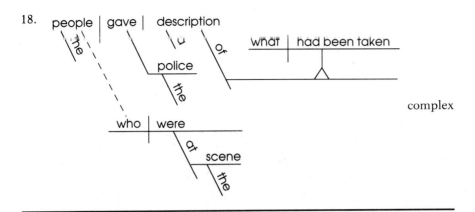

complex

■ **Exercise 4.12. Review (page 182)**

1.

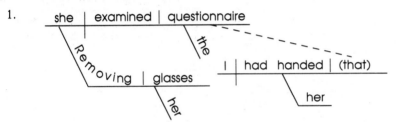

2.

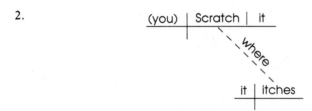

3.

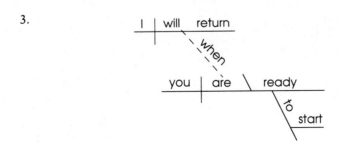

4.

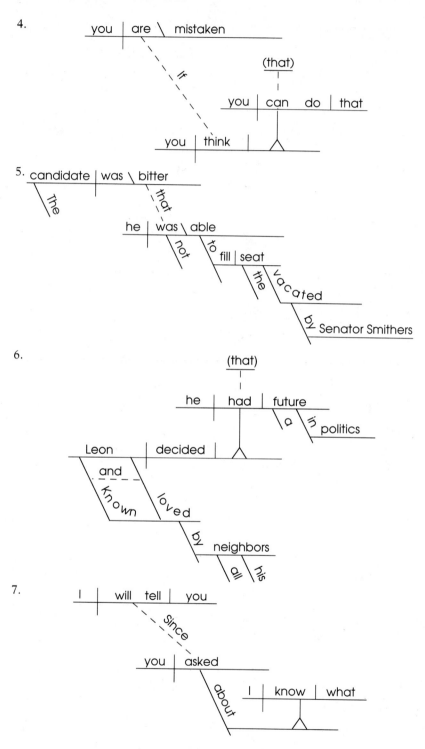

8.

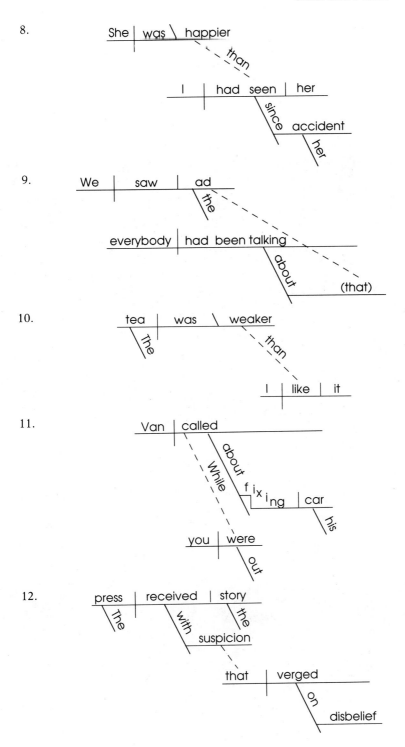

9.

10.

11.

12.

13.

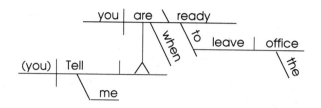

14.

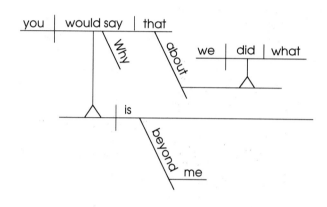

15.

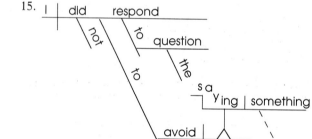

16.

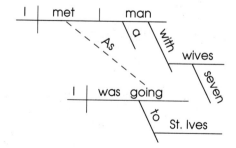

17.

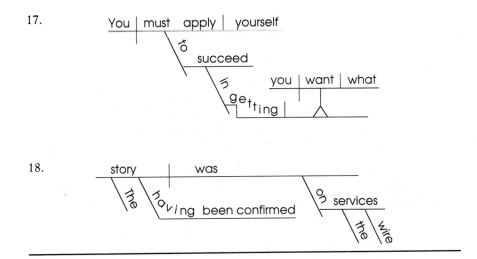

18.

CHAPTER 5   HISTORY OF GRAMMAR

■ **Exercise 5.1. Prefixes and suffixes that identify parts of speech (page 202)**

2. 1. inactive, inconsiderate, inelegant, insane, insignificant, invalid, invulnerable
   2. Adjective (proof: very inactive . . .)

3. 1. mini-cab, mini-conference, mini-session, miniskirt
   2. Noun (proof: the mini-cab . . .)

4. 1. rebuild, reform, rejoin, relocate, reproduce, resell, retell, return, rewind
   2. Verb (proof: will rebuild . . .)

5. 1. boyhood, brotherhood, knighthood, manhood, motherhood, neighborhood, widowhood
   2. Noun (proof: the boyhood . . .)

6. 1. foredoom, forejudge, foreordain, foresee, forestall, foretell
   2. Verb (proof: will foredoom . . .)

7. 1. hyperactive, hypercritical, hypersensitive
   2. Adjective (proof: very hyperactive . . .)

8. 1. booklet, cigarette, kitchenette, leaflet, piglet, starlet
   2. Noun (proof: the booklet . . .)

9. 1. outgrow, outlive, outperform, outplay, outsell, outweigh
   2. Verb (proof: will outgrow . . .)

■ **Exercise 5.2. Prefixes and suffixes that change parts of speech (page 203)**

  2. 1. Noun (proof: the blame . . .)
      2. blameless, careless, childless, hairless, harmless, restless, speechless, toothless
      3. Adjective (proof: very careless . . .)
  3. 1. Verb (proof: will contest . . .)
      2. contestant, defendant, disinfectant, informant, inhabitant
      3. Noun (proof: the contestant . . .)
  4. 1. Adjective (proof: very banal . . .)
      2. banality, curiosity, diversity, infirmity, intensity, rapidity, vitality
      3. Noun (proof: the banality . . .)
  5. 1. Noun (proof: the adjective . . .)
      2. adjectival, critical, logical, national, professional, traditional
      3. Adjective (proof: very critical . . .)
  6. 1. Verb (proof: will confirm . . .)
      2. confirmation, deportation, exploration, fixation, organization, protestation
      3. Noun (proof: the confirmation . . .)
  7. 1. Adjective (proof: very hard . . .)
      2. harden, madden, ripen, roughen, sadden, shorten, sweeten, widen
      3. Verb (proof: will harden . . .)
  8. 1. Verb (proof: will amaze)
      2. amazement, arrangement, embodiment, government, puzzlement, retirement
      3. Noun (proof: the amazement . . .)
  9. 1. Noun (proof: the compass . . .)
      2. encompass, encourage, endanger, enslave, enthrone, envision
      3. Verb (proof: will encompass . . .)

■ **Exercise 5.3. Related parts of speech (page 205)**

Note: more than one answer possible

  2. Verb: attract; Noun: attraction; Adjective: attractive; Adverb: attractively
  3. Verb: edit; Noun: editor, edition; Adjective: editorial; Adverb: editorially
  4. Verb: explode; Noun: explosion; Adjective: explosive; Adverb: explosively
  5. Verb: prefer; Noun: preference; Adjective: preferential, preferable; Adverb: preferentially, preferably
  6. Verb: sense; Noun: sensation; Adjective: sensitive; Adverb: sensitively

7. Verb: offend; Noun: offense; Adjective: offensive;
   Adverb: offensively

8. Verb: explore; Noun: exploration; Adjective: exploratory;
   Adverb: exploratorily

9. Verb: refute; Noun: refutation, refutability;
   Adjective: refutative, refutable; Adverb: refutably

10. Verb: participate; Noun: participation; Adjective: participative;
    Adverb: participatively

11. Verb: specify; Noun: specification; Adjective: specific;
    Adverb: specifically

12. Verb: enslave; Noun: slave, enslavement, slavery, slavishness;
    Adjective: slavish; Adverb: slavishly

13. Verb: organize; Noun: organization; Adjective: organizational;
    Adverb: organizationally

14. Verb: inform; Noun: information; Adjective: informative;
    Adverb: informatively

15. Verb: criticize; Noun: critic; Adjective: critical; Adverb: critically

16. Verb: credit; Noun: creditation; Adjective: creditable;
    Adverb: creditably

■ **Exercise 5.4. Phrasal verbs (page 210)**

1. John looked up the word.
2. John looked out the window.
   Question: Where did John look? Answer: out the window
3. They boarded up the windows.
4. She broke off our engagement.
5. The general looked over the situation.
6. We usually turn in after the 10 o'clock news.
7. I turned in my report.
8. Fred turned down the offer.
9. The truck turned down a side road.
   Question: Where did the truck turn? Answer: down a side road
10. The well finally dried up.
11. The assembly voted down the motion.
12. The assembly voted on the motion.
13. The assembly voted in the main ballroom.
    Question: Where did the assembly vote? Answer: in the main ballroom
14. We picked out the bad parts.
15. He always picked on smaller children.
16. We worked in the back yard.
    Question: Where did we work? Answer: in the back yard
17. I can't put up with that nonsense.

CHAPTER 6 TRANSFORMATIONAL GRAMMAR

■ **Exercise 6.1. Deep and surface structures (page 227)**

2. You Past I find Aunt Sally a table
  Kernel: You found Aunt Sally a table.
  Passive: Aunt Sally was found a table by you.
  Dative switch: You found a table for Aunt Sally.
  Dative switch + Passive: A table was found for Aunt Sally by you.

3. They Past tell me all their secrets
  Kernel: They told me all their secrets.
  Passive: I was told all their secrets by them.
  Dative switch: They told all their secrets to me.
  Dative switch + Passive: All their secrets were told to me by them.

4. I Past order you dinner
  Kernel: I ordered you dinner.
  Passive: You were ordered dinner by me.
  Dative switch: I ordered dinner for you.
  Dative switch + Passive: Dinner was ordered for you by me.

5. The owner of the restaurant Past serve us our dinner
  Kernel: The owner of the restaurant served us our dinner.
  Passive: We were served our dinner by the owner of the restaurant.
  Dative switch: The owner of the restaurant served our dinner to us.
  Dative switch + Passive: Our dinner was served to us by the owner of the restaurant.

6. We Past reserve them a place
  Kernel: We reserved them a place.
  Passive: They were reserved a place by us.
  Dative switch: We reserved a place for them.
  Dative switch + Passive: A place was reserved for them by us.

7. The operator Past read me the telegram
  Kernel: The operator read me the telegram.
  Passive: I was read the telegram by the operator.
  Dative switch: The operator read the telegram to me.
  Dative switch + Passive: The telegram was read to me by the operator.

8. His thoughtfulness Past spare us a lot of trouble
  Kernel: His thoughtfulness spared us a lot of trouble.
  Passive: We were spared a lot of trouble by his thoughtfulness.
  Dative switch: His thoughtfulness spared a lot of trouble for us.
  Dative switch + Passive: A lot of trouble was spared for us by his thoughtfulness.

9. He Past owe me some money
  Kernel: He owed me some money.
  Passive: I was owed some money by him.
  Dative switch: He owed some money to me.
  Dative switch + Passive: Some money was owed to me by him.

10. The waiter Past bring us the check
  Kernel: The waiter brought us the check.
  Passive: We were brought the check by the waiter.
  Dative switch: The waiter brought the check to us.
  Dative switch + Passive: The check was brought to us by the waiter.

11. The IRS Past do me a big favor
    Kernel: The IRS did me a big favor.
    Passive: I was done a big favor by the IRS.
    Dative switch: The IRS did a big favor for me.
    Dative switch + Passive: A big favor was done for me by the IRS.
12. The agency Past sell them the house
    Kernel: The agency sold them the house.
    Passive: They were sold the house by the agency.
    Dative switch: The agency sold the house to them.
    Dative switch + Passive: The house was sold to them by the agency.
13. The pitcher Past throw the catcher the ball
    Kernel: The pitcher threw the catcher the ball.
    Passive: The catcher was thrown the ball by the pitcher.
    Dative switch: The pitcher threw the ball to the catcher.
    Dative switch + Passive: The ball was thrown to the catcher by the pitcher.
14. She Past offer me her hand
    Kernel: She offered me her hand.
    Passive: I was offered her hand by her.
    Dative switch: She offered her hand to me.
    Dative switch + Passive: Her hand was offered to me by her.
15. We Past teach old dogs new tricks
    Kernel: We taught old dogs new tricks.
    Passive: Old dogs were taught new tricks by us.
    Dative switch: We taught new tricks to old dogs.
    Dative switch + Passive: New tricks were taught to old dogs by us.

■ **Exercise 6.2. Present and past tense (page 232)**

1.

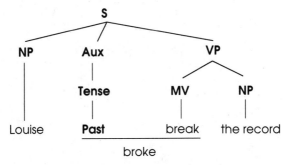

2.

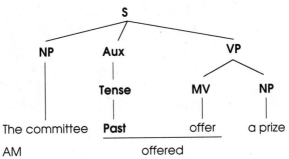

3.

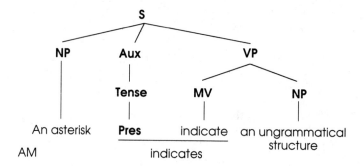

4.

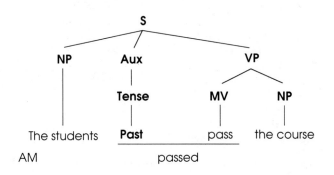

5.

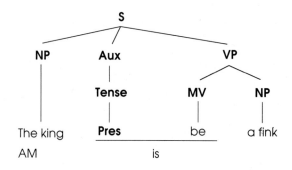

6.

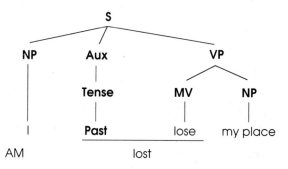

7.

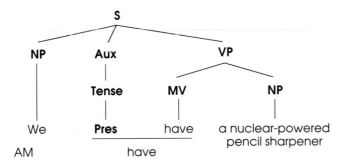

8.

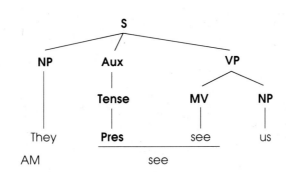

9.

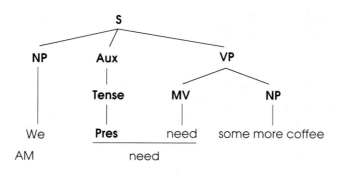

10.

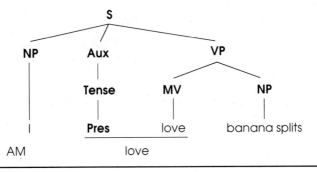

■ **Exercise 6.3. Modals (page 234)**

1.

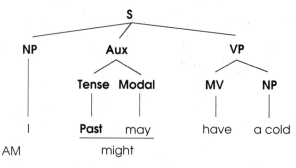

2.

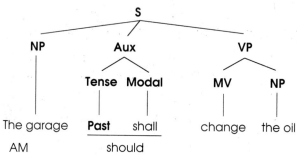

3.

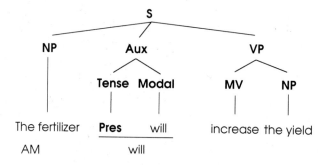

4.

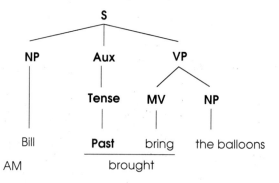

5.

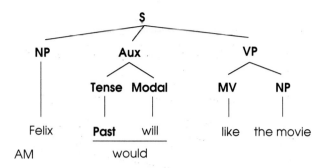

6.

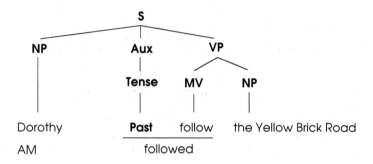

7.

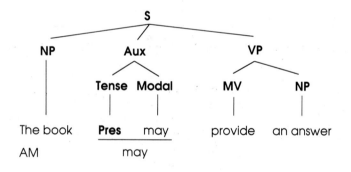

8.

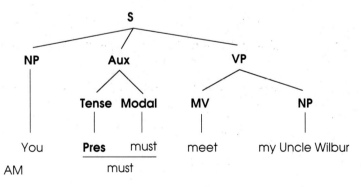

9.

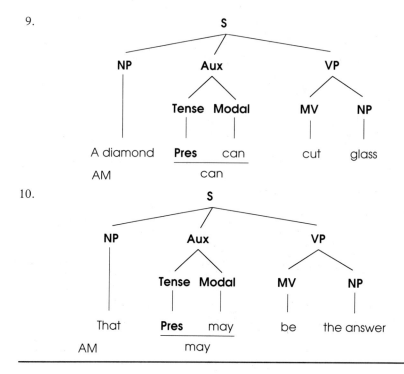

10.

■ **Exercise 6.4. Perfect (page 236)**

1.

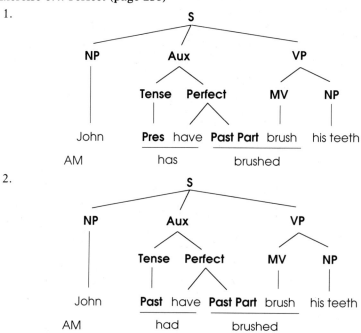

2.

3.

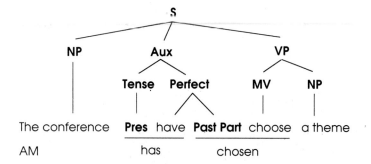

4.

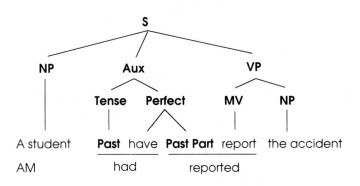

5.

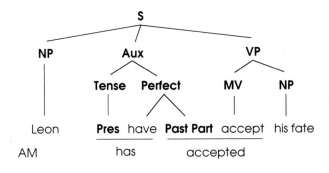

6.

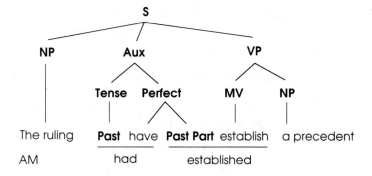

7.

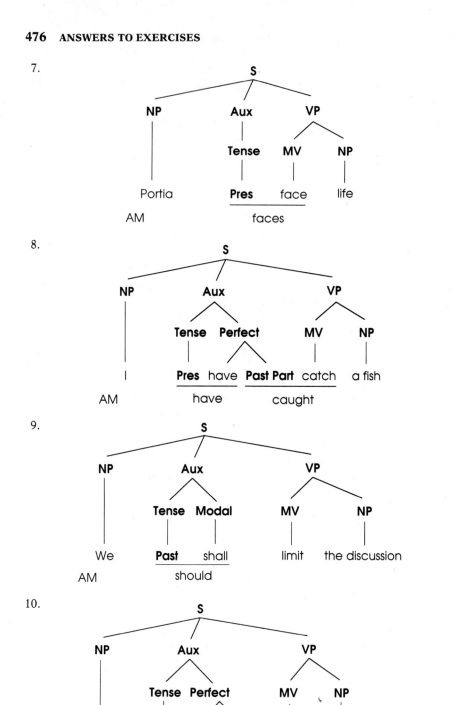

8.

9.

10.

■ **Exercise 6.5. Progressive (page 238)**

1.

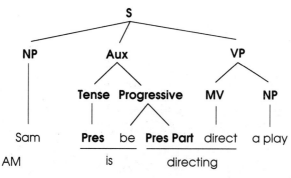

2.

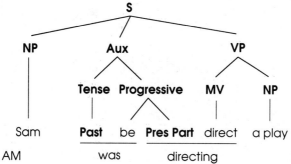

3.

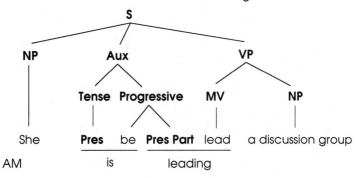

4.

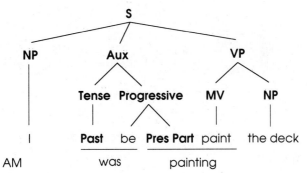

5.

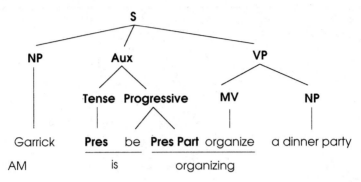

6.

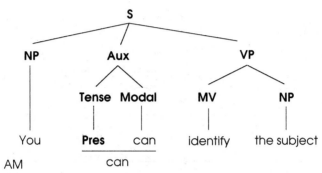

7.

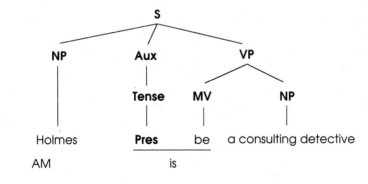

8.

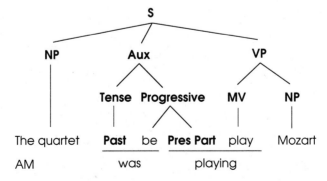

9.

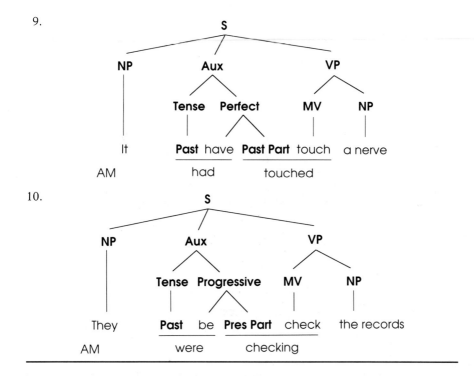

10.

■ **Exercise 6.6. Order and names of auxiliary verbs (page 241)**

2. We <u>have been avoiding</u> the issue.   Pres perfect progressive

3. The tips <u>could be touching</u>.   Past modal progressive

4. They <u>have been examining</u> the issue.   Pres perfect progressive

5. I <u>might have known</u>.   Past modal perfect

6. Leon <u>should have been working</u> in the kitchen.   Past modal perfect progressive

7. Everyone <u>will have finished</u> by now.   Pres modal perfect

8. Henry <u>had been visiting</u> his old mother.   Past perfect progressive

9. Leon <u>might have been collecting</u> bottle caps.   Past modal perfect progressive

10. The gift <u>must have surprised</u> them.   Pres modal perfect

11. He <u>should have ignored</u> the question.   Past modal perfect

12. We <u>should have been participating</u> in the activities.   Past modal perfect progressive

13. Harry <u>had struggled</u> against fate.   Past perfect

14. You <u>can afford</u> it.   Pres modal

15. They <u>may have been dancing</u>.   Pres modal perfect progressive

16. I <u>had had</u> the question before.   Past perfect

17. Louise <u>was being</u> difficult.   Past progressive

■ **Exercise 6.7. Auxiliary review (page 243)**

1.

```
                              S
        ┌─────────────────────┼──────────────────────┐
       NP                     Aux                     VP
        │          ┌──────────┼──────────┐        ┌───┴───┐
        │        Tense    Perfect    Progressive  MV      NP
        │          │        ╱╲          ╱╲        │       │
       We         Pres have Past Part be Pres Part draw  trees
      AM            have        been        drawing
```

2.

```
                          S
        ┌─────────────────┼──────────────┐
       NP                Aux             VP
        │              ╱─────╲        ╱───╲
        │           Tense  Modal     MV    NP
        │             │      │        │     │
  The advertisement  Pres   will   attract a crowd
      AM              will
```

3.

```
                        S
        ┌───────────────┼──────┐
       NP              Aux      VP
        │               │     ╱───╲
        │             Tense  MV    NP
        │               │     │     │
   The clutch         Pres  engage the gears
      AM               engages
```

4.

```
                          S
        ┌─────────────────┼──────────────┐
       NP                Aux             VP
        │           ╱──────╲          ╱───╲
        │         Tense   Perfect     MV    NP
        │           │       ╱╲        │      │
      They        Pres have Past Part file  a motion
      AM            have        filed
```

5.

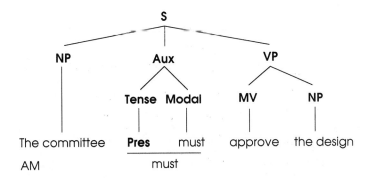

6.

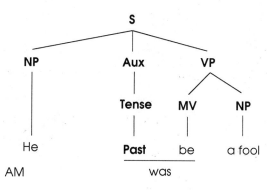

7.

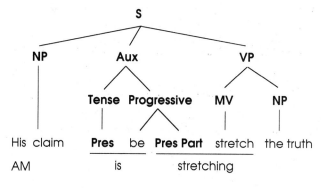

8.

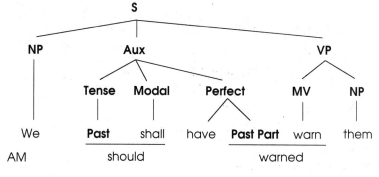

9.

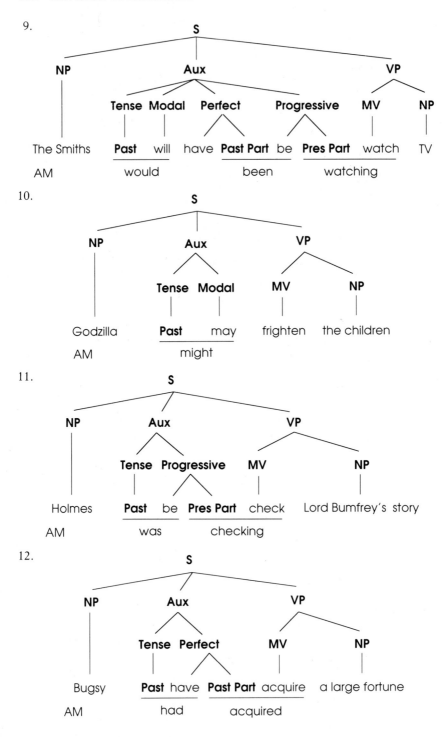

10.

11.

12.

13.

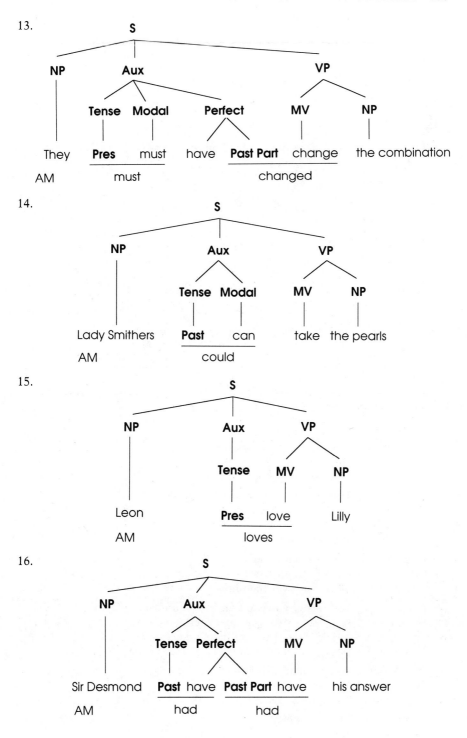

14.

15.

16.

17.

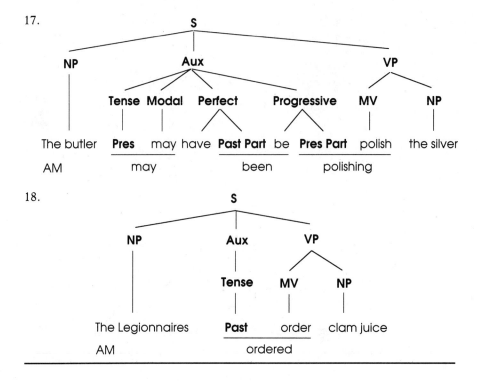

18.

■ **Exercise 6.8. Questions (page 248)**

3. *Deep:*   He Past justify his answer
   Question: Past he justify his answer
   do support: Past do he justify his answer
   Affix Mov: Did he justify his answer?

4. *Deep:*   They Past wax the car
   Question: Past they wax the car
   do support: Past do they wax the car
   Affix Mov: Did they wax the car?

5. *Deep:*   I Pres shall answer the phone
   Question: Pres shall I answer the phone
   Affix Mov: Shall I answer the phone?

6. *Deep:*   Your sister Pres want an ice-cream cone
   Question: Pres your sister want an ice-cream cone
   do support: Pres do your sister want an ice-cream cone
   Affix Mov: Does your sister want an ice-cream cone?

7. *Deep:*   You Past can wait here
   Question: Past can you wait here
   Affix Mov: Could you wait here?

8. *Deep:*   They Past enlarge the prints
   Question: Past they enlarge the prints

do support:	Past do they enlarge the prints
Affix Mov:	Did they enlarge the prints?

9. | *Deep:* | The witness Pres will invoke the 5th amendment |
|---|---|
| *Question:* | Pres will the witness invoke the 5th amendment |
| *Affix Mov:* | Will the witness invoke the 5th amendment? |

10. | *Deep:* | You Past look up the word in the dictionary |
|---|---|
| *Question:* | Past you look up the word in the dictionary |
| *do support:* | Past do you look up the word in the dictionary |
| *Affix Mov:* | Did you look up the word in the dictionary? |

11. | *Deep:* | The flowers Pres bloom in the spring, tra-la |
|---|---|
| *Question:* | Pres the flowers bloom in the spring, tra-la |
| *do support:* | Pres do the flowers bloom in the spring, tra-la |
| *Affix Mov:* | Do the flowers bloom in the spring, tra-la? |

12. | *Deep:* | You Pres have Past Part overlook something |
|---|---|
| *Question:* | Pres have you Past Part overlook something |
| *Affix Mov:* | Have you overlooked something? |

13. | *Deep:* | They Past have Past Part violate the country's airspace |
|---|---|
| *Question:* | Past have they Past violate the country's airspace |
| *Affix Mov:* | Had they violated the country's airspace? |

14. | *Deep:* | You Pres have a quarter |
|---|---|
| *Question:* | Pres you have a quarter |
| *do support:* | Pres do you have a quarter |
| *Affix Mov:* | Do you have a quarter? |

15. | *Deep:* | They Past have a good time |
|---|---|
| *Question:* | Past they have a good time |
| *do support:* | Past do they have a good time |
| *Affix Mov:* | Did they have a good time? |

■ **Exercise 6.9. Negative statements (page 252)**

3. | *Deep:* | He Past accuse you of anything |
|---|---|
| *not:* | He Past not accuse you of anything |
| *do support:* | He Past do not accuse you of anything |
| *Affix Mov:* | He did not accuse you of anything. |

4. | *Deep:* | That approach Pres will earn a penny |
|---|---|
| *not:* | That approach Pres will not earn a penny |
| *Affix Mov:* | That approach will not earn a penny. |

5. | *Deep:* | The contractor Past install a sprinkler system |
|---|---|
| *not:* | The contractor Past not install a sprinkler system |
| *do support:* | The contractor Past do not install a sprinkler system |
| *Affix Mov:* | The contractor did not install a sprinkler system. |

6. | *Deep:* | Paul Pres like coffee |
|---|---|
| *not:* | Paul Pres not like coffee |
| *do support:* | Paul Pres do not like coffee |
| *Affix Mov:* | Paul does not like coffee. |

7. *Deep:*   I Pres know all the answers
   not: I Pres <u>not</u> know all the answers
   do support: I Pres <u>do</u> not know all the answers
   Affix Mov: I <u>do</u> not know all the answers.

8. *Deep:*   They Pres will arrive on time
   not: They Pres will <u>not</u> arrive on time
   Affix Mov: They <u>will</u> not arrive on time.

9. *Deep:*   The Congressman Past avoid the question
   not: The Congressman Past <u>not</u> avoid the question
   do support: The Congressman Past <u>do</u> not avoid the question
   Affix Mov: The Congressman <u>did</u> not avoid the question.

10. *Deep:*   Leon Past have Past Part finish the exam yet
    not: Leon Past have <u>not</u> Past Part finish the exam yet
    Affix Mov: Leon <u>had</u> not <u>finished</u> the exam yet.

11. *Deep:*   Scrooge Past contribute to the Christmas Fund
    not: Scrooge Past <u>not</u> contribute to the Christmas Fund
    do support: Scrooge Past <u>do</u> not contribute to the Christmas Fund
    Affix Mov: Scrooge <u>did</u> not contribute to the Christmas Fund

12. *Deep:*   The piece Past fit into the puzzle
    not: The piece Past <u>not</u> fit into the puzzle
    do support: The piece Past <u>do</u> not fit into the puzzle
    Affix Mov: The piece <u>did</u> not fit into the puzzle.

13. *Deep:*   Watson Past blink an eye at Holmes's strange suggestion
    not: Watson Past <u>not</u> blink an eye at Holmes's strange suggestion
    do support: Watson Past <u>do</u> not blink an eye at Holmes's strange suggestion
    Affix Mov: Watson <u>did</u> not blink an eye at Holmes's strange suggestion.

14. *Deep:*   You Past shall have Past Part compare their stories
    not: You Past shall <u>not</u> have Past Part compare their stories
    Affix Mov: You <u>should</u> not have <u>compared</u> their stories.

15. *Deep:*   We Pres be Pres Part go
    not: We Pres be <u>not</u> Pres Part go
    Affix Mov: We <u>are</u> not going.

■ **Exercise 6.10. Recognizing passives (page 256)**

1. The committee reviewed the book.
2. Everyone appreciated his contributions.
3. The President informed the Cabinet.
4. The committee had estimated the total.
5. No change.
6. The whole family was washing the dog.
7. The editor had threatened the writers.
8. Adults must accompany children.

9. A retired policeman owned the gun.
10. Everyone had noticed Corla's embarrassing slip.
11. No change.
12. They will catch us.
13. Proper planning could have prevented the accident.
14. No change.
15. The committee should approve the plan.

■ **Exercise 6.11. Deriving Passives (page 256)**

1. *Surface:*   The book was reviewed by the committee.
   Kernel: The committee reviewed the book.

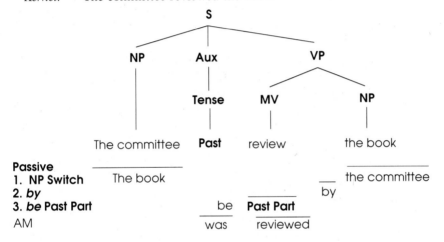

2. *Surface:*   His contributions were appreciated by everyone.
   Kernel: Everyone appreciated his contributions.

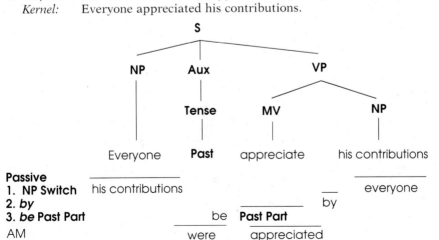

3. *Surface:* The Cabinet was informed by the President.
   Kernel: The President informed the Cabinet.

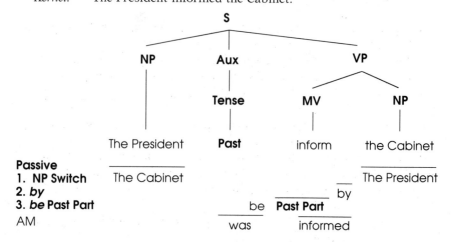

Passive
1. **NP Switch**   The Cabinet   The President
2. *by*   __   by
3. *be* **Past Part**   be **Past Part**
AM   was   informed

4. *Surface:* The total had been estimated by the committee.
   Kernel: The committee had estimated the total.

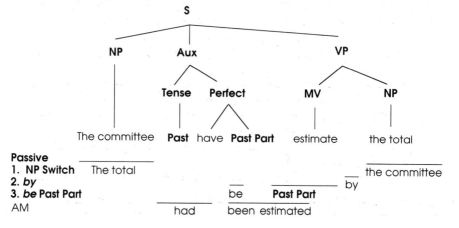

Passive
1. **NP Switch**   The total   __   the committee
2. *by*   by
3. *be* **Past Part**   be   **Past Part**
AM   had   been estimated

5. *Kernel:* The scientists had defined the problem.

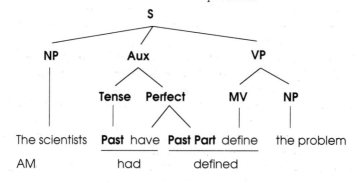

6. *Surface:*   The dog was being washed by the whole family.
   Kernel: The whole family was washing the dog.

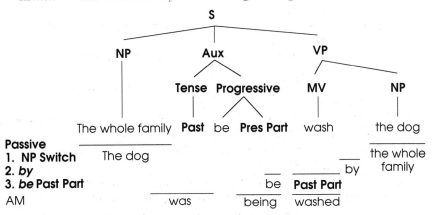

7. *Surface:*   The writers had been threatened by the editor.
   Kernel: The editor had threatened the writers.

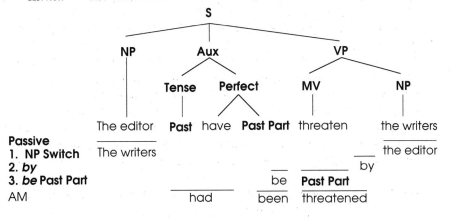

8. *Surface:*   Children must be accompanied by adults.
   Kernel: Adults must accompany children.

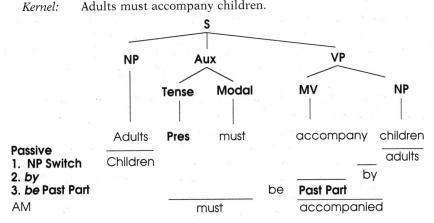

9. *Surface:* The gun was owned by a retired policeman.
   Kernel: A retired policeman owned the gun.

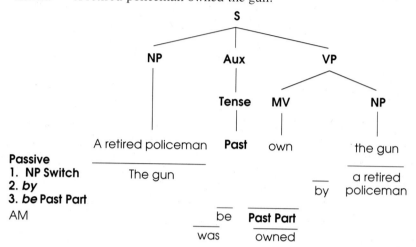

10. *Surface:* Corla's embarassing slip had been noticed by everyone.
    Kernel: Everyone had noticed Corla's embarassing slip.

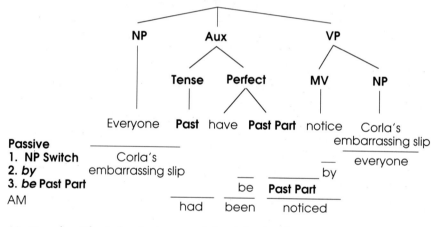

11. *Kernel:* The judge had granted the defendant's request.

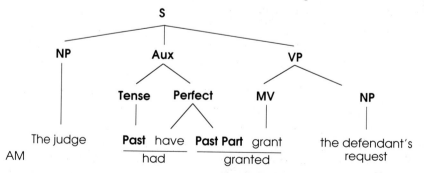

12. *Surface:* We will be caught by them.
    Kernel: They will catch us.

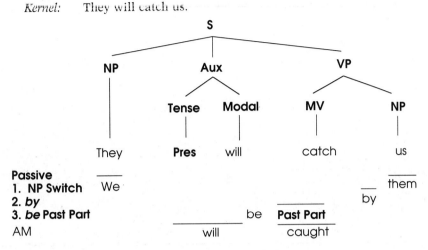

13. *Surface:* The accident could have been prevented by proper planning.
    Kernel: Proper planning could have prevented the accident.

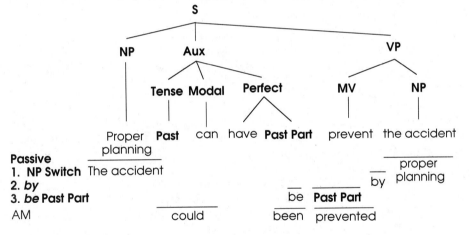

14. *Kernel:* A microphone was recording the conversation.

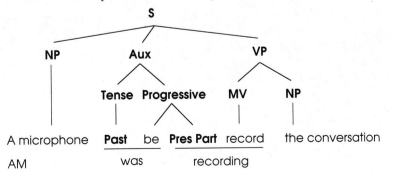

15. *Surface:* The plan should be approved by the committee.
    Kernel: The committee should approve the plan.

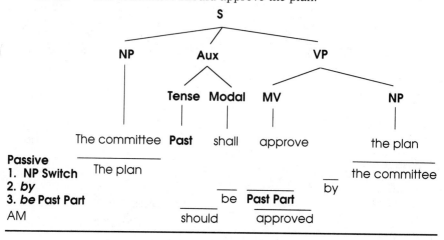

Passive				
1. NP Switch	The plan			the committee
2. by				by
3. be Past Part		be **Past Part**		
AM		should	approved	

■ **Exercise 6.12. Applying optional transformations (page 261)**

1. Sally Past tell the children a story
    1. Kernel: Sally told the children a story.
    2. Question: Did Sally tell the children a story?
    3. Passive: The children were told a story by Sally.
    4. Passive + Question: Were the children told a story by Sally?
    5. Dative: Sally told a story to the children.
    6. Dative + Passive: A story was told to the children by Sally.
    7. Dative + Question: Did Sally tell a story to the children?
    8. Dative + Passive + Question: Was a story told to the children by Sally?

2. I Past find her an apartment
    1. Kernel: I found her an apartment.
    2. Question: Did I find her an apartment?
    3. Passive: She was found an apartment by me.
    4. Passive + Question: Was she found an apartment by me?
    5. Dative: I found an apartment for her.
    6. Dative + Passive: An apartment was found for her by me.
    7. Dative + Question: Did I find an apartment for her?
    8. Dative + Passive + Question: Was an apartment found for her by me?

3. He Past may sell me Boardwalk
    1. Kernel: He might sell me Boardwalk.
    2. Question: Might he sell me Boardwalk?
    3. Passive: I might be sold Boardwalk by him.
    4. Passive + Question: Might I be sold Boardwalk by him?
    5. Dative: He might sell Boardwalk to me.
    6. Dative + Passive: Boardwalk might be sold to me by him.
    7. Dative + Question: Might he sell Boardwalk to me?
    8. Dative + Passive + Question: Might Boardwalk be sold to me by him?

CHAPTER 7   SENTENCE COMBINING

■ **Exercise 7.1. Forming relative clause (page 268)**

2. They took a risk (the risk Past be totally unjustified)
   Rel Repl: They took a risk (that Past be totally unjustified)
   Affix Mov: They took a risk (that was totally unjustified)

3. Alexander (Alexander Past have a terrible day) turned in early
   Rel Repl: Alexander (who Past have a terrible day) turned in early
   Affix Mov: Alexander (who had a terrible day) turned in early

4. I finally saw the bear (we Past have Past Part see the bear's tracks earlier)
   Rel Repl: I finally saw the bear (we Past have Past Part see whose tracks earlier)
   Wh- fronting: I finally saw the bear (whose tracks we Past have Past Part see earlier)
   Affix Mov: I finally saw the bear (whose tracks we had seen earlier)

5. The teacher changed the sentence (we Past have trouble with the sentence)
   Rel Repl: The teacher changed the sentence (we Past have trouble with that)
   Wh- fronting: The teacher changed the sentence (that we Past have trouble with)
   Affix Mov: The teacher changed the sentence (that we had trouble with [or: The teacher changed the sentence (with which we had trouble)]

6. The Latin (Latin Past be Past Part speak in the Middle Ages) was "Church" Latin
   Rel Repl: The Latin (that Past be Past Part speak in the Middle Ages) was "Church" Latin
   Affix Mov: The Latin (that was spoken in the Middle Ages) was "Church" Latin

7. We had a question about the route (we Past have Past Part decide on the route)
   Rel Repl: We had a question about the route (we Past have Past Part decide on the route)
   Wh- fronting: We had a question about the route (that we Past have Past Part decide on)
   Affix Mov: We had a question about the route (that we had decided on) [or: We had a question about the route (on which we had decided)]

8. My brother (my brother's aim Past be unreliable) broke a window
   Rel Repl: My brother (whose aim Past be unreliable) broke a window
   Affix Mov: My brother (whose aim was unreliable) broke a window

9. Leon's ballet (he originally Past write the ballet for radio) amused the critics
   Rel Repl: Leon's ballet (he originally Past write which for radio) amused the critics

   Wh- fronting: Leon's ballet (which he originally Past write for radio) amused the critics

   Affix Mov: Leon's ballet (which he originally wrote for radio) amused the critics

10. The lawyer found the discrepancy (the discrepancy Past be in the witnesses' testimony)

   Rel Repl: The lawyer found the discrepancy (that Past be in the witnesses' testimony)

   Affix Mov: The lawyer found the discrepancy (that was in the witnesses' testimony)

11. They found the horse (the stranger Past have Past Part ride out of town on the horse)

   Rel Repl: They found the horse (the stranger Past have Past Part ride out of town on that)

   Wh- fronting: They found the horse (that the stranger Past have Past Part ride out of town on)

   Affix Mov: They found the horse (that the stranger had ridden out of town on)

   [or: They found the horse (on which the stranger had ridden out of town)]

12. His belief had been badly shaken by the events (the events Past have Past Part take place)

   Rel Repl: His belief was badly shaken by the events (that Past have Past Part take place)

   Affix Mov: His belief was badly shaken by the events (that had taken place)

■ **Exercise 7.2. Reducing embedded sentences with** *be* **as a main verb (page 277)**

2. Please get the book (the book Pres be on the top shelf)
   Rel Repl: Please get the book (that Pres be on the top shelf)
   Rel Cl Red: Please get the book (on the top shelf)

3. The audience (the audience Past be strangely silent) began to take notice
   Rel Repl: The audience (which Past be strangely silent) began to take notice
   Rel Cl Red: The audience (strangely silent) began to take notice
   Adj Switch: The (strangely silent) audience began to take notice

4. With the money (the money Past be a gift from his parents) he bought a tuba
   Rel Repl: With the money (that Past be a gift from his parents) he bought a tuba
   Rel Cl Red: With the money (a gift from his parents) he bought a tuba

5. The jury ignored the story (the defendant Past give the story)
   Rel Repl: The jury ignored the story (that the defendant Past give)
   Affix Mov: The jury ignored the story (that the defendant gave)

6. The soldiers (the soldiers Past be exhausted) returned to camp

   Rel Repl: The soldiers (who Past be exhausted) returned to camp

   Rel Cl Red: The soldiers (exhausted) returned to camp

   Adj Switch: The (exhausted) soldiers returned to camp

7. Mike (Mike Pres be a bartender at a place (the place Pres be in town)) called me over

   Rel Repl (twice):   Mike (who Pres be a bartender at a place (that Pres be in town)) called me over

   Rel Cl Red (twice): Mike (a bartender at a place (in town)) called me over

8. The heat (heat Pres be intense) had broken all records

   Rel Repl: The heat (which Pres be intense) had broken all records

   Rel Cl Red: The heat (intense) had broken all records

   Adj Switch: The (intense) heat had broken all records

9. Baseball (baseball Pres be America's favorite sport) has been played for years

   Rel Repl: Baseball (which Pres be America's favorite sport) has been played for years

   Rel Cl Red: Baseball (America's favorite sport) has been played for years

10. Adam (Adam Past come to the door first) is the oldest brother

    Rel Repl: Adam (who Past come to the door first) is the oldest brother

    Affix Mov: Adam (who came to the door first) is the oldest brother

11. They objected to delays (the delays Pres be costly and unnecessary)

    Rel Repl: They objected to delays (which Pres be costly and unnecessary)

    Rel Cl Red: They objected to delays (costly and unnecessary)

    Adj Switch: They objected to (costly and unnecessary) delays

12. Everyone appreciated the effort (you Past put in the effort)

    Rel Repl: Everyone appreciated the effort (that you Past put in)

    Affix Mov: Everyone appreciated the effort (that you put in)

13. The collectors recognized the value (the value Pres be obvious)

    Rel Repl: The collectors recognized the value (which Pres be obvious)

    Rel Cl Red: The collectors recognized the value (obvious)

    Adj Switch: The collectors recognized the (obvious) value

---

■ **Exercise 7.3. Present participles and present participial phrases (page 280)**

2. The judge (the judge Past be Pres Part uphold the dignity of the court) called for order

   Rel Repl: The judge (who Past be Pres Part uphold the dignity of the court) called for order

   Rel Cl Red: The judge (Pres Part uphold the dignity of the court) called for order

   Affix Mov: The judge (upholding the dignity of the court) called for order

3. Watson (Watson Past be Pres Part nurse a severe headcold) reluctantly followed Holmes into the wet sewer

> *Rel Repl:* Watson (who Past be Pres Part nurse a severe headcold) reluctantly followed Holmes into the wet sewer
>
> *Rel Cl Red:* Watson (Pres Part nurse a severe headcold) reluctantly followed Holmes into the wet sewer
>
> *Affix Mov:* Watson (nursing a severe headcold) reluctantly followed Holmes into the wet sewer

4. The crowd (the crowd Past be Pres Part cheer) spilled out of the stadium

> *Rel Repl:* The crowd (which Past be Pres Part cheer) spilled out of the stadium
>
> *Rel Cl Red:* The crowd (Pres Part cheer) spilled out of the stadium
>
> *Affix Mov:* The crowd (cheering) spilled out of the stadium
>
> *Adj Switch:* The (cheering) crowd spilled out of the stadium

5. The sheriff (the sheriff Past be Pres Part check his pistols) turned to face the angry mob

> *Rel Repl:* The sheriff (who Past be Pres Part check his pistols) turned to face the angry mob
>
> *Rel Cl Red:* The sheriff (Pres Part check his pistols) turned to face the angry mob
>
> *Affix Mov:* The sheriff (checking his pistols) turned to face the angry mob

6. I was sourly greeted by a clerk (the clerk Past be Pres Part complain)

> *Rel Repl:* I was sourly greeted by a clerk (who Past be Pres Part complain)
>
> *Rel Cl Red:* I was sourly greeted by a clerk (Pres Part complain)
>
> *Affix Mov:* I was sourly greeted by a clerk (complaining)
>
> *Adj Switch:* I was sourly greeted by a (complaining) clerk

7. The driver (the driver Past be Pres Part look at his map) nearly missed the freeway exit

> *Rel Repl:* The driver (who Past be Pres Part look at his map) nearly missed the freeway exit
>
> *Rel Cl Red:* The driver (Pres Part look at his map) nearly missed the freeway exit
>
> *Affix Mov:* The driver (looking at his map) nearly missed the freeway exit

8. The kids (the kids Past be Pres Part risk life and limb) climbed up the cliff

> *Rel Repl:* The kids (who Past be Pres Part risk life and limb) climbed up the cliff
>
> *Rel Cl Red:* The kids (Pres Part risk life and limb) climbed up the cliff
>
> *Affix Mov:* The kids (risking life and limb) climbed up the cliff

9. The conductor (the conductor Past be Pres Part bow to the audience) motioned for the soloists to rise

> *Rel Repl:* The conductor (who Past be Pres Part bow to the audience) motioned for the soloists to rise
>
> *Rel Cl Red:* The conductor (Pres Part bow to the audience) motioned for the soloists to rise
>
> *Affix Mov:* The conductor (bowing to the audience) motioned for the soloists to rise

10. The ghost (the ghost Past be Pres Part manifest herself as a Rockette) appeared in the hallway again

Rel Repl: The ghost (who Past be Pres Part manifest herself as a Rockette) appeared in the hallway again

Rel Cl Red: The ghost (Pres Part manifest herself as a Rockette) appeared in the hallway again

Affix Mov: The ghost (manifesting herself as a Rockette) appeared in the hallway again

11. The senator glared at the audience (the audience Past be Pres Part snicker)

    Rel Repl: The senator glared at the audience (who Past be Pres Part snicker)

    Rel Cl Red: The senator glared at the audience (Pres Part snicker)

    Affix Mov: The senator glared at the audience (snickering)

    Adj Switch: The senator glared at the (snickering) audience

---

■ **Exercise 7.4. Past participles and past participial phrases (page 285)**

2. They lived in a miserable apartment (incompetent builders Past construct the apartment)

    Passive: They lived in a miserable apartment (the apartment Past be Past Part construct by incompetent builders)

    Rel Repl: They lived in a miserable apartment (which Past be Past Part construct by incompetent builders)

    Rel Cl Red: They lived in a miserable apartment (Past Part construct by incompetent builders)

    Affix Mov: They lived in a miserable apartment (constructed by incompetent builders)

3. John (the wind Past bother John) missed the target completely

    Passive: John (John Past be Past Part bother by the wind) missed the target completely

    Rel Repl: John (who Past be Past Part bother by the wind) missed the target completely

    Rel Cl Red: John (Past Part bother by the wind) missed the target completely

    Affix Mov: John (bothered by the wind) missed the target completely

4. Captain Midnight received a message (somebody Past hide the message)

    Passive & by del: Captain Midnight received a message (the message Past be Past Part hide)

    Rel Repl: Captain Midnight received a message (which Past be Past Part hide)

    Rel Cl Red: Captain Midnight received a message (Past Part hide)

    Affix Mov: Captain Midnight received a message (hidden)

    Adj Switch: Captain Midnight received a (hidden) message

5. Leon (the group Past exclude Leon) finally went home

    Passive: Leon (Leon Past be Past Part exclude by the group) finally went home

    Rel Repl: Leon (who Past be Past Part exclude by the group) finally went home

Rel Cl Red: Leon (Past Part exclude by the group) finally went home

Affix Mov: Leon (excluded by the group) finally went home

6. Aunt Sally (the news Past depress Aunt Sally) unplugged the radio

Passive: Aunt Sally (Aunt Sally Past be Past Part depress by the news) unplugged the radio

Rel Repl: Aunt Sally (who Past be Past Part depress by the news) unplugged the radio

Rel Cl Red: Aunt Sally (Past Part depress by the news) unplugged the radio

Affix Mov: Aunt Sally (depressed by the news) unplugged the radio

7. We collected the tents (something Past damage the tents)

Passive & by Del: We collected the tents (the tents Past be Past Part damage)

Rel Repl: We collected the tents (that Past be Past Part damage)

Rel Cl Red: We collected the tents (Past Part damage)

Affix Mov: We collected the tents (damaged)

Adj Switch: We collected the (damaged) tents

8. Near the village there is a fort (Crusaders Past build the fort in the 14th century)

Passive: Near the village there is a fort (the fort Past be Past Part build by the Crusaders in the 14th century)

Rel Repl: Near the village there is a fort (that Past be Past Part build by the Crusaders in the 14th century)

Rel Cl Red: Near the village there is a fort (Past Part build by the Crusaders in the 14th century)

Affix Mov: Near the village there is a fort (built by the Crusaders in the 14th century)

9. The movement (somebody Past discredit the movement) eventually collapsed

Passive & by Del: The movement (the movement Past be Past Part discredit) eventually collapsed

Rel Repl: The movement (which Past be Past Part discredit) eventually collapsed

Rel Cl Red: The movement (Past Part discredit) eventually collapsed

Affix Mov: The movement (discredited) eventually collapsed

Adj Switch: The (discredited) movement eventually collapsed

10. Marcia (every paper in the country Past interview Marcia) began to hit the talk shows

Passive: Marcia (Marcia Past be Past Part interview by every paper in the country) began to hit the talk shows

Rel Repl: Marcia (who Past be Past Part interview by every paper in the country) began to hit the talk shows

Rel Cl Red: Marcia (Past Part interview by every paper in the country) began to hit the talk shows

Affix Mov: Marcia (interviewed by every paper in the country) began to hit the talk shows

■ **Exercise 7.5. Review of noun modification (page 288)**

[Some grammatically possible but stylistically inept forms have been ignored.]

2. The steps (the steps Past be in the back yard) needed to be fixed
   Rel Clause: The steps that were in the back yard needed to be fixed.
   Adj Phrase: The steps in the back yard needed to be fixed.

3. Yelling at the referee was a foul (the foul Past be certain)
   Rel Clause: Yelling at the referee was a foul that was certain.
   Adjective: Yelling at the referee was a certain foul.

4. The people (the people Past be Pres Part come through the door) were dressed in costumes (the costumes Past be outlandish)
   First embedded sentence:
   Rel Clause: The people who were coming through the door . . .
   Pres Part Phrase: The people coming through the door . . .
   Second embedded sentence:
   Rel Clause: . . .   in costumes that were outlandish
   Adjective: . . .   in outlandish costumes

5. The road (someone Past oil the road) was much better than before
   Rel Clause (passive):   The road, which was oiled, . . .
   Pres Part Phrase: The road, being oiled, . . .
   Pres Part (Adjective):   The oiled road . . .

6. The picture (the picture Past be a seascape (the seascape Past be bright)) was perfect for my office
   [Do deepest embedded sentence first]
   Adjective: . . . the picture was a bright seascape . . .
   Rel Clause: The picture, which was a bright seascape, . . .
   Appositive: The picture, a bright seascape, . . .

7. Holmes (Holmes Past learn little from the butler) turned his attention to the footprints
   Rel Clause: Holmes, who learned little from the butler, . . .

8. We followed the trail (someone Past mark the trail)
   Rel Clause (passive):   We followed the trail that was marked.
   Past Part (Adjective):   We followed the marked trail.

9. Again Watson heard the noise (the noise Past be a tapping (the tapping Past be mysterious) under the floorboards)
   Deepest embedded sentence:
   Adjective: . . . a mysterious tapping . . .
   Highest embedded sentence:
   Rel Clause: Again Watson heard the noise, which was a mysterious tapping under the floorboards.
   Appositive: Again Watson heard the noise, a mysterious tapping under the floorboards.

10. The bike (the bike Past be Pres Part speed hopelessly out of control) left the path and jumped the curb (the curb Past be steep)
    First embedded sentence:
    Rel Clause: The bike, which was speeding hopelessly out of control, . . .
    Pres Part Phrase: The bike, speeding hopelessly out of control, . . .
    Second embedded sentence:
    Adjective: . . . jumped the steep curb

11. Lestrade (Lestrade Past be Pres Part grow increasingly uneasy at Holmes's explanation (Holmes's explanation Past be strange)) turned to Watson in frustration
    Deepest embedded sentence:
    Adjective: . . . Holmes's strange explanation . . .
    Highest embedded sentence:
    Rel Clause: Lestrade, who was growing increasingly uneasy at Holmes's strange explanation, . . .
    Pres Part Phrase: Lestrade, growing increasingly uneasy at Holmes's strange explanation . . .

■ **Exercise 7.6.** *That* and *wh-* noun clauses (page 293)

3. The computer keeps track of (you log on or off <u>whenever</u>)
   Wh- fronting: The computer keeps track of (whenever you log on or off)

4. (you said <u>whatever</u> about our problems) made quite an impression on them
   Wh- fronting: (whatever you said about our problems) made quite an impression on them

5. (you were not hurt worse) is a miracle
   (that you were not hurt worse) is a miracle

6. We want to know (they cannot finish their jobs on time <u>why</u>)
   Wh- fronting: We want to know (why they cannot finish their jobs on time)

7. Can you tell me (I can get to the train station <u>how</u>)?
   Wh- fronting: Can you tell me (how I can get to the train station)?

8. The question is (<u>who</u> will clean this mess up)
   The question is (<u>who</u> will clean this mess up)
   [*wh-* word is already in first positon]

9. (we will win) is a foregone conclusion
   (that we will win) is a foregone conclusion

10. They were asked about (they wanted <u>what</u> for dinner)
    Wh- fronting: They were asked about (what they wanted for dinner)

11. (you decide <u>whatever</u>) is OK with me
    Wh- fronting: (whatever you decide) is OK with me

12. (there is a will <u>where</u>), there is a way
    Wh- fronting: (where there is a will), there is a way

13. We wondered (the game would start on time)
    We wondered (whether/if the game would start on time)

14. I don't understand (you put up with all that <u>why</u>)

    Wh- fronting: I don't understand (why you put up with all that)

15. I know (you know (he knows))

    [Do deepest embedded sentence first]

    I know (you know (that he knows))

    I know (that you know (that he knows))

16. He knew (I was right about (the Giants won the pennant <u>when</u>))

    [Do deepest embedded sentence first]

    Wh- fronting: He knew (I was right about (when the Giants won the pennant))

    He knew (that I was right about (when the Giants won the pennant))

■ **Exercise 7.7. Gerunds and gerund phrases (page 296)**

2. (the flowers Past burst into sudden bloom) made it seem like spring in the kitchen

    Tense Repl: (the flowers Pres Part burst into sudden bloom) made it seem like spring in the kitchen

    Affix Mov: (the flowers bursting into sudden bloom) made it seem like spring in the kitchen

    Subject: (the flowers' bursting into sudden bloom) made it seem like spring in the kitchen

3. Our trip was nearly ruined by (Leon Past have Past Part lose the map)

    Tense Repl: Our trip was nearly ruined by (Leon Pres Part have Past Part lose the map)

    Affix Mov (twice):   Our trip was nearly ruined by (Leon having lost the map)

    Subject: Our trip was nearly ruined by (Leon's having lost the map)

4. (Watson Pres assist Holmes in his investigation) is a necessary, but artificial, plot device

    Tense Repl: (Watson Pres Part assist Holmes in his investigation) is a necessary, but artificial, plot device

    Affix Mov: (Watson assisting Holmes in his investigation) is a necessary, but artificial, plot device

    Subject: (Watson's assisting Holmes in his investigation) is a necessary, but artificial, plot device

5. (the wind Past be from the north) forced the Admiral to return to port

    Tense Repl: (the wind Pres Part be from the north) forced the Admiral to return to port

    Affix Mov: (the wind being from the north) forced the Admiral to return to port

    Subject: (the wind's being from the north) forced the Admiral to return to port

6. (the children Past have Past Part eat earlier) made our meal more pleasant

   Tense Repl: (the children Pres Part have Past Part eat earlier) made our meal more pleasant

   Affix Mov: (the children having eaten earlier) made our meal more pleasant

   Subject: (the children's having eaten earlier) made our meal more pleasant

7. We resented (they Past object to the proposal) very much

   Tense Repl: We resented (they Pres Part object to the proposal) very much

   Affix Mov: We resented (they objecting to the proposal) very much

   Subject: We resented (their objecting to the proposal) very much

8. The recruits practiced (they Past salute) all afternoon

   Tense Repl: The recruits practiced (they Pres Part salute) all afternoon

   Affix Mov: The recruits practiced (they saluting) all afternoon

   Subject: The recruits practiced ((their) saluting) all afternoon

9. (we Past be always anxious about the time) prevented us from really enjoying ourselves

   Tense Repl: (we Pres Part be always anxious about the time) prevented us from really enjoying ourselves

   Affix Mov: (we being always anxious about the time) prevented us from really enjoying ourselves

   Subject: ((our) being always anxious about the time) prevented us from really enjoying ourselves

10. (I Pres diet) is not much fun

   Tense Repl: (I Pres Part diet) is not much fun

   Affix Mov: (I dieting) is not much fun

   Subject: ((my) dieting) is not much fun

11. He appreciated (she Past fix dinner for a change)

   Tense Repl: He appreciated (she Pres Part fix dinner for a change)

   Affix Mov: He appreciated (she fixing dinner for a change)

   Subject: He appreciated (her fixing dinner for a change)

12. He appreciated (he Past fix dinner for a change)

   Tense Repl: He appreciated (he Pres Part fix dinner for a change)

   Affix Mov: He appreciated (he fixing dinner for a change)

   Subject: He appreciated ((his) fixing dinner for a change)

■ **Exercise 7.8. Infinitives and infinitive phrases (page 302)**

2. (the weatherman Past predict snow) seemed absurd at the time

   Tense Repl: (the weatherman to predict snow) seemed absurd at the time

   Subject: ((for the weatherman) to predict snow) seemed absurd at the time

3. (the runner Pres hesitate between first and second) is a sign of poor coaching

   Tense Repl: (the runner to hesitate between first and second) is a sign of poor coaching

   Subject: ((for the runner) to hesitate between first and second) is a sign of poor coaching

4. John offered (John Past resign)

   Tense Repl: John offered (John to resign)

   Subject: John offered (to resign)

5. (they Past leave without saying goodbye) was really rude

   Tense Repl: (they to leave without saying goodbye) was really rude

   Subject: ((for them) to leave without saying goodbye) was really rude

6. (he Past wash the dishes without making a fuss) was a real switch

   Tense Repl: (he to wash the dishes without making a fuss) was a real switch

   Subject: ((for him) to wash the dishes without making a fuss) was a real switch

7. (the company Past redesign the front entrance) was surprisingly expensive

   Tense Repl: (the company to redesign the front entrance) was surprisingly expensive

   Subject: ((for the company) to redesign the front entrance) was surprisingly expensive

8. Kafka wanted (a friend Past burn his works)

   Tense Repl: Kafka wanted (a friend to burn his works)

   Subject: Kafka wanted (a friend to burn his works)

9. The plan was (Fred Past impersonate the Secretary of State)

   Tense Repl: The plan was (Fred to impersonate the Secretary of State)

   Subject: The plan was ((for Fred) to impersonate the Secretary of State)

10. (he Past have Past Part return our call so promptly) came as a real surprise

    Tense Repl: (he to have Past Part return our call so promptly) came as a real surprise

    Affix Mov: (he to have returned our call so promptly) came as a real surprise

    Subject: ((for him) to have returned our call so promptly) came as a real surprise

11. We decided (we Past go out for dinner)

    Tense Repl: We decided (we to go out for dinner)

    Subject: We decided (to go out for dinner)

12. Mary asked John (John Past pass her the potato salad)

    Tense Repl: Mary asked John (John to pass her the potato salad)

    Subject: Mary asked John (to pass her the potato salad)

13. I want (I Pres be alone)

    Tense Repl: I want (I to be alone)

    Subject: I want (to be alone)

■ **Exercise 7.9. Abstract noun phrases (pages 305)**

[Note: if the subject is deleted, the abstract noun is automatically used with *the*.]

2. (she Past conceive the idea) astonished the critics
   Ab Noun: (she conception of the idea) astonished the critics
   Subject: ((her) conception of the idea) astonished the critics

3. (we Pres calculate the net present benefit) is included in our project proposal
   Ab Noun: (we calculation of the net present benefit) is included in our project proposal
   Subject: ((our) calculation of the net present benefit) is included in our project proposal

4. Everyone was painfully aware of (Harry Past refuse to face reality)
   Ab Noun: Everyone was painfully aware of (Harry refusal to face reality)
   Subject: Everyone was painfully aware of ((Harry's) refusal to face reality)

5. The press was caught off guard by (the government suddenly Past impose martial law)
   Ab Noun: The press was caught off guard by (the government sudden imposition of martial law)
   Subject: The press was caught off guard by (the (government's) sudden imposition of martial law)

6. (the farmers Past employ migrant workers) was a common practice in the small farming community
   Ab Noun: (the farmers employment of migrant workers) was a common practice in the small farming community
   Subject: (the (farmers') employment of migrant workers) was a common practice in the small farming community

7. Once we entered the door (we Past disrupt the gathering) was immediately apparent
   Ab Noun: Once we entered the door (we disruption of the gathering) was immediately apparent
   Subject: Once we entered the door ((our) disruption of the gathering) was immediately apparent

8. (they immediately Past recover the stolen bonds) was naturally the primary concern of the insurance company
   Ab Noun: (they immediate recovery of the stolen bonds) was naturally the primary concern of the insurance company
   Subject: ((their) immediate recovery of the stolen bonds) was naturally the primary concern of the insurance company

9. The city council approved (the company Past expand its plant in Easton)
   Ab Noun: The city council approved (the company expansion of its plant in Easton)
   Subject: The city council approved (the (company's) expansion of its plant in Easton)

10. The Mayor expected (Leon Past retract his statement)

   Ab Noun: The Mayor expected (Leon retraction of his statement)

   Subject: The Mayor expected ((Leon's) retraction of his statement)

11. (Sir Mortimer despicably Past seduce Lady Cravencroft) filled the readers with foreboding

   Ab Noun: (Sir Mortimer despicable seduction of Lady Cravencroft) filled the readers with foreboding

   Subject: ((Sir Mortimer's) despicable seduction of Lady Cravencroft) filled the readers with foreboding

---

■ **Exercise 7.10. Review of nominalization (page 306)**

2. (Leon Past reject the bottle caps) was an unexpected development

   Noun clause: That Leon rejected the bottle caps . . .

   Gerund: Leon's rejecting (of) the bottle caps . . .

   Infinitive: For Leon to reject the bottle caps . . .

   Ab Noun phrase: Leon's rejection of the bottle caps . . .

3. We all noticed (he Past behave strangely)

   Noun clause: . . . that he behaved strangely

   Gerund: . . . his behaving strangely

   Ab Noun phrase: . . . his strange behavior

4. (the test Past be on verbals) upset all the students

   Noun clause: That the test was on verbals . . .

   Gerund: The test's being on verbals . . .

   Infinitive: For the test to be on verbals . . .

5. There was quite a debate about (the company Past exploit the shoreline)

   Gerund: . . . the company's exploiting the shoreline

   Ab Noun phrase: . . . the company's exploitation of the shoreline

6. A likely outcome was (the legislature Past create new districts)

   Gerund: . . . the legislature's creating new districts

   Infinitive: . . . for the legislature to create new districts

   Ab noun phrase: . . . the legislature's creation of new districts

7. (They Past disrupt the elections) was reported by the newspaper

   Noun clause: That they disrupted the elections . . .

   Gerund: Their disrupting (of) the elections . . .

   Ab noun phrase: Their disruption of the elections . . .

8. We had grown used to (the truck Past have a loud muffler)

   Gerund: . . . the truck's having a loud muffler

9. After yet another truly appalling meal, Lady Crumhorn decided (Lady Crumhorn Past give the cook her notice)

   Infinitive: . . . Lady Crumhorn decided to give the cook her notice

10. (The court Past reverse the decision) was expected at any time

  Gerund: The court's reversing the decision . . .

  Infinitive: ?For the court to reverse the decision . . .

  Ab noun phrase: The court's reversal of the decision . . .

11. (You Past forgive your enemies) will drive them crazy

  Noun clause: That you forgive your enemies . . .

  Gerund: Your forgiving your enemies . . .

  Infinitive: For you to forgive your enemies . . .

  Ab noun phrase: Your forgiveness of your enemies . . .

12. I tried (I Past start the engine)

  Gerund: I tried starting the engine

  Infinitive: I tried to start the engine

13. We asked the professor (the professor Past postpone the test)

  Infinitive: We asked the professor to postpone the test

14. (Holmes Past demonstrate how the crime was committed) astonished Inspector Lestrade

  Noun clause: That Holmes demonstrated how the crime was committed . . .

  Gerund: Holmes's demonstrating how the crime was committed . . .

  Infinitive: For Holmes to demonstrate how the crime was committed . . .

  Ab Noun phrase: Holmes's demonstration of how the crime was committed . . .

■ **Exercise 7.11. Absolutes (page 312)**

2. The court announced its decision (two justices Past dissent)

  Tense Repl: The court announced its decision (two justices Pres Part dissent)

  Affix Mov: The court announced its decision (two justices dissenting)

3. (the game Past be out of reach) the crowd began to leave

  (a) Absol Del: (the game out of reach) the crowd began to leave

  (b) Tense Repl: (the game Pres Part be out of reach) the crowd began to leave

   Affix Mov: (the game being out of reach) the crowd began to leave

4. (Karen Past have Past Part compile the names) we began to address the envelopes

  Tense Repl: (Karen Pres Part have Past Part compile the names) we began to address the envelopes

  Affix Mov: (Karen having compiled the names) we began to address the envelopes

5. (their noise Past disturb the neighbors) they received many complaints

  Tense Repl: (their noise Pres Part disturb the neighbors) they received many complaints

Affix Mov: (their noise disturbing the neighbors) they received many complaints

6. They fell into formation (their uniforms Past be stiff with starch) (their shoes Past be Past Part polish) (their brass Past gleam)

Absol Del (twice):   They fell into formation (their uniforms stiff with starch) (their shoes Past Part polish) . . .

Tense Repl: . . . (their brass Pres Part gleam)

Affix Mov: They fell into formation (their uniforms stiff with starch) (their shoes polished) (their brass gleaming)

[Comment: it is grammatically possible (but stylistically awkward) to apply tense replacement to the first two embedded sentences, producing the following nonparallel version: They fell into formation (their uniforms being stiff with starch) (their shoes being polished) (their brass gleaming)]

7. The car went into the ditch (its wheels still Past spin)

Tense Repl: The car went into the ditch (its wheels still Pres Part spin)

Affix Mov: The car went into the ditch (its wheels still spinning)

8. They waited patiently (legs Past be Past Part cross) (arms Past be past Part fold) (eyes Past be Past Part close) (faces Past be utterly blank)

Absol Del (4 times):   They waited patiently (legs Past Part cross) (arms Past Part fold) (eyes Past Part close) (faces utterly blank)

Affix Mov: They waited patiently (legs crossed) (arms folded) (eyes closed) (faces utterly blank)

9. (their passports Past have Past Part be Past Part check) the passengers were allowed to go

Tense Repl: (their passports Pres Part have Past Part be Past Part check) the passengers were allowed to go

Affix Mov: (their passports having been checked) the passengers were allowed to go

10. (the scaling ladders Past be in position) the attack on the walls began

(a) Absol Del: (the scaling ladders in position) the attack on the walls began

(b) Tense Repl: (the scaling ladders Pres Part be in position) the attack on the walls began

Affix Mov: (the scaling ladders being in position) the attack on the walls began

11. (no other issues Past be Past Part present) the meeting was adjourned

(a) Absol Del: (no other issues Past Part present) the meeting was adjourned

Affix Mov: (no other issues presented) the meeting was adjourned

(b) Tense Repl: (no other issues Pres Part be Past Part present) the meeting was adjourned

Affix Mov: (no other issues being presented) the meeting was adjourned

■ **Exercise 7.12. Distinguishing present participial, gerund, and absolute phrases (page 315)**

Pres participial

1. The plant, having already manufactured a similar product, was an obvious choice for the contract.

Gerund

2. The plant's having already manufactured a similar product was an advantage.

Absolute

3. The plant having manufactured a similar product, we bid for the contract.

Gerund

4. Holmes's becoming suspicious of the blind beggar was the turning point in the case.

Pres Participial

5. Holmes, becoming suspicious of the blind beggar, immediately gave chase.

Absolute

6. Holmes becoming suspicious of the blind beggar, Watson began to make inquiries about him.

Absolute

7. The alarm sounding, the firemen quickly donned their gear.

Pres Participial

8. The alarm, sounding throughout the building, aroused the firemen.

Gerund

9. The alarm's sounding aroused the firemen.

Gerund

10. The plan's attaining quick success was our only hope.

Pres Participial

11. Attaining quick success, the plan changed everything.

Absolute

12. The plan attaining quick success, we immediately sought out a tax shelter.

Pres Participial

13. The elderly man hesitating at the door slipped into the room unnoticed.

Gerund

14. The elderly man's hesitating at the door went unnoticed.

Absolute

15. The elderly man hesitating at the door, the waiter bustled forward.

■ **Exercise 7.13. Identifying absolutes, participial phrases, and gerunds (page 316)**

Gerund

1. The President's authorizing the appointment caused considerable controversy.

Participial phrase

2. The agreement assuring future cooperation has been accepted by all parties.

Absolute

3. The SEC has been in the news a lot lately, insider trading being on TV every night.

4. Unexpected developments delayed <u>our announcing our decision.</u>
   Gerund

5. The reporters <u>investigating the story</u> were criticized for <u>spreading</u>
   Participial phrase
   <u>groundless rumors.</u>
   Gerund

6. Students <u>transferring from other institutions</u> often lose credits in the
   Participial phrase
   process.

7. The experiment <u>resolving the question,</u> the researchers began
   Absolute
   <u>writing up their project.</u>
   Gerund

8. <u>Anticipating the questions</u> is half the battle in <u>dealing with reporters.</u>
   Gerund   Gerund

9. <u>Revenues exceeding expectations,</u> the company declared a dividend.
   Absolute

10. The key to the company's <u>succeeding</u> was <u>constantly incorporating new ideas</u>
    Gerund   Gerund
    without <u>losing contact with the dealers.</u>
    Gerund

11. <u>Reserving judgment for the moment,</u> Ronald turned to other matters
    Participial phrase
    <u>demanding his attention.</u>
    Participial phrase

12. The spokesman <u>having admitted</u> *the government's continuing involvement,*
    Absolute   Gerund
    Congress called for an investigation of all activities <u>relating to the sale.</u>
    Participial phrase

13. <u>Making a good impression on his date</u> was Leon's motivation for
    Gerund
    <u>sending her the singing telegram.</u>
    Gerund

■ Exercise 7.14. T-units (page 319)

Passage 1

> I'm going to tell you how to play and live the game of Dungeons and Dragons.
> / You must find your way through maze. Slay dragons and unknown foes./
> You will find yourself a new role of another person./ Here are some of the
> characters that you might play the Swordsman, War Lord, Sorcerer and
> Wizard./ To gain in this game you must collect spells gold and jewels from
> the maze./ Before you start to play Dungeons and Dragons you should buy
> a Dungeons and Dragons playing guide which costs $11.95./ Then you can
> start it with mazes which cost $5.50 a maze./ Now I think you are ready to
> play/ have fun/ may your spells be many and your adventures be great./

Passage 2

Twister comes in a box about a foot long./ The game has the instructions on the box /it has a long plastic sheet with different colors such as green, yellow, blue, and red./ The first thing you do is take out the plastic sheet and spread it across the floor/ now take out the spinner/ you might have to put it together /after you have done that you have four squares with the spinner in the middle/ each square has something left foot red, yellow, blue, and green/ each square has the same colors/ the second square would have left hand and the same amount of colors in that square / the third square would have right foot/and the fourth square would have right hand./ Now you are ready to play twister./ You can play all by yourself/ you can have three people playing the game /and you can have four people playing too./ Now you are ready to play/ you need a friend or a parent to referee the game/you and your partner get anywhere on the sheet/now have your friend or parent spin /say it lands on right foot green /you and your partner put your foot on the green/ you keep doing this until your partner falls out of the game/ and this means you have won the game./

Passage 3

You deal five cards to each player, /then the dealer will ask you if you want to trade any number of cards. For the ones that don't follow a number right after the other card./

After all the players have traded. You start the bidding./ After all the players have quit, because the bid went too high. You show them your cards./ You may have won/ or someone else has. / It all depends on the cards./

Index on Usage

Index